CONSTITUTIONS IN THE GLOBAL FINANCIAL CRISIS

Few see any substantial connection between the global financial crisis and national constitutions. But, in this impressive and timely book, a strong collection of talented constitutional experts from Europe and North America reveal the essential dynamics of this connection and scrutinize the varying responses to the crisis under different constitutional regimes. It offers a provocative and penetrating comparative analysis that should be read by financial scholars and constitutional jurists alike.

Allan C. Hutchinson, York University, Canada

Constitutions in the Global Financial Crisis

A Comparative Analysis

XENOPHON CONTIADES

Centre for European Constitutional Law, Greece

Routledge
Taylor & Francis Group
LONDON AND NEW YORK

First published 2013 by Ashgate Publishing

2 Park Square, Milton Park, Abingdon, Oxon OX14 4RN
711 Third Avenue, New York, NY 10017, USA

Routledge is an imprint of the Taylor & Francis Group, an informa business

First issued in paperback 2016

British Library Cataloguing in Publication Data
Constitutions in the global financial crisis : a comparative analysis.
1. Global Financial Crisis, 2008–2009. 2. Financial crises – Europe. 3. Constitutional law – Europe. 4. Comparative economics. 5. Comparative government.
I. Contiades, Xenophon.
342.4–dc23

The Library of Congress has cataloged the printed edition as follows:
Constitutions in the global financial crisis : a comparative analysis / by Xenophon Contiades.
pages cm.
Includes bibliographical references and index.
ISBN 978-1-4094-6631-4 (hardback)
1. Constitutional history—Europe—21st century. 2. Constitutional law—Economic aspects—Europe. 3. Europe—Economic policy.
4. Financial crises—Europe. 5. Global Financial Crisis, 2008-2009. I. Contiades, Xenophon I., editor of compilation.

KJC4431.C658 2013
342.4—dc23

2012042528

ISBN 978-1-4094-6631-4 (hbk)
ISBN 978-1-138-25570-8 (pbk)

Contents

Notes on Contributors vii

Introduction: The Global Financial Crisis and the Constitution 1
Xenophon Contiades

PART I CONSTITUTIONAL REACTIONS IN COMPARATIVE PERSPECTIVE

1 How Constitutions Reacted to the Financial Crisis 9
Xenophon Contiades and Alkmene Fotiadou

PART II FIRST PATH: ADJUSTMENT

2 The Constitution and the Financial Crisis in Ireland 63
David Gwynn Morgan

3 The Constitutional Consequences of the Financial Crisis in Italy 89
Tania Groppi, Irene Spigno and Nicola Vizioli

4 Financial Crisis and the Constitution in Latvia 115
Ringolds Balodis and Janis Pleps

5 The Spanish Constitution in the Turmoil of the Global Financial Crisis 141
Agustín Ruiz Robledo

6 The Constitution and the Financial Crisis in the UK: Historical and Contemporary Lessons 167
John F. McEldowney

PART III SECOND PATH: SUBMISSION

7 The Impact of the Financial Crisis on the Greek Constitution 195
Xenophon Contiades and Ioannis A. Tassopoulos

8 The Sovereign Debt Crisis and the Constitution's Negative Outlook: A Portuguese Preliminary Assessment 219
Jónatas E.M. Machado

PART IV THIRD PATH: BREAKDOWN

9 Breaking and Making Constitutional Rules: The Constitutional Effects of the Financial Crisis in Hungary 245
Zoltán Szente

10 The Impact of the Financial Crisis on Icelandic Constitutional Law: Legislative Reforms, Judicial Review and Revision of the Constitution 263
Björg Thorarensen

PART V FOURTH PATH: STAMINA

11 The United States Constitution and the Great Recession 287
Mark Tushnet

Index 301

Notes on Contributors

Ringolds Balodis, Professor of Law, University of Latvia
Xenophon Contiades, Professor of Public Law and Dean, University of Peloponnese, Director, Centre for European Constitutional Law
Dr Alkmene Fotiadou, Research Associate, Centre for European Constitutional Law
Tania Groppi, Professor of Public Law, University of Siena
John F. McEldowney, Professor of Law, University of Warwick
Jónatas E.M. Machado, Associate Professor of Constitutional Law, University of Coimbra
David Gwynn Morgan, Professor Emeritus of Law, University College Cork
Janis Pleps, Lecturer of Law, University of Latvia
Agustín Ruiz Robledo, Professor of Constitutional Law, University of Granada
Irene Spigno, Doctor of Comparative Public Law, University of Siena
Zoltán Szente, Professor of Law, University of Győr, Hungary
Ioannis A. Tassopoulos, Associate Professor of Public Law, National and Kapodistrian University of Athens
Björg Thorarensen, Professor of Law, Faculty of Law, University of Iceland
Mark Tushnet, Professor of Law, Harvard University
Nicola Vizioli, Researcher in Public Law University of Siena

Introduction

The Global Financial Crisis and the Constitution

Xenophon Contiades

There have been oppression and luxury,
There have been poverty and licence,
There has been minor injustice.
Yet we have gone on living,
Living and partly living.

T.S. Eliot, *Murder in the Cathedral*

Setting the Table

The study of constitutions in the context of the global financial crisis can be structured through two distinct questions: how can constitutions help in the crisis and what happens to constitutions during such crises? Much is expected from constitutions, perhaps more than they can achieve, and even more happens to them as they are impacted in multiple ways. How a crisis is experienced and the implications it has are bound to surface in response to the 'what happened to you' question.

Beyond its economic impact, the 2008 financial crisis has been producing *new constitutional stories*. If we wish to encapsulate into one single question what this book is about, that question is 'How does the global financial crisis affect constitutions and their enforcement?' Nonetheless, one could begin by asking the exact opposite, that is 'Can constitutions affect the course and consequences of the financial crisis?' The interaction between the financial crisis and constitutions differs in each legal order as it is correlated to the exact form the crisis took in each country, varying in terms of intensity and symptoms, and also because constitutions and political systems have their own safety valves in response to such challenges.

Economists often compare the current recession to the 1929 Great Depression. Nonetheless, comparing the constitutional dimensions of the two crises would be a mistake, leading to false generalizations, because much has changed since 1929. Democracy operates differently, the functions of constitutions have evolved, and so have state functions and the global economy. Still, the inevitable reminiscence of that era carries connotations of major constitutional repercussions. Looking back to the 1930s, the New Deal constitutional moment and the collapse of the Weimar Constitution are suggestive of the interaction between major financial crises and constitutions, indicating that *completely adverse reactions may occur*.

What happens depends on a combination of constitutional design and multiple external factors. The US Constitution being short and open to informal change was able to resist the crisis, while the Weimar Constitution crumbled under the interaction of inherent faulty constitutional design and external political and social conditions. Revisiting the past thus, not in search of some sort of cyclic recurrence of constitutional reactions but in order to pin down factors that underlie such reactions, indicates the importance of studying the exact correlation between state-specific internal constitutional factors and external influences in real time. Approaching constitutions from the financial crisis perspective reveals the strengths and shortcomings of constitutional design, for such crises simultaneously activate multiple constitutional mechanisms. The need for or desirability of intervention in the constitutional text may surface, while a *deeper understanding of the financial crisis viewed from a constitutional aspect* is also possible, which is important as the need to manage the crisis and its side-effects persists.

This attempt to document how constitutions responded to the 2008 global financial crisis is structured by addressing a series of questions that aim to reveal what dominated the country-specific dialogues. Constitutional revision proposals, sovereignty issues, fundamental rights protection, regulatory reforms, the augmentation of executive power and changes in the party system have different weight in each dialogue. Some countries are characterized by ground-breaking court decisions, others by constitutional reforms, changes in governance or diminishing constitutional normativity. The crisis-based dominant constitutional debate in each jurisdiction serves as a guide to discover the actual constitutional reactions. The following questions are explored:

- What is the constitutional timeline of the financial crisis in each country (that is the series of crucial moments such as the enactment of austerity measures, elections, constitutional revisions, landmark supreme or constitutional court decisions)?
- How was constitutional jurisprudence affected?
- Did issues of fundamental rights protection, including individual, socio-economic and political rights, become the object of litigation?
- Were issues touching on standing, allocation of state powers and constitutional doctrines revisited?
- Did a dialogue between law-maker and judge take place?
- Were there informal amendments to the constitution?
- Did constitutional rights provide a shield against legislative measures or were they (treated as) impediments to policies?
- Did the financial crisis translate into a political, judicial or constitutional crisis as well?
- Did constitutional moments occur?
- Did the relationship between the executive and the legislature undergo transformations?
- Was there an enhancement of technocratic governance?

- Did the financial crisis cause fragmentation or on the contrary concentration of political power?
- Has a fear of constitutional deconstruction and loss of normativity emerged?
- Did the crisis diminish faith in the ability of the constitution to offer a shield in times of crisis?

From Financial Crisis Narratives to Constitutional Narratives

Comparing how constitutions react to a global financial crisis is based on an *externalist comparability foundation.* The point of departure is the common stimulus set by the crisis and not structural commonalities between constitutional orders. Instead, commonalities and differences are revisited under the prism of *what causes, underlies or explains the varying constitutional reactions*. Numerous similarities among the reactions that can be detected in different constitutional orders seem to reverse the famous quote from the opening of Tolstoy's *Anna Karenina*, 'Happy families are all alike; every unhappy family is unhappy in its own way.' When it comes to crisis-struck constitutional orders it seems that happy families differ, but unhappy families are unhappy in similar ways.

Financial unhappiness, which began to develop following the sub-prime mortgage market meltdown and the burst of the housing bubble in the United States, showed its potential effects after the collapse of Lehman Brothers in 2008. The USA, where it all began, is not only the strongest economy in the world, but also has the oldest constitution, which plays a central role in American culture. Iceland's collapse came soon afterwards and it was the first country to seek aid from the International Monetary Fund (IMF), followed by Hungary and Latvia. The eurozone sovereign debt crisis marked the entrance into the game of the Troika, composed of the European Central Bank, the European Commission and the IMF, as Greece, Ireland and Portugal entered the support mechanism. Spain and Italy are currently faced with the possibility of also seeking bailout, and the UK has been profoundly struck in terms of GDP per capita, while it also has the highest gross foreign debt of any European country. These countries, selected for this volume's comparative analysis, diversely impacted in terms of their economy and at different moments, have constitutions that although they fulfil comparability prerequisites differ in terms of age, flexibility and design. Yet, the financial crisis narrative was everywhere *translated into a constitutional narrative*, and striking constitutional developments soon followed.

Ever since the financial crisis broke out, fleeting images of constitutional activity have kept surfacing, to be overshadowed by financial commentary. Discussions on the US debt-ceiling crisis, Iceland's 'crowd-sourced' constitution, the constitutional enshrinement of fiscal discipline clauses in Italy and Spain, the annulled Greek referendum plan, Hungary's notorious new constitution, the emblematic decisions of the Latvian Constitutional Court, the Irish referenda, the UK's financial regulation, the Portuguese inability to reach consensus on amending the constitution and so forth were taking place parallel to the main recession theme. How such stories connect to the financial crisis and what their constitutional implications are is explored in the following chapters.

Many scenarios exist: the financial crisis may *ignite constitutional developments* or perhaps provide the pretext for them to be induced. Conversely, constitutional design may have caused or underpinned the financial crisis. Constitutional change could simply coincide with the financial crisis or it may be the *crisis-plus-other-factors* that carves out new constitutional routes. The distinction between interpreting the financial crisis *as a result, cause or pretext of constitutional change* is not always prima facie clear. The extent to which constitutions successfully provide the arena for political conflicts and demonstrate self-preservation skills or are sacrificed and lose their legitimacy, allowing the political class to survive at their expense, may determine that. What sometimes turns out to be difficult to discern where constitutions are concerned is whether the financial crisis simply *unveils what already exists or creates something new.*

Paths of Constitutional Reaction

The financial crisis has been setting continuous challenges to the functioning and interpretation of constitutions, leaving behind conspicuous marks. The range of changes taking place within the crisis-struck constitutional orders encompasses multiple areas that have been affected in different ways and in varying degrees. Sweeping legislative responses to the crisis have been constantly creating constitutionality issues. Shifts in constitutional interpretation are employed by both law-makers and judges. Changes in the constitutional capabilities of state organs, along with changes in their relationship and the allocation of powers among them, are clearly detectable. Decision-making processes are revisited along with rule production. The relation between state and economy has become different, directly impacting regulation. Party systems have been undergoing multilevel transformations. Sovereignty issues have acquired novel aspects through the interaction of international lenders, supranational entities and financial markets. The functions of constitutions have evolved in new directions. Constitutional texts have changed by way of revision, and some constitutions have reached the end of their journey and have been replaced or are under total reconstruction.

An overview of the constitutional landscape since the financial crisis broke out provides a record of multifarious changes. Among the different paths followed by constitutions since the financial turmoil began, the birth of new constitutions has been the only conspicuous assault on constitutional durability. More subtle facets of the unfolding changes are vast informal amendments, visibility of faulty design that could not be repaired due to stringent amendment formulas or lack of consensus, the chilling effect of the financial crisis on the functions of constitutions, constitutional adjustments hastily adopted without clear impact assessment that are bound to have unpredictable future side-effects on constitutional practice and jurisprudence, and erosion of state sovereignty.

How long constitutional reactions last and how deep are the imprints they make on the fabric of constitutions relate to the possibility of the occurrence of constitutional crises, constitutional hardballs, changes of constitutional order and even constitutional moments, or consist of more subtle changes. Disagreement or synergy between constitutional actors may make the difference, since unresolved judicial and political crises may culminate in constitutional crises. What is ultimately tested is the capability of constitutions to provide guidance to state organs and constitutional actors, and to convey the impression that no impasses exist blocking the way to financial crisis management.

The attempt to grasp how constitutions have been reacting to the financial crisis, while it still unfolds, equally entails privileges and risks. Only in real time can the immediate responses and their importance be captured before they are set aside because of new developments and reinterpreted from a distance. Yet reversals may happen, and the end is neither fixed nor foreseeable, so the attempt to make predictions is best abandoned and focus placed on comprehending and explaining how the financial crisis connects to constitutions so far.

Four years have passed since the outbreak of the crisis, and by now (September 2012) distinct paths of constitutional reaction can be discerned under the rationale of interrelated shifts in the functions of constitutions and the relationship of state organs: *adjustment, submission, breakdown and stamina.* Constitutions adjusted to the requirements of the financial crisis, became submissive, succumbing to its demands, broke down under the pressure or remained intact, demonstrating stamina. Part I of this book presents these reactions analytically, and the parameters that determine how constitutions react. Structured along these four paths, the four sections that follow offer a full account of the interaction between the financial crisis and national constitutions, revealing the overall constitutional landscape and the concomitant perspectives in each country. How and why constitutions took each path and formed their reaction in the face of the financial crisis becomes apparent through the course of each chapter.

PART I
Constitutional Reactions in Comparative Perspective

Chapter 1
How Constitutions Reacted to the Financial Crisis

Xenophon Contiades and Alkmene Fotiadou

> In my beginning is my end. In succession
> Houses rise and fall, crumble, are extended
> Are removed, destroyed, restored, or in their place
> Is an open field, or a factory, or a by-pass.
>
> T.S. Eliot, *East Coker*

An overview of how constitutions responded to the global financial crisis based on the comparative study of political systems and power configurations, litigation and fundamental rights, constitutional reforms and the performance of constitutional functions brings forth *four types of constitutional reaction*: adjustment, submission, breakdown and stamina.

Can the political systems in the countries struck by the financial crisis get through it unscathed? The first part of this chapter addresses the inevitable *interaction between political systems and financial crisis*. How resistant to the effects of the crisis the political system appears to be may in itself provide explanations as to the particularities of the way in which the financial crisis materialized in each separate country. Patterns of authority may change, *the executive, the legislature and the judiciary may redefine their operational scope*, and the party system may undergo transformations that could eventually turn out to be either deep or superficial. Such rearrangements may enter the text of the constitution or affect its application – even by triggering informal change.

The second and third parts of this chapter map out formal and informal constitutional change occurring during the financial crisis, which ranges from the enactment of new constitutions and total revisions to modifications and adjustments, while examples of inertia are also approached. *Narratives of constitutional reform are a separate incident of the financial crisis*, sometimes corresponding to the changes actualized and sometimes proving unfeasible yet suggestive of the journeys of constitutional faith. Informal change brought about by the vast bulk of the legislative output adopted to tackle the crisis, bearing the mark of urgency and commonly containing measures of questionable constitutionality, complements the financial crisis legal scenery. Often challenged before courts, the crisis-induced legislation has led to a series of judgments addressing the permissibility of rights limitation in light of financial emergency, *thus reassessing indirectly the scope of judicial self-restraint*. Distinct areas where developments activated by the financial crisis are traced include the nature of regulation, the doctrinal dictates of proportionality and legal certainty, the endangerment of social rights, the constitutional enshrinement of fiscal discipline clauses and the fade-out of state sovereignty.

The fourth section examines *how the financial crisis affects the functions of the constitution*: constitutionalism is challenged, the allocation of powers is undergoing rearrangement and the symbolic function, being intrinsically bound to what people expect from the constitution, is reactivated or threatened with decline. How constitutions react to the financial crisis is documented in the final part of this chapter, where four distinct paths of constitutional reaction toward the crisis are analysed under the prism of multilevel transformations.

Crisis, State Powers and the Political System

The Judiciary: Interpretative Shifts

The role of the judge as guarantor of the rule of law and of fundamental rights is tested by the financial crisis. Claims of constitutional violations accumulate before courts, as the rights of the weak as well as the rights of the strong are subjected to legislative limitations. For example, infringements of property rights might include cutting down pensions but also the rights of creditors such as banks. Judges are faced with difficult choices, as the stakes are high and their choices determine their court's profile. The characterizations of activism and, conversely, of backing up governmental choices hang overhead and in that context judges may demonstrate an unusual degree of self-restraint, while there is also a chance that *activism might merely entail applying traditional doctrines in the traditional way*. When asked to decide on the scope of constitutional protection in the course of the financial crisis, courts are actually handling the very notion of constitutional normativity and thus influence constitutional faith.

Courts themselves are susceptible to change due to crisis-induced litigation that urges them to interpret constitutional principles and rights under the shadow of emergency. When they rule on the constitutionality of legislative measures taken as a result of the financial crisis, courts are faced with *choices that could change their profile*. This may happen either because judges alter their interpetation or because they abide by their prior jurisprudence under newly created circumstances. What is perhaps difficult to trace in the crisis case law is where *genuine crisis-related changes in the application of constitutional doctrines and rights are detectable*. That is, where courts altered their stance due to the financial crisis, where they adopted an unexpected stance and where what is criticized as either activism or passivity is only the true identity of a court viewed under the magnifying lenses of the crisis. Interpretative shifts may also result from the efforts a court makes to maintain its profile. Self-restraint in the midst of the financial crisis might entail such shifts: *maintaining doctrinal precedent and maintaining the same profile might turn out to be incompatible.*

Alongside moral and legal dilemmas judges may be faced with external pressures from the political class that vary from strong criticism to attempts to curtail the power of the court. The extreme facet of change in a strong court's profile has been the externally forced change in the Hungarian Constitutional Court, whose powers have been significantly reduced by way of constitutional amendment exactly because its prior consistent jurisprudence signalled that it would proclaim the unconstitutionality of governmental measures.[1] The protection the Constitutional Court had given to pension rights as property rights that may only be limited in accordance with the proportionality doctrine prerequisites, alongside proclaiming unconstitutional retroactive taxation due to violation of good morals, sketches out the stance the Court would have taken *if government had not curtailed its power to review public finance cases*. This limitation of the Court's jurisdiction, which threatens rule of law guarantees, *is a non-voluntary change in a court's profile*. Although such extreme external interference with judicial power is unique, it is not the only example of attempts to exert pressure on the judiciary. In Latvia, the judiciary accused the legislature of being vindictive against the Constitutional Court due to its rights-friendly jurisprudence, when the legislator openly considered the non-application of case law regarding the compensation of judges.

When such interventions do not exist, it is left to the judiciary to determine, and in certain cases maintain or re-invent, their profile under the challenge of the crisis. Non-interference with the expediency of governmental policies has always been a major concern and a somewhat hard to handle goal in the age of balancing and proportionality, *yet it has become particularly grave in the context of the crisis as the repercussions of invalidating legislation are amplified*, and more so, since the scheme of interference with the law-makers' goals is rendered more complex when the goals stem from obligations undertaken due to commitments made to international or supranational entities.

The Latvian Constitutional Court, which is a strong court enjoying the trust of the people, chose the path of confronting the law-maker through its crisis rulings in order to maintain its role as a champion of rights. Thus, it shielded constitutional rights from financial crisis erosion by finding unconstitutional the impugned norms in 25 per cent of the crisis cases it heard.

In contrast, the Portuguese Constitutional Court and the Greek Council of State, by upholding the constitutionality of legislative measures enacted to fulfil the obligations undertaken through the 'Memoranda of understanding', that is the bailout agreements, are examples of *strong courts opting for judicial minimalism, extreme cautiousness and self-restraint*. The reluctance of these courts to interfere

1 Throughout this comparative chapter, the approach of each country, unless otherwise indicated, is based on the analysis and data provided by the contributions in this volume.

with governmental decision-making, underlying their respective case law, signals the stance they are inclined to keep regarding crisis legislation. Even when the Portuguese Court, in the exercise of abstract review of the budget, demonstrated what is perceived as a will to confront the law-maker and engage in rigorous constitutional review, adopting a more robust attitude than expected in light of its original reaction to crisis litigation, it did so cautiously. It pinpointed the unconstitutional disproportionalities but nonetheless left the 2012 budget intact, prescribing changes for 2013. Fear of the unpredictable results that may stem from overturning fiscal policy is conspicuous in the ruling, which strives to strike a balance between championing rights and not placing insurmountable obstacles in the path of the government's endeavour to reach its financial goals.

In the Greek example things are even more complicated due to the existence of a diffused system of constitutional review, in which, although the Council of State has traditionally played the role of a quasi-constitutional court virtually exercising concetrated constitutional review, all courts have the power to rule on the constitutionality of a provision when hearing a specific case. This opens up a wide range of options. Thus, a ruling of unconstitutionality pronounced by a Justice of the Peace finding wage cuts that had been imposed due to the Memorandum disproportional gained the same publicity as the Council of State judgments, and their two rationales are widely juxtaposed despite the difference in the hierarchy of the courts that issued them.

The stance courts adopt during the financial crisis and the case law they produce may be viewed from several angles. From the aspect of the legislator, the question is *how to ensure that legislation passes constitutionality review*. This may involve exerting external pressure on the court or contrarily drafting legislation in such a way that it can withstand judicial evaluation. From the aspect of judges, *interest in the legitimacy of courts inevitably comes into play*. From the aspect of rights claimants, the question boils down to *what convinces judges to invalidate*. How to deal with judicial concerns over legitimacy, and in certain occasions even with concerns regarding their individual reputation as judges, could turn out to be a very important consideration. From the aspect of constitutional evolution, questions may emerge with regard to whether the financial crisis case law amounts to informal constitutional change. The role of the judiciary in handling the crisis may have multifaceted consequences as it impacts on the people's faith in the constitution and it may also provide a *safety valve* against the results of the disappointment and anger caused by the crisis.

In their struggle to tackle the strain put on constitutional rights under the pending accusation of an activism that may have more detrimental consequences than anticipated, judges engage in a *financial crisis-induced bricolage*.[2] An underlying common jurisprudential thread has emerged due to the crisis, which cannot be accurately described as judicial borrowing but rather as unavoidable

2 M. Tushnet, 'The Possibilities of Comparative Constitutional Law', *Yale Law Journal* 108 (1999): 1225-1310.

bricolage, since judges employ comparative constitutional jurisprudence to solve the problem in hand. Its distinct feature is that it does not consist of citing foreign authority or making explicit references to foreign jurisprudence. Filtered through the litigants' argumentation, this unique type of borrowing constructs a *sort of implied dialogue between courts that address the same constitutional issues in hard cases under the pressure of emergency, the political implications of their rulings and the publicity and attention these rulings draw*. Questions regarding the knowledge and information judges have about the legal orders and the courts they are glancing towards are secondary compared to the linkages the financial crisis has created, as bailout agreements dictating the same line of fiscal policies create similar issues and produce unexpected and perhaps bizarre comparability transcending its traditional notion. How knowledgeable justices are varies,[3] and so does the degree of sophistication of the filtering that borrowed arguments and concepts undergo. Answering legal questions is linked to a current emergency rather than the deeper linkages between constitutional arrangements and the ratio and history of provisions.[4]

The attitude of openness is not confined to crisis-struck jurisdictions: whatever works bricolage techniques lead to the usage of notions such as 'minimum subsistence' and 'Existenzminimum', which are incorporated as terms and even referred to in quotations without reference to their controlled designation of origin, but interpretatively built into the constitution being applied. Nonetheless, judges do not pick and choose as randomly as it appears.[5] *A unique stream of information has started to flow regarding the constitutional issues faced by crisis-struck legal orders and especially their case law*.

Relevance and comparability are thus produced by the crisis itself, since identical constitutional problems are litigated and agreements with international lenders obey the same rationale, placing similar threats on fundamental rights. First aid tools used by judges blend into their jurisprudence remarkably quickly. These foreign ingredients are absorbed into the national cuisine, not losing their original flavour but producing distinct local dishes. What's more, the environment in which judges pronounce their rulings has evolved: suddenly a supreme court decision in Spain or Portugal upholding or invalidating austerity measures makes headline news in Greece and Italy, and vice versa. It is not just attorneys who borrow arguments to which inevitably judges must respond; *it is the people as*

3 On the possibility of judges understanding foreign law, see M. Tushnet, 'When is Knowing Less Better Than Knowing More? Unpacking the Controversy over Supreme Court Reference to Non-U.S. Law', *Minnesota Law Review* 90 (2006): 1275-1302.

4 S. Choudhry, 'Globalization in Search of Justification: Toward a Theory of Comparative Constitutional Interpretation', *Indiana Law Journal* 74 (1999): 819-892; V.C. Jackson, 'Constitutional Comparisons: Convergence, Resistance, Engagement', *Harvard Law Review* 119 (2005): 109-128.

5 D. Robertson, *The Judge as Political Theorist: Contemporary Constitutional Review* (Princeton University Press, 2010).

well who accumulate expectations regarding the feasibility of constitutional rights protection. The backlash of judgments is seriously influenced by foreign jurisprudence. The stage for the financial crisis bricolage is thus set. And even when judges do not follow the example of their foreign colleagues, they are under a burden to provide sound justification for the reasons why not.

Exploring how this bricolage affects jurisprudence is not easy. A common theme is emerging, producing a shared jargon stemming from the way constitutional rights are subjected to limitations that serve the public interest, the concomitant construction of the common good notion in terms of facing a financial crisis, novel conceptualizations of emergency and the deviations it permits, and inventive uses and misuses of proportionality creating a case law with distinct characteristics. *Often within this jurisprudence more commonalities may be found than between the crisis-related rulings of a specific court and its prior case law.* What legacy this jurisprudence will leave is far from clear. Nonetheless, constitutional doctrine will not be left intact, and perhaps the discussion on juristocracy will be influenced as well, since the role the judiciary choose to play in various legal orders has the potential to influence the very course of the financial crisis. For example, invalidating bailout agreements due to unconstitutionality or contrarily upholding them regardless of the strain they might place on fundamental rights lies at the heart of the activism–self-restraint dipole. *The financial crisis is forging a case law culture of its own; and this culture seems to trample the prerequisites of comparative propriety in judicial borrowing due to the extraordinary context it creates.*

The Legislature: An Ambivalent Pragmatic Turn

The manner, quality and form of law-making has changed during the financial crisis. The changes are profound and have thus impacted the function of the legislature. The traditional role of parliament as the law-making body that produces legislation through deliberation is being tested. The subsequent ratification of austerity measures and reforms became a mainstream function of legislatures, which thus appear to be undergoing a *downgrade of their law-making power.* The substantial relocation of law-making power in the executive branch alters the profile of parliaments. Conversely, *the importance of the legislature's oversight role in monitoring economic regulation is revisited.*

The situation created by the financial crisis demands swift legislative responses to what is perceived as an emergency situation. Standing Orders of Parliaments, which in many cases have been modified in that direction, demonstrate that this change is becoming a permanent mode of law-making. Swiftness of response can be rephrased as haste in law-making. The connotations are different as the quality of law-making deteriorates, time for impact assessment vanishes and the effectiveness of legislation adopted under such conditions becomes doubtful. Acceleration in the pace of law-making making leads to hastily drawn legislation, which in the long run betrays its original goal of achieving quick results by proving to be ineffective.

Fast-track law-making often corresponds to augmented use of decree laws, wherein rules are drafted by government and subsequently ratified by parliament with limited opportunity for either elaboration or debate. The role of parliament is thus reduced with regard to the substance of rule production. Nonetheless, the crisis legislation, touching upon constitutional rights and principles, *is impacting constitutions to a degree that amounts to inducing informal change.* Novel regulatory demands along with the need to re-evaluate regulatory practices demonstrate an important aspect of the law-making problems, which are linked to the existing constitutional arrangements and their degree of flexibility. It could be argued that these changes in the role of parliament correspond to a *pragmatic turn dictating the adaption to the new requirements created by the financial crisis*, that is the ability to respond quickly to the risks posed by the financial markets and to monitor the financial regulatory system.

A variety of cunning tricks has been employed to stretch the procedural possibilities and allow speed to become the key element of law-making in most of the examined legal orders. The Icelandic 'Emergency Act', which brought about severe modifications to financial legislation, was prepared and passed under conditions of extreme haste. Drafted in a few days and debated in a few hours it is exemplary of extremely hastily adopted legislation. The need to react swiftly to imminent dangers also underlies the rationale of the High Court, which upheld the Act's constitutionality.

Budget-related draft laws were the vehicles employed in Latvia, where draft laws aiming to bring about reforms to tackle the crisis were packed together with the national budget or with amendments to this law so that they would be passed quickly. This allowed a fast-track process to be followed, which facilitated quick reforms addressing a wide variety of topics. Speed of this kind led to harsh criticism of the quality of the legislation by the judiciary, which targeted *haste and unprofessionalism in the preparation of the legislation.*

In Spain and Italy, much of the crisis legislation adopted was in the form of decree-laws. In Spain, a remarkable number of decree-laws were enacted containing wide-ranging measures to handle the crisis. The 'extraordinary and urgent necessity' required by the Constitution for the use of decree-laws was identified with the need for urgency dictated by the financial situation. The use of this tool was so extensive as *to impact the very system of sources of law*, since decree-laws acquired a novel position in it. It is important that during the crisis decree-laws became *qualitatively different* as they no longer addressed urgent matters of limited national significance, but on the contrary mostly tackled wide-ranging matters of national importance such as banking law and labour law. Furthermore, they are of a permanent nature, as they are not intended to be implemented over a short period of time only.

The use of decree-laws had been mainstream in Italy for years, yet during the financial crisis they became the main vehicle for passing legislation, subtly gaining permanency. All major crisis-related legislation, including the 'Save Italy' piece of legislation, which was pursued to achieve a balanced budget, is in the form of decree-laws. Such decrees enacted by government lose force if not adopted by parliament within 60 days and it is common practice for governments to employ votes of confidence to ensure their passage. This results in very limited time for consideration or debate and very little room for amendments.[6]

When fast-track law-making by government with subsequent parliamentary approval becomes upgraded to a frequent procedure it strips parliament of its traditional role. Haste in the production of rules does not merely change the quality of the rules themselves, but also *erodes the identity of the legislature* insofar as it confines its participation in the subsequent approval of measures, and substantially limits debate and deliberation prior to the adoption of rules. Regardless of the impact this may have on the quality and effectiveness of the rules produced, *it alters the manner in which they acquire legitimation.*

In the extreme case, change in the functioning of the legislature could lead to the straightforward curtailment of the role of parliament, which occurred in Hungary. The new Constitution provides for a two-thirds majority requirement for all major financial issues, while a Budget Council with constitutional status has been conferred veto power over the state budget in specified cases, thus limiting the budgeting power of the legislature and upsetting the traditional role of a legislature in a democracy.

In countries where the financial crisis did not lead to a general dismantling of constitutional safeguards, the augmented production of rules by government was counterbalanced through the *enhancement of parliamentary scrutiny* to secure transparency and legitimation. In the UK, parliamentary scrutiny was strengthened by the Fiscal Responsibility Act 2010. As part of that new phenomenon, more focus is placed on the authority of select committees of the House of Commons. Characteristic of the tendency to strengthen parliamentary scrutiny over the executive is the creation of a new committee, the Backbench Business Committee, which is chaired by a member of a non-governing party and is designed to give more voice to backbench MPs. In Iceland, proposals for the new Constitution include the enhancement of the controlling role of parliament over the executive. Changes in the processes followed by legislatures reflect the new reality. In Ireland, improvement of the Lower House processes is underway, including enhancement of oversight and scrutiny over state agencies and strengthening the position of the Speaker. In Greece, the Standing Orders of Parliament have already been modified to allow swift law-making on the one hand and enhanced oversight on the other, whereas more radical changes in that direction have been announced. Although it is too early to know whether such enhancement of monitoring authorities will materialize into a substantial oversight power or fade away as a spontaneous

6 See E. Piccardi, 'The Economic Crisis and the National Parliaments: The Italian Experience'; available at http://www.parlamento.it/documenti/repository/affari internazionali/ecprd2012/4_Piccardi_EN.pdf.

reaction to experiencing the crisis, it shows a *wider trend towards the pursuance of transparency.*

The above changes in the role of legislatures are not a one-way street. In the United States, despite the extensive delegations of authority channelling power to the executive, the power of the legislature was not threatened. This is demonstrated by the deep involvement of Congress in the discussion of the terms of the bank bailouts, since the response to the financial markets crisis was a task belonging to both the executive and the legislature. Political polarization within a strict separation of powers system led to conflicts between the President and Congress, over which he has no control, as usually happens in parliamentary systems. These confrontations did not diminish the role of the US legislature.

The Executive: In Battle Position

The executive branch was asked to play a key role during the financial crisis, involving multiple tasks, many of which were quite novel. Interminable negotiations with international lenders and the EU have become an integral part of the job, subtly *displacing traditional social deliberation.* Markets, whose confidence acquired major importance, became a permanent dialogue partner, and a hard one to convince. The legislative production of the executive branch was augmented greatly in response to the requirement of speed. *The scope of government powers expanded* through the enhancement of scrutiny and regulatory functions to enable response to the demands of the crisis, leading to *the emergence of new governmental agencies* mandated to perform regulatory and oversight tasks. *The functioning of governments themselves* has undergone transformation in light of the new political landscape, as their collective functioning acquires different characteristics within coalition government settings induced by the crisis. In this changed environment, *unprecedented reactions by heads of state*, who attempted to redefine the role of the president in parliamentary republics, became part of the picture in some countries.

The scope of activity of the executive is undergoing a steady crisis-driven growth. The requirement that the state intervene in the financial markets and produce effective financial regulation has led to the establishment of new supervisory authorities and to reflection on the nature and expediency of regulation.[7] Attributing the financial crisis to regulatory failures underlies this tendency. A clear example is the overall reconstruction of the Financial Services Authority in the UK, renamed the Financial Conduct Authority, and the focus on consumer protection and market oversight, while its main task of banking supervision has moved on to an independent subsidiary within the Bank of England. This break-up of tasks and authorities and the enhancement of the Bank of England's role in

7 J. Black, 'Managing the Financial Crisis – The Constitutional Dimension', LSE Law, Society and Economy Working Papers, 12-2010; available at http://eprints.lse.ac.uk/32895/.

view of the fact that it is deemed to be best equipped to deal with the functioning of financial entities and markets, although as yet untested, shows the importance placed on the change of the state apparatus in dealing with its new mandate. The establishment of an independent Banking Commission to report on British banks and the discussions on how the Bank of England governor should be appointed, along with the intensification of the use of penalties and prosecutions, are also characteristic.

This enhancement of the role of the executive in financial regulation along with vesting new tasks to independent authorities appears to be a general phenomenon. In the Irish example, where failures in financial regulation were also given major importance, the focus is on ways to improve regulation. The Central Bank Reform Act 2010 has been introduced to address the problems caused by the previously existing division in tasks between the Regulator and the Central Bank, while financial scrutiny of public expenditure has been enhanced through the establishment of a Fiscal Advisory Council and an independent Electoral Commission. The power of the Federal Reserve in the United States became clearly visible during the crisis, as its monetary policy has enormous political implications.[8] Dodd-Frank, the Obama regulation reform introduced after the 2008 financial crisis to promote financial stability and transparency, increased regulation significantly.

The formation of coalition governments in countries with no prior experience in this kind of governance created the need for ground rules for decision-making, amplified by the requirements of speed and efficiency and the newly emerged negotiation mandate stemming from the crisis. This seems to have worked in two directions: in the UK, the revision of the Cabinet Manual to provide detailed rules that enable the smooth functioning of government in response to the new demands of collective workings of government suggests that collectivity based on clearly drawn procedures is achievable. Conversely, the Greek experience demonstrates that coalition does not necessarily lead to collective decision-making, as it is strongly suggested that governmental policies are decided by the leaders of the parties that have formed the coalition government rather than by the collective functioning of government.

The extent to which *the crisis has pushed, and probably legitimized, state organs to act in unpredictable ways* and in deviation of prior practice is traceable; there are even specific examples of heads of state who have behaved in unprecedented ways under the strain of the crisis. In Iceland, an authority never applied before by the President of the Republic was employed for the first time as he refused to sign legislation. By twice refusing to sign bills passed by parliament, the President triggered the constitutional dictate that in case of rejection bills must be put to referendum. This development inevitably brought about a debate on the scope of presidential powers. In Latvia, presidents during the financial crisis became

8 G.N. Magliocca, 'The Deep State', 8.8.2012; available at http://balkin.blogspot.gr/2012/08/the-deep-state.html.

engaged in efforts to overcome it in ways that enhanced their authority. These involved calling for negotiations between political parties to urge them to come to agreement and ultimatum-type speeches addressing the need for constitutional amendments.

In the search for ways in which the crisis has affected constitutional rules, overtly or subtly changing the constitution and its operation, several examples have surfaced. What remains to be seen is whether such changes are of a permanent character, as well as what factors will determine that, differentiating spontaneous fleeting reactions from structural changes.

The Political System: A Whodunit Story

The way in which the financial crisis has influenced the political systems of the countries it has struck has all the ingredients of a whodunit story. There is a victim, there are also multiple suspects who connect to the victim and to each other in multiple ways, past secrets are revealed, distrust grows, strange coalitions emerge, the solution is expected from a wise outsider and reversals are a lingering possibility.

A crisis of values and disenchantment with the political class followed the outbreak of the financial crisis. *Party system restructuring* occurred as the governing parties experienced significant decline in their share of votes, and in certain instances major parties collapsed while new political parties appeared, some of which belong to the extremes of the political spectrum. The emergence of hung parliaments resulted in the formation of coalition governments, where this had been unprecedented. The need for some sort of catharsis was expressed through impeachments of public officials and the quest to enhance accountability mechanisms. Most countries experiencing financial crisis found themselves in a changed political landscape, consisting of a matrix of interacting developments that demand alterations in practices, regulations and even political ethos.

The growing dismay with politics, which in most countries preceded the crisis, culminated and concretized into *delegitimation of the political class, accompanied by distrust in state institutions*. Within the newly emerged political reality disappointment in certain instances also took the form of social upheaval. In Iceland, overreaching distrust of political parties and MPs followed the crisis and was targeted not only against the government and parliament, but also against the state institutions deemed responsible for monitoring the financial market. Distrust of institutions also grew in Ireland, supplemented by a general attitude of mistrust of politicians. In the UK, the reputation of parliamentarians suffered a blow, due to corruption scandals having to do with MPs' expenses, and put in question the efficacy of parliamentary scrutiny. This development, combined with the increasing frustration against public institutions and distrust of expert systems flowing from the failures of the regulatory system, created a climate of overall disillusionment. Political scandals have also totally dismantled trust in politicians and political parties in Portugal, as institutional failures in the operation of oversight mechanisms became apparent. Likewise, in Spain the financial crisis is attributed by the people to poor governance and the failures of the political class.

Disenchantment with the political class took the form of *social upheaval* and was expressed through protests and demonstrations primarily in Greece, Portugal, Spain, Italy, Iceland and Hungary. At the institutional level, *early elections were called in several countries*. It is quite remarkable that in Spain the Prime Minister announced in June 2011 that general elections would be held in November, contrary to all prior practice according to which early parliamentary dissolutions always came as a surprise. In Iceland, early elections were called due to strong public pressure. In Portugal and Greece, early elections were also held. In the case of Greece, early elections were called in 2009, at the beginning of the crisis, and in May 2012 in its midst. That election, where total dismay towards the major parties was expressed, resulted in a hung parliament. Since the formation of a government proved impossible, new elections had to be held in June 2012.

The financial crisis brought about changes in the party systems of the affected countries. *The collapse of long-lived major parties* and the formation of new ones marks a striking break from the past. The change of scenery, however, has also produced remarkable *deviations from party discipline* and the enhancement of extreme right-wing or left-wing parties and populist narratives. In Ireland, the party that had formed the government for 61 of the 79 years since 1932 was punished by the electorate and in 2011 suffered a crushing election defeat that endangered its very survival. In Greece, the two major pro-bailout parties suffered extensive losses as their share of the vote dropped spectacularly to almost half, a radical left-wing coalition quadrupled its power to become a key player and an extreme right-wing party entered parliament for the first time. In Spain, the ruling socialist party suffered unprecedented losses, which was also the case in the post-crisis elections in Iceland, where the ruling party, which had been in power for 18 years, also suffered remarkable losses. In Hungary, the collapse of the ruling socialist party was followed by dramatic changes in the party system as the rightist coalition gained a supermajority and established parties failed to enter parliament, while new parties including an extreme right-wing one succeeded. The defiance of party discipline is a feature that also marked the political developments in several countries, the most striking examples being Greece, Ireland and Portugal; and it might not be a mere coincidence that these are the countries where the severest austerity measures were passed by parliament.

No such developments occurred in the United States. Nonetheless, the recession impacted politics by *further enhancing polarization*. Ideological differences in fiscal matters became more acute. As the President applied policies to manage the financial crisis, the extremely conservative Tea Party faction acquired a dominant role within the Republican Party, which led to the sequence of events of the debt-ceiling crisis. The characteristics of the political system became more conspicuous due to the financial crisis and polarization resembling that of parliamentary systems was revealed: the political parties act like those in parliamentary systems *but with the advanced weaponry provided by the legislative rules resulting from the stricter separation of powers system.*

The formation of *coalition and technocrat governments* in countries where it was not common practice has been a crisis-related phenomenon,[9] which has led to discussions about changing electoral laws. In Hungary, the formation of a technocrat government comprising both experts and politicians with the task of managing the crisis lasted only for one year; this unpopular government was swept away by the landslide victory of a rightist coalition. In Greece, an interim coalition government under a technocrat prime minister was formed to manage the bailout, and was followed after two consecutive general elections by a coalition government composed of three political parties with unwavering pro-Euro agendas. In Italy, a technocrat government totally composed of experts succeeded the collapse of the Berlusconi government in November 2011. This government enjoyed the vast confidence of both Houses and was mandated to manage the crisis. Finally, the first coalition government in modern times in the UK was formed after the general election of 2010, led by the Conservative Party.

A side-effect of changes in the political system was that pre-existing electoral laws were put under scrutiny and criticism. In Greece and Italy, the new political party landscape and the current trend of coalition governments have led to serious discussions about *changes in the electoral laws*. In the UK, a major constitutional innovation has been proposed, that is recall elections for MPs. This proposed change reflects the new coalition government rationale, which corresponds also to the growing need for efficient accountability mechanisms. In line with this tendency the financing of political parties was put on the table in many countries.

Ensuring accountability became a focal issue during the financial crisis. In Iceland, a Special Investigation Commission was given the task of searching for the reasons for the collapse of the banking system, and provided a detailed report on the failures that had occurred. On the basis of this report the former Prime Minister was impeached and convicted for negligence in office. The importance of attributing responsibility is also demonstrated by the establishment of a new office for the investigation of alleged criminal conduct related to the events which led to the crisis, and by the enhancement of accountability provided for by the constitutional draft prepared by the Constitutional Council.[10] In the UK, the Treasury Committee is investigating the rigging of the LIBOR rate by Barclays, and it is noteworthy that the Opposition suggested that the inquiry should be made by a judge-led independent committee. After the banking crisis the Financial Services Authority changed its approach to prosecutions and become much more favourable to this means of control. In Ireland, the financial crisis resulted in strong calls for enhanced accountability. Nonetheless, a referendum

9 In certain countries, for example in Iceland and Ireland, coalition governments were formed during the crisis but this did not constitute an unusual practice.

10 T. Gylafson, 'From Collapse to Constitution: The Case of Iceland (June 2012)', CESifo Working Paper Series No. 3770; available at http://ssrn.com/abstract=2034241.

aiming to confer on parliament the power to hold inquiries failed. This outcome, although seemingly contradictory, can be explained by distrust of parliament and the popular perception, underpinned by the crisis, that parliament and government are not in reality distinct from one another. In Greece and Portugal, discussions about enhancing accountability are ongoing but have not as yet materialized into the activation of control mechanisms.

The role of *punishment in times of crisis* is as sensitive as it is important. Two alternative ways of dealing with the responsibility of the political class with regard to the financial crisis can be detected. The first is to hold investigations and impose sanctions. The second is to enhance the accountability mechanisms provided for by the constitution. This second path suggests that people attribute the crisis more to systemic malfunctions than to individuals, although it might also indicate a reluctance to stir up political passions in the midst of a trying situation. Catharsis is sought through attempts to ensure that the constitution will not allow the future recurrence of bad practices rather than through punishment.

The Crisis as a Trigger of Constitutional Reforms

The Spontaneous Move towards Constitutional Revisions

Any major crisis endangers constitutional endurance, and more so when a crisis is attributed (even partly) to the function of the political system, which is regulated by the constitution. It is thus not surprising that the outbreak of the crisis was soon followed in several legal orders by a *frenzy about constitutional reform*, which in most cases eventually cooled off and was succeeded by discussions on rectifying and rationalizing specific provisions. Thus, the initial reactions, which varied from calls for replacement, total revision and even use of constituent power, faded away and more targeted interventions were scheduled. In certain cases the initial enthusiasm was confined to words, lingering in political party agendas and plans for the future, whereas in others it was realized through the initiation of processes that did not, however, proceed as smoothly as anticipated.

Understanding the spontaneous need for reform as a reaction to the financial crisis brings forth the question of constitutional faith: *is it faith or lack of faith in the constitution that urges people to press for radical constitutional change?* On the one hand it might indicate lack of trust in the existing arrangements with regard to the function of the polity, but on the other it might be indicative of a deeper adherence to constitutionalist ideals expressed in the romantic belief that changing the constitution will offer an exit from the crisis. The turn in the direction of rationalizing constitutional provisions expresses a tendency towards efficiency-oriented constitutional change.

From a comparative perspective, amendment mechanisms do play a role: availability (or lack of availability) of mechanisms that allow immediate revision and, conversely, stringency of the amending formula are crucial. They may either facilitate or rule out spontaneity and impose a time of sober reflection, while there is a chance that over-strict prerequisites may trigger deviations from the formula. In other words, constitutional amendments that were proposed or came about as a response to the financial crisis *offer a test area for the ratio of amending formulas* that are notoriously striving to strike the proper *balance between adaptability and protection against whimsical change and temporary majorities*. On the one hand, the major demand of responses to any crisis is speed and efficiency enhancement, while on the other speed may coincide with the side-effects of hasty decisions sometimes made under the additional pressure of a general spirit of malaise and disappointment induced by the recession. Constitution writing in that context may have far-reaching consequences.[11]

A distinct aspect of the impact of the financial crisis on constitutional change is the *constitutional adoption of a balanced budget clause* and the way this is performed and treated in different legal orders. State sovereignty issues are raised, and the balanced budget clause may be regarded differently where it is viewed purely as a product of external pressure, as opposed to being part of the constitutional dialogue or considered by theory as implied by the constitution. Its compatibility with the constitutional enshrinement of social rights is questioned, as it may set serious impediments to the realization of those rights even when they are regarded as policy goals. The big question raised is *whether it is actually an undue limitation imposed on democratic decision-making or can be part of the checks and balances system*, setting limits on the executive. The constitutionalization of balanced budget clauses, being the most obvious crisis-induced amendment, itself bears the imprint of a change made without much impact assessment or much clarity as to the way it will be enforced in practice. Interesting lessons in that direction may be learned from the debt-ceiling crisis and the balanced budget rule discussion in the United States.

Sweeping Changes

Perhaps the most striking example of constitutional reform triggered by the financial crisis is the case of Iceland, not only because the initiation of reform qualifies as a *direct result of the crisis* but because the reform process itself and the unique form of popular participation it entailed may be attributed to crisis. The ingredients of the pressing demand for therapeutic change were an aged constitution – which had not been the product of a constituent assembly but was unilaterally established by a king – practical malfunctions caused by lack of clarity in the allocation of powers, a problem in constitutional design which became conspicuous during the

---

11 R. Congleton, 'The Political Economy of Crisis Management: Surprise, Urgency, and Mistakes in Political Decision Making', in Peter Kurrild-Klitgaard (ed.), *The Dynamics of Intervention: Regulation and Redistribution in the Mixed Economy* (Advances in Austrian Economics 8) (Emerald Group, 2004), pp. 183-203.

financial crisis and a feeling of disappointment in the Constitution, which was blamed as a contributing factor to the crisis.

The reaction was sweeping: a Special Constitutional Assembly and a Constitutional Commission were formed to organize a National Forum selected through random sampling from the National Register. The accumulation of viewpoints on the Constitution from almost 1,000 citizens who attended the Forum, along with the opportunity given to the people at large to express their opinions on the pending reforms through the social media, created a strong outset of democratic participation. In that context the low turnout in the Constitutional Assembly election (36 per cent of the electorate, whereas participation in general elections normally exceeds 85 per cent) was the first setback in the process; a second blow came soon after, when following complaints about the conduct of the election the Supreme Court nullified the election.

The initial idea of a constitution written by the nation's representatives was thus compromised. What followed was a legislative bill containing proposals by the Constitutional Council to parliament based on proposals by the Constitutional Commission and on the original points that had come up in the National Forum. These proposals themselves bear the mark of haste – the most conspicuous general symptom of the crisis. Despite such problems, no expert advice was sought and the next step, decided in the midst of heated political confrontations, is a consultative referendum on the proposals scheduled to be held in the autumn of 2012.

What commenced as a novelty in constitution writing at this point faces the possibility of turning out to be something quite different. However, it provides a *chronicle of crisis response through a constitutional path* and as such it has unique value. Treated originally as an experiment in 'crowd-sourcing' the Constitution, with a strong therapeutic function, an image conveyed also through the fanciful use of social media, the ongoing reform appears to be succumbing to a more conventional process. Shortcomings and weaknesses that may enter the text will perhaps thus be treated with less sympathy than they would be had they been the direct product of popular involvement. The exercise of constituent power under the dynamics of the financial crisis, which had been the original conceptualization of the process, became a search for compromises and consensus that turned out to be difficult to achieve, while the current Constitution suffered a lethal blow. The basic directions of the proposed revision are a clearer delineation of powers, the enhancement of checks and balances, and the adoption of more direct-democratic features through referenda processes. Distrust of the political class and political parties is reflected in the overall spirit of the proposals, rendering the Icelandic constitutional reform a true child of the financial crisis. As the outcome of this spontaneous innovative approach to constitutional change is still open, multifarious effects of the crisis with regard to the functions of the Constitution continue to emerge.

The Hungarian Constitution suffered the most detrimental change within the context of the financial crisis. A constitutional revision that took place in 2011, severely changing the character of the Constitution, will have long-lasting effects on Hungarian constitutionalism and rule of law guarantees. The basic axes of this change are a total rewrite of the constitutional rules regarding public economy and finance, the curtailment of the power of the Constitutional Court, severely limiting the scope of judicial review, including its elimination on all public finance issues for as long as the state debt is not reduced to below half of the GDP, and the introduction of a constitutional requirement of a two-thirds parliamentary majority for any changes in the basic directions of economic policy, reducing the policy-making power of any future government.

The adoption of a new constitution was made possible by the sweeping victory of a right-wing party, which acquired a two-thirds majority in parliament allowing it to alter the Constitution at will. The result of the restructuring of the party system, expressed in this election following the outbreak of the financial crisis, offers a blunt demonstration of *what a supermajority can do when empowered to remove all constitutional obstacles to its political goals*. Thus, the introduction in the constitutional text of amendments directly linked to handling the crisis combining unorthodox rules with mainstream ones, like the balanced budget clause, is overshadowed by the simultaneous removal of rule of law guarantees.

Uprooting not only the pre-existing Constitution but also the jurisprudence that went with it, by diminishing the scope of constitutional review and by changing the synthesis of the Constitutional Court and conferring on parliament the authority to elect the Court's head, which replaced the pre-existing system of election by the Court itself, amounts to a complete overturn of the checks and balances system. Hence it is difficult to soberly evaluate the crisis-induced constitutional provisions in light of their expediency or rationality. The profound impact of the financial crisis on the content of the Constitution correlates to the effects of unbridled constitution-writing power exercised by a supermajority. Tracing on the one hand the interrelation between the crisis and the formation of this supermajority, and on the other how it relates to the pre-existing function of the changed political landscape is a challenging task.

The temptation to juxtapose opposite reactions to the crisis when viewing the cases of Iceland and Hungary is difficult to resist. Is the dismantling of constitutional fetters to handling the crisis, supplemented by the reduction of the Constitutional Court's powers, actually going to allow a strong executive to handle the crisis better than governments constrained by constitutions? Or will the only result be the far-reaching endangerment of democracy and the rule of law? Has the crowd-sourced constitution-writing experience offered *some kind of catharsis and healing* in Iceland, allowing it to deal better with the consequences of the financial crisis?

Modifications and Updating

Constitutional adjustment to address a variety of issues raised by the financial crisis is the path followed in several legal orders. Two issues can be explored in documenting constitutional changes that have been taking place due to the crisis in the UK: the uncodified nature of the UK Constitution and the fluidity of its constitutional arrangements may provide an answer to the question of *how the crisis impacts the constitution when what needs to be done can be done quite easily*. This may be rephrased into the question of what occurs when the executive and legislative powers face no procedural or material constraints in making constitutional alterations. The way in which the ability to respond promptly is employed may shed light on the actual value of swift constitutional reactions during the crisis, perhaps revealing also the advantages of a certain degree of difficulty of change. On the other hand the very fluidity of the Constitution makes it more difficult to distinguish *what rearrangements will endure long enough to qualify as genuine crisis-induced constitutional reforms*.

Pinning down what constitutes constitutional change is difficult, since what is actually part of the UK's uncodified Constitution is in itself subject-dependent and sometimes hard to trace. Nonetheless, the introduction for the first time in UK history of a fixed five-year parliamentary term, resulting from the formation of a coalition government, and the concomitant tendency to give written and codified form to the procedure and practice of government appear to qualify as such. The passage of the Fixed-Term Parliaments Act 2011 and the Draft Recall Bill 2011 (which is expected to be passed in 2012), along with the revision of the Cabinet Manual, mark constitutional changes.

Upcoming reforms in the House of Lords and its relationship with the House of Commons are also linked to the context of the crisis, which rendered it crucial to rule out the possibility of government bills passed by the Commons being blocked by the unelected House of Lords. In particular, when the formation of a single party government proved impossible following the election of May 2010, the Cabinet Manual was re-drafted and published by December 2010 to provide solutions for the eventuality of a hung parliament, making conspicuous changes to prior practices with regard also to the role and function of the civil service.[12] The codification of rules performed by the revision of the Manual is a landmark point in what can be perceived as the gradual transformation of the UK's Constitution into written form, while its adoption is closely linked to, and motivated by, the effects the financial crisis has had on the political system and the reality of a hung parliament. It is therefore possible that the financial crisis will influence the route and future of the passage of the Constitution into a written, codified form.

Another lesson the UK has to offer is *the constitutional importance of regulation*. In the context of the Constitution's unwritten nature autonomous regulation and regulators occupy an eminent position. Consequently, much weight was put on evaluating and refurbishing regulation, and changes in that area are perceived as having a constitutional nature. The discussion on regulatory failures and rearrangements in regulation accompanied by changes in the type of

12 R. Blackburn et al., 'Who Governs? Forming a Coalition or a Minority Government in the Event of a Hung Parliament' (Hansard Society and the Study of Parliament Group, 2010). Available at http://www.hansardsociety.org.uk/.

regulation, along with a re-evaluation of principles-based regulation, as part of the UK's constitutional reaction to the financial crisis not only shows the major influence the crisis is having in the area of regulation but also reveals a very important facet in exploring the variety of constitutional responses to the crisis.

In Ireland, where popular involvement is a prerequisite of constitutional change and so people are accustomed to taking part in constitutional change, crisis-induced amendments have a different quality. The Irish Constitution may only be amended with the agreement of the people expressed by way of referendum. Furthermore, ceding any degree of sovereignty requires constitutional amendment, while a wide variety of issues also demand constitutional amendment in order for any alteration to be made. The examples of the Nice and Lisbon ratification referenda, which failed initially and succeeded subsequently when put again before the people, are indicative of the attitude of the people towards referenda as well as of the political problems faced by governments due to this direct-democratic requirement. These features are demonstrated in the amendments passed during the crisis. The Treaty on Stability, Coordination and Governance in the Economic and Monetary Union, which thus required constitutional amendment, was passed by 60.3 per cent on a 49.1 per cent turnout. The Judicial Pay Amendment was passed by 79.7 per cent on a turnout of 56.0 per cent. Touching upon the independence of the judiciary, the no argument failed to convince the people despite the fact that the yes amendment was obviously hastily drafted as a consequence of the crisis.

Contrarily, a proposed amendment aiming to give more power to MPs to set up inquiries into matters of public importance failed. The people, distrusting politicians, considered the difference between parliament and the government to be but fictitious, so they rejected this amendment not perceiving it as a true enhancement of accountability. What this series of crisis-related amendments seems to suggest is that *the financial crisis has already left a clear imprint on the Constitution*, which underwent modifications. It is also apparent that haste, the omni-present problem of rule-drafting during crisis, has impacted these changes, exerting influence on the sensitive area of referendum preparation, which is in itself a challenging task and a decisive element in direct-democratic procedures. The question here is whether an electorate accustomed to directly tackling all constitutional and state sovereignty issues perceives the constitutional changes dictated by the financial crisis differently.

In Latvia, throughout the crisis several constitutional reform proposals were made by the political parties and by the President of the Republic. The President's proposals that were submitted to parliament aimed at the enhancement of presidential competences. Yet, the only constitutional amendment adopted addressed the right of the people to propose the dissolution of parliament. Discussion on major reforms of the Constitution revived after a new President took office, as he suggested that a new constitution should be enacted with major alterations to the allocation of powers among branches of government. What remains to be seen is whether these proposals for serious changes will be acted on, leading indeed to major reforms induced by the crisis, or be eventually restricted to more minimal interventions.

Adopting the Balanced Budget Rule

In a straightforward sense, the formal constitutional amendment that has taken place directly as a result of the crisis is the enshrinement in various constitutions of balanced budget clauses. Such changes to the constitution usually aim *to restore the confidence of the markets and to respond to international demands*, such as the requirements set by the Fiscal Compact, that is the Treaty on Stability, Coordination and Governance in the EMU, and the Treaty establishing the European Stability Mechanism. Fiscal discipline is perhaps the most overtly crisis-related change to constitutions, as commitments of this kind are binding on all future governments and set serious limits to future policy choices.

Setting constitutional limitations on political decision-making margins by clauses adopted in the shadow of time pressure and in response to external motivation is a stereotype of the kind of hasty rule-drafting that takes place during a crisis. Approaches involving fiscal discipline clauses through the aspect of state sovereignty, by placing weight on the source of the rules and not on their content, may result in *focusing on sovereignty narratives rather than on the actual repercussions of such clauses and their potential impact on systematic constitutional interpretation*. Bearing the mark of urgency, weight is put on *the symbolic function of the constitutionalization of fiscal discipline rules* and on the communicative extroversion of their enshrinement rather than on technical perfection and applicability. Aggravated future consequences may thus stem from their heightened status.

In Italy, Constitutional Law 1/2012 amended Articles 81, 97, 117 and 119 of the Constitution. The revised Art. 81 imposes on national government as well as on local governments the obligation to balance the budget. The amendment of these articles followed fast-track parliamentary procedures and was thus made rapidly, having the consent of most political parties. The new rule is scheduled to come into effect by 2014 through the enactment of the necessary legislation. Ever since their adoption the Italian Constitution's original arrangements with regard to the budget have provided grounds for theoretical and political debate on the existence of an implied balanced budget rule. This must be considered when addressing what may have facilitated the quick response to international factors that demanded the adoption of the balanced budget rule, the question being *whether pre-existing doctrinal discussion can be a substitute for the ad hoc debate and impact assessment that major constitutional reforms require*. Moreover, it remains to be seen whether it will influence the legitimation of the reform not only during its enshrinement but also at a later stage, when the required measures for its application in practice will start being adopted.

A fast-track procedure was also used in Spain, which adopted the balanced budget rule in September 2011 following a single reading. Extreme haste marked this amendment, which was passed by parliament within 15 days of its first announcement by the Prime Minister. Given that the Spanish Constitution of 1978 had only once been amended before, the adoption of the balanced budget and the public debt cap acquires particular importance. Absence of dialogue with the Autonomous Communities and local authorities, and lack of prior elaboration by the Council of State are the major side-effects of haste.

In Latvia, an amendment of the Constitution to enshrine fiscal discipline is underway, while it is considered that through its ratification the Fiscal Compact has acquired constitutional status. Furthermore, it is widely supported by theory that fiscal discipline rules are already implied in the Constitution.

In the USA, a balanced budget amendment is among the constitutional aspirations of Conservatives, who afford much weight to fiscal responsibility.[13] Nonetheless it does not seem to have much chance of acquiring the mainstream configuration it has recently gained in Europe in the financial crisis context. State sovereignty has quite a lot to do with the way in which fiscal discipline is conceived, and in the US context the conceptualization of the merits and shortcomings of a balanced budget rule is much different, *being detached from sovereignty narratives and in the light of the strong checks and balances system that exists*. The practical difficulties of enforcing such a rule and the availability of remedies to give effect to it seem thus to be given much greater importance.

A balanced budget rule and debt-ceiling provisions have also been enshrined in the new Hungarian Constitution. It is characteristic of the new era that the right to work, deemed outdated, was omitted from the revised text. The particularities of the Hungarian case lie, first, in the paradox that the adoption of fiscal discipline rules coincided with the removal of all relevant issues from judicial control, thus leaving no clear safeguards as to their implementation, and, second, in the subsequent passage of new constitutional legislation postponing their entry into force until 2014, as they were considered to be inconveniently over-rigid. The exact nature of this piece of legislation is not clear as yet, and both the above-mentioned particularities are related to the formation of a political supermajority with constitution-making power.

In Greece, the external pressure for the adoption of a balanced budget rule did not lead to its enshrinement within the Constitution, since no constitutional amendment process can start before May 2013 due to a mandatory time interval between two consecutive amendments imposed by the stringent amending formula. Thus, despite the debate it triggered with regard to the limits it sets to political decision-making along with sovereignty issues, it could not be adopted because of the prerequisites of the revision process. This situation can be viewed as *a test of the proper level of difficulty of changing the Constitution*: the amending formula provides a serious obstacle to sending a clear message to the markets and the other eurozone countries, yet it is also a fetter against the hasty adoption of norms.

13 See J.E. Fleming, 'The New Constitutional Order and the Heartening of Conservative Constitutional Aspirations', *Fordham Law Review* 75 (2006): 537-544.

In light of the procedural hurdles, hasty enshrinement of rules has aggravated importance since their correction is in itself hard to achieve.

What remains to be seen, in comparison to the examples of Italy and Spain, is whether having time to speculate on the desirability and probably the form of constitutional fiscal discipline rules will indeed make a difference, and if so in what direction. Moreover, it will become apparent *whether such clauses are differently perceived in states with strong decentralization*, where the constraints they impose on the executive and the legislative powers can operate as part of the checks and balances system, which is less possible by far in centralized states.

Rigidity Halts Constitutional Reform

Immobility following the immediate constitutional reform proposals made at the outbreak of the crisis characterizes Portugal. The two-thirds majority requirement set out by the amending formula, dictating a degree of consensus that could not be achieved, led to the abandonment of the initial proposals and the postponement of amendment discussions. The content of the frozen proposals targeted the status of social rights, which were to be downgraded, and in 2010 the abolishment of the right to free universal education and health care was proposed along with the relaxation of the prerequisites for firing workers. Meeting with strong opposition, these proposals were abandoned. Their adoption would have facilitated the drafting of austerity measures without the need to circumvent the Constitution but would have also *changed the identity of the document itself.*

The postponement of constitutional reforms due to the stringency of the amending formula explains the situation in Greece as well. What this obligatory period of reflection will produce is not as yet obvious. Constitutional reform talk has been intense ever since the crisis broke out, amounting to proposals for exercising constituent power or circumventing the amending formula to revise the Constitution. Such narratives are of particular importance, first because they were employed by key political figures and members of the government and, second, because such deviations had marked Greece's turbulent political history prior to the restoration of democracy in 1974.

Documenting how the discussions on constitutional change unfold while major changes in the party system occur, until they can be formalized into constitutional text, could provide evidence *for comparison between immediate and delayed reactions*. What may be explored through such a juxtaposition is whether there is a difference in the degree of actual elaboration of proposals, whether experience from constitutional orders that rushed into crisis-related reforms might be of help to others, and how reforms on the one hand and inertia on the other during a major crisis impact on the people's faith in the constitution.

The Impact of the Crisis on Fundamental Rights and Constitutional Litigation

The Focus of Fundamental Rights Protection Shifts

The financial crisis has had a growing impact on fundamental rights. Budgetary considerations, bailout agreements, hastily drawn legislation, rearrangements of policy priorities and an underlying all-encompassing notion of emergency have put a *severe stress on the exercise of rights*. Constitutional normativity is tested under this pressure, and so are the courts. Although an overall assessment of the crisis' transformative effect on rights may only be done in its aftermath, and it is possible that not merely limitations and infringements but also enhancement and expansion towards new interpretative directions may occur, a distinct crisis-related litigation has already developed. The basic features of this case law are the high profile and publicity of cases, the influence decisions have on the issuing court's profile (and the awareness of that impact by judges), claims of fundamental rights violations, the multifaceted use of Art. 1 of the First Protocol to the European Convention on Human Rights (First Protocol ECHR), the transformation of legal principles and a recurring demand to tackle the issue of haste.

Part of the drama of the financial crisis is thus played out in courtrooms. The extent to which this happens depends on the legal culture and also on the system of judicial review. Claims of unconstitutionality lie at the heart of this litigation, ranging from fundamental rights protection to sovereignty issues, sometimes disguised as challenges against the procedure used to ratify bailout agreements or to adopt measures in order to abide by them. In that process traditional doctrines like equality, legal certainty and proportionality are revisited in a new light, and the state of emergency acquires a new meaning.

The crisis litigation and the exchange of dialogue between judge and legislator in that context creates a new stream of comparability criteria. Courts of legal orders that prima facie would not be compared handle identical problems and are faced with similar doctrinal dilemmas due to the crisis. Judicial borrowing is inevitable as legal strategies to preserve the increasingly threatened rights are sought. Simply put, lawyers must come up with arguments that can win cases. To do so they explore the rationale of judgments that handle challenges brought against legislative measures enacted due to the financial crisis regardless of their country of origin, rather than seeking domestic precedent dealing with the rights at stake. What convinces judges to pronounce unconstitutionality in the particular context of the financial crisis is a matrix with multiple parameters.

Notwithstanding that the influence of the financial crisis on constitutional rights and principles unfolds in multiple arenas, courts are the place where it becomes visible and detectable. It is self-evident that salary and pension cuts would be the first issues to become objects of litigation. It is possible that *the crisis may turn out to be a trigger for re-enforcing rights where strong courts are willing to protect them*. The ability of rights to withstand the pressure, even scarred, strengthens their normative content. Already in Italy the Constitutional Court, although not yet faced with massive crisis litigation regarding infringements of constitutional rights, has recognized the extraordinary circumstances created by the crisis and used it as a basis not to curtail rights but to enhance their protection by upholding provisions that would otherwise be ruled unconstitutional. In allowing the temporary rearrangement of competence between the state and the regions due to the promptness of response dictated by the crisis, the Court has used the need for haste in a pro-social rights manner.

Yet, the impact of the crisis on rights is not limited to the area of socio-economic rights, as deeper transformations occur in the way fundamental rights operate. And although rights directly dependent on economic resources are the obvious victims, as changes in the health and education systems, the social security system and so on are triggered by the crisis, civil rights also undergo changes. What is difficult to trace is the relation between the two areas of rights, that is *whether the shift in focus towards threats against the rights most related to the well-being of the economy influences the practice and development of other rights as well.* For example, when the rights discussion moves away from topics like the right of same-sex couples to marry, the protection of the environment or the rights of immigrants and is directed towards the constitutionality of salary cuts, a question emerges as to what happens to the issues left behind. The development of rights interpretation is influenced not only by jurisprudence, but also by possible major changes in the party system caused by the crisis. The rise of extreme right-wing and left-wing political parties, with particular ideological frameworks regarding the content and protection of fundamental rights, may alter the reality of rights. Furthermore, changes in the application of principles such as proportionality, equality and security of law, and their adaptation to the crisis rationale, will inevitably have far-reaching implications.

Transformations of Proportionality

Under the burden of the knowledge that legislative limitations of rights are made in conformity with commitments undertaken by loan agreements that may be at stake, the use of proportionality varies. Thus, its rigour is used either to impede hastily drawn interventions or conversely to furnish legislative choices with extra legitimation. The latter requires *adjustments in the application of the test.*

The Constitutional Court of Latvia addressed the problem of legislative choices made in response to commitments undertaken towards international lenders by concluding that all proportionality considerations are still to be made by the legislator, as it is just the goals that are set by the agreements. How these goals are achieved and the choice of the most appropriate and necessary measure, based on the examination of alternative ways to reach them, is left to the discretion of the law-maker. According to the Court, hastily taken and insufficiently considered decisions risk the violation of fundamental rights to the same degree as excessive delay in reforms. Proportionality was thus used to invalidate hastily drawn legislation.

In upholding the constitutionality of rights limitations the Portuguese and the Greek courts alike shrunk the second step of proportionality, that is the examination of necessity when evaluating salary cuts. An underlying notion of emergency seems to erode the necessity doctrine, making flexible the obligation to seek less restrictive means to reach the legislative objective. *By relaxing the second tier of the proportionality test*, these courts refuse to address the issue of hastily drawn legislation, as they appear willing to accept the simple invocation of necessity by the legislator (Portugal) or are satisfied by the mere existence of other measures taken simultaneously (Greece).

If haste, which is a distinct characteristic of crisis legislation,[14] is left beyond judicial evaluation, or even worse accepted as a limitation of the rigour of proportionality, *the hands of the law-maker are unbound.* This could inflict wounds on constitutional normativity, as the very least legislatures are expected to do when handling constitutional rights is to afford them due consideration. On the other hand, it is the very use of proportionality that may allow the limitation of rights during a severe crisis without loss of their normative content. *It is exactly in drafting legislation hastily that proportionality can supply an efficient mechanism for the respect of rights*, as it provides clear guidelines on what to look for, formulated into ready-made steps to follow.

This mechanism has an additional asset: its worldwide acceptance as a fundamental doctrine renders it user-friendly for evaluating legislation drafted in line with commitments undertaken at the international level. From a symbolic standpoint the aspiration of preserving normativity is exactly why Greek and Portuguese courts have opted to use proportionality to evaluate the impugned legislation even though they have not been led to a ruling of unconstitutionality. By pronouncing the limitation of rights proportional, even through a tricky application of necessity, courts declare that the protective scope of rights shall withstand the crisis. Whether this is convincing depends on a variety of factors, the most important of which is perhaps *the impression left that on another occasion the court would be willing to invalidate.* In the Greek and Portuguese examples proportionality was used to back up governmental choices, while in the Greek case it is noteworthy that the Council of State went as far as to employ the third step of the test, something it rarely does in its case law, and thus found the measures *stricto sensu* proportional as well. This stance may be read in different ways that could impact both the legitimacy and the popularity of the judiciary, that is *as an expression of self-restraint or as a failure to protect rights.*

14 C. Coyne, 'Constitutions and Crisis', *Journal of Economic Behavior and Organization* 80(2) (2011): 351-357.

Proportionality, by allowing the possibility of ad hoc judgments, has immense potential during a crisis.[15] It allows courts to hand down specific judgments offering guidance to law-makers when limitations are taken too far, *without signifying an irreversible break with previous case law and without binding themselves to invalidate all similar measures in the future*, since the balancing acts performed in the application of proportionality can be very precise. This utility of proportionality can be seen in the decision of the Portuguese Constitutional Court, which exercising abstract review of the 2012 Budget opted to adopt a firmer stance compared to its prior jurisprudence, and it did so by employing proportionality. Discussing the salary and pension cuts of public servants and pensioners it read the principle of equality as prescribing that the hardship of the crisis must be equally distributed among citizens in the light of the proportionality dictates. Although the Court did not question the imperative of compliance with the Troika programme, it nonetheless stated that the goals must be reached through respect for proportionality, which requires that all departures from the principle of equality due to the crisis must be temporary.

An underlying question is whether the use of proportionality and the application of constitutional principles and rights at large can indeed be the same regardless of who the beneficiaries of the infringed rights are. The evaluation of property rights through the application of proportionality in the Council of State 'Memorandum case' in Greece has many similarities with the way in which the test was applied to scrutinize the constitutionality of property rights limitations in Iceland, both leading to the contested measures being upheld. Yet, a major difference exists: the former case is about salary and pension cuts, while the latter addresses the property rights of banks limited by a provision redefining the claims of owners of deposits in brands located in Iceland as priority claims. According to the Icelandic Court's assessment, more lenient options that would burden the creditors less would not achieve the same result, that is the legitimate goal of avoiding a bank run. Thus, proportionality was employed to scrutinize legislative choices regarding two remarkably distinct facets of the right to property.

The constitutional protection of property interpreted in light of Art. 1 of the First Protocol ECHR may have a *totally different backlash depending on the right holder*, as the people's perception of the weak–strong claimant dichotomy is much more sentiment-driven than the lawyer's. It is noteworthy that the private property protection of Art. 1 of the First Protocol ECHR has been invoked in the UK in the legal challenge brought by aggrieved shareholders who, following the nationalization of Northern Rock plc, were afforded very little compensation or were left with no compensation at all. Although the shareholders' claims of disproportional limitation of their rights were dismissed both by the domestic courts and eventually by the European Court of Human Rights (ECtHR), the very

15 X. Contiades and A. Fotiadou, 'Social Rights in the Age of Proportionality: Global Economic Crisis and Constitutional Litigation', *International Journal of Constitutional Law* 10(3) (2012): 660-686.

choice of legal basis marks a shift, as the case was not construed in terms of company law but as a question of fundamental rights infringed due to the financial crisis.[16]

No such dilemmas reached the judiciary in Hungary. Before the problem of offering the same degree of protection to constitutional rights regardless of the right-holder's identity had a chance to reach the Hungarian Constitutional Court, which would evaluate the legislation that set fixed exchange rates for private loans, the authority was removed from the Court through constitutional revision. If this had not been done and the Court had followed its case law, the decision might have put obstacles in the way of governmental policy.

The Notion of Emergency and Legal Doctrines

A conspicuous difference among legal orders lies in the way in which the notion of emergency appears. The very title of the Icelandic impugned legislation is 'Emergency Act', bearing the connotation of extraordinary circumstances, while in the Greek and Portuguese examples the idea of emergency underlies the rationale of the austerity legislation and court rulings, but is not expressly put into words so that it can acquire a more precise meaning. In Italy, although the Constitutional Court has been reluctant to explicitly refer to the crisis, when it did invoke emergency it used it to favour rights protection. In that novel context of emergency, where it is accepted as a reality and thus has a profound impact on legal reasoning, but is not a declared status with delineated legal consequences, *proportionality could provide a way of controlling its potentially detrimental impact on rights*.

The case of Ireland, where the legislator seems to be abandoning the traditional silence of the common law lawyer and has begun to explicitly state the exact aim of each piece of legislation so that it may withstand judicial review, demonstrates this potentiality. Nonetheless, *this undeclared yet accepted emergency situation inevitably impacts the factual evaluations necessary for the application of proportionality*, while it also influences the use of other traditional legal doctrines such as equality and legal certainty. Alongside proportionality, the doctrines of equality and legal certainty provide the most obvious source of arguments in favour of the protection of constitutional rights in the midst of the crisis. Yet, if applied as usual by judges they could lead in the particular circumstances to jurisprudence considered activist, since it could result in invalidating legislative measures of major importance for handling the crisis and for abiding by the obligations undertaken towards international lenders.

The Latvian example is characteristic, as the Constitutional Court denied the legislature's claims that the principle of legal certainty is limited under conditions of severe financial crisis, thus conferring in that exact context even greater

16 R.A. Tomasic, 'Shareholder Litigation and the Financial Crisis – The Northern Rock Shareholder Appeal', *Company Law Newsletter* 262 (2009): 1-5.

importance to this legal doctrine. Nevertheless, when applied legal certainty is pitched against the public interest at stake, the evaluation of the actual stability of the normative regulations relied on is considered as a prerequisite for offering protection to individuals. The result is twofold: on the one hand *the principle is strengthened due to the crisis*, but on the other it is elaborated to become *more precise and in a sense more narrow*. The starting point makes a difference: where the use of the doctrinal toolkit by courts was normally *in the direction of favouring the state*, the financial crisis did not require changes in its application.

Hence the application of equality did not lead the Irish High Court to find unconstitutional financial emergency measures that imposed a levy on all public servants. The Court counterbalanced the far-reaching content of the principle by placing on the applicant the burden to prove the unequal treatment, even though this would entail evidence requiring extreme expertise. The common law tradition of setting the balance in favour of the state in reviewing administrative decisions facilitated allowing law-makers a wide scope of decision-making in the context of the crisis too, without the need for principles to be restructured. Who bears the burden of proof determines to a great extend the outcome of unconstitutionality claims.

When such pro-state interpretations do not exist, doctrines are remoulded under the burden of the crisis as courts prepare to face the contingency of further litigation and the judge becomes more conscious of the link between rights protection and the availability of financial resources. The Greek Council of State placed on claimants the burden of proof regarding the lack of necessity of measures taken by the legislature. In doing so *it relaxed the rigour of the proportionality test in favour of the state*. The Portuguese Constitutional Court's equality-based ruling, that salary cuts and the suspension of holiday and Christmas bonuses for public servants and pensioners only were unconstitutional, led the Prime Minister to state that the argument of inequality may be bypassed by extending cuts to the private sector.

Levelling equality downward, an option already elaborated by the Italian Constitutional Court so that equality-based rulings would not interfere with legislative budgetary considerations, appears to be becoming consolidated as a concept in the context of the financial crisis. Although the crisis invocation has not as yet fully appeared in Italian jurisprudence, its debut is still remarkably relevant to the refurbishing of judicial doctrines. In the 'Alitalia case', where the Constitutional Court ruled that a law allowing an economic concentration was reasonable in exemption to communitarian antitrust rules – whereas under other conditions it would be deemed unconstitutional – *the crisis erodes proportionality from within*. Penetrating the test in the form of factual considerations the financial crisis conditions determine what is found proportional or disproportional in a direction other than in a non-recession context. *The potential erosion and reshaping of constitutional principles during the crisis may have even more severe consequences than the limitation of specific rights*.

The Constitutional Court of Spain, although not yet fully engaged in reviewing austerity legislation, has already displayed the tendency to be extremely cautious and exercise self-restraint. The alleged violation of the right to collective bargaining was brought before the Constitutional Court in a challenge against a decree law, which by adopting extraordinary measures due to the financial crisis reduced the salaries of public employees, thus modifying collective agreements. The Court ruled that there had been no infringement of the right, as none of its essential elements had been affected. Finding no interference with the right on this basis, the Court demonstrated a total reluctance to interfere with policies tackling the crisis. The burden seems to be placed on the severity of the consequences that a ruling of unconstitutionality could potentially have. Thus, despite the fact that the Constitutional Court of Spain is a strong court that has traditionally guaranteed fundamental rights and mirrored the ECtHR protection, it shows a clear inclination not to stand in the way of the legislator, accepting that the crisis creates an exceptional situation.

The right to collective bargaining is one of the rights most endangered by the crisis and its shrinkage may have far-reaching consequences. This may explain the wide publicity gained by a ruling of unconstitutionality in Greece, although it was pronounced by a low-ranking court. Finding that there had been a violation of constitutional provisions and the International Labour Treaties ratified by Greece that enshrined the right to collective bargaining, the Court stressed that the impugned measure, that is, the obligatory reduction of salaries, interferes with collective bargaining and must thus not only serve the general interest but should also contain an expiry clause as well as compensatory measures in order to satisfy the necessity prerequisite of the proportionality test. Since among the commitments undertaken by Greece towards the Troika regarding the labour market is 'levelling the playing field in collective bargaining', extreme legal sophistication will be required to determine *what constitutes permissible and proportional limitation* of this fundamental right and what amounts to its extinction.

Social Rights

Underlying the financial crisis jurisprudence is the deterioration of social rights protection. The function of a strong socio-economic rights constitutional shield during a period of severe recession is ambivalent, since it might offer a certain degree of protection but *it might also turn out to be inoperative.* Where constitutional protection is detailed and strong, as in Greece and Portugal, constitutional normativity is challenged by its inevitable shrinkage and much depends on how sophisticated limitations are. Lack of constitutional protection of socio-economic rights, as in the US Constitution, which due to its age does not entail such provisions, may allow a wider range of policy-making choices during a serious recession, without causing constitutional problems.

Wage and benefit cuts, pension cuts and austerity measures inevitably lead to reduced protection of social rights, the fulfilment of which is closely linked to budgetary considerations. Beneath challenges to austerity measures lies the increase of poverty caused by the crisis. Nonetheless, the inherent obstacles to the realization of social rights *do not allow them a place in the heart of judicial reasoning*. Although in cases challenging the austerity packages claims of social rights violations are usually included and arguments combining social rights with human dignity protection, minimum subsistence and minimum core narratives are employed, such argumentation is usually only found in dissenting opinions, whereas the courts, when they do invalidate measures due to unconstitutionality, mainly invoke property rights (the increasing use of Art. 1 of the First Protocol ECHR being a distinct trend), equality and proportionality.

The important steps made towards the justiciability of social rights have not had direct influence on the crisis jurisprudence. Perhaps judges, faced with the far-reaching political consequences that the invalidation of legislation has during the financial crisis, are hesitant to openly ground such reversals on the still contradictory basis of social rights. Protection against the adverse consequences of recession is thus channelled through widely accepted principles and rights. Social rights are thus visible in the crisis jurisprudence, yet *by themselves* they still seem *unable to offer grounds for rulings of unconstitutionality* without the support of more mainstream mechanisms.

In the area of social rights, which are the most endangered among constitutionally enshrined rights, as opposed to social acquis and minimum content considerations that are country-specific, the law-maker's obligation to respect proportionality is undisputable – thus it cannot be argued that international lenders have an expectation for the commitments undertaken by states to be kept by way of imposing disproportional limitations on constitutional rights. Although its full potential has not been as yet explored, when social rights are afforded judicial protection it is often through some finding of disproportionality.

State Sovereignty before Courts

The drafting of legislation in response to obligations undertaken through loan agreements with international entities brought the evaluation of the legal nature of such agreements before the courts. Underlying any legal evaluation of the form of international bailout agreements are sovereignty issues. EU member states had already come to terms with the idea of loss of sovereignty in the process of European integration, as their constitutions were amended where interpretation did not suffice for the necessary transfer of sovereignty to happen. Bailout agreements, however, marked a darker side of sovereignty loss, and thus challenges brought against the Memoranda before courts, questioning the way in which the commitments were made, reflect dismay at this loss.

In Latvia, where the commitments were made by a letter of intent not passed by parliament, it was the government and not parliament that made the promise. As these commitments were often referred to in draft laws, the authority of the government to undertake them was challenged before the Constitutional Court on several occasions. According to the Court, the separation of powers doctrine dictated that the need and conditions of such an international loan should be debated in parliament, which had to authorize the Cabinet to take out the loan. The Court also maintained that the international lenders did not limit state sovereignty in a formal sense. As political instability resulted from the Court's finding of unconstitutionality, the Prime Minister turned to the expertise of the Presidential Commission on Constitutional Law to resolve the issue. The Commission tried to find a middle way, on one hand being concordant with the Court that the agreement of the parliament was necessary, yet indicating that this agreement could be expressed in various formats, thus leaving much room for manoeuvring.

In Greece, the constitutionality of the form of the loan agreement was questioned per se, when a law under the title 'Measures for the Implementation of the Mechanism in Support of the Greek Economy from the Member States of the Eurozone and the IMF' was challenged before the Council of State. The Memorandum was integrated into that piece of legislation as an attachment. Yet, it was supported that this was not sufficient, since it made concessions of sovereignty and transferred state competences to international organizations (the Troika). Thus, according to that view its vote required a three-fifths enhanced majority, as provided by Art. 28 of the Greek Constitution referring to international treaties and agreements. The Council of State rejected this argument characterizing the Memorandum as a political programme and not an international treaty. Doing so had two consequences: on the one hand the Court evaded the question as to whether there had indeed been a transfer of sovereignty, and on the other hand it recognized that it was up to the legislator to find ways in which the goals set could be reached, and thus the considerations on proportionality, equality and legitimate expectations were for the legislature to make and were reviewable. The repercussions of invalidating the Memorandum as a whole where thus avoided. In addition, no words about lost sovereignty were uttered by the judge.

Compared with the Latvian case, where parliament had no part in the agreement, in Greece the Memorandum had the support of parliament. What was therefore sought by challenging the law was an even stronger approval through an enhanced majority. Regardless of the interpretation of the relevant constitutional provision, the ruling of the Court betrays the dilemmas faced regarding the identity of the Court itself. If the Court had rejected the loan agreements based on this line of argumentation, *it would also have reinvented its identity and role.*

The other side of the coin sovereignty-wise is represented by Ireland, where strong constitutional assertions of sovereignty have been enhanced by landmark past jurisprudence in such a manner that any sovereignty transfer must be decided on by popular referendum. All agreements targeting an exit from the financial crisis would thus have to be put before the people, and since it is not easily imaginable that a solution at a European level could be reached through a single agreement touching on sovereignty, continuous referenda must be called. This illustrates the difficulties that may arise when no room for manoeuvring is left to the executive or even to the legislature in light of the main side-effect of the financial crisis, time acceleration. The requirement of popular involvement for ceding any degree of sovereignty may be viewed *either as ideal in terms of democratic decision-making or as a troublesome process*, where the inherent problems linked to the use of referenda and the way in which questions are put before the people are amplified by the crisis context.

The legalistic aspects of sovereignty and the way they are tackled in each country under the pressure of the financial crisis, along with the form and nature of bailout agreements and mechanisms, are adding a new facet to the *fading state sovereignty narrative* and one that may influence it in unpredictable ways. The translation of state sovereignty transfer and loss *into a justiciable matter* bears many difficulties and is different in character to fundamental rights claims, even when their protection would entail judicial activism. *A different tint of judicial activism would be required for the resolution of state sovereignty issues.* Even if judges were keen to address state sovereignty questions in a legalistic manner, it is highly doubtful that they could make a difference in the course of sovereignty dilution. It would probably be a waste of activist energy. The fading of state sovereignty is a multifaceted and elusive process, and courts are ill-suited to handle it.

Are the Functions of Constitutions Affected by the Crisis?

Constitutionalism Challenged

The limitation of government through legal rules is one of the primary functions of the constitution, understood as constitutionalism. Limits on the power of government correspond to the rule of law and the protection of constitutional rights. Rights protection as an integral element of constitutionalism influences people's perception of the constitution and their faith in it. Any change in the constitutionalist function is bound to interact with constitutional faith. To trace such transformations in real time requires parallel monitoring of legislative intrusions upon rights, the judicial handling of such intrusions, the degree to which rights are influenced, shrink or give way, and the manner in which the tools used by courts to assess rights infringements are applied. Rights are developed through their balancing with other rights and legitimate aims, and each separate battle won or lost is imprinted in the protective scope of the right, which is perpetually redefinable. This puzzle of rights protection allows rights to grow and expand, and still to be subject to limitations that allow the expansion of other rights and the pursuance of various aspects of the general good.

Yet, *if the common good becomes identified with exit from the financial crisis*, and rights start to lose every battle when balanced against a repetitive and overwhelming goal, the constitutionalist function starts to undergo transformation. From a legal aspect the shrinkage of the protective scope of rights and the concomitant modification of the tools employed to evaluate limitations – for example changes in the way courts apply proportionality, equality and legitimate expectations in the course of the crisis – are critical aspects of this transformation. With regard to the way the people conceptualize the constitutionalist function *the line between perceiving its failure or its endurance may be much thinner*: a seminal judicial decision may suffice to create a narrative of rights being guaranteed despite the overall gloomy landscape. The role of the judiciary in that light becomes more complicated and the long-standing distinction between activism and self-restraint is itself undergoing changes.

Symptoms already detected include the subtle erosion of the limitations set on governments due to the overshadowing and somewhat nebulous emergency situation that allows the executive to trespass on or bend legal rules, supported by a judiciary contriving ways to allow such trespasses under the imperative of self-restraint. In crisis-struck constitutional orders the landscape of rights protection is being rearranged. The impression of rights protection moving perpetually forward, remedies against violations becoming more expedient, the ECtHR creating a unified culture of protection, the justiciability of social rights gaining ground and the basic justification for rights limitations lying in the competition with other rights seems to have come to an end. *A large-scale retreat of rights protection is taking place*; doctrines used as protection tools are being subtly redefined to allow this retreat and the specificity of purposes demanded for allowing rights limitation is being replaced by the *all-encompassing fiscal emergency*. The temporary character of infringements is not secured and the boundaries between what is transitory and what is transitional, signifying a passage to new interpretative realities, are unclear.

Informal constitutional change, perceived before in relation to rights primarily as their expansion through judicial interpretation, is being transformed into the legislative shrinkage of rights tolerated by the courts. Changes that occur in the area of the rights more susceptible to the contingency of economic conditions relate to the stance of courts and the elaboration of legal doctrines in directions imposed by the crisis, and may create a *spillover effect* with regard to the overall handling of fundamental rights by both the legislature and the judiciary. When under financial crisis conditions the constitution is 'taken away from the courts' and delivered into the hands of the legislator (or of whomever produces legal rules), who in many cases is bound by commitments made to international lenders, interventions on the spectrum of rights are made under a *general rationale of meeting fiscal goals* and in terms of pressure and haste. Which changes will acquire such permanence as to amount to informal constitutional amendment will become more evident as the financial crisis unfolds, but changes in the quality of informal change have already become visible.

Judicial activism and self-restraint are being remodelled. Repercussions-conscious self-restraint is bred by the conditions of the crisis. The financial risks that judicial rulings of unconstitutionality may create matter greatly, and when international commitments come into play, the stakes become higher. The practical facet of these dilemmas comes down to the observation that the more specific the unconstitutionality claim is, the better chance it stands of succeeding, as it allows judges to maintain a legalistic approach, while *the more specific a finding is, the less overall influence on policy-making it has*. The counter-majoritarian difficulty thus becomes even more complicated in financial crisis conditions.[17] To the extent that a modern version of the counter-majoritarian difficulty suggests that the difficulty lies not merely in going against elected and accountable representatives but also in going against public opinion,[18] judges are faced with a hard-to-solve puzzle. On the other hand the burden of overturning policies that may determine the outcome of the crisis might become too heavy for the judiciary to bear, even if endorsing policy choices contrary to prior constitutional interpretations may signal a decline of constitutional normativity.

The potential backlash against the courts' constitutional output during the financial crisis is unpredictable: media coverage is vast and austerity packages are often passed by votes subject to strict party discipline and are highly unpopular. Multiple dangers exist both in striking down and in supporting major economic reforms. Constitutionalism is thus being rearticulated through the route courts opt to follow in addressing constitutional claims.[19] Hard cases become harder in the context of the crisis and different courts, by treating them differently, have a part in determining the way in which the constitution navigates through the crisis.

Decline or Activation of the Symbolic Function?

The most intangible and fluid function of constitutions is their symbolic function. Constitutions provide a set of values around which a collective identity is formed. A basis of consensus with regard to political sovereignty is built, and clashes are transformed into politics. Accordingly, the people have expectations of the constitution that reach beyond its normative function (although they are not detached from it). People count on the constitution to unify their society as a polity.[20] Expectations stem from faith. Constitutional faith entails belief that the constitution will fulfil its promises.[21]

---

17 B. Friedman, *The Will of the People: How Public Opinion has Influenced the Opinion of the Court and Shaped the Meaning of the Constitution* (Farrar, Straus and Giroux, 2009).

18 O. Bassok, 'The Two Counter-majoritarian Difficulties', *St. Louis University Public Law Review* 31 (2012); available at http://papers.ssrn.com/sol3/papers.cfm?abstract_id=2097475.

19 On how the Great Depression impacted conceptions of the constitutionalist claims for government conducted in ways that secure the ordinary citizens' material conditions, see W.E. Forbath, 'The Will of the People? Pollsters, Elites, and Other Difficulties', *George Washington Law Review* 78 (2010): 1191-1206, at 1204.

20 D. Grimm, 'Integration by Constitution', *International Journal of Constitutional Law* 3 (2005): 193-208, at 194.

21 S. Levinson, *Constitutional Faith* (Princeton University Press, rev. edn, 2011); J. Balkin, *Constitutional Redemption: Political Faith in an Unjust World* (Harvard

Financial crises have the potential to undermine societal unity and at the same time test the normativity of the constitution. This twofold strain may work in two directions: it may either cause a decline in the symbolic power of the constitution, stimulating a disintegration effect, or contrarily activate the symbolic power towards the creation of a communal spirit. The determinant factor with regard to the constitution's symbolic function is *whether the people have faith in its ability to contribute in overcoming the crisis*. Where the constitution is perceived as having the capacity to be a vehicle for combating the crisis its symbolic function is enhanced, but if it is deemed to be incapable of offering support its symbolic-integrative power fades. When its symbolic-integrative power is diminished, it is possible that the constitution will collapse as well. Although the perception that the constitution can help overcome the crisis may be but a fiction, belief in this fiction may prove to be a powerful tool against the crisis.

Putting the blame for the crisis on the constitution is linked to the belief that the constitution has failed to efficiently organize the state and allocate powers so that checks and balances can provide a shield against malfunctions. Regardless of the actual share of responsibility a constitution may have in a country's economic woes, once the citizenry assign blame to it its symbolic glow is lost and the danger of constitutional populism surfaces. Constitutional replacement or total revision may then be the only way for symbolic-integrative power to be reactivated.

Unwavering faith in the constitution throughout the financial crisis and preservation of its symbolic power may be a safeguard against crisis-induced social disintegration. On the premises of a deep-rooted commitment to constitutional dictates the symbolic function may be reinforced. *The perception that the constitution is not ignored* or set aside in the process of decision-making to tackle the crisis enhances its symbolic function, which may in turn contribute to channelling the political tensions regarding crisis management in accordance with the rules of the game set by the constitution.

The preservation of symbolic power may also be sought through constitutional maintenance and updating. Constitutional revision introducing specific modifications aimed to enhance the efficiency of the constitution during the crisis is a pragmatic stance, which preserves the symbolic function by ensuring that *the constitution does not become obsolete* or treated as irrelevant because of the severe situation. Such interventions in the text of the constitution may have practical value, where they ensure that the demands set by the crisis can be pursued without need to violate or circumvent constitutional provisions, or more symbolic expressive content. The very achievement of the consensus necessary to amend the constitution in the midst of the crisis has the potential to reinforce its symbolic function.

The adoption of fiscal discipline clauses is the most recognizable direct impact of the financial crisis on constitutional texts. From the aspect of its relation to

University Press, 2011); J. Balkin, 'The Distribution of Political Faith', *Maryland Law Review* 71 (2012): 1144-1172.

the symbolic function of constitutions the constitutional enshrinement of fiscal discipline rules prima facie entails a paradox: it expresses the faith of markets and international leaders in national constitutions at a time when their normativity and symbolic strength is endangered. With regard to EU member states the signature of the Fiscal Compact does not seem sufficient to produce equal symbolism with the actual enshrinement of a debt cap in national constitutions. The puzzling consequence is that *viewed from the 'outside' the importance of national constitutions is reinforced*, however the constitutionalization of debt clauses when perceived by the citizenry as constitutional change in response to external pressure *may in itself undermine constitutional faith as part of the diminishing state sovereignty narrative.* Conversely, where seen as an addition to the checks and balances system that can help prevent the repetition of the past mistakes that led to the financial crisis, it might reinforce the symbolic function. In several constitutional orders the hasty adoption of fiscal discipline rules, which did not allow time to afford much attention to crucial considerations as to their applicability, suggests that *more importance has been placed on its expressive and symbolic power.* This could potentially strengthen the image of constitutions as vehicles to overcome the crisis. It is thus uncertain whether introducing fiscal discipline rules by way of constitutional revision will eventually lead to the enhancement or decline of the symbolic function of constitutions.

As the financial crisis unfolds, it continuously exerts influence on the symbolic function of constitutions. Whether the constitution is perceived as part of the problem or as a way out of it shapes its symbolic-integrative power. The activation or decline of the symbolic function impacts not only the fate of constitutions but the course of the crisis as well.

Reallocation of Powers

Constitutions separate state authority and allocate it to different branches. During the crisis this function of constitutions has acquired a *relaxed configuration*, to allow state powers to adapt to the emerging challenges. A subtle realignment of constitutional powers is occurring, and in many constitutional orders the rules of the game set by constitutional texts are undergoing informal change due to the financial crisis. Rearrangements in the boundaries of authorities, their functioning and the relations between state organs have been taking place. Ground rules governing decision-making processes, deliberation, law-making, regulation, oversight and control, and legitimation channels are becoming blurred, and the tension between judge and law-maker is often eased. These developments do not happen simultaneously nor do they appear in all constitutional orders. Different facets of adaptation surface in each country, indicating where the weight is put or where its weaknesses lie. How rearrangements of this function of constitutions take place depend also on the way in which each constitution sets out patterns of authority.

Fluidity encompassing the allocation of powers emerges from a stream of changes. Modes of decision-making have adapted to the crisis circumstances. Governments attempt to influence the markets and negotiate with international debtors, while they make quick decisions in line with this new deliberative process. In that context a turn towards technocrat decision-making takes place, going as far as the participation of technocrats in governments. The boundaries of executive power have expanded through extensive law-making, which reduces the legislatures' participation in the rule-making process to ex post approval. Rule-making of this type is becoming the main source of informal constitutional change during the financial crisis, claiming priority over judicial decisions. This impacts the legislatures' profile as the law-making branch, while it also undermines the way in which legislation is legitimized through parliamentary voting and its democratic connotations, and thus the legitimation role of parliament is also influenced. In certain contexts traceable changes have occurred in the way the authority of heads of state has been used to counterbalance the powers of the government and/or the legislature, complementing the overall fluidity by opening new or long forgotten possibilities.

The shrinkage of the law-making role of legislatures is counterbalanced by a distinct enhancement of their monitoring role over the executive branch. The whole consort is signalling a change in the relationship between the executive branch and the legislature. The enhancement of independent controlling agencies complements the shifting equilibrium. Focus on regulatory failures has highlighted the importance of oversight mechanisms endorsing the reliance on experts and technocrats. Checks and balances are thus under reorganization.

The judiciary, forced by litigation to confront matters of outstanding political significance, being called to make decisions with far-reaching consequences, is caught between legitimizing governmental policies on one hand, and losing legitimacy or even suffering retribution on the other. Bottom-up judicialization of mega-politics[22] has increased, as loan agreements and austerity measures find their way to the courts regardless of models of review and standing prerequisites. Nevertheless, *the response of the judiciary is not as 'juristocratic'* as the prior course of judicial decision-making would suggest. A tendency of the judicial branch towards a reinforced self-restraining attitude involves shifts in constitutional interpretation to allow minimalist jurisprudence. The judiciary appears reluctant to be the final arbiter of what the general interest under the pressure of the crisis allows constitution-wise.[23] It is characteristic that the Chairman of the Greek Council of State, shortly before being appointed caretaker Prime Minister, stated that although the emergency situation demands that the judge decide whether deviations from legality are justified and therefore tolerable, the judge cannot

22 R. Hirschl, 'The Judicialization of Mega-politics and the Rise of Political Courts', *Annual Review of Political Science* 11 (2008): 93-118.

23 On the reluctance shown by courts during times of crisis, see, T. Poole, 'Courts and Conditions of Uncertainty in "Times of Crisis"', *Public Law* 234 (2008): 234-259.

be rendered the sovereign in a Schmittean sense, that is judges cannot undertake the task to decide on emergency situations.[24] Where courts did not signal that they would exercise self-restraint to allow the government to have the final say, there were examples of explicit confrontations between courts and the executive, ranging from criticism and threats of salary cuts (Latvia), to the extreme reaction of dismantling the Constitutional Court by stripping it of its jurisdiction and lowering the retirement age to achieve a change of the composition of the judiciary (Hungary).[25]

Breaking down the three-partite relationship between branches into three distinct relationships and tracing how each separate interaction has been affected brings forth the dynamics of the unravelling reallocation of powers. Where rearrangements in the distribution of powers cannot be achieved in times of crisis and this function of the constitution cannot be relaxed to allow some fluidity in the correlation between branches, the very durability of constitutions may be threatened.[26]

Constitutional Reactions towards the Crisis

The Four Paths Forward

The combinations of changes that occur within specific legal orders are endless and evolve as a financial crisis unfolds. The overall reaction of a constitution towards the crisis is revealed in the way ongoing changes connect. Reaction assessment may be attempted through the use of three criteria encompassing all signs of unravelling transformations: whether the constitution underwent *formal change* and to what extent, whether *informal constitutional change* has been induced by law-maker and judge, affecting rights and principles as well as the operation and allocation of state powers, and whether the *functions of the constitution* have been altered. When the mixture of evolving shifts and alterations amounts to change classifiable under the above criteria, the way in which each constitution responds to the crisis begins to acquire specific shape.

---

24 See also the discussion on the Commonwealth executive crisis during the financial crisis in the High Court Decision in *Pape* v. *Commissioner of Taxation*, where the Court 'drew an analogy between the powers of the executive to respond to a national crisis, such as war or natural disaster, and the power to deal with a financial crisis', in A. Twomey, 'Pushing the Boundaries of Executive Power – Pape, the Prerogative and Nationhood Powers', *Melbourne University Law Review* 34 (2010): 313-343, at 315.

25 K.L. Scheppele, 'How to Evade the Constitution: The Case of the Hungarian Constitutional Court's Decision on the Judicial Retirement Age', 8.8.2012; available at http://www.comparativeconstitutions.org.

26 Z. Elkins, T. Ginsburg and J. Melton, *The Endurance of National Constitutions* (Cambridge University Press, 2009), p. 109.

Documenting how constitutions have responded to the financial crisis reveals distinct reactions: a constitution confronted with the crisis may remain intact, or adjust to the new circumstances, or suffer breakdown under the strain, or become submissive but still hold on. The path followed is dependent upon the correlation of multiple parameters, thus these paths intersect and constitutional responses may change direction in the course of the financial crisis. The barriers between types of constitutional reaction to the crisis are permeable. A constitutional map of forking paths with infinite endings stretches out. Changing paths at intersections is possible: a constitution that initially seems to adjust can later fall into inertia, a submissive one may at some point regain its strength, and when constitutions collapse anything goes. Nonetheless, the initial reaction is crucial, as in all traumas: first response and recovery are inevitably connected.

Adjustment

Some constitutions adjust to the requirements of the crisis. Adjustment takes place through the *combination of formal and informal change as the constitution adapts to keep up with developments*. The aim of adaptation is that the constitution should not become obsolete so that it can continue to perform the functions it is designed to perform. Success or failure in that respect depends on persistent endeavour, since adjustment is a slow process encompassing successive steps, each entailing risks. Determination to use constitutional adjustment as a tool and exploit its dynamics, instead of treating constitutional change as a means to blow off steam, or to attempt rebirth, marks this type of constitutional reaction towards the financial crisis.

The answer to the question of whether anything that needs to be changed in the constitution may indeed be changed is provided by the UK reaction, due to the uncodified nature of the UK Constitution and the concomitant lack of procedural constrains. Prompt extensive adjustments took place emphasizing the ability of the Constitution to give shape to the realignments necessitated by the financial crisis. Ranging from the introduction of the Fixed-Term Parliament Act and the reform of the Cabinet Manual, aimed to ensure that the unprecedented request for a smooth functioning of coalition governments would be resolved through constitutional rules, to regulatory innovation, the Constitution's adaptation has been narrowly tailored to the unravelling crisis. The capacity to make continual swift adjustments, as a safeguard against normativity impairments, allowed the Constitution to continue to perform its functions and even to somewhat strengthen its symbolic power.

In Ireland, where any formal change of the Constitution requires popular referendum and any transfer of sovereignty requires formal amendment, the Fiscal Compact was put before the people and met with approval. This twofold requirement means that every step of the way towards a possible European solution to the crisis will trigger formal change of the Constitution through popular participation. The first steps of constitutional adjustment were successful, and although the original attitude towards the crisis involved demands for constitutional replacement and radical change, what prevailed was making practical alterations; current tendencies are in the direction of adopting modifications that serve constitutional efficiency. The strengthening of independent authorities and scrutiny mechanisms, as well as the modification of the Lower House processes to enhance oversight, complement the pragmatic adaptation of the Irish Constitution to keep up with the reality of the financial crisis.

Two distinct major developments directly attributable to the crisis can be detected in Spain. The first is formal change of the Constitution to enshrine the fiscal discipline rule, which acquires extra importance in view of the rarity of constitutional revisions, this being the second since the enactment of the Constitution in 1978. The second development is the rearrangement of the sources of law to accommodate decree-laws, which acquired different characteristics, becoming the basic means to address the crisis-related issues even in the area of fundamental rights. Legislative limitations of rights, in the light of the emergency created by the financial situation, are backed up by the Constitutional Court and changes in political practice. Formal and informal constitutional adaptation aims to preserve constitutional normativity. The Constitution adjusts to the conditions of the financial crisis in order to provide the framework for decision-making and politics as well as for rearrangements in the checks and balances between executive, legislative and judicial authority.

The introduction of the balanced budget principle in the Italian Constitution, which is rarely formally amended, through the fast-track process and with very large majorities, expresses the determination to make use of the Constitution's symbolic and normative power in fighting the financial crisis. Textual adjustment is complemented by extensive use of all procedural margins, allowing fast decision-making, including the systematic use of decree-laws. Both formal and informal change are thus in the service of an operative constitution that adapts to the unravelling crisis requirements.

Among the numerous and radical proposals for constitutional amendments that resulted from the financial crisis, the one adopted and those underway show that the path followed by the Latvian Constitution was that of adjustment. Enshrining the right of the people to propose parliamentary dissolution and the expected constitutionalization of the already interpretatively recognized balanced budget rule indicate that cautious adaptation marks formal change. Informal change played a major part in this adjustment process. The distinctive Latvian feature that the harsh measures taken due to the crisis were often found unconstitutional by the Constitutional Court, which adhered to its role as the champion of rights, created a thin balance between informal change induced by the executive and backed up by the legislature, and informal change in the opposite direction induced by the judge. Through this adversarial interpretative approach, constitutionalism and the symbolic function of the Constitution survived the crisis.

Submission

Constitutions may become submissive to whatever the crisis demands. Constitutions may react to the crisis by adopting sleep-mode, conveying the impression of being stunned by the new demands. Exposed to informal change brought about by the crisis-induced rule production, *some constitutions pathetically witness the erosion of their functions*. Normativity starts to fade and drags down with it the symbolic function of the constitution along with faith in constitutionalist safeguards. As shrinkage of rights and realignments in the allocation of powers dictated by the crisis occurs, the constitution seems to simply succumb to all deviations without authoritatively providing guidance and limits. Absence of formal constitutional change contributes in that direction, and a danger lurks that if the constitution retains a submissive stance for a prolonged period it will become doubtful whether a delayed revision can restore what has been lost.

Since the beginning of the financial crisis the constitutions of Portugal and Greece have not undergone any textual modifications and have been experiencing a loss of normativity, yet they have gone on living, living and partly living. *Constitutions go on living, still providing the basic framework of the polity, but undergo lawmaker-driven informal change*, which exerts enormous influence on their functions. In Portugal, the degree of consent required by the stringent formula for revising the Constitution was not achieved. As trust in the political class, which operated the Constitution, was completely lost, and the overall institutional system was held responsible for failing to provide oversight mechanisms able to prevent the financial crisis, the credibility of the Constitution itself suffered a tremendous blow. The major crisis of faith in the Constitution was also bolstered by the stance of the Constitutional Court, which kept a self-restraining attitude towards the impugnment of austerity measures, conveying the impression that the protection of social rights, which characterizes the Portuguese Constitution, has been rendered inoperable. Inertia complemented by fading credibility and sovereignty loss are signs of a constitution submissive to the financial crisis.

In Greece, rigidity of the amendment formula did not allow formal change. Need for such change, to counterbalance disappointment in the political class attributable also to institutional malfunctions, was expressed through strong constitutional reform dialogue. Due to procedural hurdles this need was left unattended. As austerity measures curtailing rights are constantly introduced and their constitutionality is upheld by a self-restrained judiciary reluctant to interfere in mega-politics, the citizenry's constitutional faith – largely dependent on rights protection – seems to be jeopardized. The Constitution appears immobilized in the face of the crisis, unable to offer either institutional support or some sort of catharsis through change, and is subordinated to informal interventions made by the law-maker in accordance with commitments undertaken by loan agreements. In the midst of an environment of extreme political and economic uncertainty all functions of the Constitution seem to have slowed down instead of unfolding their full potential. As Greece is at a turning point with regard to the crisis and the threat of exiting the eurozone is looming, the situation in which it will find itself when procedurally capable of revising its Constitution will perhaps determine the very future of this Constitution. Remaining in the eurozone will require adjustments, possibly including the adoption of fiscal discipline rules, while an exit would bring reversals of pre-existing certainties that could potentially lead to a constitutional moment.

Breakdown

Financial crises may provide the context for or trigger *constitutional replacement, total revision or the establishment of a new constitutional order*, that is, constitutions may crumble during a crisis. Constitutional breakdown corresponds to major reversals in all functions of the constitution. The end of a constitutional era may be the pathway to a brighter and at least more hopeful future, or may contrarily mark darker developments. Who takes responsibility for constitutional change, that is whether it is the people themselves who decide or other political actors, is a determinant factor in the outcome. The substantial content of such changes necessarily reflects interpretations of what constitution-wise causes, facilitates or allows a financial crisis to get out of hand and also what constitutions can do to help manage it or remedy its results.

In Iceland, weaknesses of the aged Constitution suddenly became visible and a participatory, inclusive constitution-writing process began, so that constitutional faith could be restored. An experiment in constitution-writing, often described as 'crowd-sourcing' the Constitution, made even more fascinating by the use of social networking to increase public participation and deliberation, was Iceland's constitutional reaction to the financial crisis. Translating anger into a constructive process and seeking restart and democratic renewal through the creation of a new Constitution is still a work in progress. The outcome may have shortcomings, since the content of the Constitution under construction might entail weakness in design in attempting a novel allocation of powers and a renewed checks and balances system. Furthermore, the aspired level of democratic participation will most probably not be as high as originally envisaged. Yet, the *symbolic value of this experiment* has already benefited the healing process. In the meanwhile, during the transition, all weaknesses of the old Constitution have been in the spotlight and this seems to have abolished its symbolic function, unification being served instead by the slow, experimental constitution-writing process. Breakdown of the current Constitution results from taking perhaps much more of the share of blame than it actually deserves by absorbing the outrage against the political class.

A sequence of events, correlated to the situation created by the financial crisis, led in Hungary to the enactment of a new Constitution, which totally dismantled the pre-existing allocation of powers and removed fundamental constitutionalist guarantees. Austerity along with political scandals and mismanagement by the socialist governments that had been in power for years resulted in a sweeping victory for the centre-right party, which thus obtained through a free and fair election a supermajority enabling it to change the Constitution at will. Economic depression and political disillusionment thus triggered a constitutional crisis, and the repercussion of these intersecting crises will stretch into the future as Hungary seems to have abolished the features of a constitutional democracy.[27] The question here is whether this development is attributable solely to the ruling party supermajority and the financial crisis landscape, or whether its explanation lies also in the features of the collapsed Constitution. Hungary is the only post-communist country where the transition to democracy was not expressed through the enactment of a new constitution. This *incomplete constitution-making* may provide a deeper explanation for why the Constitution crumbled when faced with financial crisis.

Stamina

Constitutions demonstrate stamina when they are able to *face the demands of the financial crisis and remain intact*. Nothing changes in the constitution, which retains its functions, and the relationship between state organs continues to be the same. Neither formal nor informal amendments occur that result in actual modifications. The constitution is tested as it is called to provide directions and mechanisms, and in that sense it may be subject to varying interpretations and criticism or be caught in the midst of political conflicts. The ability to stretch and contract back into place is crucial, allowing the constitution to help manage the financial crisis while preserving its normativity and symbolic force.

What was spoken of by US constitutional scholars as the 'debt-ceiling crisis' left the US Constitution intact. The US Constitution is very difficult to formally amend, but is nonetheless subject to informal change by way of judicial interpretation. Informal changes in the Constitution that took place after 9/11, leading to a new form of governance based on surveillance, increased presidential power and limited accountability of the executive,[28] and created perhaps more serious challenges to the US Constitution than the financial crisis.

Although the United States has been experiencing a great recession, which created novel governance issues and caused tensions construed through constitutional arguments, the Constitution was not threatened in any way by loss of normativity or symbolic power. The way the US Constitution evolves, despite the serious difficulty of making formal changes, and acquires flexibility, thus demonstrating the ability to provide new solutions whenever new problems arise, explains how it went through the recession unscathed. Lacking the wordy protection modern constitutions often offer to social rights and in the absence of fiscal provisions, it is less susceptible to normativity impairment as it leaves room for manoeuvring. The dilemmas set by the debt-ceiling crisis and the bank bailouts were comfortably addressed within the constitutional framework.

27 K.L. Sheppelle, 'Hungary's Constitutional Revolution'; available at http://krugman.blogs.nytimes.com/2011/12/19/hungarys-constitutional-revolution/.

28 See J. Balkin, 'The Constitution in the National Surveillance State', *Minnesota Law Review* 93(1) (2008): 1-25.

The augmentation of executive power present in most crisis-struck legal orders did appear in the United States. The broad discretionary power required by the executive to implement policies was indeed employed through the use of delegation. Still the non-delegation doctrine had already been interpretatively relaxed, requiring merely the existence of intelligible standards to guide the executive. As part of a broader phenomenon of accretion of power and use of this power by the President to implement policies within a polarized political environment, when the relevant need emerged due to the recession the Constitution could accommodate it.

The constitutional hardball played through the departure from previously taken-for-granted norms, when the Republicans who controlled Congress refused to raise the debt ceiling and threatened to go against routine practice, was eventually politically resolved without harm to the Constitution. Threats of an impasse were faced by scholars through the creation of new constitutional arguments based on a quite forgotten constitutional provision, Section Four of the Fourteenth Amendment, stating that the validity of the public debt of the United State shall not be questioned.[29] Constitutional argumentation in favour of the President unilaterally raising the debt ceiling or ignoring it never materialized in practice, as the President chose not to face the problem as a constitutional one. Regardless of how convincing the arguments are and to what extent this dysfunctionality could potentially turn into a constitutional crisis,[30] the dialogue proved that when in trouble people turn to the Constitution for arguments, and in doing so its power is most typically reinforced. Able not only to stretch without being deformed, but also to contain tensions by allowing them to be played out by providing the source for constitutional argumentation, the US Constitution displays stamina through such episodes.

Constitutional Reactions vs Constitutional Crises

Constitutional reactions towards the financial crisis sometimes *entail constitutional crisis, constitutional hardball, change of constitutional order or even constitutional moments*, and sometimes consist of more subtle changes. Questions that need to be addressed are: what causes a constitution to react in a specific way instead of

29 For discussion on Section Four prior to the recession, see M. Abramowicz, 'Beyond Balanced Budgets: Fourteenth Amendment Style', *Tulsa Law Review* 33 (1977): 561-612 and *Perry* v. *United States*, 294 U.S. 330, 354 (1935). For turning towards Section Four in search of solutions appearing as an effort to put on the table off-the-wall arguments, see M. Tushnet, 'Structural Similarities Between Conservative and Liberal Constitutional Arguments', 30.6.2011; available at http://balkin.blogspot.gr/2011/06/structural-similarities-between.html.

30 See J. Balkin, characterizing it in the aftermath as a phony crisis, in 'The Not-So-Happy Anniversary of the Debt-Ceiling Crisis'; available at http://www.theatlantic.com/politics/archive/2012/07/the-not-so-happy-anniversary-of-the-debt-ceiling-crisis/260458/.

following a different route and in what manner does the financial crisis relate to each specific reaction? How long do constitutional reactions last – can they be temporary or do they become integrated in the constitutional order? How do different constitutional reactions impact the connection between financial crisis and constitutional durability? Although a full-fledged answer to such questions can only be sought in the aftermath of the financial crisis and even perhaps in the more distant future, the attempt to address them in real time may document elements and causalities that might fade with the passage of time.

What distinguishes a financial crisis from other types of crises and emergencies is that *it touches upon the whole fabric of the constitution*, that is the allocation of powers, the authority of state organs, the fundamental rights and principles protection, as well as its normativity and symbolism. Thus, there are multiple levels at which a constitutional crisis may be ignited. Diagnosis of a constitutional crisis is not an easy task. In general terms 'constitutional crises arise out of the failure, or strong risk of failure, of a constitution to perform its central functions'.[31] Numerous variations exist, all presupposing an exit from ordinary politics. The constant invocation of the term, being disanalogous to the actual frequency of constitutional crises, has come to suggest all conflicts of constitutional tint involving intense emotions.[32] Since several of the more concrete components of constitutional crisis definitions, as well as most of the abstract and intangible ones, are bound to appear when a financial crisis breaks out, the temptation to employ the term to describe constitutional reactions is strong. Disagreement between constitutional actors about the ambit of their power, in the course of which they may even directly claim the necessity of acting outside the constitution or conversely refuse to go outside the constitution even if reality dictates so doing, are clear signs of a constitutional crisis.[33] Moreover, judicial and political crises that remain unresolved may eventually amount to constitutional crises. Judicial crises occur when judicial decisions are met with non-compliance by the other branches and even trigger retaliation, whereas political crises occur when strong conflicts arise among political authorities with regard to who decides on a particular area of policy.[34] Austerity legislation creates an environment friendly to judicial and political crises, however more is required for their culmination into constitutional crises.

31 K.E. Whittington, 'Yet Another Constitutional Crisis?', *William & Mary Law Review* 43 (2002): 2093-2149, at 2099. On different approaches of the definition and the way it is invoked, see A.G. Ristroph, 'Is Law? Constitutional Crisis and Existential Anxiety', Constitutional *Commentary* 25 (2009): 431-460.

32 See S. Levinson and J.M. Balkin, 'Constitutional Crises', *University of Pennsylvania Law Review* 157 (2009): 707-753.

33 Ibid.

34 M. Gerhardt, 'Crisis and Constitutionalism', *Montana Law Review* 63 (2002): 277-299, at 286.

Although manifest characteristics of constitutional crises are often spotted, such as issues and conflicts surpassing ordinary politics, claims of the necessity to go beyond the constitution, as well as the probable need to actually go outside the constitution, what has rarely occurred in the context of the current financial crisis is cleavage between state organs. The examination of how constitutions have behaved during the financial crisis shows that most often *the strain triggers synergy between constitutional actors* in the way in which they operate the constitution. A more expansive formulation of the definition of constitutional crisis might offer a different prism. A broad definition focused on the functions of constitutions rather than on conflicts among branches, according to which a constitutional crisis occurs when the constitution does not provide a way out to guide and bind the actors, opens up more possibilities.[35] From this aspect the financial crisis tests the capability of constitutions to offer guidance on different assessment criteria. Even so, it is crucial to detect whether lighter versions of rifts among constitutional actors are more likely to appear.

Pre-constitutional understandings, that is things considered self-evident until times of crisis make them not only visible but also contestable, lie at the core of constitutional hardball, a concept introduced by M. Tushnet. Hardball, being 'political claims and practices – legislative and executive initiatives – that are without much question within the bounds of existing constitutional doctrine and practice but that are nonetheless in some tension with existing pre-constitutional understanding' takes place when political actors attempt 'to put in place a new set of deep institutional arrangements', which Tushnet calls constitutional orders.[36] J. Balkin redefines constitutional hardball as 'attempts by political actors to make significant changes to the constitutional order or to extend and further entrench an existing one'.[37] More instantaneous and dense in terms of time are Ackerman's transformative constitutional moments, which emphasize the importance of informal change of the constitution.[38] Understanding the New Deal as a constitutional moment inevitably sets forth the possibility of the current financial crisis creating the conditions for the occurrence of constitutional moments. Pinning down whether constitutional moments or a succession of constitutional orders through the change of institutional arrangements have been attempted by resetting the rules of the game and changing what previously went without saying provides a tool to explore constitutional reactions to the financial crisis.

The term perhaps most constantly employed by the legislative, executive and judicial branches since the beginning of the current financial crisis is that of emergency. What distinguishes an emergency from a constitutional crisis is that

35 Ibid., 285.

36 M. Tushnet, 'Constitutional Hardball', *John Marshal Law Review* 37 (2004): 523-553, at 523.

37 J.M. Balkin, 'Constitutional Hardball and Constitutional Crises', *Quinnipiac Law Review* 26 (2008): 579-598, at 581.

38 B. Ackerman, *We the People: Foundations* (Harvard University Press, 1991).

an emergency lies in the real world, and although it may create the preconditions for a constitutional crisis it does not necessarily result in one.[39] Rather it creates a challenge for the constitution to prove competent to provide solutions and for branches of government to seek and implement solutions within the options and boundaries laid down by the constitution.

Linking reactions of constitutions towards the financial crisis to the rationale of constitutional crisis reveals the essence of what happened in each separate example. *Constitutional breakdown is strongly suggestive of constitutional crisis.* In Hungary, a full-blown constitutional crisis led to the enactment of a new constitution, which marked the passage to a new constitutional order introducing a new checks and balances system in favour of the executive branch. A two-thirds majority requirement for policy changes in several areas, including tax and fiscal policy, makes the political choices of the party that designed the new constitution extremely hard to reverse. The conflict between the government and the Constitutional Court marked a parallel constitutional crisis, resolved by a reform that stripped the Court of its power.

In Iceland, a state of constitutional limbo is lingering through a prolonged constitutional moment. A paradox is thus created by the continuance in operation of a constitution totally discredited through a constitutional crisis that emphasized its flaws and led to the initiation of a constitution-making process much celebrated for its democratic aspiration. This unfinished business, which suggests that the people have experienced a constitutional moment without yet having a new constitution, is still unfolding through the slow, seemingly irreversible transition to a new constitutional order.

Adjustment as a constitutional reaction to the financial crisis is closely related to the perception of emergency as a premise for introducing problem-solving changes. The conceptualization of *emergency as a pre-constitutional-crisis-situation creates the imperative for the necessary adjustments to be made*, so that constitutional crises are avoided. The financial crisis emergency provides a conceptual lens through which basic features of the constitution are revisited, evaluated and modified where necessary. The UK, Ireland, Italy, Spain and Latvia went through this sort of reflective approach to the constitution in their efforts to address the issues set by the financial crisis through adjustment. With the exception of Latvia, where two conflicts arose that could be viewed as games of constitutional hardball played between the President of the Republic and parliament, and between the government and the Constitutional Court respectively, in the rest of the countries that followed the adjustment path state organs cooperated to face the emergency.

The submission of constitutions to the demands of the financial crisis *offered an alternative route to avoid the possibility of a constitutional crisis*. In Greece and Portugal the respective constitutions have not failed to perform their functions,

39 For the distinction between constitutional crises and emergencies, see Levinson and Balkin, 'Constitutional Crises', 717.

but are nevertheless exposed to subtle erosion marking a slow transformation. Emergency provides the grounds for rule production and informal change, which without meeting serious obstacles from any branch of government corresponds to the requirements of the financial crisis, yet wears away pre-constitutional understandings about fundamental rights and principles. One could be tempted to read a *passage into a new constitutional order* encompassing a changed landscape of rights protection, yet it is too soon to judge whether the current tendency in that direction will be realized.

Constitutional stamina allows the constitution to remain intact even if a constitutional crisis looms or is averted at the last minute. The strong sense that in the United States government officials were hurtling towards a constitutional crisis[40] and that constitutional hardball was played in the debt-ceiling affair did for a while create fears of an impasse. The threats of congressional Republicans that they would refuse to raise the debt ceiling contrary to routine practice, unless Democrats would agree to spending cuts detrimental to their policies, seemed to bring the President to a constitutional cliff. Attempts of a transformation were made and pre-existing assumptions were defied. Nonetheless, the Constitution prevailed and political solutions were found without the need for far-fetched constitutional behaviour. Constitutional stamina works in the direction of avoiding the culmination of a constitutional crisis and is in turn boosted by the Constitution's ability to withstand games of hardball.

Factors Affecting Constitutional Reactions

How a constitution reacts in the face of a severe financial crisis depends on a number of entwined external and internal factors. An internalist account of what explains the choice of route focuses on constitutional design. The level of *separation of powers* and the way it is built into the constitution, which is different in *presidential and parliamentary systems*, influences not only the response time to the input of the financial crisis but also the probability of constitutional crises and constitutional hardballs taking place. The stricter the separation of powers is, and *the more veto players exist*, the greater the possibility of constitutional hardball, or even of a constitutional crisis entailing conflict between branches of government.

The difficulty of implementing formal change plays a major part in the range of available choices with regard to constitutional reactions,[41] as is demonstrated in the Portuguese example. *How long and detailed a constitution is* can also be

40 S. Levinson, 'So are We Moving Toward a "Constitutional Crisis"?', 13.7.2011; available at http://balkin.blogspot.gr/2011/07/so-are-we-moving-toward-constitutional.html.

41 See X. Contiades and A. Fotiadou, 'Models of Constitutional Change', in X. Contiades (ed.), *Engineering Constitutional Change: A Comparative Perspective on Europe, Canada and the USA* (Routledge, 2013), pp. 417-468.

crucial: lack of fiscal provisions and absence of enumerated socio-economic rights may allow more flexibility without the threat of loss of normativity, something illustrated in the US reaction. Whether the judge is a key actor in the drama depends on *the system of constitutional review* – for example in the UK model it would be unimaginable to expect the judge to take the lead. The differences between the constitutional structure of *federations and unitary states* are also relevant, as illustrated by the example of the constitutional enshrinement of fiscal discipline clauses: where autonomous units exist, as in Spain and Italy, the debt ceiling is read foremost with regard to the equilibria between central state and sub-state units, leading to different connotations than in unitary states.

Constitutional design interacts with external factors and determines how each constitution reacts. The *type and severity of the financial crisis* in each country is a crucial exogenous factor, as it creates differentiated demands and tensions. *Constitutional culture* is also significant in shaping the behaviour of political actors, underpinning distinct constitutional reactions. The grasp a constitution has on political actors can make a difference: the degree to which they have internalized the ability to set constitutional limits on themselves, stemming from the history and functioning of a constitutional order, and their willingness to commit to certain shared values is vital.

The *political system* offers another important extraneous parameter. Polarization and distrust as well as the credibility of institutions and political actors construct the environment in which courses of action are decided upon. Who decides and how strategies are built relates also to the *electoral system*, which influences the political system, as happened in the case of Hungary. *Sovereignty* not only underlies but also accounts for constitutional reactions. In the Greek example, the quick abandonment of the idea of calling a referendum on the bailout plan and the concomitant austerity measures after the negative reaction of European leaders,[42] not only indicates sovereignty loss but also delineates the way sovereignty relates to the range of available constitutional reactions. Finally, of utmost importance is the degree of *flexibility available through informal change*, as in the US example, where the Constitution despite the great difficulty of formal change adapts through informal amendments. How and by whom subtle informal change of the constitution can be channelled complements the rest of the parameters that explain the road travelled by each constitution.

The length of time that constitutional reactions pervading the constitution last varies. Constitutional breakdown marks the *end of an era* and is characterized by permanency. Likewise, the ability of a constitution to display stamina in the face of the demands of the financial crisis leaves a *permanent imprint*, serving as a renewal of its normative and symbolic force. How far into the future the effects

42 Characterized by S. Levinson as 'The Death of Democracy in Greece'; available at http://balkin.blogspot.gr/2011/11/death-of-democracy-in-greece.html. See also J. Habermas, 'Rettet die Würde der Demokratie', *Frankfurter Allgemeine Zeitung*, 4 November 2011.

of constitutional adjustment could last relies on the *actual applicability of the modifications made* and the way in which they interact with other constitutional provisions in the course of systematic interpretation. The potential to induce major shifts in practice exists, but a turn in the direction of oblivion is also possible, modifications having served their purpose by the mere symbolic statement made by their adoption. The most *transitory constitutional reaction* is that of submission: being a pause impregnated with change in many directions, it is the most unpredictable reaction in terms of its final outcome.

Conclusions

Constitutional expectations arising out of the global financial crisis reflect different notions of the constitution as well as different requirements from its functions. A constitution can neither cause nor resolve a financial crisis. Still, the financial crisis *brought to light malfunctions and faulty constitutional machinery* that influenced the course of events, and *aided identification of what is required from constitutions* in times of financial crisis. The people as well as government officials turned at one point or another to the constitution, which was somehow *expected to walk them through the unfolding crisis.*

The people, simply put, expected constitutions to delimit state power and to shield fundamental rights, thus they anticipated that *oversight and accountability mechanisms would work and that constitutionalism would prevail.* Failures caused loss of faith in the constitution, and for those for whom the limitation of constitutional rights has translated into severe deterioration of their living conditions, street protests or civil disobedience have become a way of expressing that loss of faith.

Governments had more practical requirements. They wanted constitutions not only to allow them to act, but also to facilitate their actions. *Expediency and efficiency were requested from constitutions.* Assessment of malfunctions had to do with what should or could be changed. Interpreting the constitution to find out permissible courses of action became a task with many repercussions, ranging from revisions and informal changes to circumventions of the constitution. Looking to the constitution as an ally in tackling the crisis was also an option – the *symbolic force of constitutions was explicitly employed* to send messages to the international markets through revisions.

The judiciary, often faced with very hard choices as the constitutionality of loan agreements and austerity legislation was challenged, had to look to the constitution for ways out. Since even the customary accusation of juristocracy would have to be reinvented if court decisions had caused the cancellation of bailouts, only *intricate interpretational machinery* could allow courts to demonstrate self-restraint without betraying their role. Judges expected the constitution to provide this machinery.

The mixture of expectations with abrupt realizations of what a constitution can or cannot do underlies distinct constitutional reactions corresponding to breaking down, adjusting, submitting or demonstrating stamina in the face of the financial crisis. Exploring constitutional reactions to the global financial crisis reveals how much a constitution can do.

PART II
First Path: Adjustment

Chapter 2
The Constitution and the Financial Crisis in Ireland

David Gwynn Morgan

Two elements of the background are significant to the case of Ireland. First, in the broadest of outlines, Ireland has a very simple constitutional framework.[1] The Head of State is the (non-executive) President. The executive power of the state is exercised by the government, composed of the Prime Minister and 14 other members, each of whom heads a Department of State. In addition, there are a multitude of executive agencies. The government is formally responsible to parliament, which makes the laws. The judicial branch is housed in a system of four general courts. Beyond this one can say that state power is highly centralized, geographically and otherwise. With a population of five million, there is no requirement for federalism and even the autonomy of local authorities is not very well-respected.

Most (though not all) of the thought and innovation in public law has gone into developing individual constitutional/human rights, mainly by way of interpretation and application of the Constitution. This has been taken, by the senior judiciary, to an extent which can certainly be characterized as judicial activism. Where there has been less development is in the field of the institutions of government and their proper functioning. And, in the extreme conditions of the Celtic Tiger, the claims of powerful individuals or interest groups were pitted against the protection of the (unorganized) public community. Ireland's institutions often failed this robust test.

Second, is the economic-financial background. There are two preliminary points. Everyone knows what follows hubris and in Ireland the excess of the Celtic Tiger period (mid-1990s-2008) played a major part in causing what is usually known sombrely as the post-Tiger years;[2] and consequently the two must be discussed together. One should add that, particularly in an economy as unusually open and trade-dependent as Ireland's, EU and international factors, especially low interest-rate policies, played a huge part in both the boom and the bust. Without going into an economic history, one can say that, long after political

1 The standard authority is G. Hogan and G. Whyte, *J M Kelly: The Irish Constitution* (4th edn, LexisNexis Butterworths, 2003).

2 The Irish are the most articulate and even literary of people and the failure to come up with a less utilitarian and more imaginative, allusive or wry title speaks volumes for the national shock engendered by the economic crash.

independence from Britain in 1922, Ireland remained an economic pensioner of Britain.[3] In particular, Ireland lacked an indigenous industrial sector, because after Ireland became independent, the industrial part of the island, Ulster, remained part of Britain. Thus, Ireland's only big industry was agriculture and its largest export market was Britain, where Irish prices were kept artificially low by virtue of Britain's 'cheap food' policy. Ireland was also able to export some of its unemployment in the form of many hungry, young men.

The first bit of economic luck granted to Ireland was entry to the Common Market and its Common Agricultural Policy (CAP) in 1973. The CAP was good for Ireland's small farms, which up to the 1980s provided 20 per cent of Irish employment. But the real lift-off for the Irish economy did not come until the Celtic Tiger years. It was fuelled by multinationally-owned pharmaceutical and IT industries. The result was that, whereas traditionally Ireland was among the poorest countries in Western Europe, from the mid-1990s onwards the state enjoyed unaccustomed wealth. In net terms, the average Irish income, on entry in 1973, was 40 per cent of the EU average but by 2008, it was the third most prosperous state in the EU and the fifth in the world (with a GDP that had doubled between 1995 and 2005).

But the fall was also unusually steep: in 2005, Ireland's growth rate was 5 per cent, but by 2009, the rate of decline was −9 per cent. Comparable figures throughout the Euro-15 zone are 2 per cent (2005) and −4 per cent (2009). Unemployment for each of the years 2000-2007 was historically at its lowest, with figures of 4-5 per cent, compared with a figure of 14 per cent for 2012. However, each of these figures rather understates the true position in that the 2011 figure is lower than it would otherwise be, because of a resumption of the historic pattern of high emigration; whereas during the Tiger era, there was a population increase of around 10 per cent, because of emigration from new members of the EU such as Poland, as well as returned Irish emigrants, bringing new ideas and experiences with them. Gross public debt is projected to peak at around 117 per cent of GDP (more so than in most states, Ireland's GDP is substantially higher than its GNP) in 2013. Approximately a quarter of the state's present indebtedness arises from the state guarantee given to cover the banks' debts and the remainder results from deficits between the government's own income and expenditure, accumulated mainly during the Celtic Tiger years.

The following simple chronology of the Crash and the post-Tiger years is designed simply to provide a framework for the legal events and comments outlined in the remainder of the chapter:

- 1994-2007: Celtic Tiger – economic growth, unprecedented by Irish or even most international standards.

3 The economic crash has produced a lot of literature: see, for example, B. Lucey, Ch. Larkin and C. Gurdgiev (eds), *What if Ireland Defaults?* (Orpen, 2012); C.Ó Gráda, *A Rocky Road: The Irish Economy since the 1920s* (Manchester University Press, 1997).

- 2008: Recession, extent and nature of which is still emerging.
- September 2008: the state guarantees the debts of five leading Irish banks.
- February 2009: (first) Financial Emergency Measures in the Public Interest Act passed. These empower government to reduce public service salaries and pensions and to increase contributions paid by ministers or public servant employees to pensions.
- Early 2010: National Asset Management Agency becomes operational, acquiring €73bn from five major banking institutions.
- June 2010: Croke Park Agreement between government and public sector unions, regulating cut-backs but also requiring greater productivity.
- November 2010: Rescue agreement for Ireland funded by the IMF and the European Central Bank (ECB).
- February 2011: General election removes Fianna Fáil party from power by a landslide.
- October 2011: Referendums to allow decreases to judges' salaries and pensions (passed) and to establish parliamentary enquiries (rejected).
- May 2012: Referendum to allow ratification of fiscal responsibility treaty passed.

So far as one can identify a consensus-narrative in a field that is naturally affected by a good deal of special pleading and blame-transfer, it is that the crash was caused or more likely exacerbated by misconduct by 'the elites' (meaning the top government, business or professional groups) and, second, that there was significant failure by public institutions whose duty it was to police the boundary between enterprise and dishonesty, and to take timely steps to prevent, or minimize, the consequences of misconduct. To take some examples: failure of regulation, by specifically established public agencies: huge and unjustifiable increase in numbers employed in the public service and, especially at the top levels, in their salaries, pensions and expenses; over-generous contracts between the professions (of law, medicine, pharmacy and so on) and the biggest and most reliable consumer, the government; generous grants for big business, tax breaks; failures by the Regulator to rein in reckless lending by banking institutions; grant of excessive number of planning permissions;[4] planning permission granted for construction on unsuitable sites, such as flood plains or environmentally-sensitive areas.

Because the period of prosperity was so sudden and relatively short, the Irish polity had insufficient time in which to develop rules and a culture of probity to moderate the temptations and excesses brought by the Celtic Tiger: to take the nearest analogy, the City of London had more than two centuries to develop (largely unwritten) rules, an opportunity denied to Ireland. In addition, in a small

4 Indeed, there was zoning for 42,000 hectares of new development land, enough to house four million people, at a time, 2008, when, coincidentally, this was the same size as the existing population: *State of the Nation: A Review of Ireland's Planning System 2000-2011*, An Taisce survey, published April 2012.

country like Ireland, there was too close a relationship between the elites and the politicians or regulators. And the 'herd instinct' is rather strong, so that there may have been a strong belief that whistle-blowers or contrarians would be informally sanctioned or at least ignored, regardless of the quality of their analysis or their place in organizations.[5]

It is especially easy to give examples of this misconduct because over the last two decades there have been several long-running public inquiries into various forms of misconduct or the failure of regulation.[6] It is only fair to emphasize that – broadly speaking – the reason why Ireland has had these inquiries is not that Irish public authorities are more corrupt or incompetent than those elsewhere, but simply because inquiries are seen as an aid to open government. In addition, there is in Ireland a reluctance to prosecute for white-collar crimes, and such inquiries, since they involve a public 'naming and shaming', are seen as a sort of substitute. As a result of this widely accepted analysis, the general view is now taken (or at any rate stated) that, first, those who committed acts of misconduct as well as those who failed in their duty to prevent them should be sanctioned And, second, efficient forms of accountability should be put in place to minimize the chance of repetition.

But, so far as the first of these views is concerned, we can dispose briefly of the practical outcome. Apart from a good deal of public and media indignation, little or nothing has happened and it is easy to see why. Put simply, the Constitution, as enforced by a pro-individual judiciary, contains unusually strong protections for the rights of the individual. Take a hypothetical, though likely, example. It is suggested that the government ought to withhold the pension of an official of a regulator's staff, who is thought not to have done his duty during the Celtic Tiger years. This might well have been provided for in the terms and conditions of employment (whether in legislation or contract). However, whatever these say, the official can be dismissed only by a process that follows the principles known as fair procedure or, in Ireland, as constitutional/natural justice. These require that the official should be informed in detail of the case against him and afforded every opportunity to put his side of the case, including an independent forum (possibly an administrative tribunal). In addition, in whatever forum the proceedings commence, they would certainly end up before the High Court and probably the Supreme Court, by way of judicial review. Given the circumstances, there would probably be a substantive defence along the lines that the state had encouraged light touch regulation and so the official had a 'legitimate expectation'

5 P. Nyberg, *Misjudging Risk: Causes of the Systemic Banking Crisis in Ireland: Report of Commission of Investigation* (PRN No A11/0460), para 5.5.6.

6 The most significant are *The Tribunal of Inquiry into Certain Payments to Politicians* (2011) set up in 1997, under the chairmanship of Mr Justice Moriarty; and *The Tribunal of Inquiry into Certain Planning Matters and Payments* (2006 and 2011) set up in 1997, under the chairmanship of Mr Justice Flood, who was replaced, on his retirement, by Judge Mahon.

(to invoke a growing area of public law) that following the principle of light touch regulation would not attract liability. All this would be going on in public, over a period of months and probably years, during which it would be raising old ghosts that many members of the political or business elite would wish had remained in their graves. In addition, many would deprecate this path of rough justice because of a preference for avoiding 'lynch justice' or 'trial by television'. In the end, nothing happens.

Constitutional Development by the Political Organs

In Ireland, the financial collapse has produced no violence and very little unrest or civil disobedience, perhaps because, at some level, many private individuals believe that their own extravagance and unpopularity has contributed to the Crash. In any case, the strongest part of the public's reaction to the country's fall from economic grace was to remove Fianna Fáil from power, at the 2011 general election, by such a huge margin as to leave a question mark over its survival. Fianna Fáil had formed the government for 61 of the 79 years since it first came to office in 1932, and was arguably the most successful party in modern European democracy. But even then, it is notable that despite incontrovertible evidence of financial incompetence and, in some cases, worse, and (based on consistent public opinion polls) the prospect of catastrophe at the next general election, the government continued over the period commencing with public awareness of the crash in mid-2008 until late 2010[7] to present a united front: party discipline largely held up across an unlikely coalition government of Fianna Fáil and the Greens. Admittedly, in response to this, it could be said that there was an element of the ministers hanging together lest they hang separately, but the fact that, through two years of the greatest unpopularity of any Irish government, even backbenchers did not step away from the sinking ship, when it might have been in their personal interest to do so, speaks of the ingrained instinct for party unity.

At the 2011 general election, Fine Gael and Labour (formerly the two major opposition parties) were elected as the government, with a massive majority. This happened because the electorate held the outgoing government responsible for the economic crash (even more so than is usually the case in such situations) and despite the fact that the then opposition parties' manifestos for dealing with the crisis did not differ radically from that of the outgoing government. On the constitutional front, each had proposed quite radical constitutional reform. In

7 Though for detail on both the withdrawal of the Green ministers in November 2010 and, in January 2011, the replacement of deputy Brian Cowen as leader of Fianna Fáil, while remaining as Prime Minister until the election, see Eoin Daly, 'Residual Conventions of the Irish Constitution: The Incongruous Example of Collective Responsibility', *Public Law* (2011): 703-729, at 715-719.

addition, proposals for reform (often a little incoherent)[8] emerged at least as much from civil society, such as 'We the Citizens', as from the political parties, with a number of organizations being established specifically for this purpose.[9] At their highest, proposals were made that there should be a Constitutional Convention through which a range of individuals would draft a new constitution to be put before the people during 2016, the centenary of the Easter Rising against British Rule.

But the mountain laboured and brought forth a mouse. In mid-2012, the government set down a series of six areas in which the 'the options for reform are to be examined'. These measures are, with the exception of review of the electoral system,[10] rather minor and by no means add up to a coherent policy or theme. The machinery is also rather low key, consisting of a group of 66 'ordinary citizens', 28 Members of Parliament (whether Upper or Lower House) and one member of the Legislative Assembly, from each of the political parties in Northern Ireland, with an expert advisory group of political scientists and constitutional lawyers. (It should be emphasized that this review is separate from the constitutional amendments covered in the following sections.) It is all a far cry from the electoral commitments to entrust the process of reform to the citizenry itself.

Why has what might have been regarded (because of the economic shock to the system) as a 'constitutional moment' been shirked? The government's attitude seems to be that it is already facing an unprecedented crisis in the economic field, without voluntarily seeking out other potential sources of strife. From the perspective of the 'ordinary citizen', the flurry of interest, which came to a head at the time of the 2011 election, seems to have ebbed. In general, lay people do not have much interest in laws and constitutions, often cleaving to the notion: 'For forms of government let fools contend/What e'er is best administered is best.'[11]

For historic reasons, perhaps arising from Ireland's colonial history, this may be less true in Ireland than elsewhere. However, in the present uncharted waters, the radical reversal in their economic fortune has left most people too numbed and cowed to have much thought for anything else; and the common perception is that the course of events depends mainly on international forces, way beyond the influence of domestic governments or laws. Some concern at the limited character

8 Cf. *King Lear* (2.4.305-309): 'I will do such things/What they are, yet I know not: but they shall be/The terrors of the earth.'

9 See, for example, www.politics.ie; www.politico.ie; www.2nd-republic.ie; www.PoliticalReform.ie.

10 The other five topics are reducing the (non-executive) President's term to five (from seven) years, aligning it with local and European Parliament elections and giving citizens abroad the vote in presidential elections; reducing the voting age generally from 18 to 17; removing blasphemy from Art. 40.6.1; providing for same-sex marriage; encouraging greater participation of women in public life and generally giving women a more equal position than is represented in the present system (unamended since 1937).

11 Alexander Pope, *An Essay on Man*, Ep. (iii).1.303.

of the constitutional review has been expressed by academics, a spokesman for whom remarked: 'there may be welcome reforms of things such as lobbying or whistleblowing but none to the basic structure of the system that serves the people very badly but political machines very well'.[12] But this view has not attracted much popular support. Nevertheless, what the recent trauma seems to have left is a diminution of trust in institutions and, on the constructive side, a craving for greater accountability. The changes, mainly on the sub-constitutional level, which have been made or suggested, may be regarded as directed at making existing institutions more accountable, rather than anything more radical. They can be put under the following heads.

Parliament

From an international perspective, the most obvious candidate as a watchdog over government, in its various forms, would be parliament. And, sure enough, the Irish Constitution (1937) gives parliament prime position. Following the traditional British-Westminster model, the Lower House (Dáil) is the entity to which the government is made responsible: the Dáil appoints and may remove and (if a majority is available for a new government without the need for a fresh general election) may replace the government. Superimposed on this is the separation of powers, as expressed in Art. 15.2.1 of the Constitution, which states that parliament is the only law-making authority in the state.

The reality is otherwise. As has been remarked by an experienced Irish parliamentarian, 'Modern Ireland was born in an age of party government and its parliamentary institution has never acquired the dignity and respect of older bodies which knew real power in the Nineteenth Century. [Parliament lacks] any but the most nominal role in the formulation of public policy and the management of the State.'[13] Thus, the feat of removing a government and replacing it by a new one, without an intervening general election, has been achieved only once (1994) since Independence. Again, as few as 11 Private Members (= non-government) Bills have navigated the tortuous course to the status of law. And the power, usually provided as a safeguard when delegated legislation is being made, that enables either House to pass a resolution negating delegated legislation has seldom been attempted, and never successfully.

In line with what was said earlier, the programme[14] of the government of 2011 makes a number of relevant proposals, some of which have already been implemented. Thus, at a sub-constitutional level, the processes of the Lower House

---

12 F. O'Toole, 'Tammany Hall Lives on in Feeble Reforms', *Irish Times*, 26 May 2012.

13 B. Desmond, 'The Houses of the Oireachtas – A Plea for Reform', *Administration* 23 (1975): 425.

14 New Government for National Recovery 2011-2016 (Programme for Government, 2011).

would be improved, including strengthening the position of the Speaker, and the parliamentary questions system and the parliamentary committee system would be extended, to ensure that all state agencies are answerable. Parliament will have full scrutiny powers over EU draft proposals and the way in which they are to be transposed into Irish law. A new parliamentary committee on 'Investigation, Oversight and Petitions', will link parliament and ombudsman, the Data Protection Commissioner and the local Government Auditor.[15] In order to empower citizens, a petition system will be introduced, so that citizens may raise cases illustrative of failures or gaps in public service.

However, at the constitutional level, the record of achievement is very mixed. In the first place, a constitutional amendment which would have given parliament the same powers to hold inquiries that are taken for granted elsewhere in the democratic world recently failed by a narrow majority at the referendum stage, which is required for all constitutional amendments. The background to this referendum is that the Supreme Court, in a landmark (or landmine) decision,[16] had ruled that parliament could not, constitutionally, be empowered to hold inquiries, resulting in adverse findings against individual public officials. The Joint Parliamentary Committee on the Constitution proposed vigorously that there should be a constitutional amendment to reverse this position.[17]

The reader may well ask why, given that the people have just been said to be in favour of greater accountability, they rejected this proposed amendment. So far as one can say, it seems that the major reason why the measure failed is that a major feature underlying the Irish political and constitutional system is that (possibly more than in other states) many people do not trust politicians. A number of voters seem to have regarded the difference between parliament and government as entirely theoretical and perceived the grant to parliament as the government's trying to give itself more power, with the main opposition parties supporting it, on the calculation that some day they would be in power. In response, one of the (populist) arguments relied on by the yes-side was that in many cases the alternative to a parliamentary inquiry would have to be a judicial inquiry. And, because of the requirement of fair procedure, in particular the audi alteram partem ('hear the other side') principle, this would require lawyers to cross-examine before any judicial inquiry on behalf of all parties whose conduct is under investigation.

---

15 PRN A12/0001 (2012).

16 *Maguire and Ors* v. *Ardagh and Ors* [2002] 1 IR 385.

17 The full title of the bill was the Thirtieth Amendment of the Constitution (Houses of the Oireachtas Inquiries) Bill 2011. The Oireachtas Inquiries Amendment was rejected by 46.7 per cent to 53.3 per cent, with a turnout of 55.9 per cent. For a full overview of results, see Department of the Environment, Community and Local Government, *Referendum Results: 1937-2011* (2011); available at http://www.environ.ie/en/LocalGovernment/Voting/Referenda/.

This would prolong the inquiry and cost the state a fortune.[18] In cartoon terms, one might say that the amendment was portrayed as an issue of rich lawyers versus distrusted politicians, with the people preferring the former, by a small majority.

Second, the present government promised, in late 2012, to put before the people an amendment to remove the Seanad (or Upper House of Parliament). This is justified on the straightforward grounds of economy, coupled with the fact that Ireland is the only small, non-federal state to have an Upper House. To take comparable jurisdictions, New Zealand and Denmark have removed theirs. In addition, the Irish Seanad has been in search of a role, pretty much since Independence, as testimony to which none of the numerous committees set up to consider reform of the Seanad has reached any firm conclusion. Nevertheless, critics of the proposed amendment have raised strongly the rhetorical question: how does amputating a substantial piece of parliament strengthen it?

'Politically Neutral Zones'

We use this term to embrace official watch dogs whose task is to police the executive-legislature and to prevent it from abusing its authority: plainly to perform this role each entity must be independent. In view of the lack of trust in government, it is not surprising that such entities have been increased and this process continues. Over the last decade or two, there have been some changes in the apparatus of state, including legislation to control political parties, to give independent authority and responsibility to (civil servant) heads of government departments over (elected) ministers;[19] to vest the selection of civil servants in a politically neutral body;[20] and to establish an independent body to run the courts service.[21] Finally, a proposed law on judicial standards and discipline (a 'first' for Ireland) has been in the pipeline for some years. It is true that these developments pre-date the financial collapse. However, inasmuch as they strengthen the fabric of the state, in order to try to ensure proper conduct by political leaders and other 'over mighty subjects', they are broadly part of the present theme.

The sort of thing that can happen when a politically neutral zone is not given a properly designed and comprehensive pedestal is illustrated by the following episode, involving the Ombudsman for the Public Service. In 2009, during the time of the discredited Fianna Fáil-led government, the Ombudsman was forced to publish a special report,[22] because, for the first time, her recommendation had not been accepted. This recommendation arose out of the 'Lost at Sea' Scheme. This scheme gave the owners of fishing boats lost at sea the opportunity

18 To take the most recent example, it is estimated that the Mahon Inquiry, referred to in footnote 6, will cost €250 million.

19 Public Service Management Act 1997.

20 Public Service Management (Recruitment and Appointments) Act 2004.

21 Courts Service Act 1998.

22 Lost at Sea Scheme (December 2009), PRN A9/1507.

to apply to the Minister for Agriculture and Fisheries for grant aid. Numerous applications under the scheme had been made successfully by fishermen living in the Minister's own (coastal) constituency. The complainants were a family who had lost two family members, as well as their boat. Their application had been rejected by the Minister, on the grounds that they had missed the deadline. The Ombudsman's report criticized several aspects of the administration of the scheme, including the advertising procedure, which she found had not been extensive enough. She recommended compensation of almost €250,000. The Department, however, rejected her recommendation (which, as is the way with most national ombudsman schemes, is not legally binding). Significantly, this was the first time this had happened since the establishment of the Ombudsman in 1984. The matter was referred to the Parliamentary Committee on Agriculture, Fisheries and Food, which by a (government party) majority voted to reject the Ombudsman's decision.[23] Following this debacle, as noted already, in the 2011 parliament, a Joint Parliamentary Committee on Investigation, Oversight and Petitions was set up as a formal channel of consultation and communication between parliament and the Ombudsman.

In the light of this sort of lapse and including the negligence of the Financial Regulator outlined in the following section, a number of (admittedly fairly minor) improvements have been made by the new government, or reliably promised. Financial scrutiny of public expenditure has been enhanced through an Irish Fiscal Advisory Council, which has been set up independently of the government, and comprehensive spending reviews of all public spending. An independent Electoral Commission will be established to oversee spending for elections, reduce limits on donations to political parties and candidates, and ban corporate donations altogether. In view of the findings of the Moriarty and Mahon Inquiries into corruption, mentioned above, the Standards in Public Office Commission is to be strengthened. To enhance transparency and reduce conflicts of interest the Official Secrets Act will be amended and a statutory register of lobbyists will be established, together with rules regulating the practice of lobbying. Legislation will also be enacted to protect whistle-blowers. This is necessary because just after the Celtic Tiger era, there were a few cases of 'insiders' – often accountants or auditors – who, despite a prevailing 'cloud of unknowing' regarding misconduct, spoke out and in some cases were dismissed. Finally, Ireland's Freedom of Information Act was passed in 1997 but authority in respect of this legislation lay under the control of a (right-wing) Minister for Finance who brought in amending legislation in

23 Initially, the Lower House rejected a motion to refer the matter to a Committee. Then, following protests, the matter was referred: *Irish Times*,10.3.2010 and 25.3.2010. For the report, see *Joint Oireachtas Committee on Agriculture, Fisheries and Food – Third Report on Ombudsman's Special Report* (Prn. A10/1500 Oct. 20, 2010), 7 (five lines of rationalization); possibly the Committee's attitude was affected by the involvement of the Minister.

2003.[24] This somewhat clipped the wings of the original Act. The government has promised to restore the original position.

Financial Regulator[25]

Although the business and commercial regulators[26] may appear to be operating in a relatively narrow field, the far-reaching consequences of their actions (more usually inactions) in regard to the present crisis are plain to see in the opening section. Here, we are going briefly into the failure of the Financial Regulator and the improvements that have been suggested. There have been three stages of evolution. Originally, there were several different regulators in particular financial fields. Then in 2003, with the establishment of the Central Bank and Financial Services Authority of Ireland, all these sectors were brought under a unified system. Finally a new framework has been introduced by the Central Bank Reform Act 2010. Each of these overhauls was in response to recognized limitations in the previous model. It was during the middle period (2003-2010) that mistakes were made and this is the period with which we are concerned here.

All three reports[27] into the causes of the financial crisis, while emphasizing the responsibility of other factors, many international and other actors, in particular the directors of the leading commercial banks, found that the failure of the Regulator had contributed. Two features were particularly significant, the first structural and the other 'light touch' regulation.

(i) During the 2003-2010 period the overall authority was the (joint) Central Bank and Financial Services Authority of Ireland, with the Regulator (Irish Financial Services Regulatory Authority) independent so far as its own functions were concerned. Thus, each institution had its own board, though the legislation required a good deal of overlapping membership. This semi-autonomy was based on the idea that if there were not some independence, the Authority might be subject to a conflict of interest between the financial institutions and their clients; accordingly, the McDowell advisory group[28] had recommended complete

24 M. McDonagh, *Freedom of Information Law* (2nd edn, Thomson Round Hall, 2006), para 2.06-07.

25 This section draws heavily on M. Donnelly, *The Law of Credit and Security* (Round Hall, 2011), ch. 4.

26 For a sketch of the group of regulators, see G. Hogan and D.G. Morgan, *Administrative Law in Ireland* (4th edn, Thomson Round Hall, Reuters, 2010), ch. 6, part E.

27 Various aspects of this failure have been the subject of three official inquiries, which are referred to later in this section: P. Honohan, *The Irish Banking Crisis: Regulatory and Financial Stability Policy 2003-2008* (Government Publications Office, 2010); K. Regling and M. Watson, *A Preliminary Report on the Sources of Ireland's Banking Crisis* (Government Publications Office, 2010); Nyberg, *Misjudging Risk*. The first two enquiries were cast as preliminary reports providing a basis for the terms of reference of the third.

28 This new system had been the subject of an Oireachtas Joint Committee on Finance and Public Services report of 1998 and the Report of the Implementation Advisory

autonomy. This recommendation was vigorously opposed by the Central Bank, supported by the then Minister for Finance. And the outcome was the compromise just described.

The Nyberg Commission's judgment was that the division in operations between the Regulator and the Central Bank was deleterious. The Central Bank was charged with overall financial stability matters while the Regulator was responsible for identifying and bringing to the Central Bank any bank-specific or prudential concerns, of potentially system-wide significance. (Individual consumer complaints, with which we are not concerned here, because they usually do not have a wide impact, are under the jurisdiction of the Financial Services Ombudsman.) The Central Bank had taken the view that it would not be appropriate for it to raise issues unless these had been brought to its attention by the Regulator and that acting otherwise would have been an unacceptable intrusion on the Regulator's autonomous status. This narrow view was not shared by the Nyberg Commission (para 4.4.3) which held that this view created 'a situation where financial stability problems could not be addressed'. Again, the Honohan Report (para 1.19) found that at a structural level, 'the institutional separation of the Regulator from the rest of the organisation may have contributed to an insufficient appreciation of the micro-macro linkages involved in financial stability analysis'. In addition the report noted the possibility that institutional rivalry may have contributed to failure to communicate on occasion. Because of these views, under the 2010 Act, there is now a fully integrated Central Bank.

(ii) Many people have identified 'light touch regulation' (sometimes called principle-based regulation), that is leaving management and boards to act in the best interests of their respective institutions, an approach which is by no means particular to Ireland, as among the causes of the failure. For example, Mr Nyberg remarks at para 4.3.2:

> The financial regulator was unwilling to engage in a process of (what was possibly perceived to be) intrusive verification to establish whether institutions were in fact behaving in a prudent manner and managing this appropriately. Instead the FR relied on principle-based regulation. Given that the FR did not perform the required detailed scrutiny of lending practices, it is very unlikely that it would at any time have formed an adequate understanding of bank exposures or the risks arising from the 'procedures creep' [namely greater risks were taken to retain borrowers].

Coupled with this, when it came to enforcement, the Regulator's 'general policy was not to act unless a legally watertight case could be made.' (Nyberg, para 4.3.3).

Group on the establishment of a Single Regulatory Authority for the Financial Services Sector, known as the McDowell Report (Pn. 7271, 1999). This group was chaired by Michael McDowell who was then a Senior Counsel and later Attorney General and Minister for Justice.

In addition (para 4.3.10) 'It appears that concerns about a loss of market share by Irish banks to potentially less regulated foreign competitors may have inhibited forceful action by the FR. However, fears on this score may have been overstated. It is not clear to the Commission why cooperation from relevant foreign Regulators could not have been sought to help discourage imprudent behaviour specifically in Irish financial markets.' Reinforcing this trend is a particular Irish factor. As a people with deep historical memory and a troubled colonial past, the Irish have a difficult relationship with state authority, including the law. As protector, guardian or disciplinarian, the first recourse was traditionally the family and community, coupled with the (Catholic) Church. Respect for the state and its institutions was also undermined by the fact that its real jurisdiction excluded the six counties of Northern Ireland (which after Independence remained part of the UK), whereas traditional Irish patriotism depended on the notion of the Irish nation embracing the entire island. Finally, the Irish had little enthusiasm for the state regulation of activities traditionally regarded as 'private law' in character. So far as they have thought about the matter, in their attitude to capitalism and 'free enterprise', the Irish have plumped for Boston over Berlin.

Corporate Governance

This is not a book about corporate governance. Nevertheless, given that we are speaking about state regulation of financial-commercial activities, it is pertinent to say that the design and operation of such machinery in Ireland, as elsewhere, assumes that there already exist private law safeguards. This is especially true in the light of modern reforms to corporate law, designed to promote probity, openness and accountability, as well as external values, such as respect for the environment. Yet, in Celtic Tiger Ireland, such systems failed to function effectively. As has been said: 'Questions are being asked regarding the judgment of directors, boards and other officers and their accountability for risk-taking.'[29] In addition, in a small jurisdiction, it proved very difficult to find persons to serve as 'independent directors' who were genuinely both independent and informed.

Again, in significant cases, external auditors, whose duty it is to give an annual true and accountable picture of a company's affairs, were found to have been asleep at the wheel.[30] In one typical episode, a number of companies in the Zoe development group had debts of €1.3 billion and applied for the appointment of an examiner. The independent accountant's report which accompanied the application predicted a surplus of €10 million over the following three to five year period, on the assumption of a recovery in the Irish property market. In refusing the application, Kelly J stated that '[the] degree of optimism of the independent

29 I. Lynch-Fannon and G. Murphy, *Corporate Insolvency and Rescue* (2nd edn, Bloomsbury, 2012), para [1.03].

30 V. Browne, 'Scrutiny of Audit Firms Over Crisis is Critical', *Irish Times*, 30 May 2012, p. 16.

accountant borders, if it does not actually trespass, on the fanciful ... The valuations in question are out of date [author: some were seven months old] and can hardly be described as truly independent' (Re: Vantive Holdings [2009] *IEHC* 384).

In summary, state regulators are regarded as safety nets, designed to complement and reinforce internal systems. In Celtic Tiger Ireland, neither these internal – nor the external – safeguards worked properly.

Planning Control

At a broad level, the failures of the financial and business regulator and of the land use planning regulatory system have a good deal in common. About each, at the time when the errors were being made (rather than in the steady, clear light of hindsight), an elected politician might well have said: 'No one was asking questions about this on the doorstep.' This is surely true, given the fact that such control is unloved by many Irish voters and that elected local councillors are involved in its administration. Lack of interest was increased by the lack of discussion of the real issues, which resulted from the media's feel that the public was not interested, coupled with the strength of Irish defamation law. Yet, planning control is sorely needed in a country in which the population is relatively sparse and houses are frequently spread over the countryside, putting great pressure on roads and other services.[31]

Consequently, planning permission was granted too freely for speculative development, a factor which indirectly contributed to the economic collapse. One of the many recent post-mortems remarks:
there has been a catastrophic failure of the planning system ... Planning should provide checks and balances to the excesses of development and act for the common good, even if that means taking unpopular decisions. However, during the Celtic Tiger period, a laissez faire approach to planning predominated at all levels of governance ... As a result not only was there an unsustainable growth in property prices, but this was accompanied by a property building frenzy.[32]The paper goes on to refer to 'charges of localism, cronyism and clientelism'.

Amending the Constitution to Accommodate the Fiscal Treaty, 2012

The particular Irish feature regarding the Fiscal Treaty is that, because the Treaty violates Irish state sovereignty, in order to empower the government to ratify it,

---

31 A planning decision is largely determined by zoning regulations, which are made by elected councillors, for the particular area. These have been the subject of substantial controversy.

32 Kitchin et al., *A Haunted Landscape: Housing and Ghost Estates in Post Celtic Tiger Ireland* (National Institute for Regional and Spatial Analysis, 2010), 2. See also *Annual Report Ombudsman for 2000*, 6-7 and for 2009, 15.

a constitutional amendment was necessary; and for this Art. 46 always requires a referendum. In mid-2012, the Referendum was passed by a three to two majority[33] on what by Irish standards was a fairly low turn-out, following a fairly energetic campaign on both sides over the preceding two months.

The reader may respond that the EU, with its integrated approach to law, governance and policy-making, is a standing affront to state sovereignty, such that this conflict must have arisen before. (Admittedly, the EU was not directly involved on this occasion, but it is likely that it may be in other developments in this field.) This is a cue to call on stage the landmark case of *Crotty* v. *An Taoiseach* [1987] IR 713 in which the Supreme Court held that for Ireland to ratify the Single European Act (SEA) 1987 would be unconstitutional. There were two features to this case. The first concerned the fact that the Irish Constitution, having been drafted following eight centuries of British colonization, naturally contains strong statements regarding sovereignty. Not only is there a broad, sweeping assertion of 'sovereignty' in Art. 5, but also there is a vesting of legislative, executive and judicial powers (the classic separation of powers categorization of government functions) in the appropriate domestic organ (Arts 15.2.1, 34.1, 28.2 and 29.4.1). This vesting bars these organs from alienating or abdicating their powers to external bodies. This meant that the SEA obligation to align foreign policy among all EU states violated Irish sovereignty.

Second, in view of the provisions just summarized, in order for Ireland to enter the EU in 1973 it was necessary for the Constitution to be amended. This was done following a 1972 Amendment which introduced a new saving provision, Art. 29.4.10. This states that the other provisions in the Constitution already mentioned could not be read as invalidating laws, acts or measures 'necessitated by the obligations of membership of [the EU]'.

In *Crotty* a majority of the Supreme Court held, in respect of the first feature, that for the institution which in 1972 was called the 'European Economic Community' to adopt a foreign policy competence was plainly in violation of Art. 29.2, which specifically vests this power in the (Irish) government. Second, the saving provision in Art. 29.4.10 could have no purchase since, for the institution which in 1972 was called the 'European Economic Community' to sprout a foreign policy competence would, in 1972, have been so unexpected as to be outside the saving provision. The net result was that in order for the ratification of SEA, it was necessary to augment Art. 29.4.10. Similar adjustments were necessary to permit the ratification of the Maastricht, Amsterdam, Nice and Lisbon Treaties.[34]

---

33 The Thirtieth Amendment of the Constitution (Treaty on Stability, Coordination and Governance in the Economic and Monetary Union) Act 2012 was passed by 955,000 (60.3 per cent) to 629,000 (39.7 per cent) on a 49.1 per cent turnout, amending Art. 29.4.

34 In the case of Nice (2001 and 2002) and Lisbon (2008 and 2009), the initial referendum to make the necessary amendments failed; in each case, a further successful proposal was made to amend the Constitution.

The government finds it inconvenient to have these referendums in regard to Europe. The no-side frequently uses questionable tactics; whereas the yes-side is expected to observe the 'Queensbury Rules'. The people naturally weary of being asked for the 'Nth' time a question which may appear to many of them to boil down to 'do you still love the EU?' In addition, respectable legal argument[35] could have been made against the *Crotty* precedent. But there would have been a significant risk – in the calculation of any realistic government legal advisor – in going ahead without a referendum and hoping to secure a court victory against any legal challenge. It would be this: if the challenge were successful, the government would be perceived as having lost face. It is true that the government would then have the possibility of a Plan B, namely to bring forward a referendum to amend the Constitution. But because of the government's defeat, the yes-side would start off the ensuing referendum one-nil down in sporting terms, and it might not recover from this handicap.

It does not need a crystal ball to predict that the EU's financial woes will be solved, if at all, only by a method that involves further infringements of state sovereignty. As of mid-2012, it is being said[36] that progress to a measure such as eurobonds will come about only at the end of a process of many smaller confidence-building measures. The significance of this is that it means that there will be no single point at which the people must be asked to give their assent. This opens up the awesome prospect of a series of even further referendums, carrying the risk of a low turn-out and the result being determined by extremist elements. A related range of problems for government lawyers follows from the process of actually agreeing the terms of the various international arrangements. This is best done by a government known to have the authority to commit the state, on agreement being reached. In the case of Ireland, this would require an amendment in advance of the terms being agreed. Yet, as against this, seen from the perspective of the referendum, it is better for the people to have before them a cut-and-dried agreement: otherwise, there are numerous possibilities for dispute as to what may happen after the referendum is safely passed, with the no-side claiming that the government will 'sell the country down the river'.[37]

35 The argument would be that *Crotty* had been undermined by *McGimpsey* v. *Ireland* [1990] 1 I.R. 110. The distinguishing of *Crotty* in *McGimpsey* was by no means convincing.

36 R. McCrea, 'EU Reforms Call for New Approach to Referendums', *Irish Times*, 22 June 2012.

37 For an account of a real, analogous 'chicken-and-egg' situation, centring on the referendum to authorize the 19th Amendment to allow Ireland to ratify the Belfast Agreement with Britain (an important part of the Northern Ireland Peace Process), see Hogan and Whyte, *J M Kelly*, para 8.1.09-10.

Established Constitutional Doctrine in Turbulent Times?

We have just examined constitutional or sub-constitutional changes made, or under consideration, in relation to the economic crisis. In the first two sections of the present part, we consider how existing principles of judicial review of laws and administrative acts have stood up when subjected to the robust tests presented by the current economic circumstances. The first situation discussed here is where the state is seeking to vary or terminate arrangements entered into in more prosperous times and the person or, more likely, group disadvantaged by the change takes legal action against the state. Second, faced with a financial collapse of Irish banking institutions, the Irish state (in 2008) issued a guarantee in respect of the banks' liabilities and also took over many of the debts owed to the banks. In response, some of the debtors took legal action. The third section notices briefly the judiciary's role in relation to certain high profile and highly significant private and commercial law cases thrown up by the present crisis.

Altering Arrangements and Agreements

A very great deal of state expenditure consists of the salaries, pensions, expenses and so on of public servants. Therefore, the state, in seeking to reduce its expenditure, has tried to reduce the numbers of public servants, as well as their salaries, pensions or other benefits. The government has sought to effect these changes by agreement with representative organizations representing various groups of employees or businesses. (For instance, the form of agreement with public service employees is known as the 'Croke Park Agreement' of 2010.) But, in some cases, agreement has not proved possible and since in Ireland a good deal of political contention takes the form of court cases, there have been a number of court challenges to the legality of the government's actions.

Equality

One potentially far-reaching line of argument has been based on the equality provision which in the Irish Constitution takes the form of Art. 40.1, which states: 'All citizens shall, as human persons, be held equal before the law. This shall not be held to mean that the state shall not in its enactments have due regard to differences of capacity, physical and moral, and of social function.' This is such a wide provision that, generally speaking, Irish, like other, courts, have been reluctant to rely upon it: just because 'there is a sense in which to legislate is to discriminate'.[38] The provision was, however, squarely invoked in *Unite the Union* v. *Minister for Finance* [2010] IEHC 354 (8 October 2010). The background to the case was the Financial Emergency Measures in the Public Interest Act 2009, section 2 of which imposed on almost all public service workers a significant levy. At the centre of the case was a provision of the Act that empowered the

38 *Brennan* v. *Attorney General* [1983] ILRM 449, 480.

Minister for Finance to exempt specified employees from the scope of this levy. The applicant trade union's members had sought an exemption from the Minister and had been refused.

The basis of the applicants' claim was that they were employees of the Central Bank which, in contrast to most other public servants, had its own free-standing and self-funded pension scheme, separate from the usual Civil Service Superannuation Scheme or its equivalent in other sections of the public service. The only other public servants in the same position as the applicants, in that they had their own fully-funded scheme, were members of the 'commercial semi-state bodies'; these employees – significantly – were not subject to the pensions levy. Accordingly, the applicants contended that they were in a like position with commercial semi-state employees, and since such employees were not required to pay the levy, the applicants were being discriminated against. However, the High Court (Kearns P) rejected this argument.[39] Central to the judgment was the general legal principle that, because of the far-reaching character of the equality doctrine, the burden is on an applicant to establish the unequal treatment of which it complains. Kearns J stated (at p. 26): 'The applicants' argument would necessitate expert evidence on the manner in which pensions are paid across the public service and evidence of how pension schemes operate in the commercial semi-state sector in comparison. No such evidence was advanced in these proceedings.'

Nailing the door against an argument which he clearly disliked, Kearns P added (at p. 26) that 'the Scheme is modelled on the civil service pension schemes which apply across the public service and are generally believed to be significantly more generous than private pension arrangements both in relation to the levels of contributions and benefits'. Here is a striking contrast with the strict requirement, just noted, which has been imposed on the applicant to show evidence. Underlying this contrast in judicial treatment is probably the feeling that comparing the pensions or remuneration of various sections of the public service is an inappropriate function for a judge operating within the confines of court procedure.

Legitimate Expectations

Another broad and far-reaching notion is legitimate expectations,[40] meaning broadly that the state must keep to a promise which it has made. In *J. & J. Haire & Company Limited* v. *The Minister for Health and Children*[41] the central fact was that the Financial Emergency Measures in the Public Interest Act 2009 enabled the government to reduce the amount paid by the state to a wide range of persons, including pharmacists. Pursuant to her powers under the Act, the Minister

39 An analogous argument related to a different group of public service workers (the police) met a similar fate in *Garda Representative Association* v. *Minister for Finance* [2010] IEHC 78.

40 Hogan and Morgan, *Administrative Law*, ch. 19.

41 [2009] IEHC 562; [2010] 2 I.R. 615.

introduced Regulations[42] that reduced payments made to pharmacists under a pre-existing scheme. The plaintiff-pharmacist brought proceedings challenging the constitutionality of both the 2009 Act and the Regulations.

Among the scatter-gun of arguments advanced by the plaintiff, the most significant, for present purposes, started from the basis, which is well-established law, that a contract, such as that between the plaintiff and the state medical authority, is regarded as a property right which is protected by Art. 40.3.2, which states 'The State shall protect as best it may from unjust attack … the property rights of every citizen.' The judge's main line of reasoning for rejecting the plaintiff's argument was, if anything, of even wider significance. He ruled that, given the state's motivation for altering the rates of payment – the financial emergency – the reduction of the pharmacists pay rate was not (to use the language of Art. 40.3.2) 'unjust'. McMahon J stated (at para 113):

> 'unjust' in this sense, refers to matters such as retrospectivity, lack of fair procedures, unreasonableness and irrationality, discrimination, lack of proportionality and, in some cases, lack of compensation. Suffice it to say at this point not only do I consider that there has not been an attack on the plaintiffs constitutional rights but also I consider that what encroachment the plaintiffs might complain of could not be considered unjust.

The judge continued that the Act of 2009 was a 'measured, proportionate and carefully drawn piece of legislation in response to an unprecedented economic crisis and included a number of significant safeguards'. A further relevant point is that before varying the rates, the Minister had engaged in a consultation process with the pharmacists' professional body. In summary, in the changed circumstances afforded by the collapse in the public finances, the government was justified in altering its position, though this involved dishonouring the plaintiff's expectation.

It is worth briefly comparing *Haire* with an episode from the private sector. For many decades in Ireland, it has been the practice in the case of leases of business premises to include an 'upwards only rent review clause'. In other words, a medium-or long-term fixed lease normally includes a provision by which, at a specified stage (usually every five years), the rent could be reassessed against comparable property, so as to fix the rental value for that type of premises in that sort of locality, *as at the date of reassessment*. In this way, the rent is kept in line with contemporary changes.

So far, so good. But what was problematic about these clauses is that they only applied if there was an increase in rental values: seemingly, the failure to contemplate a situation in which there was a fall in rental values was so far outside anyone's expectation as to be not thought worthy of mention by the lawyers drafting the lease. Yet, the financial collapse brought circumstances in

42 Health Professionals (Reduction of Payments to Community Pharmacist Contractors) Regulations (S.I. No. 246 of 2009).

which rental values fell by 30-50 per cent, compared with amounts at the height of the boom, when many of the leases would have been fixed. The consequences of this for business tenants, who were already suffering a reduction of income, were often calamitous. Some landlords were prepared not to insist on their full legal rights. But others were not. Tenants' organizations naturally protested to the government and parliament. The result was to change the law so that, even if the variation clause in the lease allowed only for an increase in the rent, a tenant could, in appropriate conditions, insist on a reduction. But this change of law was made to apply only to leases entered into *after* the law change. The reason for this restriction – which was hotly opposed by tenants groups – was that to include pre-law leases would be to violate the landlord's property right. This was on advice from the Attorney General in the 1997-2011 government.

A further episode, thrown up by the economic tsunami and engaging broadly similar legal policy, concerned judicial pensions. It is plainly important from the perspective of ensuring that everyone, especially such highly-regarded and well-paid members of the public service as judges, should bear an equal share of cuts being imposed on public service salaries and pensions. (Such equality might even be regarded as an aspect of the Rule of Law.) The then Attorney General, however, gave it as his (rather surprising) view that to include the judiciary in those who had to bear such cuts would be to violate Art. 35.5 of the Constitution.[43] This provision, which is part of the Independence of the Judiciary section of the Constitution, provides that 'the remuneration of a judge shall not be reduced during his term of office'. The consequence was that the cuts could be made only if the Constitution were amended and this is what was done in 2011.[44] At the referendum that was necessary for the amendment, many lawyers opposing the amendment put their case on the basis that in the unpredictable future some government might use the new power to try to manipulate the judiciary. But this argument seems to have been regarded as special pleading by the voters, who supported the amendment by about four to one.

It is worth commenting on these two episodes – the judicial levy amendment and the refusal to apply the change to rent review clauses to existing leases – together with the *Haire* authority. At a fundamental level, they all centre on the same issue,

43 There were some who contended that the Attorney's view was too literal and not supported by authority: see D. Gwynn Morgan, 'The Pension Levy and Judicial Independence', *Irish Law Times* (2009): 63. But the government naturally accepted the view of its Attorney. It should be added that some of the judges paid voluntarily; though not always the full amount.

44 The full title of the amending Act was the Twenty-Ninth Amendment of the Constitution (Judges' Remuneration) Act 2011. The results were that the Judges' Remuneration Amendment was passed by 79.7 per cent to 20.3 per cent, on a turnout of 56.0 per cent. For a full overview of results, see Department of the Environment, Community and Local Government, *Referendum Results: 1937-2011* (2011); available at: http://www.environ.ie/en/LocalGovernment/Voting/Referenda/.

namely that of whether to allow existing arrangements to be unilaterally changed for the future because of supervening economic adversity. (As noted, the need for the judicial pension levy amendment turned on its own particular circumstance, namely Art. 35 of the Constitution. At the broadest level, however, it is part of the theme under discussion here.) There is, of course, a good deal of intricate analysis that could be offered in respect of retrospectivity and cognate areas, which would not be relevant to the theme of this book. One observation that may be made is that there is a difference between a law that seeks to alter the consequence in the future of arrangements made before the law and, on the other hand, a law that goes to the extreme of affecting consequences that had occurred before the law. This last contingency would be illustrated, in the present context, if it were suggested that judges had to pay the excessive remuneration or landlords the excessive rent which had been paid to either before the change of law. However, emphatically in the present situation, it was not this contingency, but the earlier more moderate one, that was at issue.

At base, the policies at play here are, first, respect for property, including contract (or whatever wider category of agreement is at issue) in the Constitution. In particular, there is the broad, common law, notion that supervening economic difficulty is not a defence to an action for breach of contract, on the traditional basis that this is a 'slippery slope' that could lead to the unravelling of a lot of contracts. Telling in the opposite direction is the notion that where the law is seeking to regulate far-reaching issues of state economic survival, it must take account of reality: *fiat iustitiae ruat coelum* (let justice be done, though the heavens fall) will not suffice in the contemporary world. *Haire* indicates that the courts have preferred the second of these policies in the extreme conditions affecting the state at present.

So much for policy. As to authority, the reader will see that there was a divergence between the Attorney General's view – and it was the same Attorney General who advised in respect of each episode – and, on the other hand, the High Court judgment, and one should add that there were other cases agreeing with *Haire*.[45] The reader may well ask: who carries the greater authority – the Attorney General or the courts? The answer is plain: the courts (the High Court or, on appeal, the Supreme Court). The Attorney General's role is to advise the government on what the law is and that is something which, on points of constitutional interpretation, is determined by the courts. In these circumstances, accordingly, the best summation may be to say that the judges have ruled that economic crisis may constitutionally justify a unilateral variation of arrangements, but that this conclusion is viewed with some unease by some Irish lawyers, including the Attorney General, because of the strong right to property in the Constitution.

45 *Curran* v. *Minister for Education and Science* [2009] IEHC 378; [2009] 4 I.R. 300.

Transfer of Debts from Banks to NAMA

Towards the end of the boom years, a significant contribution to growth came from a major property market bubble. In addition, there was a rise in consumer spending which has now left a significant consumer debt problem. Accordingly, a significant part of the state's financial crisis arose from the fact that certain banks or other credit institutions had lent money to borrowers on a massive scale. The result was a classic 'bubble': money was lent to borrowers to purchase development land or buildings, some in Ireland and some abroad,[46] on the basis of valuations which, by 2008, had become serious overvaluations, often by as much as 50 per cent. There was thus a serious threat to the stability of credit institutions and a need to stabilize the Irish financial system by removing uncertainty regarding the value of assets of credit institutions that were of systemic importance to the economy.

The reaction of the state was twofold. First, although the banks were all privately owned commercial bodies, the Irish government in September 2008 gave a State Guarantee to cover the borrowings of these credit institutions. Second, a State agency, the National Asset Management Agency (NAMA), was set up by statute. And, as some compensation for the Guarantee just mentioned, the mortgages over land and buildings, which had been given by the developer-borrowers to the banks were now transferred from the banks to NAMA. In brief, the method followed by NAMA was as follows. At the outset, the relevant bank was free to decide whether or not to participate in the NAMA scheme. However, an eligible bank asset is not acquired by reason of this fact alone, but only if NAMA, in the exercise of its discretion, concludes that its acquisition is desirable for the purposes of the Act. The case law has centred on this second point.

It has often been observed[47] that in exercising its power of judicial review over administrative actions the Irish judiciary has sought to make up for a lack of control over substantive issues by imposing a very stringent doctrine of procedural rectitude. Each of these aspects was at issue in *Dellway Investments* v. *NAMA* [2011] IESC 14 (12 April 2011). First, on the substantive front, it was argued that the Act was unconstitutional. This was on the basis that the regulations used to determine bank assets were so broad as to leave the discretion of NAMA so untrammelled and unguided as to represent an unjust and disproportionate attack on the developer's property rights.[48] Relevant here is the fact that Irish draftsmen, in anticipation of the sort of argument considered here, had adopted the civil law style, rather than the silence of the common law, in stating explicitly the purposes of this novel public law legislation. Thus, sections 2 and 84 of the Act constituting NAMA, the National Asset Management Agency Act 2009, sets out the grounds

46 It was a particular joy to Irish developers to buy prime sites in central London, which they saw as a happy reversal of eight centuries of history.

47 Hogan and Morgan, *Administrative Law*.

48 Cf. the unsuccessful challenge by shareholders to British state take-over as being interference with property rights in Art. 1, First Protocol ECHR.

upon which the power to acquire bank assets must be exercised. These include 'the need to address a serious threat to the stability of credit institutions and the need for the maintenance and stabilisation of the financial system in the state by [removing] uncertainty about the valuation and location of certain assets of credit institutions of systemic importance to the economy and to restore confidence in the banking system'.

An alternative basis for upholding the constitutionality of the legislation is the general precept in Irish law that, as it was put in an earlier classic authority, quoted with approval by the Court: 'It is to be presumed that, when it conferred a statutory power, Parliament intended the power to be exercised only in a manner that would be in conformity with the constitution and within the limitations of the power as they are to be gathered from the statutory scheme or design.'[49] On this basis, there was sufficient guidance in the Act, in the form of the statutory principles, quoted earlier, which should guide NAMA, in deciding whether to acquire a particular asset.

The applicants' second argument, in which they did succeed, was based on fair procedure, in particular audi alteram partem (hear the other side). A preliminary point here is that the NAMA Act gave significant additional powers to NAMA, which were not possessed by the bank under the original mortgage-loan transaction. The consequence is that the applicant-developer's rights under the mortgage are altered to their detriment by the transfer, despite the fact that the obligations to repay remain the same. Accordingly, the Supreme Court held that a person whose interests are capable of being affected by the decision of a public body exercising statutory powers is ordinarily entitled to notice of the public body's intention to consider taking the decision and also to have their representations considered by the decision-maker. The liveliest point here arose from the fact that it has long been accepted that the audi alteram partem rule need not be observed where to do so would frustrate, for example by creating delay, the purpose of the exercise of the discretionary power. As to this, the Supreme Court stated as a fact that any likely delay would not be sufficient to have this effect.

Dellway was taken further in *Daly* v. *NAMA* [2011] IEHC (12 September 2011). The plaintiffs contended, successfully, that fair procedure required that they had a right to be heard, not alone in respect to the acquisition of their loans by NAMA but also prior to any subsidiary decision being taken, for instance to make demand for repayment to appoint Receivers, following default of payment. In addition, it is worth noticing that there was a preliminary point in *Daly*. Put briefly, the specialized judicial review procedure, for which the applicant-developer had opted in *Daly* is confined to issues of public law. And the respondent-NAMA had argued that since the applicant's claim was based on contract and property, it was private law in character. In short, the applicant had chosen the wrong procedure. The High Court rejected this argument. The plaintiffs had submitted that decisions relating to the exercise of powers by NAMA under the National Asset Management

49 *The State (Lynch)* v. *Cooney* [1982] IR 337, 338.

Agency Act 2009 are public law matters and, as such, amenable to judicial review. Ruling in their favour, the High Court stated that (pp. 95-96):

> Section 2 of the Act sets out purposes which are public, truly national in their scope, and aimed at securing some advantage to the state's economy and finances, and the stability of the banking sector. The Act has all the appearances of emergency legislation where a statutory body is established with unusual powers which would not, I would have thought, be contemplated as being necessary, desirable or perhaps even permissible in normal times … Decisions made under such legislation with the capacity to affect the interests of persons in such a drastic way and supposedly in the interests of the state as a whole should be capable of judicial scrutiny, where, as contemplated by the Act itself, a substantial issue is raised as to the lawfulness of decisions.

One should observe that if the judicial review route had failed, other avenues into the court would have been available to the applicant. But this, for good reasons, was his preferred route.

It is suggested that these cases show the Irish judges applying established constitutional principles steadily in the new circumstances. In terms of results, it is true that the state's defence succeeded in *Haire* and, on the substantive point, in *Dellway*. But these were cases drawing on principles that have always allowed a lot of ground to the state side. As noted, the common law has always set the balance far in favour of the state where an attack is made on an administrative decision on substantive grounds, because of the fear that otherwise a judge would be perceived as substituting his own decision for that of an elected person or an expert administrator. The other half of the historic compromise, in common law judicial review, is the strong principle in favour of fair procedure that is imposed upon public administrators. This was applied strongly in *Dellway*, by the Supreme Court, and in *Daly*. This was despite the fact that it might have seemed that in each case there was room for the judges to have taken refuge in a well-established exception to the usual principle (the need for speed and the fact that points of detail were involved, respectively). We are not here appraising the utility or worth of these established constitutional doctrines, but simply observing that fundamental judicial precepts pre-Crash look largely the same as post-Crash, which most would regard as good. As was said in a not dissimilar context, 'in this country amidst the clash of arms, the laws are not silent. They may be changed but they speak the same language in law as in peace.'[50]

Independence of the Judiciary and the Elites

It needs no emphasis that the independence of the judiciary is probably the most important aspect of the rule of law. And especially at a time when the foundation

50 *Liversidge* v. *Anderson* [1942] AC 206, 244 (Lord Atkin dissenting).

stones of the polity are quaking and political leaders are being doubted, and the citizenry needs to be reassured that the sacrifices, which are inevitable, are being shared fairly, it is important to have decision-makers in at least one field who can be trusted. Legal ideology has traditionally identified 'Leviathan', that is the state or king, as the suspect one, against whom the people must be protected. And we have noticed this aspect of the judges' duty being performed earlier in this part. However it may be that, given the unpopularity of politicians with the people and the popularity of judges, an almost equally exacting threat to judicial independence arises where cases involve figures from big business. These heroes of the Celtic Tigerhood (their image burnished in the mass media, by a lifestyle centring on helicopters or race-horses) bring with them into court quite a powerful aura. The sort of issues that have been thrown up by the exigencies of the Crash often come down to those such as whether the apartment block was really transferred to the developer's spouse or children, or, in a different situation, the spouse appreciated what she was doing when she purported to mortgage the mansion to the bank, as security for the husband's debt. Another sort of case may raise the question of whether the lifestyle of a debtor, whom it is sought to bankrupt, creates jurisdiction in the courts of one state, rather than another, with more advantageous laws, or whether a Judgment-debtor has removed assets from the jurisdiction in breach of a court order not to do so.[51] With such vital questions of fact, many of which came down to who was telling the truth and who was not, the judges have dealt fairly and without undue respect for the rich and powerful personages before them. This is no small thing.

There is a related point. In the past, the banks would always have stood as independent creditors of developers. But in the present catastrophe, because of the banks' sloppy lending policy and the unprecedented and life-risking extent of their exposure to the property sector, the banks did not enjoy an 'arm's-length relationship' with creditor-developers. The outcome was that until the effective nationalization of the Irish banks, any opposition to (say) the appointment of an examiner, however implausible the proposed rescue attempt, would come from a foreign bank. Here was another situation in which an independent and sophisticated judiciary proved vital.

Conclusions

To put it simply, the recent financial partial collapse was a considerable shock to Ireland, with consequences at all levels and in every way – individual, personal, family, artistic and literary. Yet, what takes one's notice regarding constitutional reaction to the financial crash is its moderation: as Sherlock Holmes remarked on one occasion 'the curious incident of the dog in the night-time is not that the dog barked; but that the dog failed to bark': there has been no Big New Idea. Equally,

51 See, for example, *Irish Times*, 27 June 2012, Business Section, 1.

the judges have remained true to the centuries-old principles of judicial review: insistence on fair procedures, but scant attempt to second-guess the political organs in economic fields.

This chapter also shows an example of things remaining more or less the same, but with more unfortunate consequences. Constitutions frequently look to the past. In every conventional state, the Constitution enshrines sovereignty. In Ireland, because of eight centuries of British rule, the Constitution established a particularly inflexible form of sovereignty, which has been strengthened by the literal interpretation adopted by the *Crotty* majority. And, significantly, true to the logic of sovereignty the Constitution may be amended only with the majority of citizens at a referendum. Thus the problem of moving from the nineteenth-century notion of sovereignty to a sort of supranational model, some form of which seems to offer the only basis of economic salvation, appears to be especially difficult on a political-legal plane in Ireland. And not just economic salvation, for in devising solutions to the problems set for humankind by global warming, international terrorism, the financial 'markets' or communications technology, the same difficulties, on the level of both practice and principle, have to be confronted on the supranational plane.

Chapter 3
The Constitutional Consequences of the Financial Crisis in Italy

Tania Groppi, Irene Spigno and Nicola Vizioli

Political and Socio-economic Facets of the Crisis: A Brief Introduction

The financial crisis that struck the eurozone in 2008 and which reached its peak in 2011 not only affected the economic arena, but also had highly relevant consequences at the constitutional level in most of the countries affected. This is something of a novelty if we compare today's crisis with previous ones, and it is linked, directly or indirectly, to what can be considered the main new feature of the crisis, namely the role played by supranational actors and above all the EU. In fact, since the establishment of the Economic and Monetary Union, many financial and economic functions have been the province of the EU. However, as far as constitutional and institutional reforms are concerned, the EU lacks any kind of jurisdiction and action by national governments is still required in order to enact EU reforms. In addition, democratic legitimacy still comes from the national level.[1]

Within this context, the Italian experience may be considered to be of particular interest. In fact, economic and financial crises are nothing new to Italy. In the early 1990s, for example, Italy suffered another deep crisis, which did not lead to any kind of constitutional consequences (at least from the formal point of view). The origin of the Italian economic crisis can be traced back to some weakness in the economic system dating back to the pre-Republican period, but it was further exacerbated as the main consequence of the enormous public debt that has seen a continuous and tremendous increase since the 1960s. There are both political and economic grounds for today's crisis. The causes of the growing public debt are numerous, one of which is the consociational political system that characterized the Italian political arena in the aftermath of the Second World War. This system lacked a real political opposition able to check the government majority. In fact, as a consequence of the Cold War, the main opposition political party, the Communist

1 See P. Lindseth, 'Greek "Sovereignty" and European "Democracy"'; available at www.eutopialaw.com, November 2011: 'When push comes to shove, European integration still needs democratic legitimation coming from the national level, both in a formal and substantive sense.'

Party, was excluded from the possibility of winning elections and becoming part of the government in what has been called a '*conventio ad excludendum*'.

In effect, the various governments that came to power after 1948 were all dominated by the Christian Democratic Party, and they were able to enforce spending policies geared to the maintenance of a high consensus without any form of control, in a climate of increasing political clientelism and corruption. This party system collapsed after the fall of the Berlin Wall in the early 1990s, thanks to the operation involving high level judicial investigations known as 'Clean Hands' ('*Mani Pulite*'), which involved many political actors. Since then, governments, irrespective of their political orientation, have tried to approve debt reduction measures, primarily to meet the Maastricht criteria and to allow entry and permanent national presence in the Economic and Monetary Union. This has resulted in several public administration and welfare reforms (especially concerning the pension system), which have, however, brought only limited savings. More specifically, since 2008 room for manoeuvre has decreased even more, because the government has had to face the consequences of the international economic crisis, resulting in a reduction of GDP and a consequent decline in tax revenues. In addition, Italy has at the same time witnessed an increase in public spending in order to deal with the liquidity crisis faced by the banking sector and the difficulties facing the private sector (related, apart from the economic crisis, to the 'credit crunch'), which has led to the increasing use of social safety nets (especially redundancy payments). In 2011, financial speculation led to a marked increase in the interest rates of public debt bonds and in their spread compared with those of other countries (most notably Germany).

The point in time when Italian politicians could no longer ignore the crisis was 5 August 2011, when the ECB sent a letter to the Italian government, in which it asked Italy to adopt policies to deregulate its economy, to introduce more flexibility in employment and to increase privatization. Since that moment, an incessant chain of events has been underway: a constitutional revision bill was introduced in parliament by the government in order to introduce the balanced budget principle into the Constitution; the Fourth Berlusconi government collapsed due to the political (and personal) difficulties it was already facing, and a new government, led by Mario Monti, was nominated. The main focus of the European institutions was the lack of political credibility of the Italian government especially with regard to the reduction of public debt and the adoption of the structural reforms necessary to contain public spending. Therefore, as will be further explained in the following paragraphs, the very grounds for the constitutional consequences of the crisis, especially as far as constitutional amendment is concerned, are strictly related to the need to improve the credibility of the Italian institutions in the global context.

However, this is the first time that, beyond ordinary economic and financial measures, a 'constitutional response' has been required. By 'constitutional response' we would like to indicate a series of constitutional consequences which find their roots in the financial crisis, and which can be summarized as follows. First of all, it does include formal changes to the constitutional text (the so called 'written Constitution'): as will be analysed further, in Italy, as has occurred in other European countries, a constitutional revision in order to introduce the 'balanced budget' principle into the Constitution was approved in April 2012. We will deal with this revision in the next section. The crisis influenced the 'unwritten Constitution' as well. More specifically, the 'unwritten Constitution' is regulated more by constitutional conventions than written constitutional provisions, and its main focus is the functioning of the form of government in the political realm.[2] The third section of the chapter will be dedicated to the impact of the crisis on the political and party systems. Legislative reforms impacting on constitutional provisions and the consequent judicial review of legislation could be considered as constitutional consequences. Thus, in the final section, constitutional case law on areas able to produce or improve public expenditures, such as social rights, public administration and regional government, will be considered and discussed.

The Impact of the Crisis on the 'Written Constitution'

In Italy, the financial and economic crisis has led, as in other countries, to the approval of a constitutional amendment. Constitutional Law 1/2012, of 20 April, has introduced the 'balanced budget' principle into the text of the Constitution itself, modifying Art. 81, among others. In this regard, four aspects need to be underlined: first, the timing of the revision, especially in connection with the development of the crisis; second, the analysis of previous constitutional rules on this matter; third, the content of the reform; and, finally, the first comments on, and perspectives of, the implementation of the new rules.

A Constitutional Amendment in Order to 'Reassure the Financial Markets'?

It should be emphasized that formal amendments to the Italian Constitution are quite rare due to the prevailing legal culture that is not strictly linked to the text, and also because of the complexity of the process of constitutional amendment established by the Constitution itself. In fact, according to Art. 138 of the Constitution, each of the two Chambers, the Chamber of Deputies and the Senate of the Republic, must proceed with a double reading of the constitutional bill. During the first reading a majority of the deputies or senators present at the reading is required, while during the second reading a qualified majority of two-thirds of the components of each Chamber is needed. Art. 138 provides the possibility to call for a referendum if, at the second deliberation, the qualified majority of two-thirds is not reached, but there is at any rate an absolute majority. This complex

2 An example of how the crisis affected the 'unwritten Constitution' can be represented by the very active role played by the President of the Republic, which in November 2011 led to the formation of a new government of experts with the specific purpose of putting into practice the necessary economic and administrative reforms.

procedure (whose rationale lies in the need to guarantee passage of only those amendments on which a large consensus has been reached, equally as large as that reached in the Constituent Assembly) means that in the absence of a strong political will, many proposals are abandoned after approval by one Chamber and are not even submitted to the other.[3]

In the case of the 'balanced budget' amendment, following the approval of the Euro Plus agreement on 11 March 2011 by the heads of state and government of the eurozone, later shared also by the European Council of 24-25 March of the same year, several constitutional bills have been filed in both Chambers, by the majority as well as by members of the opposition. However, only after receiving the letter sent by the ECB to the Italian government on 5 August 2011[4] did the government announce the presentation of a constitutional bill,[5] filed on 15 September 2011, to the Chamber of Deputies.[6] The amendment was finally approved by the Senate of the Republic on 17 April 2012,[7] and promulgated by the President of the Republic, Giorgio Napolitano, on 20 April 2012, thereby concluding a procedure that may be considered unique in the history of constitutional amendments in Italy. First of all, it is very rare that such revisions are brought about through government initiatives. Second, the process has been relatively fast, as shown by the dates of the deliberations,[8] and third, the majorities obtained have been very large,[9] thus obviating the necessity to call a referendum.

---

3 See T. Groppi, 'Constitutional Revision in Italy: A Marginal Instrument for Constitutional Change', in X. Contiades (ed.), *Engineering Constitutional Change: A Comparative Perspective on Europe, Canada and the USA* (Routledge, 2013), pp. 203-228.

4 In which it was indicated that 'a constitutional reform tightening fiscal rules would also be appropriate'.

5 This occurred on 11 August 2011, at the sitting of the Constitutional Affairs and Budget Joint Committee, urgently called after the interruption of parliamentary activity for the summer break.

6 Bill 4620, Chamber of Deputies, XVI legislature.

7 Constitutional Law 1/2012.

8 The Committee debate in the Chamber of Deputies began on 5 October 2011 and ended on 10 November; the debate in the Chamber itself began on 23 November and ended on 30 November. In the Senate, the Committee debate began on 7 December 2011 and ended on 14 December 2011; the senators approved the text already approved by the House with no further amendment at the first reading on 15 December 2011. The second reading in the House took a single day for examination by the Committee, on 21 February 2012, and two in the Assembly, on 5 and 6 March. The amendment was definitively approved by the Senate on 17 April 2012.

9 The amendment was approved at first reading by 464 of the 630 members of the Chamber, with 11 abstentions and no opposing votes. The rest of the members of the Chamber were not present. As this was the first vote, the large majority reached was neither relevant nor necessary from the legal point of view. The amendment was approved by the Senate at first reading on 15 December 2011, by 255 out of 315 members, with 14 abstentions and no opposing votes. At the second reading (important in the light of Art. 138 of the Constitution, as a two-thirds majority eliminates the possibility of a referendum) it

This might well be considered a 'hetero-directed' constitutional revision, insofar as it was requested by supranational institutions: this is because it was 'encouraged' by the EU (even more after the Fiscal Compact) and because, as emerged repeatedly during the preparatory works, it was requested in order to 'restore market confidence'. However, none of the above-mentioned European documents clearly requires a constitutional amendment; not even an international commitment on the part of the government which would result in no modification of the Treaties could limit the power to amend the national Constitution.[10] Moreover, it should be noted that in the Italian legal order, European obligations have immediate constitutional primacy under Art. 11 of the Constitution, according to the interpretation provided by the Constitutional Court since Decision 14/1964. Thus, to date it has not been deemed necessary to adapt the text of the Constitution to European obligations. When constitutional provisions are inconsistent with such obligations, an implicit adaptation of the constitutional text is preferred.

As far as the confidence of the market is concerned, this seems to derive more from the strong signal behind the constitutional amendment than from the new constitutional rules themselves. It is a signal that the sustainability of public finances represents a goal shared by the whole of Italian society. Therefore, it can be assumed that necessary unpopular political decisions will be adopted and implemented to this end without strong political or popular opposition.[11]

The Former Constitutional Rules on Budget

We should briefly recall the former fiscal rules deriving from the Italian Constitution. In the absence of a true 'economic constitution' (according to the German definition of *Wirtschaftsverfassung*),[12] these rules can be found in several constitutional dispositions, strictly linked to those protecting social rights. The main article we should refer to on the matter of budget is Art. 81, which is also at the core of the constitutional amendment (although the constitutional revision brings with it some changes to Art. 97 of the Constitution, by introducing the requirement

---

was approved by 489 members of the Chamber, with 3 opposing votes, and no abstentions. In the second reading by the Senate there were 235 votes in favour, 11 against, and 34 abstentions.

10 See M. Luciani, 'Unità nazionale e struttura economica. La prospettiva della Costituzione repubblicana'; available at www.associazionedeicostituzionalisti.it.

11 See F. Coronidi, 'La costituzionalizzazione dei vincoli di bilancio prima e dopo il patto Europlus', *Federalismi*, 7 March 2012.

12 For analysis of the economic constitution in Germany, see G.U. Rescigno, 'Costituzione economica', *Enc. Giur.* X (Treccani, 2001), p. 6. According to the Italian constitutionalist who dealt most with these issues, the economic constitution cannot be distinguished from other parts of the Constitution itself: see M. Luciani, *Economia nel diritto costituzionale*, *Digesto delle discipline pubblicistiche*, vol. V (Utet, 1990), pp. 373ff. See also I. Ciolli, 'I paesi dell'eurozona e i vincoli di bilancio. quando l'emergenza economica fa saltare gli strumenti normativi ordinari', *Rivista AIC* 1 (2012).

that public administrations, in line with EU directions, ensure 'balanced budgets and public debt sustainability'; 117, paras 1 and 2, granting the state exclusive legislative power over the 'harmonization of public budgets', whereas it was previously shared between state and regions; and 119, on matters of regional and local finance, where more stringent constraints on the local authorities have been introduced).

It is worth dwelling briefly on the original version of Art. 81 of the Constitution, particularly its last paragraph, to underline that the 'balanced budget' issue was not unknown to the Constituent Assembly.[13] The distinguished constitutionalist Costantino Mortati, one of the fathers of the Italian Constitution, highlighted that leaving the initiative regarding spending laws in the hands of MPs would have been too great a risk. Luigi Einaudi, a pre-eminent economist, later to become the first President of the Italian Republic, proposed two possible solutions to the problem posed by Mortati. The Constituent Assembly could either deny MPs 'the right to make spending proposals, or … force MPs to accompany them with an equivalent income proposal able to cover the expenditure, in order to give it an imprint of seriousness'. The second proposal received the approval of Ezio Vanoni, a prominent economist, later Minister of Finance, who interpreted it as 'a guarantee of a move towards a balanced budget'. He strongly pointed out the need for this principle to be always in the minds of political actors, 'also from the legal point of view'.

However, the prevailing interpretation of this provision, in the legislation, in the scholarship and in the constitutional case law, especially since the 1960s, gradually deprived this rule of its legal value, leading to a significant increase in public debt. Two aspects of this development should be underlined. First, strict coverage of the financial burden, in the case of long-term spending, was deemed necessary only for the first year; this practice allowed a probable and reasonable evaluation for the following years. Second, public borrowing was considered a possible instrument for covering expenditure.[14]

Two doctrinal positions animate the current Italian debate: on the one hand, there are those for whom a strict interpretation of Art. 81.4 would be sufficient

---

13 Art. 81(in its original version): '(1) For each year, chambers vote on the budget and final balance submitted by the government. (2) Temporary execution of the budget may not be granted except by law and for periods of no more than four months altogether. (3) In the budget law, no new taxes or expenditures may be adopted. (4) All other laws implying new or additional expenditures must set out the means to cover them.'

14 However, the assessment of this case law is not unique, because alongside those who criticize it for its lack of severity, for example G. Di Gaspare, 'Innescare un sistema in equilibrio della finanza pubblica ritornando all'art. 81 della Costituzione', in G. Di Gaspare and N. Lupo (eds), *Le procedure finanziarie in un sistema multilivello* (Giuffrè, 2005), there are those who consider it too severe; see S. Scagliarini, *La quantificazione degli oneri finanziari delle leggi tra governo, parlamento e corte costituzionale* (Giuffrè, 2006), pp. 13ff.

to avoid the expansion of the public debt;[15] on the other, a majority consider that this provision was not a sufficient obstacle to borrowing, as it was meant only to ensure that ordinary laws would not alter the balance of the budget and was not binding on the budget law itself.[16]

The Constitutional Court, despite considering public borrowing a legitimate means of covering expenditure, has several times denied since Decisions 1/1966 and 22/1968 an interpretation whereby Art. 81.4 could represent an effective constitutionalization of the 'balanced budget' principle. The interpretation provided by the Court, on the other hand, stressed how the obligation to indicate, in laws other than those referring to the budget, the means to address new or additional expenditures consists substantially in bringing about an increase in income that could ensure the maintenance of the balance between income and expenses established by approval of the budget. This balance should be strictly observed only for expenses relating to the current year, while the same degree of strictness is not required for future periods, for which the 'not arbitrary or irrational' (in the words of the Court itself) provision of a higher entry balanced with the expenditure expected in subsequent years and according to the economic and financial planning of the government[17] would be enough.

This interpretation has been compounded by the difficult justiciability of any violations of Art. 81.4, due to 'bottlenecks' in the Italian system of constitutional justice in which it is quite difficult to challenge a spending bill without proper financial coverage in the Constitutional Court. In fact it is hardly conceivable that such a challenge would take place within the 'concrete review' procedure, which can only be promoted by judges when they have to apply a law in deciding a case. As far as the 'abstract review' is concerned, parliamentary minorities or state institutions cannot challenge the law. State laws can be challenged only by regional governments, in the case of the violation of parameters relating to their competences, which do not include Art. 81. Conversely, the government can challenge regional laws for any constitutional violation, including Art. 81.4. Thus, it is no coincidence that the few laws declared unconstitutional for violation of the obligation of financial coverage are regional laws.

15 See Di Gaspare, 'Innescare un sistema in equilibrio della finanza pubblica' and G. Bognetti, 'Costituzione e bilancio dello Stato. Il problema delle spese in deficit', *Nomos* 3 (2008): 11ff.

16 See G. Rivosecchi, 'Parlamento e sistema delle autonomie all'ombra del governo nelle trasformazioni della decisione di bilancio', *Rivista AIC* 1 (2012); V. Onida, *Le leggi di spesa nella Costituzione* (Giuffrè, 1969), pp. 450ff.; A. Brancasi, *Legge finanziaria e legge di bilancio* (Giuffrè, 1985), pp. 411ff.; P. De Ioanna, *Parlamento e spesa pubblica. Profili istituzionali del bilancio pubblico in Italia* (Il Mulino, 1993), pp. 67ff.

17 See F. Coronidi, 'La costituzionalizzazine dei vincoli di bilancio prima e dopo il patto Europlus', *Federalismi*, 7 March 2012, making reference to the interpretation at that time by Onida, *Le leggi di spesa nella Costituzione*, pp. 159ff.

The Constitutional Court has long been well aware of this problem, thereby admitting, with reference to Art. 81 as a constitutional parameter, the legitimacy of the intervention of the Court of Auditors in the exercise of its role of controlling the acts of the government (Decisions 226/1976 and 384/1991) and the equalization of the financial statement of the state and the regions (lastly, see Decision 213/2008). At the same time, it also directed a stern warning to the legislator, inviting it to broaden access to the Constitutional Court regarding financial issues.[18] Neither the parliamentary instruments of control of coverage (increasingly developed during the 1980s) nor the presidential power of veto (a power rarely exercised, although some of the rare cases refer precisely to the violation of the obligation of coverage) have proved to be effective.[19]

The Amendment of Art. 81 and the 'Balanced Budget' Principle

The gradual erosion of the legal meaning of Art. 81.4 and the doctrinal and political debate that this practice has generated for decades explains the favourable response to the proposals coming from Europe in 2011. As already mentioned, the constitutional bill presented by the government followed a fast-track parliamentary procedure: few formal changes were introduced at the first reading in the Chamber of Deputies, which approved the text of the constitutional revision, and it was not amended in successive readings. Four constitutional provisions were changed.[20] We shall focus on Art. 81, even though it should be noted that it is in Arts 97 and 119 (on the public administrations and territorial authorities) that reference to 'economic and financial constraints derived from the EU' was included, a reference lacking in Art. 81.

The choice of the Italian constitutional legislator deviates from the German model and is closer to the French and Spanish models, as it introduced only a few provisions into the Constitution. According to Art. 5 of the constitutional revision law, the detailed legislation has to be enacted by an ordinary law, which must be approved by an absolute majority (in the absence of a source comparable to the organic law it can be labelled as 'reinforced law' due to the special majority required).

Although the title of the constitutional bill refers to the 'balanced budget', what has been introduced in practice is 'the balance between revenues and expenditures' of the state budget, mitigated, however, by the possibility of taking into account periods of adversity and growth (para 1). The establishment of the maximum deviation from the parameter of equilibrium is entrusted to the 'reinforced law',

18 Decision 406/1989.

19 On the interpretation and implementation of Art. 81, see N. Lupo, *Costituzione e bilancio (l'art.81 della Costituzione tra interpretazione, attuazione e aggiramento)* (LUISS University Press, 2007).

20 Arts 81, 97, 117 and 119.

under Art. 5 of the constitutional law. As has been pointed out,[21] the meaning of this provision is not in itself explicit, because it only refers to a difference between income and expenditure. Thus, a balance is always reached. In the actual budget, for example, the expenditure is matched by the revenue, with the peculiarity that among these there are a significant number of resources acquired by public borrowing.

Far more significant in the amendment is the prohibition of public borrowing: it is permitted only with parliamentary authorization (by absolute majority), with the sole purpose of considering the effects of the economic cycle and the occurrence of exceptional events (para 1). These events will be more carefully defined by the reinforced law as established in Art. 5. However, such provisions must refer to the 'net borrowing' balance, allowing the renewal of maturing bonds, not producing, therefore, any reduction of the total debt.[22]

It should be noted that as far as borrowing is concerned a stricter provision is to be introduced on regional and local finance in Art. 119 of the Constitution. Even back in 2001, borrowing was permitted only to finance investment expenditure. 'The contextual definition of the amortization schedules' is added to the limitation mentioned above, and the requirement that the balanced budget be respected by all the local governments within each region calls for close coordination. The requirement to cover expenditure laws has also been reinforced, so that every law must 'provide' the means to cover (para 3) and not simply 'indicate' such means (as in the former text). The coverage of expenditure cannot be deferred to future provisions, such as the measures adopted in the budget law package. In addition, the budget law, which has up to now been excluded, is also subject to compulsory coverage; thus, if revenues from borrowing are expected, the coverage of costs for the subsequent periods must be indicated.[23]

The mechanism for monitoring compliance with the balanced budget principle is somewhat problematic: having rejected the proposals that would have entrusted the power to appeal to the Constitutional Court to the Court of Auditors, Art. 5 provides two different types of oversight. First, it reiterates, in para 4, the already existing parliamentary oversight over the budget balance and the 'quality and effectiveness' of public spending, according to the methods prescribed by the parliamentary rules of each Chamber. Second, it introduces in para 1, subpara f), a new independent authority (in the form of a Fiscal Council) to be established within the Chambers, which will be entrusted with the 'task of analysing and verifying trends in public finance and compliance with budget assessment rules'. Finally, it is worth noting that among the contents of the reinforced law, under Art. 5.1, subpara g), the way in which the state in times of adversity or upon the occurrence of exceptional events ensures that funding from other levels of

21 See A. Brancasi, 'L'introduzione del principio del c.d. pareggio di bilancio: un esempio di revisione affrettata della Costituzione', *Quaderni costituzionali* 1 (2012).

22 Ibid.

23 Ibid.

government, essential levels of performance and the basic functions related to civil and social rights is also included.

A 'Hasty' Constitutional Amendment?

Some considerations can be advanced on the future reception of the reform and its implementation. As already mentioned, the constitutional amendment has enjoyed the widest consensus ever reached in Italy, even obtaining a positive vote from the Northern League (*Lega Nord*), the only party that still opposes the 'government of experts' led by Mario Monti. Despite the positive vote, the party leaders have repeatedly and critically pointed out the implicit transfer of national sovereignty it implies.

Two main positions have emerged among commentators and in legal scholarship. On the one hand, there are those who fear that the rule is not strict enough and is easy to get round (because, in fact, we are not speaking of 'perfect equivalence' but of 'balance').[24] On the other hand, there are those for whom the revision introduces an element of extreme rigidity that threatens to jeopardize the safeguard of fundamental rights and may even produce a recessive effect. In this context, some criticism that highlights the loss of state sovereignty on economic policies, now most certainly inspired by neo-liberal principles, has also emerged.[25]

One of the most critical aspects underlined by legal scholarship and also quoted in parliamentary debates is the absence of an adequate monitoring system concerning compliance with the new constitutional rules, due to the lack in the Italian system, as already mentioned, of the possibility for MPs or for the Court of Auditors to challenge the constitutionality of a statute directly in the Constitutional Court.[26] Moreover, some commentators have eyed with suspicion the introduction of another independent authority.[27] Finally, it should be noted that the reinforced law provided by Art. 5 is entrusted with the implementation of the new constitutional rules. This law is to be adopted by 28 February 2013.

As has already been underlined,[28] the changes introduced in the Constitution are of a 'structural' character, meaning that they are intended to work permanently, in order to avoid further public debt situations. As far as 'contingent' economic measures (necessary to find an answer to the present financial emergency) are

24 See A. Alesina and F. Giavazzi, 'Le riforme da blindare', *Corriere della sera*, 3 March 2012.

25 G. Azzariti, 'La 'regola d'oro' indiscussa', *Il Manifesto*, 6 March 2012; M. Luciani, 'Pareggio di bilancio: sei motivi per non toccare la Costituzione', *L'Unità*, 29 October 2011.

26 See N. Lupo, 'Costituzione europea, pareggio di bilancio ed equità tra le generazioni. Notazioni sparse', in L. Cavallini Cadeddu (ed.), *Il coordinamento dinamico della finanza pubblica* (Jovene, 2012), pp. 31, 36ff.

27 Ciolli, 'I paesi dell'eurozona e il vincolo di bilancio'.

28 Brancasi, 'L'introduzione del principio del c.d. pareggio di bilancio'.

concerned, they are entrusted primarily to the reinforced law, which is responsible, under Art. 5.1, subpara e) for 'the introduction of rules on expenditure that will make it possible to safeguard the balanced budgets and the cut of government debt/GDP ratio in the long run, consistent with the public finance goals'.

The Impact of the Crisis on the Form of Government and the Political System

Some Features of the Italian Form of Government

The financial crisis contributed, in late 2011, to a political crisis which saw the replacement of the resigned Fourth Berlusconi government by that led by Mario Monti, made up of experts. Apart from the succession of governments, some new issues have emerged, leading to the re-structuring of the Italian form of government in direct relation to the crisis. This is so true that an important constitutional scholar based the title of his commentary on these events: 'Art. 94 of the Living Constitution: The Government must have the Confidence of the Financial Markets'.[29]

In order to fully understand the impact of the crisis on the Italian form of government it should be noted that Italy is a parliamentary republic, characterized in practice by coalitions and unstable governments as a result of its fragmented and polarized party system. The Constitution only provides a few written rules, while most of the rules are grounded in unwritten sources (such as constitutional conventions).

Since 1994, the reform of the electoral system has basically pushed the system towards political bipolarism, with alternating to some extent between right-wing and left-wing governments. The political system remains fragmented, however, thus making it necessary to set up coalitions. The novelty compared with the previous era (often called the 'First Republic') is that coalitions have to be established prior to the elections, naming a 'coalition leader' who will be the candidate Prime Minister. However, these coalitions frequently break up just after the elections, resulting in significant power being held by smaller parties or even individual MPs, and in a highly unstable government (albeit less so than in the past).

Within this context, the role of the President of the Republic is variable. His powers are compared in the literature to an accordion, as they can be expanded or reduced depending on the political contingencies of the moment. In particular, two basic steps marked the political crisis (and its simultaneous solution) in Italy in the autumn of 2011: the fall of the Fourth Berlusconi government and the appointment

29 A. Ruggeri, 'Art. 94 della Costituzione vivente: "Il Governo deve avere la fiducia dei mercati" (nota minima a commento della nascita del Governo Monti)'; available at www.federalismi.it, 21 November 2011.

of the Monti government. These two events will be described over the following pages, starting with the difficulty the political circuit has experienced in responding to the economic and financial crisis and the climate of mistrust that has arisen for political and personal reasons around the former Prime Minister Silvio Berlusconi.

Measures Taken to Tackle the Economic Crisis and the Ineffectiveness of the Decisional Circuit

The political crisis of the centre-right coalition that won the 2008 elections dates back to 2010, when one of its components, led by the President of the Chamber of Deputies, Gianfranco Fini, left the Popolo della Libertà (the party that won the elections in 2008). However, the parliamentary '*transfughismo*' (the practice of deputies or senators deciding to move from the party they have been elected with for another one mid-term) allowed the government to continue holding the majority (and so being successful, for example, against the motion of no confidence presented in December 2010).

The situation worsened between the summer and autumn of 2011. First, we witnessed the electoral defeat of the centre-right coalition in the local elections of 15 and 16 May 2011, shortly followed by the failure suffered by the government in the referendums of 12 and 13 June (which went against political policy choices taken up to then, especially with regard to nuclear energy policies and the Prime Ministerial immunity law).

Despite these political events, judicial vicissitudes involving former Prime Minister Silvio Berlusconi also played an important role in bringing about the crisis of his government: in fact, his dubious private acquaintances whose conduct, according to the assumptions of the judiciary, exceeded the bounds of legality, contributed to worsening the already precarious government stability. But an even stronger factor of attrition was the worsening, during the summer, of the economic and financial crisis due to the increased spread on government bonds, which led to the ECB's letter of 5 August. And this despite the measures already taken in June 2011 when the government had adopted a Decree-Law (98/2011) which contained most of the financial manoeuvres necessary to achieve a balanced budget by 2014.[30]

The interaction between the political and financial crisis was evident in the widespread scepticism of the major financial players and of some supranational and foreign authorities towards the resilience of the Italian economic system. This attitude determined, at the end of July 2011, a major increase in the interest rates of the Italian public debt bonds, bringing with it the need to bring forward to 2013 the goal of achieving a balanced budget (Decree-Law 138/2011).[31]

30 While for the remaining parts, it would have been sufficient to use ordinary budgetary instruments for the period 2012-2014 and the related bills.

31 Among others, see F. Cramer, 'Sviluppo, premier allo scontro con l'asse Tremonti-Bossi', *Il Giornale*, 18 October 2011, p. 8; G. Longo, 'Sviluppo, gli antitremontiani fanno

The opposition parties and a part of the media believed that the main cause of this scepticism lay with the poor credibility of Silvio Berlusconi's government, whose international image was already tarnished due to the reasons indicated above. Furthermore, within the ruling coalition and the government itself, the conflict increased. Emblematic in this respect is the distance between two different points of view: the one held by the Minister of Economy and Finance, Giulio Tremonti, and the one held by the Prime Minister. They were discordant on the measures to be taken to address the financial emergency and the economic revitalization of the country. Thus, the government's scope for action appeared increasingly difficult, not only in terms of the ambitious reforms continuously announced by the government during the legislature, but also with regard to the urgent economic measures that international observers insistently requested Italy should take.

Between August and November 2011, the government repeatedly used the decree-law instrument which, according to Art. 77 of the Constitution, loses the force of law unless converted into law by parliament within 60 days of publication. In each case, the government resorted to confidence motions in order to have the decrees passed. This gave parliament less time and fewer chances to amend the government's measures. This practice has been going on for many years and is certainly not the outcome of the present economic crisis: even in the past it had been frequently criticized by the President of the Republic without any result and it is still going on with Monti's government. Nevertheless, it cannot be denied that following the financial crisis, parliament's decision-making power and representative autonomy have been squeezed between the decisions of the national government and those of international organizations. This grip on parliament emphasizes the challenge that markets pose to representative institutions.[32]

The 'Collapse' of the Fourth Berlusconi Government

An unequivocal split within the political majority became evident on 11 October 2011, when the Chamber of Deputies rejected by one vote the 2010 State Administration General Statement bill. Following this decision, scholars and commentators speculated about its consequences: in fact, from a technical point of view, it was not a vote of no-confidence in the government, which would have legally forced it to resign. The President of the Republic, in a letter considering the views expressed by a number of constitutional experts and in particular Professor Valerio Onida (a former President of the Constitutional Court), discounted the

slittare ancora il decreto', *Il Riformista*, 18 October 2011, p. 8; R. Petrini, 'Stallo sul decreto Sviluppo salta il Consiglio dei ministri. Ue irritata: "Misure urgent"', *La Repubblica*, 21 October 2011, p. 21.

32 See E. Piccardi, 'The Economic Crisis and the National Parliaments: The Italian Experience'; available at http://www.parlamento.it/documenti/repository/affariinternazionali/ecprd2012/4_Piccardi_EN.pdf.

possibility that as a consequence of rejection of the General Statement there would be 'a legal obligation for the government to resign'. However, he believed there was a necessity, also in the light of the precedents, for 'parliamentary monitoring of the continuance of such confidence', recalling at the same time the political forces towards a common national responsibility. This monitoring by parliament took place on 14 October, when the Chamber of Deputies approved, with 316 votes in favour and 301 against, the motion of confidence presented by the government to verify the persistence of the majority after the rejection of the General Statement (the absolute majority of the Chamber, although not legally necessary for the government to exist, is precisely 316 MPs).

As a consequence of the difficulties facing the Italian political system, the President of the Republic became the main actor on the stage. He launched two severe warnings in close succession (26 October and 1 November 2011): first, 'no Italian political party can continue to rule the country, or present itself as a candidate to rule, without being aware of the need to adopt decisions, albeit unpopular, to be taken immediately in the national and in the European interest'; second, he believed it was 'his constitutional duty to verify the conditions for the realization of this perspective'. Therefore, 'given the further deterioration of the Italian position within the financial markets', the Italian President seemed to be moving towards a less cautious approach than in the past.

In fact, the increasing number of communications, meetings, notes and statements by the President of the Republic (all these acts defined as 'informal talks with the major components of the opposition and majority forces', as the President did not have the power to proceed through 'formal consultations' whose legal prerequisites were not present) marked the time of the – first unannounced but later tendered – resignation of the Prime Minister, Silvio Berlusconi.

Here is the sequence of events. On 8 November, the Chamber of Deputies voted on the 2010 State General Statement again, a statement that had been rejected a month earlier; the opposition did not participate in the vote in order to ensure the approval of the measure, demonstrating at the same time that the government did not have the 316 votes that would have ensured the absolute majority. The Chamber approved the Statement with 308 votes in favour, none contrary and with only one abstention. Following the outcome of the vote, Mr Berlusconi went to the President of the Republic, and after this meeting the President announced that Mr Berlusconi would resign after the approval of the Stability Law.

As mentioned above, the crisis of the Fourth Berlusconi Government is anomalous for several reasons, among others the formal opening of the crisis itself. This moment cannot be identified with the Chamber of Deputies vote of Tuesday, 8 November 2011, during which the State General Statement was approved with only 308 votes. In fact, despite the General Statement being approved from a technical point of view, even if the government no longer had the absolute majority of votes in that branch of the parliament (which is not particularly relevant because the government needs a simple majority vote in order to adopt decisions fundamental to maintain confidence), what really matters is that the decision-making parliament-government circuit did not provide any stable guarantee on the commitments to be made to address the national financial crisis that threatened to overwhelm even the stability of the euro.

In order to ensure the adequate decision-making capacity of the country and to avoid 'a prolonged period of parliamentary and government inactivity' (as could have happened in the case of the immediate start of a formal crisis), the President of the Republic made it possible to ensure that the 'resigning government' obtained the parliamentary approval of one of the most fundamental political acts, the Stability Law.[33] At the same time, the President established proper 'pre-consultations', in order to quickly proceed to create a new government after the approval of the Stability Law.

The Formation of the Monti Government

This is the very peculiar scenario in which the government chaired by Professor Mario Monti was formed, influenced on one side by the deep political crisis within the coalition that had won the 2008 elections and, on the other, by the economic and financial crisis, accompanied by a deep mistrust of the financial markets.

As already stated, Prime Minister Berlusconi announced his resignation after the vote on the State General Statement, subject to the approval of the Stability Law. However, many doubted the sincerity of this announcement, which did not convince even the financial world. Thus, the performance of the markets continued to be critical. This situation led the President of the Republic to intervene to 'reassure' the international arena and to put an end to any possible temptation to procrastinate by Berlusconi. Throughout the dissemination of an official statement on 9 November 2011, the President of the Republic, in order to 'dispel any confusion or misunderstanding', outlined the authenticity of the intentions of the Prime Minister. The same day, the President of the Republic appointed Professor Mario Monti senator for life according to Art. 59.2 of the Constitution, for 'having honoured the Nation through his outstanding achievements in science and society'. This act, signed by Prime Minister Berlusconi (according to Art. 89 of the Constitution), was perceived by many as a sort of 'pre-ordination' for leading a 'Presidential Cabinet', especially if we consider that the appointment took place just a few hours after President Napolitano's declaration made clear that Berlusconi would most certainly resign straight after the approval of the Stability Law. Monti's appointment as senator for life may therefore be regarded as the first step in the process towards the solution of the government crisis.

Meanwhile, on 11 November, the Senate approved the Stability Law, after a very brief discussion, thanks to the decision of the opposition not to engage in

33 The Stability Law, introduced in the 2011 financial year, by Law 196/2009, replaced the Financial Law. The Stability Law aims to implement the economic political programme of the government and to establish the total amount of incomes and expenditures, in order to comply with the European Stability and Growth Pact.

filibustering, due to a 'sense of responsibility towards the country'. The next day, the Chamber of Deputies approved the definitive version of the Stability Law with 380 votes in favour, 26 against and 2 abstentions, after an unprecedented speeding through parliament, which allowed the conclusion of the whole debate within a week. At the same time, and with the same votes, the Budget Law was also passed. The two laws were immediately promulgated by the President of the Republic.

On 12 November, Silvio Berlusconi resigned. After only two days of consultations with political and social groups, on 16 November Senator Monti presented the members of the new government, all strangers to the political parties. They were sworn in and took their seats on the same day. That same day, the new government obtained the confidence of the Senate from all political groups except the Lega Nord, who voted against. The result marked a true record, with 281 votes in favour and only 25 against. On 18 November, the Chamber of Deputies also voted its confidence in the 'national commitment' executive with a large majority (556 votes in favour and only 61 against).

The Impact of the Crisis on Fundamental Rights and the Constitutional Review of Legislation

General Considerations

If we turn now to a consideration of another important aspect of the 'living constitution', namely the constitutional interpretation issued by the Constitutional Court, we cannot state that, to date, it has been strongly influenced by the current financial crisis. Initially, we should point out some general considerations. First, we should recall some features of the Italian system of judicial review of legislation, especially with regard to the 'bottlenecks' in access to the Court itself which we referenced above. The Constitutional Court has had very few opportunities to pronounce on the spending laws which have been challenged for the violation of the rule set forth in the former Art. 81.4 of the Constitution according to which 'All other [than the budget law] laws implying new or additional expenditures must set out the means to cover them.' As we have already mentioned, it is quite rare for state laws to be challenged for the violation of Art. 81.4. More often, it is the regional laws that are challenged for noncompliance with this provision.

If we exclude the 'abstract review of legislation',[34] 'concrete control' takes quite a long time before reaching the Court, because it needs some judicial initiative to be taken during a hearing or litigation. Thus, it is highly probable that the legal provisions adopted to face the economic crisis may well not be scrutinized by the Constitutional Court for years, with the exception of provisions that could violate the state–regions division of competences which can be challenged by the national or regional governments coming under the abstract review of legislation.

34 See Art. 127 of the Constitution.

Furthermore, we should consider that, at least for two decades, the Italian Constitutional Court has been fully aware of the need to contain public spending. In this vein, a rigorous case law has long been developing on Art. 81, mostly in deciding on regional laws challenged by the national government, according to which the coverage of new expenditures 'must be credible, secure enough, not arbitrary or irrational, and in a balanced relationship with the expense expected in future years' (see, for example, Decisions 213/2008 and more recently 70/2012).

Third, there is no doubt that the general financial situation has influenced constitutional case law since the early 1990s. However, the Court has shown a certain reluctance to use interpretative arguments in its decisions openly referring to the financial emergency. As already mentioned, during the early 1990s Italy faced a crisis even worse than the current one. It is a good indicator of its attitude that in reviewing the constitutional consistency of a special levy on bank deposits imposed by Amato's government in 1992, the Court made no reference to the point, highlighted in the conclusions of the government, concerning the 'dramatic situation of emergency public finance', preferring to dismiss the complaint using 'ordinary' arguments (Decision 143/1995).

Doubtless, even if formal references are not made in the decisions, the financial condition affects the proportionality test, considered as a 'factual issue'. More specifically, a recent example of this approach can be found in the so-called 'Alitalia case' (Decision 270/2010). In dealing with the severe business crisis faced by the Italian company, aggravated by the global financial crisis, the Constitutional Court found a law allowing economic concentration reasonable, in exemption to communitarian antitrust rules, as limitation of the freedom of competition was adequate to deal with the factual situation.

In this case – as in others where factual elements are relevant within the proportionality test – we should wonder how the Court knows about the existence and the content of these 'factual elements'. Since in this specific case we are dealing with macroeconomic variables, the main question concerns the possibility of considering them either as 'generally known issues' or as data to be acquired via special investigation activities.[35]

The habit of the Court to not refer explicitly to the current financial crisis is evident also in the Constitutional Court Annual Reports.[36] As we are not dealing with an 'exceptional' phase, no references to the crisis are made in the 2008, 2009

35 It should also be noted that the Court makes reference to the national goals of spending restraints, recalling only *ad adiuvandum* the need to respect European obligations. See A. Longo, 'Alcune riflessioni sui rapporti tra l'interpretazione conforme a diritto comunitario e l'utilizzo del canone di equilibrio finanziario da parte della Corte costituzionale'; available at www.giurcost.org, 19.

36 The Constitutional Court Annual Reports are the main instrument used by the Court through its President to relate to public opinion.

and 2011 reports. Only a brief reference is made in the 2010 report.[37] On that occasion, the former President of the Court, Professor Ugo De Siervo, pointed out the challenging environment in which the Court was operating with specific reference to the 'serious international and national economic crisis'. He explicitly referred to those cases in which the Court has justified some severe choices of containment of public expenditure approved by parliament, referring also to regional and local finance, which were included in the state competence on the 'coordination of the fiscal system'.

Furthermore, he explicitly referred to Decision 10/2010, on the so-called 'social card', whereby the Court had accepted a state provision that impacted on regional matters without seeking fair cooperation with the regions (usually required in such cases by the Court). This choice was justified in the light of the 'features of the extraordinary and exceptional situation resulting from the international economic and financial crisis which in 2008 and 2009 also affected our country'.

More specifically, that judgment is one of the few in which an explicit reference to the crisis is made, with the purpose of justifying rules that in its absence would have been unconstitutional, and it is interesting to note that the reference was made not to justify a state law diminishing social rights guarantees, but to permit state intervention in regional matters to guarantee the minimum core of a social right. Moving from this premise, in order to highlight how the (not new) need to contain public spending has been considered by the Court in recent judgments, we will focus on a) the division of competences between state and regions, b) the limits to the guarantee of social rights, and c) the cost of the Court's judgments.

State–Region Relationships and the Containment of Public Expenditure

To fully understand how the need to contain public expenditure has affected relationships between the state and the regions, we should briefly refer to the constitutional framework, pointing out that, as a result of the 2001 constitutional amendment, exclusive competence to legislate on matters mentioned in Art. 117.2 of the Constitution pertains exclusively to the state. Moreover, the state can also dictate the basic principles within the concurrent legislative competence (Art. 117.3), while the regions have residual legislative competence.

Among the exclusive state competences, one should be underlined in particular, that provided in Art. 117.2, subpara e): 'money, protection of savings, financial markets, the protection of competition, the currency system, the state taxation system and accounting, and the equalization of regional financial resources'. Among the matters included in the concurrent competence list, we can find 'harmonization of the budgetary rules in the public sector and coordination of the public finance and the taxation system' (the latter has been changed by the 2012 constitutional amendment and exclusive competence moved to the state). Furthermore, according

37 President Ugo De Siervo Report on 2010 Constitutional Jurisprudence, 10 February 2011; available at www.cortecostituzionale.it.

to Art. 119 of the Constitution, 'Municipalities, provinces, metropolitan cities and regions have financial autonomy regarding revenues and expenditures'. The last paragraph of this article (also subject to the 2012 constitutional amendment) states that 'Municipalities, provinces, metropolitan cities and regions have their own assets, assigned to them according to general principles established by state law. They may only contract loans in order to finance investment expenditure. State guarantees on such loans are excluded.'

The need to contain public spending has led to a pervasive reading of state competences established in Art. 117.2, subpara e), leading at the same time to the depletion of concurrent regional competence.[38] For many years, the trend whereby a state legislator can 'with a principle discipline' legitimately 'impose on autonomous entities, for financial coordination reasons related to national goals, also subjected to European obligations, constraints on fiscal policies, even if these inevitably result in indirect limitations of local authorities' expenditure autonomy' has prevailed in the Constitutional Court decisions (Decisions 36/2004 and 417/2005). However, the Court has set some limits: in order to make these obligations respect the autonomy of the regions and local authorities, they should refer to the amount of the current account deficit or – but only 'on a transitional basis and in the light of the specific objectives of public finances rebalancing pursued by the state legislature' – to the growth of autonomous entities' current expenditure. Ultimately, state law can only establish 'an overall limit, which leaves to local entities themselves broad latitude on how to allocate the resources among the different sectors and the expenditure targets' (Decisions 449/2005, 88/2006, 94/2009, 237/2009, 326/2010). Thus, state law, in order to be consistent with the Constitution, must be directed to rebalancing the public finances through a general containment of current spending, that is through measures that do not interfere in the individual entries.[39]

Moreover, the 'coordination of the public finance and the tax system' is not the only area in which state–regions relations have been affected by the demands posed by the difficult financial situation of the country. We may recall the 'social card' judgment (the aforementioned Decision 10/2010), which contains an explicit reference to the current financial crisis: the quoted section has a different purpose, seeking to justify a state intervention to protect social rights. In this decision, the Constitutional Court rejected the constitutional challenge filed within the abstract control of constitutional review of legislation by three regions (Emilia Romagna, Liguria and Piedmont) against Decree-Law 112/2008, which introduced the

38 See I. Ciolli, 'La "supremacy clause all'italiana". Regioni e strumenti finanziari derivati davanti alla Corte costituzionale', *Rivista AIC* 1 (2012) and in particular Decision 52/2010 on banking products.

39 See Longo, 'Alcune riflessioni', 20. See also A. Ruggeri, 'Summum ius summa iniuria, ovverosia quando l'autonomia regionale non riesce a convertirsi in servizio per i diritti fondamentali (a margine di Corte cost. n. 325 del 2011)'; available at www.giurcost.org.

so-called 'social card' (a debit card with 40 euros granted by the Italian government to citizens whose income falls below a certain minimum level, in order to provide them with credit for the purchase of foodstuffs and basic products): according to the regions, it touched on the matter of 'social policy', reserved by the Constitution to the regions.

The Constitutional Court stated that even though this discipline falls under the competence of the regions, it is deeply connected with determining the essential levels of services, an area assigned by the Constitution exclusively to the state (Art. 117.2, subpara m), Cost.) as touching on the protection of human dignity. Thus, the state was fully competent to implement this measure. Diverging from its previous case law, the Court did not ask the state to respect the loyal cooperation principle and to negotiate its intervention with the regions. The argument given by the Court was that 'the features of the extraordinary and exceptional situation resulting from the international economic and financial crisis which in 2008 and 2009 also affected our country' mandated a prompt response. However, when the situation of economic crisis comes to an end, respect for the principle of loyal cooperation must be restored.[40]

The Need to Contain Public Spending and the Guarantee of Social Rights

The need to contain public spending related to the economic crisis has also negatively affected guarantees of fundamental rights, in particular social rights. This is not only about state–region relationships, but also concerns exclusive state competence. Being considered inviolable, like civil or political rights,[41] social rights are 'positive rights'. Their effectiveness depends on legislative implementation, which in turn is affected by the availability of financial resources.[42] Focusing attention now on the constitutional jurisprudence on social rights, it is possible to identify three main phases.[43] The first phase covers the period from the beginning of Court activity in the late 1950s up to the 1980s: this is the period of the expansion of social rights, in which the Court, in the name of the principle of equality, extended guarantees to categories not explicitly

---

40 This section is taken from the commentary written by Francesco Saitto, Phd Candidate at the University of Siena. It was published on Palomar Italy. We thank Francesco for allowing it to be reproduced in this chapter.

41 The Italian doctrine is almost unanimous in this respect. See M. Luciani, 'Sui diritti sociali', in R. Romboli (ed.), *La tutela dei diritti fondamentali davanti alla Corte costituzionale* (Giappichelli, 1994).

42 For a summary of the Italian doctrine and an extensive bibliography, see G. De Vergottini, 'La protection des doits sociaux fondamentaux dans l'ordre juridique de l'Italie', in J. Iliopoulos-Strangas (ed.), *La protection des droits sociaux fondamentaux dans les Etats membres de l'Union européenne* (Ant. N. Sakkoulas, 2000), pp. 559ff.

43 On this case law, see A. Rovagnati, *Sulla natura dei diritti sociali* (Giappichelli, 2009), p. 97; and see also C. Colapietro, *La giurisprudenza costituzionale nella crisi dello Stato sociale* (CEDAM, 1996), p. 369.

considered in the legislation, without worrying too much about the financial consequences of its decisions. The second phase took place in the 1990s: the Court was aware of the financial consequences of its decisions, and it started to consider the needs of public finances in the proportionality test and developed innovative decision-making techniques, as will be discussed further in the next pages.[44] The third phase started immediately after the 2001 constitutional reform. Many issues related to guaranteeing social rights (especially with reference to the right to health) are strictly related to the division of competences between the state and the regions, particularly in the light of state exclusive legislative competence provided in Art. 117.2, subpara m) of the Constitution, which reserves to the state the 'determination of the basic level of benefits relating to civil and social entitlements to be guaranteed throughout the national territory'. In this phase, the recognition of a broad-ranging legislative discretion emerges, for example by underlining the necessary gradualism in the protection of social rights and, more generally, by the recognition of the substantial unquestionability of the allocation of resources. However, this discretionality meets a limit in the 'evident unreasonableness' that requires the respect of the 'irreducible core' of these rights.[45] This necessity determines the legislative duty to guarantee a minimum benefit at least for the more disadvantaged categories.

In this context, besides the case law on the right to health,[46] case law developed on the rights of the physically impaired must also be pointed out. Indeed, with Decision 80/2010, the Court set aside a provision (contained in the 2008 Financial Law), which, in the name of the control of public expenditure, reduced the possibility for schools to hire teachers to give special support to physically impaired students.

In fact, the Court stated that the challenged rules particularly affected the 'irreducible core of guarantees' (in that case the right to education), which represents an insurmountable limit to legislative discretion.[47]

---

44 M. Midiri, 'Diritti sociali e vincoli di bilancio nella giurisprudenza costituzionale', in *Studi in onore di Franco Modugno*, vol. III (Editoriale Scientifica, 2011), pp. 2235ff.

45 Gradually, the expression 'irreducible core' (Decision 251/2008, citing Decision 226/2000) is taking the place of 'minimally essential measure' (for example Decision 27/1998).

46 The Court stated that 'on one hand, the protection of the right to health in its perspective of benefits claims "cannot be subject to the constraints met by the same legislator in the distribution of the available financial resources"; on the other hand, "the needs of public finance cannot take on, in the balancing process effected by the legislator, such an overwhelming burden that the irreducible core of the right to health protected by the Constitution as an inviolable area of human dignity will be limited"' (as recently stated in Decision 354/2008; see also Decisions 455/1990, 267/1998, 309/1999, 509/2000, 252/2001 and 432/2005).

47 See Decision 18/2010; C.S. Vigilanti, 'Il diritto all'istruzione dei disabili come paradigma della tutela dei diritti sociali', in *Forum di Quaderni costituzionali*, 7 March 2012.

The Need to Contain Public Spending and the 'Cost' of Additive Judgments

Financial obligations may derive from a Constitutional Court decision. The majority of commentators, and the Constitutional Court itself, have pointed out that Art. 81.4 is not applicable to judicial decisions.[48] Actually, there have been very few isolated opinions whereby this constitutional provision should also be applied to Constitutional Court decisions. This point of view would result in depriving the Court of the ability to intervene in a very large number of cases, given the impossibility of indicating the means to cover the implied expenditures using new revenues or a reduction of other expenditures. However, the prevalent interpretation does not mean that the Court, in deciding on constitutional challenges, should not take into account Art. 81.4 of the Constitution. In fact, since the 1990s constitutional case law has shown an increasing sensitivity to the needs of a balanced budget.

In interpreting constitutional provisions that embody the principles of the welfare state in a context marked by the financial crisis and by economic austerity policies, the Court is trapped between a rock and a hard place. More specifically, it is stuck between the danger of losing its role as supreme guarantor of the Constitution and of the rights enshrined therein and the danger of bringing with it serious economic consequences for the state budget.

The Court's concern for the financial consequences of its decisions can be readily seen from a survey of its activities. In particular, since the late 1980s, the Court has had to face the especially delicate issue of the use of 'additive' judgments, that is decisions in which the Court declares a statute unconstitutional not because of its contents, but because of what it does *not* contain. In this way, the Court manages to insert new rules into the legal system which cannot be found in the statutory text. This kind of decision runs contrary to the Kelsenian model of constitutional review, according to which a constitutional court ought to be a 'negative legislator'. With these judgments the Constitutional Court transforms itself into a creator of legal rules, thereby playing a role that in the Italian system belongs principally to parliament. Yet in many cases, the mere nullification of an unconstitutional law would not solve the problem posed by the constitutional question, and the addition of a missing rule is the only way to remedy the violated constitutional value and, therefore, offers the only option for the constitutional law to perform its task.

A first effort to limit the creative impact of such judgments can be found in the rule under which they are considered appropriate only when, to use a poetical

48 This perspective was also shared by the legislator. In fact, according to Art. 17.13 Law 196/2009, if the Ministry of Economy and Finances considers that the implementation of legal provisions will affect public finance goals, it shall promptly take suitable legislative measures. The same procedure is applied with reference to those judicial decisions (including those handed down by the Constitutional Court) that are able to produce economic burdens. In practice, these cases have usually been resolved by the approval of a decree-law.

metaphor, the new provisions provided by the judgment and inserted into the statute are considered 'obligatory verses'. It means that the norm proposed by the Court is logically necessary and implicit in the normative context, thereby eliminating any discretionary choice. Furthermore, a look at the Court's case law developed during the second phase has shown its tendency to significantly reduce (compared to the earlier stages) the number of decisions based on the principle of equality and designed to equalize unequal situations upward. On the contrary, on some occasions the Court has chosen the opposite path; faced with challenges brought in the name of equality, it has decided to equalize the situations downward, raising *sua sponte* the question of the constitutionality of the baseline offered by the *a quo* judge (the *tertium comparationis*). In a decision on personal income tax applied to pensions of parliamentary deputies, where the exclusive favourable treatment they received was invoked as the baseline due to all citizens in a case involving the income of employees, the Court did not hesitate to question *sua sponte* the favourable treatment accorded to pensions, and to declare them unconstitutional (Decision 289/1994).

Finally, in hopes of balancing the two goals – on the one hand to fulfil its role as constitutional guardian, in particular of social rights, and on the other not to directly create state budgetary burdens without adequate financial support – the Constitutional Court has developed an innovative decision-making technique, judgments that 'add principles' rather than norms. This has been the tendency since the mid-1990s. These are known as '*additive di principio*'. In these types of decisions, the Court does not insert new rules into the legal system, but only principles that the legislature must implement through statutes that are universally effective. In its opinions in such decisions, the Court indicates a deadline by which the legislature must act, and sets forth the principles the legislature must follow. In this way, a single decisional tool manages to combine the contents of an 'additive' judgment with a sort of 'delegation' order, in order to reconcile the immediacy of the Court's 'acceptance' of the constitutional challenge with the preservation of the legislature's discretion.

These decisions are aimed at recognizing rights, but deferring to the legislature to choose the means for implementing them and the funds to meet their costs. Illustrative of this tendency is Decision 243/1993. In this judgment, the Court declared unconstitutional any norms that excluded cost-of-living adjustment from the calculation of severance pay benefits, but held that its decision could not take the form of the mere nullification of a law, or of an additive judgment. Rather, it fell to the legislature to choose the appropriate means, 'in view of the selection of economic political choices needed to provide the necessary financial resources'.

These judgments pose greater problems with regard to their effectiveness vis-à-vis ordinary judges. Although it is generally considered that legislative action is needed to apply the principle, in some cases judges have considered themselves capable of applying the Court's decision to arrive at a rule governing the case at bar.

A still open issue touches upon the instruments the Court must use in order to acquire the data on the financial consequences (costs) of its decisions.

A Crisis of Post-Second World War Constitutionalism?

The economic and financial crisis that has been affecting European economies since 2008 has put national constitutions under pressure as never before, creating new challenges for European democracies. However, these challenges are the result of a more complex set of factors, which for decades have been undermining Western constitutionalism based on the welfare state. More specifically, we should consider that the socio-economic premises and the institutional policies that characterized the Western countries in the aftermath of the Second World War have changed. Welfare policies reached their apex of success in the 1950s and 1960s. However, the system started to collapse in the 1970s, mainly because of social spending dynamics and the consequent market-oriented policies developed in the 1990s. In the 1990s, globalization and EU integration precipitated a crisis of the sovereign nation-state and of democratic representation.

The Italian Constitution, much more than other European constitutions, is a well-tailored product of post-Second World War constitutionalism,[49] born by a lucky interconnection between Keynes' perspective on the state's ability to politically govern the economy and to control welfare policies, and Kelsen's democratic theory of the state. Nowadays, those points of view have been overthrown: it is the economy that establishes the political agenda, and the democratically elected bodies are marginalized by both financial and economic forces on the one hand, and by supranational actors that are not fully democratic on the other hand.

In this way, the very deep foundation of the Italian Constitution (and one could say of European constitutionalism) is in danger. The question remains open as to the compatibility of the 'balanced budget' revision, if taken seriously, with the guarantee of fundamental social rights, which is a fundamental characteristic of the Italian form of state (in other words, the 'national constitutional identity') and cannot be changed by means of the procedure described in Art. 138. These principles represent the 'core' of the Constitution itself. Thus, they fall within the purview of the 'constituent power' (the constitution-making power) rather than within that of the 'constituted' power (the constitution-amending power).

As we have attempted to show in this chapter, the revision was enacted as a response to the financial markets, mainly to give national legitimacy to the unpopular policies required at this level. The lack of any public debate in this respect was justified by reference to the extremely technical nature of the matter and the external pressures coming from the markets and EU institutions, which would have left no room for national decisions. In this way, a potential hidden

49 See C. Fusaro, 'Italy', in C. Fusaro and D. Oliver (eds), *How Constitutions Change: A Comparative Study* (Hart, 2011), p. 212.

change in the 'core provisions' of the Italian Constitution has been enacted without the participation of civil society. At the moment, the ultimate protection of the fundamental values of the Italian Constitution lies in the hands of the Constitutional Court: its case law, up to now, seems impermeable to the effects of the economic crisis, as testified to by the fact that the main explicit reference to the crisis was included in a decision on a state law encroaching on the regional jurisdiction to guarantee a social right (the 'social card' Decision 10/2010).

Nevertheless, one wonders how long the Court can resist the pressure in favour of the dismantling of the welfare state that it receives day by day from government decrees; in the end the judiciary can slow, but not block, constitutional change. It is up to the organs of democracy to react: if they are unable to do so at a national level, due to the power of the external financial and economic actors, the only solution for the protection of national constitutional values may be found in a political reaction at EU level. But it would require a further step towards a European Federation. Is Europe ready for that?

Chapter 4

Financial Crisis and the Constitution in Latvia

Ringolds Balodis and Janis Pleps

Latvia is a unitary state based on the rule of law and the principles of proportionality, justice and legal certainty. It is a parliamentary republic with a pluralist system of political parties. There is a clear separation of powers with a system of checks and balances in place.[1] Fundamental rights are guaranteed and widely respected. The Constitution is a written, codified and single document which is quite brief and laconic. It is a flexible document in that it is quite easy to amend. International and non-Latvian legal norms (EU law) take priority over domestic legislation and can be regarded as being of the highest status. When there is conflict between such a legal norm on the one hand and a national legal norm on the other, the international or EU norm prevails.

Constitutional bodies include parliament, the President, the government, the National Audit Office and the courts. Parliament consists of 100 members who are elected for four-year terms. The President is elected by secret ballot by MPs for a term of four years. The Constitution does not mention economic matters in a direct sense, though it does secure the right to own property. The Constitutional Court has derived from the Constitution the ruling that every person is obliged to pay taxes and that the goal of tax revenues is to ensure public welfare.[2] Art. 66 of the Constitution also contains certain elements of fiscal discipline: 'Where parliament takes a decision involving expenditures that are not included in the budget, the said decision shall also allocate the funds which are necessary to cover such expenditures.'

After accession to the EU, Latvia experienced rapid economic growth for several years in a row. This was based on private consumption with loans that were provided by banks. Most of the money that was borrowed was invested in real estate and other sectors of non-exportable products. The economy could not effectively absorb such a large inflow of cash, and inflation increased. Powerful private consumption in the short term produced a positive fiscal effect in terms of rapidly increasing tax revenues. Budget expenditures expanded accordingly, and that stimulated consumption even further. Rapidly increasing wages in the

1 R. Balodis, 'Latvia', in G. Robbers (ed.), *Encyclopaedia of World Constitutions*, vol. II (U.S. Facts on File, 2007), p. 513.

2 Case No. 2011-03-01, 19 December 2011, para 25.

private and public sector occurred in parallel to comparatively slow increases in productivity, and this substantially harmed Latvia's competitiveness. The amount of loans issued by commercial banks rapidly increased the state's gross external debt, and in combination with declining competitiveness, this created the danger of insolvency among borrowers, because the new risk was that added value would not be sufficient to cover borrowing costs.

The first warnings about overheating in the economy and an approaching crisis were heard in 2007. Despite this, only in 2008 did indicators show that the crisis was approaching. Because of the global financial crisis and a decline in Latvia's credit rating, the availability of external financial resources collapsed during the latter half of 2008, which meant that Latvia required international financial assistance. At the end of the year, Eurostat and the Latvian Statistical Board released a report stating that even though inflation had declined by 0.9 per cent in August, it was still at a rate of 15.6 per cent. Latvian trade unions demanded that the government provide compensation for lost wages that were due to inflation at national budget institutions and that the government stop talking about the freezing of real wages in support of the economy.

It was in late 2008, after the government took over the Parex Bank, that it first suggested international aid was needed. The National Audit Office concluded that the collapse of the Parex Bank had had a serious effect on Latvia's financial situation. In audit reports, the Audit Office wrote about the effective use of money from international loans, concluding that the problems of the bank had substantially increased the country's external debt in 2009, because LVL265 million, or 17 per cent of the money received from the international lending programme, was used to provide term deposits so that the bank could repay its syndicated loans.[3] The Constitutional Court also expressed its views on the economic situation in the country, rejecting arguments that suggested that there was no financial crisis at all.[4] After analysing the economic situation in 2009, the Court ruled that 'during the second quarter of 2009, Latvia experienced the most rapid decline in economic activity in the EU. Thus, for instance, national consolidated budget revenues during the first six months of 2009 were 15 per cent lower than during the same period in 2008 ... The decline in gross domestic product in comparison to the first six months of 2008 amounted to 18.7 per cent.'[5]

Budget cuts at various government institutions led to a situation in which the institutions had to sack people, force them to take unpaid holidays and reduce the number of their regional branches. This inevitably affected the quality of public services. In some cases, local governments financed processes which had once been financed by the national government so as to keep the range of public services from deteriorating. The financial crisis also caused a substantial decline in Latvia's

3 The Annual Report of the National Audit Office of the Republic of Latvia; available at www.lrvk.gov.lv/upload/GP_2010_1Jul2011_LV/pdf.

4 Case No. 2010-71-01, 19 October 2011, para 6.

5 Case No. 2009-44-01, 15March 2010, para 20.

population. According to census results there were 2,377,383 people in Latvia in 2010, but by 2011 that number had dropped to 2,067,887. This meant that it was very likely that more than 300,000 people from Latvia had emigrated abroad in pursuit of a better economic life. The census also showed that the death rate in Latvia was above the fertility rate.[6] This can be attributed to the fact that people of working age were leaving the country, but also to the fact that the government was reducing subsidies for young mothers and their children.[7]

Addressing parliament in 2011, Prime Minister Dombrovskis argued that the financial crisis had been successfully overcome.[8] There are experts, however, who have a critical view about the selected solutions aimed at overcoming the crisis. They have argued that the long-term model by which Latvia exited the crisis period was not a success story, because much of the labour force was lost, and small and medium companies have problems with capital to the extent that they cannot take out loans. The international loan that was taken out to overcome the crisis led to an increase in the number of Eurosceptics in Latvia. This is because of unfulfilled hopes that the EU would help to resolve social problems. Many residents in Latvia have lost all faith in economic development in the country in the future. The decline in trust, in relation to national values, has reduced growth potential and very much increased demographic risks, thus limiting the potential for further economic growth.

Aspects of Sovereignty

In late 2008, after encountering a financial crisis and a drop in national budget revenues, and facing the need to resolve stability-related problems in the banking sector, the government voted to accept an international loan. On 18 December, Latvia submitted a letter of intent to the director of the IMF, stating its desire to receive an international loan so as to stabilize Latvia's economy, promising to limit national budget expenditures to the level of 40 per cent of GDP.[9] Latvia promised to implement a series of political reforms and to ensure major amendments to various normative acts. This would involve a review of the structure of national governance, the system of pensions and social subsidies, and a reduction in national budget expenditures. The promises were not reviewed by parliament. This meant that the government, not parliament, decided to take part in the international lending programme and to make relevant political promises. In most cases, the need for such legal amendments and reforms was explained on the basis of the promises that were given to the international lenders – promises that related to

6 *Latvijas Vēstnesis*, No. 11(4614), 19 January 2012.

7 Case No. 2009-44-01, 15 March 2010, paras 8-24.

8 Transcript of 8 December 2011, Meeting of Parliament; available at saeima.lv/lv/transcripts/view/97.

9 Available at http://www.fm.gov.lv/files/files/Letter_of_Intent_2008-12-18.pdf.

success in completing the international lending programme and to the relevant international obligations.[10] This limited the ability of parliament to manoeuvre in terms of improving the draft laws that were submitted by the government. This largely turned parliament into an institution that simply accepts the proposals made by the government. After the international loan was received, however, there was no parliamentary or public debate about whether the relevant procedures were appropriate or whether the government had the authority to make political promises to the international lenders that would be dependent on parliament in terms of their implementation. Among other things, these promises included amendments to laws that were of public importance, as well as the adoption of new laws.

The Constitutional Court examined the extent to which the government's promises were constitutional in several cases, because parliament and the government usually made reference to the promises that were made to the international lenders in relation to such cases. The Constitutional Court ruled that 'the fact that the aforementioned documents include a promise from the government to adopt the disputed norms does not in and of itself mean that these are the specific conditions that were determined by the international lenders. The international lenders define the main goals for the state in accordance with their areas of competence ... The decision on the most appropriate and commensurate resources in achieving these goals, as well as the choice of possible alternatives, is left up to the country itself.'[11]

This ruling means that the Constitutional Court was rejecting the arguments of parliament and the government in relation to limitations on their freedom of action in adopting crisis-era regulations. The Constitutional Court strictly stated that the government had made specific promises and could evaluate the constitutionality and necessity of the specific steps that were taken. It is also true that parliament had to evaluate solutions proposed by the government just as is the case with any other draft laws. Among other things, parliament had to evaluate the constitutionality and permissibility of such steps in a democratic country where the rule of law prevails. This, in turn, means that the international lenders did not limit the state's freedom of action and sovereignty in formal terms. The legislature and government were allowed to make decisions about specific reforms so as to achieve a national budget balance and to avoid the risk of insolvency. In this context, however, it is also necessary to take into account the conditions under which the loan was provided: 'No government in the world asks other countries or international organizations to provide it with a massive loan just because the government is bored. Only those countries facing bankruptcy are forced to do so.'[12] If it is clear that 'Latvia would not receive loans if it did not give the lenders the promise of fairly radical steps aimed at the stabilization and future improvement

10 Case No. 2009-110-01, para 24.3.

11 Case No. 2009-43-01, para 30.1.

12 M. Lejnieks, *Jurista Vārds* 5 (600) (2 February 2010): 10.

of the country's economic situation',[13] in turn, then the actual freedom of the state in terms of what it does under such circumstances is limited quite substantially.

The ruling from the Constitutional Court included the *obiter dictum* determination that in taking out an international loan and making promises related to political reforms, the government had ignored the separation of powers enshrined in the Constitution: 'A conceptual decision on receiving the international loan and on its conditions must be seen as an important and significant issue in national and public life. In accordance with the procedures specified in the Constitution, these decisions should have been taken by the legislature.'[14] Although parliament approved an economic stabilization programme, amended the 2009 national budget and approved the 2010 national budget, these decisions cannot replace the constitutional competence and obligation to take decisions on all essential issues that relate to the aforementioned loans, not least in terms of possible authorization for the Cabinet.[15] The Constitutional Court explained its ruling on the basis of previous legislative practices during the interwar period and after the restoration of independence: international loans were received only with the approval of the legislature. The Constitution also dictates a model of separation of powers, and the Court argued that parliament must first debate the need and conditions of such an international loan, also authorizing the Cabinet to take out the loan. 'Issues which the Cabinet resolved by concluding the relevant agreements with the international lenders must be seen as adequately important issues in terms of state and public life to ensure that they are debated via the legislative process at the parliament', the Court ruled.[16]

This ruling from the Constitutional Court created political instability in that it questioned the correctness of the political course the government was pursuing, as well as the constitutionality of the international loan. Some political parties represented in parliament wished to utilize this situation to try to change the parliamentary majority and to increase their political influence. That is why Prime Minister Dombrovskis asked the constitutional law experts from the Presidential Commission on Constitutional Law to offer recommendations to the government with respect to an appropriate resolution to the issue. The Commission agreed with the arguments of the Constitutional Court, indicating that agreements on specific international loans that substantially influence Latvia's economic situation in the long term must be confirmed by parliament. The Commission also, however, spoke to a greater opportunity for the parliamentary majority to engage in political manoeuvring than was the case with the Constitutional Court's ruling. That ruling clearly stated that the agreement of parliament as the legislature is needed in such cases, and that agreement must involve a separate law. The Commission, in turn, concluded that parliament can offer its agreement via various formats – a law, a

13 Ibid., 9.

14 Case No. 2009-43-01, para 30.1.

15 Ibid.

16 Ibid.

parliamentary resolution or conclusive activities before the loan is received, or else approving the process after the government takes the relevant decision.[17]

The flexible model proposed by the Commission allowed parliament to approve the decisions of two previous governments, without any political upheaval, by approving a specific resolution in this regard. On 21 January 2010, MPs from the parliamentary majority tabled a draft resolution on 'instructing the government to borrow financial resources as part of the international lending programme'. The resolution won the approval of parliament. The resolution formulated two limitations on what the government could do. One stated that the total loan could not exceed €7.5bn. The other stated that the money must be used to finance the national budget deficit, to ensure stability in the country's financial sector, to refinance national debt and to loan money to the national budget.[18]

This decision provided parliamentary cover for the international lending programme, clearly expressing agreement in terms of the authorization given to the government to continue to take out loans under the auspices of the programme. At the relevant parliamentary meeting, Prime Minister Dombrovskis insisted that

> in its ruling, the Constitutional Court stated that a decision on international loans that have a fundamental effect on the economy requires conceptual support from parliament. The draft resolution speaks to this instruction for the Cabinet – to continue the international lending programme ... In its decision of 18 January, the Commission on Constitutional Law clearly stated that of decisive importance here is the will of parliament, not the form in which that will is expressed. This means that, from this perspective, this debate about whether this requires a resolution or law is fairly artificial. The will is important here, not the form in which the will is expressed.[19]

On 10 November 2010, parliament amended the law on budgetary and financial management to set out precise procedures for future international loans. Art. 35.2^1 of the Law states that a loan that exceeds 20 per cent of the amount of GDP that is defined in the annual national budget law for the relevant fiscal year, or a loan and relevant conditions that are declared to be of importance to the state and society and affect tax policies, the social security system or other issues related to legislative procedure, may be taken out by the Minister of Finance on behalf of the state only after the Prime Minister or the Minister of Finance has delivered a report about the loan to parliament and a law concerning the loan has been adopted and has taken effect.

---

17 The view stated by the Presidential Commission on Constitutional Law on 18 January 2010, *Latvijas Vēstnesis* (2011): 59-66.

18 See *Latvijas Vēstnesis*, 13 (26 January 2010).

19 Minutes of the Emergency Meeting of Parliament on 21 January 2010 [in Latvian]; available at: http://saeima.lv/steno/Saeima9/100121/st100121a.htm.

Case Law of the Constitutional Court

The Crucial Role of the Constitutional Court in the Crisis

The financial crisis had a substantial effect on the agenda of the Constitutional Court. The first cases that were accepted by the Constitutional Court in this regard related to a halt to the indexation of public pensions and to a freeze on wage increases for judges. Discussions about these cases occurred in the context of the financial crisis, and the Constitutional Court was still looking for the correct approach towards rulings related to 'crisis cases'. Justice Viktors Skudra later declared that

> during a difficult time for the country, when parliament had to approve so-called crisis laws that were complicated and unfavourable for individuals, the Constitutional Court became something of a lightning rod. The Court had to deal with unjustified or, in some cases, justified negative emotions from the widest possible variety of strata and groups in society. Other countries later had to take similar decisions. In Greece, for instance, that led to extensive protests and riots. People in Latvia are far more constructive – they wrote to the Constitutional Court. They trusted the Court before the 'crisis rulings', and they have continued to trust it since then.[20]

On the one hand, the need to take steps to overcome the consequences of the financial crisis placed pressure on the Constitutional Court to provide greater freedom of action to the legislative and executive branch of the government. There were those who expected that the Constitutional Court would lower standards related to self-limitation or protection of basic rights. On the other hand, during the financial crisis, politicians, civil servants and members of the public at large believed that these were only short-term difficulties, which would soon be overcome so that people could return to their previous lifestyles. This was proven by initial legislative decisions that did not lead to fundamental changes in normative acts, instead halting the provision of specific social guarantees or services for a certain period of time. Accordingly, quite some time had to pass before people came to understand that the financial crisis was not a short-term phenomenon that could be resolved simply via frugality and without any substantial reforms in many areas of governance.

The Constitutional Court first sent a clear signal to show that even during a financial crisis, fundamental rights must be respected by the legislature. In the case related to pension cuts, the Constitutional Court ruled that the disputed norms were unconstitutional and declared them to be null and void from the moment when

20 V. Skudra, 'A Review of the Work of the Constitutional Court between Conferences', 2009 and 2010 [in Latvian]; available at www.satv.tiesa.gov.lv/upload/Skudra_parskats_10_09_2010.pdf.

they were first approved. The Constitutional Court also instructed the legislature to determine a procedure by which unpaid pensions lost during the period that was disputed would be paid to pensioners by 1 July 2015.[21]

At the same time, however, the Constitutional Court did not choose a mechanical position that would ensure merely a formal view of the effects of the financial crisis and the legislative efforts to reform certain areas. The Constitutional Court marked out a pragmatic approach which respected public interests in relation to certain steps taken by the legislature. The ruling related to the child care subsidy stated that the existing system was not socially responsible or in line with public interests as such. Because the legislature's amendments were aimed at reversing these shortcomings, the Constitutional Court declared them to be constitutional.[22] This meant that the Constitutional Court was giving its blessing to legislative attempts to reform areas in which fundamental reforms were needed, so as to protect public interests. It is interesting that in some cases the Constitutional Court called on the legislature to implement even more important reforms, indicating in its rulings that existing regulations were not fully functional or were not sustainable. For instance, the Court clearly stated that the legislature must consider serious reforms to the pension system.[23] In those cases in which the legislature clearly violated the fundamental rights of individuals and often affected the less protected strata of society, the Court did not permit any compromises with the Constitution in response to the financial crisis.

Analysis of Constitutional Court rulings on 'crisis cases' requires a separate mention of statistical data. The number of complaints filed with the Constitutional Court and the number of cases accepted by the Constitutional Court show that disputes related to what the legislature did to overcome the crisis were important at the Constitutional Court in 2009, when individual complaints rose from 300 in the previous year to 4,030, and dropped to 593 in 2010 and to 488 in 2011. In this context, 2008 could be seen as a pre-crisis year, while 2011 was the first post-crisis year.

During the course of these years, the Constitutional Court handed down 21 rulings that dealt with issues related to the financial crisis. Justices extensively criticized parliament and the government, claiming that politicians were unable to take political responsibility for the reforms that they implemented, leaving the final responsibility for such issues with the Constitutional Court. Analysis of rulings, however, shows that the Constitutional Court found disputed norms to be unconstitutional only in approximately 25 per cent of cases. Most of the steps taken by the legislature to cut national budget spending and to increase national revenues were accepted by the Constitutional Court as being constitutional. The rulings from the Constitutional Court cover a wide range of issues. The most important ones relate to an interpretation of the socially responsible state and legal

21 Case No. 2009-43-01, 21 December 2009, paras 33-35.

22 Case No. 2011-03-01, 19 December 2011, para 22.

23 Ibid.

certainty principles, as well as to the Constitutional Court's views about ensuring social and economic rights.

The Principle of a Socially Responsible State

The Constitutional Court did not define the principle of a socially responsible state in *expressis verbis* terms for a long time. It was only in 2006 that the Constitutional Court ruled that the Constitution includes this principle.[24] The practice of the Constitutional Court indicates that the principle of a socially responsible state means the following: the state is obliged to ensure a standard of living worthy of human beings; this includes ensuring social assistance and fundamental services, as well as the accessibility of educational, health care, social care and cultural institutions; the state is obliged to protect people against social risks; the state is obliged to be concerned about social justice, including concern about evening out social differences, protecting the weak and ensuring equal opportunities; the country's residents must be linked to society, which means that people have obligations vis-à-vis other people.[25] The *expressis verbis* definition of the principle of a socially responsible state in Constitutional Court rulings was of deep symbolic importance on the eve of the financial crisis. The definition set out a precise framework for the freedom of action of the legislature, limiting the economic, social and cultural rights of individuals.

In its crisis rulings, the Constitutional Court did not view the principle of a socially responsible state as an additional instrument to protect fundamental individual rights. Instead, the Constitutional Court viewed the principle as an objective guideline in defining the state's obligations in implementing social, economic and cultural rights. The Constitutional Court has ruled that the principle of a socially responsible state is broader than any of the social, economic or cultural rights that are enshrined in the Constitution, and this means that in practice it did not expand guarantees related to the protection of fundamental individual rights.[26]

The principle of a socially responsible state was the decisive argument for the Constitutional Court in criticizing thoughtless legislative decisions concerning special budget spending related to social insurance, and in calling for considered reforms that would ensure the sustainability of that budget. For instance, the Court ruled that by refusing to increase social insurance contributions, the legislature did not provide for a new type of social insurance.[27] The Court has particularly emphasized the fact that

> the social insurance system in Latvia is sensitive, and any careless decision can create serious consequences in terms of the system's long-term stability.

24 Case No. 2006-07-01, 2 November 2006, para 18.

25 A. Kovaļevska, *Jurista Vārds* 32 (537) (26 August 2008): 10-13.

26 Case No. 2009-08-01, 26 November 2009, para 14.

27 Case No. 2009-43-01, 21 December 2009, para 31.1.2.

> Accordingly, the state is obliged to take the greatest care in implementing social policies and managing special social insurance budget resources. Excessively speedy and insufficiently considered decisions have, along with the financial condition of the state, led to the current unfavourable situation in the special social insurance budget.[28]

Despite several instructions from the Constitutional Court, the legislature failed to launch reforms of the special social insurance budget. 'The excessive delay in a legislative decision on how to ensure the financial sustainability of the special budget creates risks related to the violation of public interests and fundamental rights', the Court declared. 'Steps taken in relation to the short-term arrangement of the social insurance system do not address the causes of the financial problems of the special budget. The absence of considered, balanced and long-term policies, as well as the absence of adequate and economically justified processes, indicates that the existence of the pension system and social budget can be endangered.'[29] The principle of a socially responsible state does not keep the state from reviewing the scope of social security. The state can limit the payment of subsidies if this is in line with public interests and the rights of others to receive financial support from the state. At the same time, however, the state must, under all circumstances, ensure a minimal volume of the individual's social, economic and cultural rights, and it cannot step back from this by referring to a lack of financing resources.[30]

The Constitutional Court has also reviewed legislative reforms in the context of the principle of a socially responsible state: 'The principle of a socially responsible state means that the state is obliged to establish sustainable and balanced policies to ensure public welfare. The country must ensure a balance between its financial capabilities and not just personal rights in the social area, but also the need to ensure the welfare of the entire society, creating legal regulations that are aimed at the country's sustainable development.'[31] The Constitutional Court has also set up a mechanism to ensure special examinations of the reform goals of the legislature. This means that the Constitutional Court investigates the issue of whether the legislature has chosen socially responsible solutions.[32]

> Under conditions of economic decline, the criterion that is used to evaluate disputed norms in relation to constitutionality and overall legal principles is whether the solution chosen by the legislature is socially responsible. A socially responsible solution is one that ensures that the legal interests of individuals are harmonized with public interests. That's why it is necessary to evaluate the resources the legislature has chosen to ensure a gentle transitional period in

28 Ibid.
29 Case No. 2011-03-01, 19 December 2011, para 22.
30 Case No. 2009-44-01, 15 March 2010, para 16.
31 Ibid., para 22.
32 Case No. 2011-03-01, 19 December 2011, para 24.

terms of ensuring a balance between the country's economic capabilities and the welfare of the public.[33]

The Principle of Legal Certainty

The principle of legal certainty does not exclude the possibility that the state can amend existing legal regulations. An opposite approach would mean that the state could not react to changing circumstances. At the same time, however, when amending legal regulations, the state must take into account the rights that individuals hope to preserve and implement on the basis of lawful, justified and sensible certainty. The principle of legal certainty demands that when the state amends legal regulations, it keeps in mind a sensible balance between the certainty of individuals and the interests on behalf of which the regulations are being changed.[34] Although the principle of legal certainty has been one of the most often applied legal principles in the practice of the Constitutional Court, it is also true that it took on fundamental meaning only during the financial crisis. Under normal circumstances, the practices of the Constitutional Court involved much greater meaning for the principle of commensurability, while during the crisis the principle of legal certainty attracted the greatest attention.

Initially, the legislature tried to convince the Constitutional Court that the principle of legal certainty must be limited under conditions of financial crisis and that the Constitutional Court should grant the legislature greater freedom of action to take steps against the crisis. The Court responded by saying that parliament was wrong in believing that the principle of legal certainty should be changed under conditions of economic decline or other extraordinary circumstances. In such cases, the principle of legal certainty demands a balance between the legal certainty of individuals and public interests.[35] At the same time, however, the Constitutional Court has accepted a few steps back from the principle of legal certainty. It must first be noted that the Court began a careful evaluation of whether normative regulations are really ones upon which people can rely. In this context, the Court also ruled that if normative regulations have not been typically stable, then the principle of legal certainty does not protect individuals from unfavourable changes in normative regulations, particularly in relation to national budget spending.[36]

The Constitutional Court has also, in some cases, accepted the possibility of not awarding decisive meaning in protecting the principle of legal certainty if the legislature implements the necessary reforms of legal regulations so as to prevent previous mistakes in legal policies: 'In order to prevent harm related to important

33 Case No. 2009-44-01, 15 March 2010, para 22.

34 Case No. 2002-12-01, 25 March 2003, para 2; see also Case No. 2005-12-0103, 16 December 2005, para 24.

35 Case No. 2009-08-01, 26 November 2009, para 23.

36 Ibid., para 24.

public interests, priority should be given to them in comparison to the principle of legal certainty. When government institutions see essential violations of public interests, they have not just the right, but also the obligation to act.'[37] In such cases, a gentle approach to new regulations can be ensured not just by ensuring a sensible transition period or compensation, but also by other techniques:

> In certain cases, when the scope of limitations related to legal certainty is balanced with the need and urgency of amendments to legal regulations, steps back from the rights that are guaranteed to individuals are permissible even without a transition period. What is more, the existence of a gentle transitional period cannot be the only criterion in deciding whether a sensible balance is being observed.[38]

The Legislature's Freedom of Action during a Financial Crisis

The Constitutional Court has devoted a lot of attention in its rulings to ways of overcoming the financial crisis, particularly evaluating the limits on the legislature's freedom of action. This means that the Court makes sure that the steps taken by the legislature to overcome the crisis are in line with the Constitution.

In the area of social, economic and cultural rights, the Constitutional Court has accepted a general position which says that in implementing these rights, the state is obliged to create an effective, just and sustainable system, and it is also free to choose those methods and mechanisms that will lead to the implementation of such rights.[39] This is because when it comes to the implementation of the rights, the political considerations and priorities of the legislature are of great importance. The Constitutional Court cannot take the place of the legislature and identify the most appropriate political decisions or determine the way in which national budget resources are to be spent. The Constitutional Court's duty instead is to determine whether disputed norms are sensible and harmonized, whether the state has the resources that are necessary for the implementation of the norms, whether the norms are balanced and flexible, whether they speak to short-term and long-term satisfaction of needs, and whether the norms have been reviewed and presented to the public.[40]

The Constitutional Court has also, however, clearly ruled that the country's financial situation and the need to reduce the budget deficit at a time when other legitimate goals do not exist cannot serve as a general excuse for the state stepping back from rights that have been granted to people previously.[41] In commenting on the state's plan to implement the euro, the chief justice of the Court has said that

37 Case No. 2009-44-01, 15 March 2010, para 19.

38 Case No. 2010-21-01, 1 December 2010, para 21.

39 Case No. 2009-08-01, 26 November 2009, para 15.

40 Case No. 2009-43-01, 21 December 2009, para 29.2.

41 Ibid., para 27.2.

the implementation of the euro is not a legitimate goal that would justify possible offences against fundamental human rights:

> If, for instance, an economist says that our goal is to join the eurozone in 2014, then I will say that it is not a legitimate or constitutional goal. In the sense of the Constitution, the goal is the welfare of the people. It is not constitutional for us to rush toward the implementation of the euro while ensuring that the people of Latvia will live below the survival level.[42]

The Constitutional Court has, however, ruled that 'in specific cases the financial crisis can reach a level at which the legislature must be given freedom to take adjusting steps even if they violate the fundamental rights that are enshrined in the Constitution. At a time when the state's financial resources are very limited, the state is free to change rules on pensions so as to ensure a just social insurance system.'[43] It has to be said, however, that the Constitutional Court has never declared that the scope of the financial crisis has reached the level at which the constitutional limitations on the legislature's freedom of action should be reviewed.

When it comes to national budget cuts, in turn, the Constitutional Court has emphasized the importance of the principle of solidarity, which means that compensation for various government officials must be reduced at the same level, and it is not permissible to have a situation in which the consequences of the financial crisis are borne by individual social groups at a time when other social groups do not experience any cuts in income.[44]

There were several cases that the Constitutional Court heard in terms of evaluating the changes made by the legislature in the area of taxes. The issue was the application of the individual income tax to revenues with respect to which no taxes had to be paid in advance of the crisis. In this context, the Court first wrote about the importance of taxes in pursuing the overall goals of society:

> The collection of the individual income tax has been determined in pursuit of the interests of public welfare ... These revenues can finance priorities in relation to social and economic projects, and they can also reduce inequality between the income and level of welfare of individuals. For that reason, the state uses tax policies in pursuit of social policy goals.[45]

The Constitutional Court also accepted the idea that a review of tax rates affects certain segments of society – those in which people receive sufficiently high levels of income:

42 V. Avotiņš , *Neatkarīgā*, 24 May 2011.
43 Case No. 2009-43-01, 21 December 2009, para 29.2.
44 Case No. 2009-76-01, 31 March 2010, para 6.2.3.
45 Case No. 2010-25-01, 6 December 2010, para 9.

> In evaluating the commensurability of the disputed limitation, the Constitutional Court takes into account the answer given by parliament to say that interest-based revenues are mostly concentrated in the more wealthy segment of society ... The disputed norms are mostly not focused on the income of those social groups that require particular protection from the state.[46]

The Dialogue between the Constitutional Court and the Legislature

The financial crisis led to harsher exchanges of views between the Constitutional Court and political elites. This focused on the confirmation of knowledge about constitutional law in terms of the impossibility of evaluating the constitutionality of laws without political considerations and discussions about the priorities of the country's development. It is no accident that it has been recognized that the ability of the judicial branch to evaluate the constitutionality of laws also simultaneously means that the judicial branch intervenes in issues that have been considered by legislators.[47]

When the government was drafting laws on reducing pensions, justices of the Constitutional Court told the media that this solution would not be permissible. They recalled an earlier ruling which had declared a similar solution to be unconstitutional.[48] The Court also did not avoid expressing criticisms of the quality of the prepared draft laws, the speed at which they were drafted or the professionalism of those who did so.[49] The active expression of the Court's position led some politicians to criticize the Chief Justice for becoming involved in political debates. Particularly harsh communications occurred when the Court handed down several rulings related to the compensation of judges, as well as budget procedures. The debates between the Court and politicians sometimes became so harsh that after handing down a ruling on the compensation of judges, the Court made claims that politicians were placing pressure on the Court and that debates about how possible it was to implement the relevant rulings could be seen as a type of revenge against the Court.[50]

---

46 Ibid., para 10.5.

47 J. Žilys, *The Constitutional Court: Legal and Historical Preconditions* [in Latvian] (Teisinės informacijos centras, 2001), p. 132.

48 L. Šupstika and K. Tropiņa, 'Kūtris: Pensions are Personal Property Which Must be Preserved' [in Latvian]; available at www.diena.lv/sabiedriba/politika/kutris-pensija-ir-personas-ipasums-uz-kuru-tiesibas-jasaglaba-673497.

49 G. Kūtris, *Jurista Vārds* 3(598) (19 January 2010): 4-6.

50 'Is Pressure Being Placed Upon the Constitutional Court?' [in Latvian], *Jurista Vārds* 8(603) (23 February 2010): 5-9.

The Role of the President in Overcoming the Crisis

A Presidential Ultimatum for Parliament

The Latvian Constitution defines Latvia as a parliamentary republic in which the President largely has ceremonial functions.[51] In terms of constitutional practices since the restoration of Latvia's independence, however, the country's presidents have increased their political influence and authority. Particularly under the circumstances of a financial crisis, President Valdis Zatlers and President Andris Bērziņš took several essential steps that strengthened the role of the Latvian President in the country's constitutional system.

When the financial crisis began in 2008, President Zatlers actively involved himself in efforts to overcome the crisis and to improve the political system. Later Zatlers went so far as to say that he was a 'crisis President'. Early in December 2008, Zatlers engaged in negotiations with the political parties represented in parliament to reach agreement on how to overcome the crisis. On 10 December 2008, representatives of all of the political parties signed the so-called Advent Agreement on supporting efforts to stabilize Latvia's financial situation. The document stated the promise of these representatives to overcome the financial crisis and to support steps proposed by the government in terms of doing so. That allowed the government of Prime Minister Godmanis to gain convincing support from parliament when it came to the first steps that were taken to overcome the crisis.

From then on, the activities of Zatlers involved a far clearer confrontation with the parliamentary majority. On 13 January 2009, a protest was held in Rīga against the policies of the government, and it turned into a riot during which people demolished buildings and cars and tried to attack the parliamentary building. The next day President Zatlers delivered a conceptual speech which was later described as 'Zatlers' ultimatum'. 'Parliament and the government have lost their links to the electorate,' the President declared.

> I have said several times in the past that trust can only be regained with concrete steps. We must not engage in further confrontation. We must do things that the public demands, including constitutional amendments, a plan to stimulate the economy, and reforms in the system of national governance. For that reason, as the President of Latvia and as a man who represents the interests of the Latvian people, I insist on three specific instructions for parliament and the Cabinet of Ministers.[52]

---

51 D. Iļjanova, 'The Governmental System of the Republic of Latvia', in N. Chronowski, T. Drinóczi and T. Takácz (eds), *The Governmental Systems of Central and Eastern European States* (Wolters Kluwer Business, 2011), pp. 367-429, at pp. 419-421.

52 See *Latvijas Vēstnesis* 8 (15 January 2009).

The President formulated several demands in his speech. He called for amendments to the Constitution and the law on parliamentary elections, as well as for a reorganization of the government. Zatlers set a deadline of 31 March 2009, by which time the work had to be completed. 'I will give a categorical answer to the question of what will happen if the work is not done by March 31,' he announced. 'I will propose a national referendum on the dissolution of the Parliament.'[53]

Although some politicians harshly criticized the 'Zatlers ultimatum', arguing that the President could not issue specific instructions to parliament and set a deadline for the implementation thereof, parliament and the government basically yielded before the ultimatum. Among the most important political changes was the resignation of the Godmanis government. The government of Dombrovskis was approved, and factions that had previously been in opposition became part of the governing coalition.

In an address on 31 March 2009, President Zatlers summarized what parliament and the government had done, arguing that the establishment of the Dombrovskis government and other steps taken by parliament and the government showed that necessary changes to overcome the financial crisis could be seen in the political system. At the same time, however, President Zatlers also formulated future tasks for parliament and the government.[54] The President also used his constitutional competence to convene emergency meetings of the Cabinet of Ministers and to set their agenda.

Dissolution of Parliament

On 28 May 2011, less than a month before the expiration of his term in office, President Zatlers made use of the authority given to him in Art. 48 of the Constitution to propose the dissolution of parliament, doing so for the first time since the Constitution took effect.[55]

President Zatlers appeared on live television on 28 May 2011 to announce his decision to propose the dissolution of parliament: 'I have decided to act radically,' he said. 'This decision on the eve of the presidential election was personally difficult for me, and it is also complicated in constitutional terms. I clearly understand that my decision may draw a line across my prospect of being re-elected to the presidency.'[56] The President also discussed the reasons for his decision. He pointed to several decisions taken by parliament that led him to make the decision. The dissolution of parliament gained the support of broad swathes of society, and it was no surprise that when the referendum on dissolution was held

53 Ibid.

54 See *Latvijas Vēstnesis* 51 (1 April 2009).

55 See *Latvijas Vēstnesis* 83 (29 May 2011).

56 Ibid.

on 23 July 2011, 650,518 citizens voted in favour of dissolution and only 37,829 voted against it.[57]

Art. 49 of the Constitution states that if parliament has been dissolved or recalled, MPs retain their authority until such time as the newly elected parliament takes office. The existing parliament, however, can only convene meetings if the President convenes them. The President sets the agenda for such meetings. Because this was the first time in terms of constitutional practice that parliament had been dissolved, the procedures enshrined in Art. 49 had to be applied for the first time by the new President, Bērziņš. He took office after Zatlers' term in office expired.

The new President published the procedure whereby he would convene parliamentary meetings so as to clearly explain the way in which the work of parliament would be organized until the new parliament was in place. The Presidential Chancery announced that issues for parliament meetings would be put on the agenda not automatically, but only after an evaluation, a request for additional information and a series of consultations and meetings. Thus the President hoped to control the issues parliament would consider.[58] The President also took on responsibility for political stability when parliament was dissolved. For instance, he did not put on the parliament agenda the issue of a vote of no confidence in the Minister of Justice, leaving that matter up to the Prime Minister and the electorate.

Constitutional and Institutional Reform Proposals Triggered by the Crisis

The Experience and Necessity of Policy Planning

The law on development planning defines the country's national development planning system. The law applies to state and local government institutions and covers plans related to policies and territorial development. There are 12 fundamental principles that are enshrined in Art. 5 of the statute.[59] Among the most important principles is the principle of harmonizing financial opportunities and documents, which has been of importance because of the crisis. During the years of fiscal consolidation, the most often discussed principle of legal certainty had not been cited as a separate principle; instead, it is derived from the principle of harmonizing documents. The financial crisis forced Latvia to review its policy

---

57 Decision 36 of the Latvian Central Election Commission, 26 July 2011, *Latvijas Vēstnesis* 116 (27 July 2011).

58 See *Latvijas Vēstnesis* 117 (28 July 2011).

59 These are sustainable development, harmonization of interests, participation, cooperation, financial capabilities, transparency, supervision and prevention, subsidiarity, links between developmental planning and the drafting of normative acts, balanced development, timely issues and harmonization of documents.

planning documents, and those officials responsible for them have admitted that the time has come to get a clear sense of the usefulness of the many plans that have been drafted. Planning should ensure linkage with financial planning and should be harmonized between state and local government entities so that decisions are not mutually contradictory, but in the event, the theory in this area has not been translated into reality.

The law on development planning defines types of planning documents and their hierarchy. There are three types of planning documents in Latvia – those that apply to policy, those that apply to management of institutions and those that apply to territorial development. These are divided up in terms of short-term, medium-term and long-term importance. At the top of the long-term hierarchy is Latvia's sustainable development strategy, while the national development plan is at the top of the list of medium-term importance. It appears that since the onset of the financial crisis, politicians have come to understand the meaning of planning. The government's social partners and members of the public have been actively involved in debates about the national development plan. The plan has attracted attention specifically because members of the public want to see a clear plan on how to deal with the consequence of the crisis. Public scepticism about the government's capabilities and its far-sighted policies – something that is clearly based on experience – is seen in statements about the draft document that have been presented in the media.

The director of the Chamber of Commerce and Industry has even argued that the biggest problem with the plan can be found in the constitutional system, because governments change far too often in Latvia, and that also means frequent changes in planning. Indeed, frequent changes in government and unstable coalitions with contradictory goals that require a great deal of compromise are more likely to hinder implementation of plans then stabilize the processes. Social partners have also been critical of what the government did during the years of the crisis, arguing that this was due to poor planning. The Association of Local Unions, for instance, has argued very directly that during the crisis the government appeared to be more chaotic than planned in its work, with some major decisions being taken at the very last possible moment. The Association of Local Governments, for its part, has recommended that the government review its role in these processes. It is clear that previous national planning documents have been duplications of effort, and they have also been contradictory within themselves. What is clear is that without a serious evaluation of mistakes and failures, as well as long-term planning, Latvia will not recover.

Crisis Legislation

The legislature and the executive branch at first saw the financial crisis as a short-term difficulty that would require a review of specific functions and a reduction in national budget spending. This was mostly done via temporary regulations that set out special rules for the period of the crisis. One law spoke to compensation for officials and employees from state and local government institutions in 2009, while another spoke to the payment of public pensions and subsidies between 2010 and 2012.

Some experts proposed the drafting of a special law to overcome the crisis – one that would set out special regulations aimed to resolve the crisis.[60] The same proposal came from the Association of Local Unions, which suggested a special crisis law to define all of the ways in which the country would step back from existing legal norms, and to ensure that this process would be monitored more easily and more transparently. The government sent to parliament a draft law on local government operations between 2009 and 2012, but parliament rejected this approach towards existing laws that regulated local government operations, instead proposing that a special law be adopted in relation to consolidation of the national budget. A separate law was not drafted, however, because steps aimed at overcoming the financial crisis were instead organized on the basis of amending the relevant normative acts.

It was the government that took the main decisions on what should be done, and submitted the necessary draft laws for parliamentary consideration. Usually, the government submitted reform-related draft laws together with the draft law on the national budget or amendments to that law, including all of the proposals in a single packet. The aim was to ensure that the draft laws could be approved quickly and that the government could maintain control over improvements to the laws being discussed by parliament.

The packet of budget laws included laws accompanying the budget – ones that amended other laws to make it possible to trim the budget and to engage in structural reforms (structural at least in the sense of the government's understanding). The law on budget and financial administration set out the procedure and procedural movement of packets of budget-related draft laws. The law stated that the budget was a resource for implementing national policies with financial methods. The goal of the budget would be to identify and justify the resources that were needed by the government, other state institutions and local governments in terms of implementing their obligations in relation to those areas in which financing was dictated in normative acts. This would ensure that revenues would cover costs during the period of time to which the law applied.

The chief justice of the Constitutional Court criticized the process of implementation of reforms via budget-related draft laws. He argued that the packets of such laws often included issues that had nothing to do with the national budget, but did have a substantial influence on the rule of law in terms of making decisions on publicly important issues while debating the budget – a process that required rapid decisions by the legislature.[61] It must be noted, however, that

---

60 A. Stucka, *Jurista Vārds* 17 (570) (28 April 2009): 12-14.

61 'When Laws Unrelated to the National Budget are Adopted in a Package of Budget Laws, Budgetary Procedures are Mixed Up' [in Latvian], *LETA News Agency*, 17 January 2011.

the Constitutional Court did, in general terms, accept the legislative practice of implementing reforms urgently and with the help of the packet of budget laws.[62] This essentially meant acceptance of the existing practice of implementing substantial reforms in the packet of budget laws. Nor did the Constitutional Court oppose the urgent review of draft laws, ruling that the 15 minutes given to MPs who wished to submit amendment proposals between readings of laws were a constitutional period of time.[63]

The scope of reforms proposed by the government in the packet of budget laws can be determined by comparing the number of draft laws in each packet of budget-related laws. In 2009, the packet of draft budgetary laws was more or less in line with the accustomed scope, but amendments to the 2009 national budget and the draft budget laws for the 2010 and 2011 national budget involved the necessary consolidation of budgetary spending by the government, substantially restructuring many aspects of life in the country. Experts who have reviewed the steps that were taken by the government and the legislature have quite frequently emphasized the fact that the reforms were implemented in a great hurry. Former Ministry of Finance state secretary Bičevskis, for instance, has said that during the years of the crisis, the government and parliament were forced to work very quickly on solutions that created much better prerequisites for government and oversight institutions in terms of acting quickly to stabilize the financial sector, thus strengthening the trust that the international community, ratings agencies, lenders and shareholders in the financial sector had in the stability of Latvia's financial sector. The Association of Local Unions, for its part, has said that during the initial phase of the crisis, when the government had to take quick steps to prevent insolvency of the state, decisions taken by the government were often incomprehensible, adopted too quickly and approved without much thought.

It must be said, however, that the legislature did implement several major reforms during the financial crisis that had been delayed in the past. On 18 December 2008, for instance, a new law on administrative territories and populated areas was approved. This implemented major reforms to the system of local government, moving from two levels of local governance to just one, merging local governments into larger territorial units and reducing the number of local governments. On 3 June 2010, the legislature amended the law on the courts to establish a Judicial Council which helps to draft policies and strategies for the judicial system and also works to improve the way in which the relevant work is organized. The need for an institution that represents the judicial branch was understood even before Latvia joined the EU in 2004, but it was only in 2010 that the legislature established the Council.

62 Case No. 2011-03-01, 19 December 2011, para 18.

63 Case No. 2009-08-01, 26 November 2009, para 17.1.

The Law on Compensation

One of the most important laws to be approved during the financial crisis was the one regarding compensation for officials and employees of state and local government institutions. Prior to Latvia's Soviet occupation, the wages of all public employees were regulated via a single normative act – regulations on wages for state employees which were approved in 1929. The government was instructed to draft the new law in the transitional rules of a law on compensation for the officials and employees of state and local government institutions in 2009. The authors of the draft law argued that it would bring greater order to the compensation system so that it would become more transparent, that all regulations concerning the wages and social guarantees of public sector workers would be placed under a single 'umbrella', that the number of systems related to wages would be reduced substantially, and that the overall system in the country would become more simple and understandable.[64] In commenting on the conceptual version of the law on compensation, constitutional law expert Pastars concluded that the law, which took effect on 1 January 2010, 'had a very ambitious goal – correlating all of the guarantees from other laws in a single law and substantially limiting the freedom of action of the relevant institutions'.[65] It is also very important in this context that the draft law was prepared as an independent regulation, as opposed to a step aimed at overcoming the financial crisis: 'The compensation law is not just a crisis law, even though the transitional rules do speak to several transitional periods.'[66]

After the compensation law was approved, it was amended several times to expand its scope by directly or indirectly covering nearly all people who were employed in the public sector. One of the most extensive reforms in this regard was the integration into the law of the compensation system for judges and prosecutors so as to ensure comparable and balanced development in all branches of government. It was specifically the reform of the system of compensation for judges and prosecutors that pointed to several shortcomings in previous regulations that were addressed by the law on compensation.

It is only natural that the government's social partners are not satisfied with the law on compensation, because they believe that the only result of this is an elimination of resources of motivation, making it impossible to ensure normal personnel management. The compensation law has also created a peculiar situation in the wages of the national governance system. Motivation of employees has been replaced by fear of being sacked under the crisis conditions. The Association of Local Unions, for its part, argues that the state is still interfering in the conclusion of joint labour agreements, thus limiting the constitutional rights of workers to engage in collective bargaining and violating the principle of autonomy for local

64 Annotation to the Draft Law. Available at www.titania.saeima.lv/LIVS/SaeimaLIVS.nsf/ 0/971F0E7A788C9469C225766200358B2B?OpenDocument.

65 E. Pastars, *Jurista Vārds* 6 (601) (9 February 2010): 6.

66 Ibid.

governments, in terms of state and local government capital enterprises being limited in their ability to do their work freely.

Irrespective of criticism about the compensation law, the Constitutional Court accepted its principles. It also accepted the approach the legislature chose in terms of regulating the compensation of state and local government officials and employees.[67] It would have been peculiar if someone had praised the compensation law, because the wages of every single person involved in the system of national governance have shrunk in practical terms.

At a time when Latvia was forced to review its spending and to borrow money so as to avoid bankruptcy, budget consolidation was implemented, and the preferred option was to increase the tax burden substantially while also implementing linear cuts in all areas of spending. The role of social partners increased during the financial crisis when it came to budgetary planning; the government involved them in planning structural reforms. An audit was conducted for governmental functions with the aim of increasing the effectiveness of the process, reducing budget expenditures, ensuring the utility of budget spending and preserving or improving the quality of the relevant services. The audit was supposed to make note of functions or jobs that the state could eliminate or delegate to the private sector. The functional audit commission which evaluated the preservation, reorganization or elimination of certain institutions and structural units involved representatives of the National Chancery, several Ministries and the social partners. The representatives of these organizations were also included in a reform management group which discussed financial and administrative reforms in national governance, as well as options for budget cuts.

The government has undertaken to continue with the rationalization of the number and structure of government institutions, and it has declared that it will implement the results of the functional audit so as to avoid any duplication of functions. The government declaration also includes the promise to get rid of functions that are atypical for the public sector, delegating some of them to the private sector and to NGOs while also monitoring the quality and availability of the relevant services.

Proposals on Constitutional Amendments

Reform of the Political System

Aspects of improvements to the Constitution attracted additional attention during the financial crisis as several political parties tried to reform the Constitution to introduce the popular election of the President and to expand the President's authority. President Zatlers, in particular, devoted attention to such amendments. On 16 March 2011, the President submitted major proposals on constitutional

67 Case No. 2011-10-01, 28 March 2012, para 27.

amendments to parliament. These spoke to the review of a series of elements in the President's authority. He proposed that the President be able to nominate two members of the Constitutional Court, the national auditor, the Ombudsman and the President of the Bank of Latvia for parliamentary approval. He also called for the ability of the President to control the make-up and activities of the government, adding once again that Art. 48 of the Constitution should be amended. The President also proposed the introduction of an impeachment procedure to protect the President against the risk of losing his job. Finally, he proposed the establishment of a system for the popular election of the President.[68]

Also, several political parties have regularly proposed amending the Constitution to institute a system for popular election of the President. None of the amendments were approved, however. In a speech dedicated to the restoration of Latvia's independence, Parliament Speaker Āboltiņa particularly focused on ways of improving the structure of state: 'The founders of the Republic of Latvia had no doubt that the new country must be a parliamentary republic,' she said. 'The path of parliamentarianism is not an easy one. It does not provide ready-made answers and does not point to a single smart person who knows all of the correct choices. No single leader takes decisions on issues that are important for the country. This is entrusted to the people and to us as representatives of the people.'[69]

After taking office, President Andris Bērziņš also focused on reforms to the Constitution. On 8 February 2012, he announced that over the next several years Latvia would draft a new constitution in line with the modern-day situation. He also said that he would be prepared to take the initiative in proposing reforms to the Constitution so that the process would be finished before the beginning of the term in office of a new parliament.[70] A little later the Presidential Chancery issued a more extensive explanation as to why a new Constitution was needed:

> If Latvia is to survive and develop not just in economic but also in political terms under conditions of globalization, it is necessary to implement qualitative changes to the model of national governance. These changes must facilitate responsibility and ensure a clearer distribution of responsibility among the branches of government, also ensuring that decisions are taken at the level that is closest to the population, thus ensuring a more compact system of national governance. The upcoming referendum and the vast social and economic problems which exist in our country confirm that such changes are needed.[71]

---

68 Available at http://www.president.lv/images/modules/items/PDF/iniciativa-satversmes-grozijumiem.pdf.

69 Available at http://www.saeima.lv/lv/transcripts/view/117.

70 L. Grundule, 'Bērziņš Prepared to Initiate New Constitution for Latvia' [in Latvian], *LETA News Agency*, 8 February 2012.

71 For the text of the announcement, see http://www.president.lv/pk/content/?cat_id=603&art_id=19098.

The only constitutional amendments that were approved during the financial crisis related to the right of the people of Latvia to propose the dissolution of parliament. Art. 14 of the Constitution was amended to say that one-tenth of the electorate could propose a national referendum on recalling parliament. Parliament would be dissolved if the majority of voters in the referendum supported the dissolution and if at least two-thirds of the number of people who had voted in the previous parliament election took part in the vote. The right to propose the referendum on a recall would not exist during the first year after a new parliament had taken office or during the last year before the end of the relevant term in office, during the last six months of the term in office of the President or sooner than six months after the previous national referendum on recalling parliament.

Fiscal Discipline

As the EU seeks to overcome the financial crisis, fiscal discipline has been seen as something of a panacea. Nearly all of the things that member states do to ensure fiscal discipline are seen as a solution for all economic problems. Nearly all EU member states signed a Treaty on Stability, Coordination and Governance in the Economic and Monetary Union. This agreement states that after it takes effect, signatory countries would be obliged to approve norms that would guarantee the absorption of rules related to fiscal discipline that are enshrined in Art. 3.1 of the agreement, preferably at the constitutional level.

Implementation of principles of fiscal discipline is not just something that relates to the new agreement; this has also been a conscious choice for Latvia as it has sought to overcome the financial crisis. That is why the government began to work on the relevant constitutional amendments and on a law on fiscal discipline even before the Treaty was signed. A draft law on fiscal discipline was submitted to parliament by the government on 6 December 2011, and consideration of the proposal has continued in parallel to the ratification of the agreement.

The fiscal discipline law speaks to the implementation of medium-term budgetary planning. The intention is to ensure that the fiscal policy planning instrument is a framework law on medium-term budgetary planning. This law would be prepared each year to cover the next three years, defining the maximum spending of the consolidated national budget during the first and second year of the medium-term budgetary framework law period, as inherited from the second and third year of the previous period of the medium-term budgetary framework.

The government has also drafted constitutional amendments to make sure that the new fiscal policy initiatives are in line with the Constitution. Art. 66.1 would be amended to say that parliament is responsible for a frugal budget and for the establishment of savings aimed at the development of the country and its financial stability. In advance of the beginning of each fiscal year, parliament would take a decision on national revenues and spending under the framework of a multi-year budgetary plan. Draft budgets would be submitted to parliament by the government, which would ensure a balanced approach to financial affairs in the country.

These amendments to Art. 66.1 would initially ensure a constitutional strengthening of parliament's responsibility for a frugal budget and for savings related to national development and financial stability. It would instruct parliament to consider the state's revenues and expenditures each year in advance of the beginning of the new fiscal year, with proposals on this submitted by the government. It would also insist that the government take a balanced approach to financial affairs in the country. The enshrining of these principles at the constitutional level, according to the authors of the proposed amendments, would help to avoid a situation in which, during an upswing in the economic cycle, the government and parliament do not have sufficient motivation to cut the national budget deficit, as well as a situation in which, during a period of economic decline, they do not have financial opportunities to stimulate economic development. Parliament has not yet begun a review of the proposed constitutional amendments because experts in the area of constitutional law have said that principles of fiscal discipline can be ensured via the ratification of the European agreement and the approval of the law on fiscal discipline, without any need at this time to amend the Constitution.[72]

Essential in the context of the constitutional amendments is that current constitutional regulations in this area can be determined not just at the level of Art. 66 of the Constitution, but also by a review of materials related to the drafting of the Constitution, as well as interpretations offered by the Constitutional Court. The use of these materials suggests that an interpretation of the Constitution can make it possible to develop necessary guidelines in the area of fiscal discipline without actually amending the Constitution itself. First, parliament approved the agreement in accordance with the constitutional procedures that are referred to in Art. 68.2 of the Constitution. The chairman of the Parliament Foreign Relations Committee, Kalniņš, said in debate about the agreement that 'the Foreign Relations Committee reviewed this agreement on 9 May, and the first thing that we did was discuss the procedure for confirming it. We … agreed that this agreement might delegate some of the competences of our government institutions to the institutions of the EU, which means that approval of this agreement by parliament requires a constitutional majority.'[73] This means that after its ratification, the agreement became an Act at the constitutional level, and its regulations are comparable to those that are enshrined in the Constitution. The principles of fiscal discipline that are found in the agreement, in other words, have become a part of constitutional regulations. The Constitutional Court has ruled on several occasions that international agreements ratified in accordance with Art. 68.2 of the Constitution do achieve the constitutional level.[74]

72 *Jurista Vārds* 20(719) (15 May 2012): 5-11.

73 Available at http://www.saeima.lv/lv/transcripts/view/119.

74 See, for example, Case No. 2007-10-0102, 29 November 2007, para 56.3; Case No. 2008-35-01, 7 April 2009, para 10.4.

Second, Art. 66.2 of the Constitution also states that when parliament approves a decision that involves unexpected budgetary expenditures, it must simultaneously allocate the funds that are needed to cover such expenditures. One of the authors of the Constitution explained the need for the principle as a member of the Constitutional Convention:

> If an owner does not wish his business to collapse, then he must act in accordance with his resources. Clearly that also applies to the state, and so when we decide on expenditures, we must speak to the sources from which resources to cover the expenditures shall come … This supplement is needed to ensure propriety in finances, because our financial circumstances are very dire.[75]

Prior to the global financial crisis, these constitutional regulations had not been thoroughly evaluated or analysed by legal scholars. Today, however, it is possible to declare that principles of fiscal discipline were enshrined in the Constitution on 15 February 1922, 90 years ago, and all that is necessary today is to find an appropriate interpretation thereof. It can be declared that the Constitution strictly demands that the country's financial resources be utilized in a sensible and commensurate way, and that expenditures be in line with the resources that are available. It is from this demand that we can derive the principle of fiscal responsibility among constitutional institutions, noting that this principle includes two elements: the principle of balance in the national budget and the duty to observe fiscal discipline.[76]

75 Minutes of the Constitutional Convention meeting of 15 February 1922.

76 D. Amoliņa, *Jurista Vārds* 33 (680) (16 August 2011): 11-12.

Chapter 5
The Spanish Constitution in the Turmoil of the Global Financial Crisis

Agustín Ruiz Robledo

Political, Economic and Social Facets of the Crisis

In 2007 Spain was a country where everything seemed to be going well, with the economy growing at a good pace, receiving hundreds of migrants because of the many employment opportunities, and confident citizens borrowing, optimistic about future prospects. It is true that some experts, including Commissioner Joaquin Almunia, warned of a Spanish housing bubble, but almost no one paid them any attention. One year later, on 15 September 2008, Lehman Brothers went bankrupt. Thereafter nothing was the same. In December the US government officially announced that the US had entered recession. None of that seemed to affect Spain, or so said its government, which argued that those distant events would not negatively affect the country.[1]

In March 2008 general elections were held in Spain; the Socialist Party (PSOE) won again as in 2004, without an absolute majority, but as it only lacked seven seats (it won 169 out of 350), the Prime Minister, Jose Luis Rodriguez Zapatero, considered it a 'sufficient majority' to govern without making a legislative pact. So, for the first time in the short political life of the 1978 Constitution, a Prime Minster was elected by a simple majority of the Congress of Deputies. As the months passed, this strategy proved very dangerous because the Socialists had to negotiate a pact for each bill, thus giving the image of some improvisation, if not a constant image of weakness.[2]

In purely economic terms, the new government had to correct its previous economic forecasts downward. The Minister of Finance, Pedro Solbes, in March 2008 reduced his growth forecasts for 2008: no longer the 3.1 per cent that was calculated in the general budget, but 2.3 per cent. Throughout the year,

---

1 For the economic context that brought about the reform of the Spanish Constitution, see J. Ruiz Heurta, 'Algunas consideraciones sobre la reforma del artículo 135 de la Constitución española', in E. Álvarez Conde and C. Souto Galván (eds), *La constitucionalización de la estabilidad presupuestaria* (Universidad Rey Juan Carlos, 2012), pp. 145-168, at p. 146.

2 J.R. Montero Gibert and I. Lago Peñas (eds), *Elecciones generales 2008* (CIS, 2010).

the forecast proved overly optimistic: GDP grew by only 0.9 per cent, and many other economic indicators also deteriorated. In January 2009 Standard & Poor's downgraded the AAA rating that it had given Spain until then. This rating has not stopped falling since then, given the huge budget deficit, which in 2010 was 11.2 per cent and in 2011 8.5 per cent of GDP (€85bn for a GDP of €1,073,383 million). It seems unlikely that a 5.4 per cent deficit will be achieved, as forecast by the new conservative government and the Eurogroup in 2012, because by 30 May a deficit of €36,364,000 or 3.41 per cent of GDP had accumulated. In June 2012, following the rescue of the Spanish banks with a loan of up to €100bn, Moody's downgraded the rating given to Spain's sovereign debt to 'Baa3' (low approval), placing it in a negative perspective because, in its opinion, the bailout 'will increase' the burden of debt and not improve the 'limited' access to financial markets or the 'continued weakness' of the Spanish economy.

In 2008 the socialist government adopted measures to stimulate the economy, estimated at 5 per cent of GDP, designed to combat the 'economic downturn' (the term used by government institutions instead of 'crisis'). In that way, Spain aligned itself with the group of states that responded to the crisis with more spending. Thus, it declared a general reduction in income tax of €400, granted a 'baby cheque' of €2,500 to each newborn or adopted child, and launched an infrastructure plan of €8bn. The impression of most economists is that these measures did not yield any result: Spain increased public spending to €67.264 million between 2007 and 2011, 6.4 per cent of GDP, but that same GDP fell by 3.3 per cent in 2009 and unemployment increased exponentially.[3]

Another economic front, opened up by the government in 2008, was the financial sector, hitherto described repeatedly as the most solvent in the world. For this the government created a rescue fund, the FROB, for troubled banks, with €99bn. Previously, the Bank of Spain had had to rescue the Savings Bank of Castilla la Mancha, and in the following years there was a policy of bank mergers that led to the 45 banks that existed in 2007 being reduced to 16 by 2011. But the worst was to come in 2012, when Bankia, a bank established in December 2010 by the merger of seven savings banks and the fourth biggest bank in Spain, had to be partially nationalized to prevent bankruptcy. It is calculated that €19bn is needed to save it, in addition to the €4.5bn the state has given it already. Specifically to meet this rescue and that of other smaller banks (such as Caixa Catalunya) the Eurogroup decided on 16 June 2012 to give Spain a credit line of up to €100bn, an operation considered by the vast majority of political, economic and social experts, except for the Popular Party, as a rescue.

In January 2009 the Bank of Spain announced that the country had gone into recession, which had not happened since 1993. And in February of that year the Ministry of Employment reported more bad data: an increase in unemployment of 6 per cent. A year later, in March 2010, the unemployment rate had reached

3 F. Parra Luna, 'Cuatro errores de la política económica en España', *Economistas* 128 (2011): 73-81.

20 per cent of the workforce, 4.6 million people out of work; and two years later, in March 2012, that figure had risen to 24.4 per cent, 5,639,500 unemployed. The projections for the future, at least until the end of 2013, are also negative.

In May 2010 Prime Minister Zapatero admitted for the first time that there was a financial crisis and announced a radical change in his economic policy:[4] austerity measures would be taken amounting to about 1.5 per cent of GDP. There would be a cut in civil servants' salaries, the 'baby cheque' would disappear and pensions would be frozen. VAT was increased from 16 per cent to 18 per cent. In addition, in June 2010 there was a reform of the labour laws, which was criticized by the trade unions. After winning the November 2011 elections, the Popular Party (which had opposed the reforms of the Socialist Party) made further reforms, in February 2012, that were much more favourable to business interests, especially by facilitating hiring workers at lower cost, weakening the worker's permanent connection with the company and reducing workers' redundancy pay. The reaction of the trade unions to both reforms and the higher retirement age (which would materialize in January 2011) was a call for general strikes, one on 29 September 2010 and another on 29 March 2012. The general impression is that the latter was much more popular than the former, reflecting the growing unrest of the Spanish people.

In June 2011, Prime Minister Zapatero announced that the general elections would be held on 20 November, thus not waiting until the end of the legislature in March 2012. Never before had the dissolution of parliament been announced so far in advance; on the contrary, previous early dissolutions had been made unannounced. The election result was a spectacular victory with an absolute majority for the opposition party, the conservative Popular Party (PP), and the collapse of the ruling Socialist Party (PSOE). Since the new conservative government took office on 21 December 2012, its policy has been similar to that of the last socialist government: fiscal austerity, increased taxes and legal reforms that cut social rights in order to contain public expenses and so reduce the deficit.

In September 2011, that is during a 'time out' of a legislature that was about to end, parliament very quickly approved the reform of Art. 135 of the Constitution to constitutionalize a limit on public debt and to strengthen its payment guarantees. The new text was agreed between the two major parties, the PSOE and the PP, who initiated reform by themselves, without consulting the other parties, thus departing from the precedent of 1992, when Art. 13 of the Constitution was amended in consultation with all relevant parties in the Congress of Deputies.

4 He gave his own explanation for the change in his economic policy in J.L. Rodríguez Zapatero, 'La España de las reformas en el horizonte 2020', in F. Jáuregui and M. Menéndez (eds), *La España que necesitamos, del 20-N a 2020* (Almuzara, 2012), pp. 25-34. My opinion on that is in A. Ruiz Robledo, 'La grandeza de Zapatero', *El País*, 31 May 2010.

How the Crisis Affected Constitutional Interpretation and Jurisprudence

The Reactions of Citizens and Social Forces

The financial crisis has affected, in the first place, what we might call the 'popular interpretation of the Constitution', as citizens have seen their living conditions worsened by the crisis, and legislative changes to combat it have reduced some of their socio-economic rights, which had been seen as independent of the situation and fully consolidated, such as the retirement age. Thus, there has been a feeling that the Constitution has been devalued and has become in the eyes of many citizens a text that is unable to protect them, as they understand it, to maintain a certain standard of living. It turns out that not only do many social rights have to be included in the supreme law of a legal system, but also that there must be economic development to meet their economic costs.

On the other hand, according to the Spanish political tradition, the Constitution has been used in the political conflict against some anti-crisis measures, both by challenges brought to the Constitutional Court by legitimate organs[5] and by using the Constitution in the political debate in which the government was accused of violating the supreme law. Although in Spain it is common for the opposition parties and the trade unions and other social forces to appeal to the Constitution to criticize the decisions of the government majority with which they are unhappy, branding them as 'unconstitutional', it is quite different to invoke the Constitution to criticize the actions of individuals. However, in these times of economic turmoil, in which so many people have lost their homes because they cannot pay the mortgage that financed the purchase, various social groups, such as the Association of People Affected by Foreclosures and Auctions (AFES) and the Platform of People Affected by the Mortgage (PAH), have repeatedly cited the 'right to enjoy decent and adequate housing' in Art. 47 of the Constitution to oppose evictions pursued by the banks when their clients fail to meet their mortgage payments. And the truth is that this argument has been partially accepted by the conservative government, partly due to the Constitution and partly due to the force of their requests: Decreto-Ley 6/2012, on urgent measures for the protection of mortgagors without resources, provides a number of mechanisms to allow the restructuring of mortgage debt of those with special difficulties in meeting payment. In particular, it set up a Code of Good Practice, to which banks may voluntarily subscribe, and established the DATION, a system to prevent situations in which, if a person's mortgage debt exceeds the value of the property, the mortgagor not only loses the

5 Fifty Deputies, fifty Senators, the Autonomous Governments and Parliaments, and the Defender of the People (the Ombudsman) (Art. 162.1 of the Constitution). As the trade unions could not lodge this appeal, as they usually do (normally with scant success), they asked the Ombudsman to do it. See, for example, the controversial petition of the UGT (General Union of Workers) to appeal against DL 3/2012; available at http://www.ugt.es/actualidad/2012/abril/Recurso%20inconstitDPueblo.pdf.

property, but also continues to maintain a debt for the difference between the value of that property and the higher amount of the loan. As the Code of Good Practice is only a recommendation and not a binding rule, social groups have considered this to be an insufficient measure, and in April 2012, following an acceptance by the Central Electoral Board, they started to collect the 500,000 signatures required to process a citizens' initiative bill in Congress entitled 'on Regulating the DATION, to Halt Evictions and Social Rent'.[6]

The Extensive Use of Decree-Laws

The last four years have produced a number of regulations having the force of law to tackle the financial crisis. Most of them were originally decree-laws approved first by the socialist government, then by the conservative government: Decreto-Ley (decree-law) 2/2008 on measures to boost economic activity; Decreto-Ley 7/2008 on Urgent Economic and Financial Matters concerning the Concerted Action Plan of the eurozone countries; Decreto-Ley 3/2009 on urgent measures on taxation, finance and bankruptcy to changing economic conditions; Decreto-Ley 8/2010 adopting extraordinary measures to reduce public deficit; Decreto-Ley 16/2011 establishing the Deposit Guarantee Fund for Credit Institutions; Decreto-Law 19/2012 on urgent measures to liberalize trade and certain services; and so on.

Undoubtedly, all these decree-laws (69 in the period 2007-2011) were motivated by the need to address the serious economic situation promptly, so that it was easy to argue that they met the requirement of 'extraordinary and urgent necessity' demanded by Art. 86 of the Constitution, which had been described by the Constitutional Court itself in the 1990s as 'problematic economic situations' (STC 23/1993). However, from the standpoint of legal theory that practice assumes that a legislative instrument as exceptional as the decree-law can be commonly used, and fills a normative technical position hitherto unknown in our system of sources. It is enough to note that while traditionally it was uncommon for more than 15 decree-laws to be approved in any given year, 20 were approved in 2011 and 19 in the first five months of 2012 alone. But if the amount is important, no less so is the quality: in Spanish constitutional history there have always been very important decree-laws, but most were motivated by the urgency of addressing social needs of limited national significance (such as natural disasters in particular areas). Some of the most important were intended to apply only once, such as Decreto-Ley 2/1983 on the expropriation of Rumasa for reasons of public utility and social interest. However, currently the proportion is reversed, and most of the decrees dictated by the government regarding core aspects of Spanish social life, such as labour relations and banking regulation, are intended to be permanent.

---

6 The legal aspects of this legislative initiative can be followed on the web page of Junta Electoral Central at http://www.juntaelectoralcentral.es. For political and social aspects, see the web pages of the AFES and the PAH at http://asociacionafes.com and http://afectadosporlahipoteca.wordpress.com.

From the perspective of separation of powers, this implies an accentuation of the preponderance of the executive over the legislature, the former being already very powerful in the Spanish parliamentary system combined with strong party discipline. This dominance of the state executive is also replicated in the Autonomous Communities, such as Catalonia and Andalusia; under their new Statutes of Autonomy, approved since 2006, their governments are authorized to issue decree-laws, which they do often.

Several of the decree-laws passed by the Spanish government profoundly altered the Workers' Statute, such as the Decreto-Ley 10/2010 on urgent measures to reform the labour market, the Decreto-Ley 7/2011 on urgent measures for the reform of collective bargaining (Zapatero's government) and the Decreto-Ley 3/2012 for urgent action to reform the labour market (Rajoy's government). This emergency legislation is a problem for the theory of sources to the extent that if not directly unconstitutional, it forces a reinterpretation of what matters are barred from legislation by decree-law. According to Art. 86.1 of the Constitution, these are 'the fundamental legal system of the state institutions, the rights, freedoms and duties of the citizens contained in Part I, the system of Autonomous Communities, or the general electoral law'. Constitutional doctrine[7] has always considered that these rights in Part I cannot be regulated by decree-law. The Constitutional Court also appears to share that opinion, because when it had to judge whether the Constitution allowed the expropriation by decree-law of private property, which is guaranteed in Art. 33, it held that a decree-law could not regulate the legal system of private property, although it could, as in this case, 'affect' a particular situation, that is, that of the expropriated companies.[8] As a more recent case puts it,

> it should be noted also that, as regards the interpretation of the material limits of the use of the decree-law, we have always maintained a balanced position that avoids extreme views, so that the restrictive clause of Art. 86.1 of the Constitution ('cannot affect ...') must be understood in a way that neither reduces the decree-law to nothing, though it is a legal instrument provided by the Constitution, or permits decree-laws to regulate the general system of rights, duties and liberties of Part I.[9]

If, then, the Workers' Statute develops the right to work in Art. 35 of the Constitution and the right to collective bargaining in Art. 37, it seems very difficult to see that the amendments made by the various executive orders to date are not a general

7 A.M. Carmona Conteras, *La configuración constitucional del Decreto-Ley* (CEPC, 1997).

8 STC 111 /1983, Decreto-Ley de expropriación de RUMASA.

9 STC 100/2012, Prórroga de la Tarifa Especial del Arbitrio Insular Canario por el Decreto-Ley 7/1993.

regulation of these two rights,[10] as indeed is evident not only in the decree-laws of the same title, but also in its explanatory memorandum. Thus, Decreto-Ley 7/2011 on urgent measures for reform of collective bargaining states:

> It is, in short, a reform of collective bargaining to provide more and better collective bargaining, more orderly and better collective agreements, so they can fulfil a more useful and effective role for the regulation of labour relations and working conditions, and contribute in the short, medium and long term to the growth of the Spanish economy, improved competitiveness and productivity in Spanish companies, and thus, employment growth and reduced unemployment.

It does seem, therefore, that the theory can be applied that these are rules that do not affect the general system of rights, as the Constitution itself has been bent to reduce salaries of employees of public companies ordered by decree-law.[11] Should we now change our interpretation of rights that cannot be regulated by decree-law and restrict them only to Division 1, of Part I of the Constitution? Or should we simply continue maintaining our traditional theory that the rights of Divisions 1 and 2 cannot be regulated by decree-law, and bypass in silence all these decree-laws issued in exceptional economic circumstances, a break with the juridical life of the state?

In any case, if the Constitutional Court ends by handing down judgments in which it examines whether any of these decree-laws, which undoubtedly affect

10 The Workers' Statute had already previously been amended by decree-law but never to the degree to which it has been done in these years of crisis. The Constitutional Court has analysed some of the articles so modified, but not from the perspective of procedural matters that prohibit it from being regulated by decree-law, but only from the material perspective to see if its content was contrary to the Spanish Constitution. See, for example, STC 253/2004, *Art. 12.4 of the Law on the Statute of Workers*. This constitutional perspective is still an indirect way to validate the amendment of the Workers' Statute by decree-law because although the plaintiffs did not argue the violation of the limits of Art. 86 of the Constitution, the Constitutional Court could have done it *ex officio* as permitted by Art. 84 of the Organic Law on the Constitutional Court.

11 Decreto-Ley 8/2010, by adopting extraordinary measures to reduce the budget deficit, reduced the salaries of public employees by 5 per cent. The National Court presented a question of unconstitutionality on the grounds that as the decree-law modified collective agreements of public enterprises it had violated the right to collective bargaining. However, the Constitutional Court gave an emphatic negative: 'the legal provisions questioned are not an "involvement" in the constitutional sense of the term, the right to collective bargaining recognized in Art. 37.1 of the Constitution, as no general rules governing this right, nor the sanctity of the collective agreement stands as one of its essential elements, so they have not crossed the material border that Art. 86.1 of the Constitution imposes on the decree-law to not violate the rights, duties and freedoms of Part I of the Constitution' (Decision 85/2011); this doctrine was then repeated in 12 other cases rejecting similar questions of unconstitutionality in other courts.

the general system of the right to work and the right to collective bargaining, have overstepped the boundaries marked by Art. 86 of the Constitution, it is most likely that it will have no legal or political effect, beyond the expected declaration of unconstitutionality of laws which have already been repealed.[12] This is because when these hypothetical judgments are made, it is highly probable that the decree-laws will not be in force, and many of their normative contents will have again been modified. This will happen not only because they were processed as laws after being validated by Congress,[13] but because the Constitutional Court gives judgments with such an excessive delay that when adopted, several changes in government and a number of new laws will have occurred, so that it is not surprising that it declares unconstitutional laws which have already been repealed. We shall return to this issue later; now, we shall limit ourselves to taking as examples three recent judgments that resolve cases of economic matters more than ten years behind schedule, and rule on laws that at the time of the judgment were no longer in force: the aforementioned STC 100/2012, dealing with Decreto-Ley 7/1993, which has its origin in a question of unconstitutionality of the High Court of the Canary Islands lodged in 2001; STC 137/2011, *Real Decreto-Ley 4/2000 medidas urgentes de liberalización en el sector inmobiliario y transportes*, which pronounced the unconstitutionality of Art. 1 of this decree-law which had been repealed 11 years before and STC 19/2012, *Ley 40/1998 del impuesto sobre la renta de las personas físicas*, which declared the unconstitutionality of various provisions repealed in 2004. In my opinion, the stance adopted by the Constitutional Court of pronouncing sentence on laws already repealed would be very commendable if these decisions were issued within a reasonable time, but with the long delay that has accumulated in the High Court, they only serve to delay their decisions about laws that are in force, thus demonstrating the truth of Voltaire's assertion that the best is the enemy of the good. This also creates a stimulus for governments who do not respect the Constitution to pass notoriously

12 The Constitutional Court has maintained that the fact that a rule has been abrogated does not prevent it from ruling on it. So for the specific case of a decree-law appealed by the Catalan parliament for lack of the prerequisite of urgent and extraordinary need, it stated: 'The fact that Art. 43 of Royal Decree-Law 6/2000 has been repealed by Act 1/2004 on business hours, does not render this process pointless because, according to the approach taken by this Court (STC 189/2005 and doctrine cited therein), it follows that the repeal of that Art. 43 does not prevent us controlling whether the exercise of the power conferred on the government by Art. 86.1 of the Constitution was performed following the requirements of that constitutional provision, because we do so to ensure the proper exercise of the power to issue decree-laws within the constitutional framework, deciding on the validity or invalidity of the challenged rules without regard to whether it is in force or repealed at the time judgment is pronounced (STC 31/2011, Royal DL 6/2000, on urgent measures to intensify competition in the markets in goods and services).'

13 For example, the Royal Decree-Law 3/2012 on urgent measures for labour market reform has been filed as a bill and was finally adopted by Congress on 27 June 2012.

unconstitutional laws, safe in the knowledge that when the Constitutional Court gives its judgment much time will have passed.

Judicial Interpretation

To date, the Constitutional Court has not had occasion to make any judgment on a regulation having the force of law that was designed to combat the financial crisis that began in 2007. Admittedly, it has given some decisions, like the one on the reform of Art. 135 of the Constitution, which will be discussed later, and another refusing an appeal against the declaration of a state of emergency. I have already mentioned the decision holding that Decreto-Ley 8/2010, by adopting extraordinary measures to reduce the deficit, would not result in a general regulation of the right to collective bargaining. I now add, at my own risk, that in addition to purely legal arguments provided by that decision of the Constitutional Court, it seems that it also reflects *the will not to make an interpretation that would hinder the government's measures against the crisis* and to meet its European commitments on the maximum deficit: we can imagine the economic impact that would have resulted if the Court had accepted the thesis that the government could not unilaterally cut the pay of public employees. This accounting for political, social and economic decisions in exceptional situations, far from being novel, is perfectly theorized by constitutional theory, which considered it permissible mainly because the Constitutional Court has 'a political responsibility to maintain the rule of law and its functional capacity'.[14]

It is expected that the coming years will produce decisions in which the Court analyses some of the laws now being passed to overcome the financial crisis, for these laws are far from being adopted by consensus and organs with standing to bring a constitutional challenge to the Constitutional Court are using it through the various routes allowed by Art. 162 of the Constitution.[15] Interestingly, the challenges to the anti-crisis legislation being presented to the Constitutional Court do not usually come from 50 Deputies or Senators, although the opposition voted against the majority of these rules, first the PP against the PSOE and now the current parliamentary majority of the PP against the PSOE, an attitude that responds to different sensitivities when interpreting the Constitution and reflects what we might call ideological conflicts. On the contrary, these challenges come from more autonomous institutions that believe that the laws have invaded their area of responsibility or, conversely, from the central government invoking EU law.[16]

14 K. Larenz, *Metodología de la Ciencia del Derecho* (Ariel, 1994), p. 504.

15 So the Report of the Constitutional Court of 2011 included 31 appeals and 51 questions of unconstitutionality in that year. We can thus say that roughly one-third of appeals and one-tenth of the questions concern laws issued to combat the crisis.

16 See, for example, the appeal of unconstitutionality no. 1886-2012, promoted by the Generalitat of Catalonia against the Royal Decree-Law 8/2011 on measures to

Although there is still no Constitutional Court ruling on anti-crisis legislation, the Court has in recent years adopted some decisions containing a doctrine that seems readily applicable to the interpretation of that legislation, such as the judgments on Law 44/2002, on measures to reform the financial system, which carried out a thorough reform of the legal system of the savings banks.[17] These decisions also show the delay of the Constitutional Court and its effects as discussed above: the bulk of its legal reasoning hinges on the claim of Law 44/2002 to prevent the Andalusian government from exercising its legislative and executive powers over the savings bank, the Caja de Ahorros de Cordoba, founded by the Church, a controversy that was very important in 2002, but had no real significance in 2011, when the Constitutional Court gave judgment in favour of the Andalusian government, since control of Cajasur had been taken over in May 2010 by the Bank of Spain, which then gave all its property rights and obligations to the Caja de Ahorros de Bilbao-Bizcaya. The Andalusian government took no part in this process, beyond a few conversations and courtesy visits to the President of the Autonomous Community.

Another group of judgments of the Constitutional Court during 2011 that will be useful in interpreting the new legislation is that relating to Law 18/2001 on General Budgetary Stability. Its doctrine is undoubtedly applicable to the recently approved Organic Law 2/2012 on budgetary stability and financial sustainability. The first judgment on the Law 18/2001 is STC 134/2011, in which the Constitutional Court dismissed the appeal of unconstitutionality lodged by the Catalan parliament against Act 18/2001 and Law 5/2001, 'Supplemental to the

---

support mortgage borrowers, public expenditure control and cancellation of debts owed by companies and autonomous communities; the appeal of unconstitutionality no. 6642-2011, sponsored by the Canaries Government against Law 2/2011. Of course, sometimes the same appeal is motivated by both ideological and regional differences. For example, the positive conflict of competences that the government has brought against the Autonomous Community of Andalusia for the Order of the Andalusian Ministry of Education 13 February 2012, announcing a selection process of 2,389 places for non-university teaching staff. In this case, the central government formally attributed to the Junta de Andalusia (controlled by the PSOE) violation of the basic state legislation on employment, but there was an *ideological* conflict underlying the controversy: the Andalusian PSOE's decision not to increase the number of students per class, against the state law adopted by the PP.

17 The first judgment is STC 118/2011, which was followed by STC 138/2011 and 139/2011, 151/2011 and 160/2011. Apart from the controversy over Cajasur mentioned in the text, in STC 118/2011 the Constitutional Court fixed the limits between state and Autonomous Communities in the area of the internal organization of the savings bank. Thus it considers that the state has the competences to fix the limits of public participation in the savings bank's governing organs and the groups of depositors and employees. However, it considered that this was a matter of precepts that are not basic and therefore the Arts of Law 44/2002 that fix the maximum and minimum limits of appointment periods of the Council Members, the maximum duration of the mandate and the restrictions on re-election.

General Law of Budgetary Stability'.[18] The doctrine laid down in this judgment was then completed with STC 157/2011, which for the first time considers the amendment to Art. 135 of the Constitution. Eleven other decisions were issued later on the same legislation: STCs 185/2011 to 189/2011, 195/2011 to 199/2011, and 203/2011.

To resolve the appeal against the laws of budgetary stability, STC 134/2011 started from the consideration that they were adopted to implement EU law in this area and found their support in the constitutional mandate of Art. 149.1.13, which gives the state competence for the basis and coordination of general planning of economic activity, a competence for overall direction of the economy, which includes the budget. Therefore, the definition of 'budgetary stability', understood as a situation of 'balance or surplus', is configured as a general economic policy orientation for which the state is authorized by Art. 149.1.13 of the Constitution. Equally constitutional is the provision for an inter-administrative compensation system in the case of the state's financial responsibility to the EU in terms of budgetary stability.

The law on budgetary stability that was appealed established a procedure for a quantitative determination of the objective of budgetary stability that should be calculated within the Council of Fiscal and Financial Policy, and occurs only when no agreement in this body is reached; then the Autonomous Communities were required to approve their budgets as, at least, balanced. According to the Constitutional Court, these decisions do not violate the autonomy of the Communities because these are decisions that affect the general economic equilibrium and, for that matter, should be adopted uniformly for the entire system; a uniformity of law that first ensures the imposition of, at least, a balanced budget and, second, through a process in the Fiscal Policy Council, where every one of the Autonomous Communities is represented.

The Constitutional Court also rejected the unconstitutionality of other provisions of the stability laws that were challenged because they sought to establish controls that, in the opinion of the appellants, violated the financial autonomy of the Autonomous Communities, but which the Constitutional Court always considered justified by the state powers on the basis of credit and general management of the economy: for example, the necessary authorization from the state of credit operations undertaken by those Autonomous Communities that failed to achieve the aim of budgetary stability; or the obligation imposed on the Communities to conduct a financial and economic plan for correcting the imbalance when the principle of budgetary stability was not respected, either in budgeting or in their implementation. Moreover, the application of the basic findings of the General Budgetary Law to local authorities is also fully constitutional, and the

---

18 See F. Uría Fernández, 'Una sentencia oportuna e imprescindible', in E. García de Enterría Martínez-Carande et al. (eds), *Administración y justicia: un análisis jurisprudencial: liber amicorum Tomás-Ramón Fernández*, vol. 1 (Civitas, 2012), pp. 373-395.

state intervention that this law permits, based on the competences of economic coordination, does not invade the powers of financial supervision of the Government of Catalonia and other executive bodies of the Autonomous Communities.

Also due to the delays in resolving cases, the ordinary courts have had few opportunities to rule on anti-crisis laws that are being challenged in court. In my opinion, the two most important laws of this type for which the Supreme Court has already given decisions have been Royal Decree 1565/2010 for regulating and amending certain aspects of the activity of production of electric power in the special regime, and Royal Decree 1673/2010, which declared a state of emergency for the normalization of the essential public service of air transport. These two have been considered lawful, justified by legal arguments behind which we can also discern the *theory of consequences*, already mentioned in connection with the opinion of the Constitutional Court Decreto-Ley 8/2010 leading the Supreme Court to avoid a decision to annul some decisions that might have very negative economic and political consequences for the state.

Royal Decree 1565/2010, reducing subsidies to photovoltaic companies, modified what the government had approved in Royal Decree 661/2007, which was immediately considered by these companies and their association, the National Association of Renewable Energy Producers (Anpier), to be unconstitutional, since they argued that it violated legal certainty and non-retroactivity of provisions restrictive of individual rights (Art. 9 of the Constitution). At first glance, the complaint seemed well founded; if the holders of the 56,000 photovoltaic installations in Spain in 2010 – so many that Spain had become the third largest photovoltaic power producer in the world – had decided to invest in them, it was because they were attracted by subsidies that the government had offered in the Decree of 2007; if in 2010 the government reduced the period of time that it would pay the premium, legal certainty was affected in the most painful way that could happen to a company: by producing grave financial loss.

Meanwhile, the Supreme Court, which studied the issue in more depth, concluded that no violation of any constitutional provision or principle of law had occurred because the new law still maintained a 'reasonable return' for photovoltaic companies. The argument used has to be considered in the light of the economic situation of general crisis in Spain, but it does add some language implying that if the companies do not earn what they expected it is their fault for relying on the government:

> The virtual elimination of business risk that accepts the regulated rate, without competing on price with other market players, is in itself an advantage over the electricity industry that is subject to the vicissitudes of competition, an advantage whose reverse, among others, is the possibility of the alteration of administrative actions to changing circumstances (with respect to minimum levels of profitability that is currently not the case). Officials or private operators who abandon the market, even if they do so more or less 'induced' by generous

> compensation offered by the regulatory framework, without consideration for the assumption of significant risks, knew or should have known that the regulatory public framework, approved at one time, was consistent with the conditions then prevailing with regard to the economic scenario and the electricity demand forecasts made at that time, and they could not subsequently be oblivious to changes in relevant economic data, or the logical reaction of the authorities to bring it into line with new circumstances. If these involve adjustments in many other productive sectors, with obvious difficulties for their activity, it is not unreasonable for those also to extend to the renewable energy sector that wants to continue receiving regulated rates instead of submitting to market mechanisms (bilateral contracts and sale in the organized market). This is even more so in situations of widespread economic crisis and in the case of electricity, with the growth of tariff deficits that, in some part, derives from the impact on the calculation of the access fees on the compensation of those by way of the regulated tariff, as costs attributable to the electrical system.[19]

For its part, Royal Decree 1673/2010 was issued to end the undeclared covert strike of air traffic controllers that was blocking the Spanish skies, to the extent that on 3 December 2010 the authorities agreed to the closure of Spanish airspace. This was a protest against their new working conditions established by Law 9/2010, regulating air traffic services, establishing the obligations of the civilian providers of such services and laying down working conditions for civil air traffic controllers. Royal Decree 1673/2010 declared a state of emergency for the normalization of essential public service aviation for 15 days, and various measures were taken, basically consisting of militarizing the air traffic controllers, submitting them to the authority of the Air Force Chief of Staff and establishing that the Code of Military Justice applied to them. With these measures, the government immediately brought an end to a strike that had caused great economic and social damage and was deeply unpopular. But when the 15 days expired, which is the maximum period for which the government itself may declare a state of emergency, and the state of emergency had to be lifted, there was a risk of the resumption of the strike, and the government decided on 15 December 2010 to ask Congress for an extension of one month. Congress granted it with the support of the PSOE, the Convergence and Union Party (CiU), the PNV (the Basque Nationalist Party) and the Canarian

---

19 STS (3-3) 4253/2012. Before this, some 20 similar sentences were handed down, the most important being STS (3-3ª) 2320/2012. The Supreme Court doctrine did nor convince Anpier, whose lawyer wrote a rather critical commentary: J. Castro-Gil Amigo, 'Comentarios a la sentencia del Tribunal Supremo o la indefensión de los canijos', *Diario La Ley* (2012): 7895. The truth is that the government was not very clear as to when that level of 'reasonable profit' would be reached because in Royal Decree 1673/2010 a period of 25 years was established, which later was increased, first to 28 years (Royal DL 14/2010 for urgent measures for the correction of the tariff deficit of the electric sector) and afterwards to 30 years (Law 2/2011 on Sustainable Economy).

Coalition (CC), with the abstention of the PP and the United Left (IU), and the Union, Progress and Democracy (UPD) and other minority parties voting against. A dispassionate comparison of the Decree to the Organic Law 4/1981 on the States of Emergency, Exception and Siege (LOEAES) leads one to conclude that the measures adopted therein were not allowed either by LOEAES or the Constitution, since in Art. 117.5 it states that military jurisdiction is exercised in the strictly military ambit and only in cases of siege.[20]

However, the Supreme Court avoided comparing the texts by considering that the proclamation of a state of emergency is a political act solely controlled by Congress and not by the judicial power:

> [The Decree] was issued by the Government of Spain as the constitutional body exercising functions under the aforementioned Part V of the Constitution. Let the government account for its actions to the Congress of Deputies and, thus, offer it the possibility of exercising all means of control that the law allows. And so Congress has to decide, at the request of the government, whether to authorize the extension of the state of emergency in the same terms as was declared by Royal Decree 1673/2010 which is challenged here. The final conclusion must be, therefore, that the decision taken by Congress is not an administrative action that can be controlled by the contentious-administrative system: it is beyond the generic scope defined for judicial review in Art. 106.1 of the Constitution, and does not fit within the scope specific to the contentious-administrative courts as defined by the LJCA Arts 1 & 2.[21]

Constitutional and Institutional Reforms Triggered by the Crisis

Some Problems in the Processing of Constitutional Reform

If, in the summer of 1992, the first reform of the Spanish Constitution of 1978 relating to Art. 13.2 was made hastily, the second reform was even more rapid, dizzyingly so, or '*express*', as the media have described it: the former Prime Minister announced in the Congress of the Deputies on 23 August 2011 that he

20 See C. Vidal Prado and D. Delgado Ramos, 'Algunas consideraciones sobre la declaración del estado de alarma y su prórroga', *Revista Española de Derecho Constitucional* 92 (2011): 243-265. My opinion, coinciding with the majority critical of the Decree, has been expressed in 'Mucho ruido y pocas condenas', *El País*, 10 December 2010.

21 Decision of the Supreme Court, Contencioso, 857/2011, which was then followed by 12 other decisions, all on the same lines. The controllers tried to lodge an appeal of unconstitutionality to the Constitutional Court, but this too was disallowed because it was considered that the decision to extend it adopted by Congress was an act equivalent to laws with the force of law and therefore could not be appealed by private citizens (Decision 7/2012).

had agreed with the PP on a constitutional amendment to 'establish a rule to ensure budgetary stability in the medium and long term' and by 7 September it had been fully approved by parliament. By way of anecdote, he did not announce it in a special appearance, but while arguing the validation of a decree-law. In between those two dates, on 26 August, the PSOE and the PP jointly submitted a proposal for reform of Art. 135, requesting it be submitted to the fast-track procedure and approved in a single reading. Four days later it was considered by Congress, which agreed to deal with it directly, in a single reading with a very short period of only two days for the submission of amendments. On 2 September, Congress rejected 24 amendments that had been tabled and approved only a grammatical correction proposed by the President of Congress in consultation with the director of the Royal Academy of Language.[22] Two compromise amendments proposed by the PSOE-PP to two amendments proposed by the CiU could not be voted on because such amendments can only be passed unanimously, and the IU opposed them, a position endorsed by the Parliamentary Standing Orders but which does not seem to square very well with appeals to consensus. The text was adopted by 316 votes in favour and five against. There were no abstentions, but there were groups that failed to vote due to the method by which the reform was processed: some chose to leave the chamber (like the Galician nationalists) and others remained but did not vote (the CiU, the PNV and the IU).

In the Senate, the reform bill was dealt with equally rapidly, none of the 29 amendments being accepted since in that case the text would have had to be sent back to Congress, and neither party wanted the matter to be delayed more than absolutely necessary. So, the full Senate approved the amendment on 6 September by 233 in favour and three against. Again, the representatives of the small parties did not vote, either because they were absent (the Galician Nationalist Bloc (BNG) and the Republican Left of Catalonia (ERC)) or because they did not push the voting buttons (the CiU, the PNV and the Catalan Green Socialists and Communists (ICV)). As within 15 days neither one-tenth of the deputies (35) nor one-tenth of the senators (26) had demanded the calling of a referendum as provided for in Art. 167.3 of the Constitution, the final text of the reform was sent to the King, who on 27 September approved, promulgated and ordered its publication, which took place the same day, as well as its entry into force. On that same day, 27 September, the Official Bulletin of Spain (BOE) published the decree of dissolution of parliament and the calling of elections for 20 November. From this coincidence, it seems clear that the urgency of the reform process was marked by the desire to maintain the date of 20 November as election day.

22 In Art. 135.3, there was a slight grammatical error: 'en relación al producto interior bruto del Estado', when the correct form is 'en relación con'. However, the most important semantic error of that expression was not corrected: the interior product is not of the state, but of Spain. My opinion on these questions and the way to process the reform is in A. Ruiz Robledo, 'Por qué lo llaman Estado cuando quieren decir España', *El País*, 6 September 2011.

In addition to the criticism from the small parties, which led to the unusual situation of their not voting for the reform and their subsequent appeal, which was not admitted by the Constitutional Court,[23] this *express* procedure provoked doctrinal criticism because with its speed a national debate on the desirability of a clause in the Constitution of budgetary stability was missed, and unlike the 1992 reform it was done without consensus, especially avoiding any dialogue with both the Autonomous Communities and the local authorities, all profoundly affected, and was not even presented with the support of a technical report from the Council of State. And if criticisms abounded about the procedure, there were no fewer on the content: the drafting of the new Art. 135 is too open to have legislative effect, so its usefulness is void and its inclusion in the Constitution superfluous; also its provisions will not be fully effective until 2020 and it constitutionalizes a liberal policy that was adopted not by the free decision of the parliamentarians but by market pressure and *Merkozy*, the portmanteau nickname of the German Chancellor and the French President who at their meeting on 16 August expressed concern about Spanish finances.[24]

My opinion about the procedure is not as fiercely negative as that of most academics. In August 2011 Spain was in an extremely difficult financial situation, with markets reluctant to buy Spanish debt, not because of any conspiracy or because they are 'dictators', but for a reasonable concern only to lend to those who can pay back the loan. Therefore it was necessary and urgent to send a signal to those markets of the political and legal commitment to pay, but the reform also sent a signal inward towards the Spanish public administration, indicating that a policy of austerity was essential. Of course, had there been sufficient time it would have been necessary to consult with the Autonomous Communities and municipalities, and seek the opinion of the Council of State, avoiding the urgent procedure of one sole reading, and even calling a referendum.[25] But when the house of the state is

23 Order 9/2012 held in the appeal against unconstitutionality 5241/2011 lodged by the deputies of the IU. On this and on the procedure in general, see P. García-Escudero Márquez, 'La acelerada tramitación parlamentaria de la reforma del artículo 135 de la Constitución (Especial consideración de la inadmisión de enmiendas. Los límites al derecho de enmienda en la reforma constitucional)', *Teoría y realidad constitucional* 29 (2012): 165-198.

24 For all the doctrinal criticism on the procedure followed, two articles are worth reading, with their very expressive titles: F. de Carreras, 'Useless, Empty and Wrongly Processed' [in Spanish], *La Vanguardia*, 1 September 2011; R. Blanco Valdés, 'The 2011 Reform: The Temple of the Muses' [in Spanish], *Claves de la razón práctica* 16 (2011): 11-15.

25 See E. Álvarez Conde, 'Presentación: la reforma (preventiva) constitucional de 2011', in Conde and Galván, *La constitucionalización*, p. 30. Two surveys made in September 2011 revealed that most Spaniards (68 per cent) wanted a referendum on the reform, although they would have voted in favour of budgetary stability (60 per cent). See the barometers of opinion of Metroscopia for *El País* (12 September 2011) and of GESOP for *El Periódico De Cataluña* (27 September 2011).

on fire, you do not ask the fire-fighters to waste time and obtain an injunction. Moreover, in making this reform, Spain followed in the wake of the German reform of 2009 and brought forward a measure that was then included in Art. 3 of the Treaty of Stability, Coordination and Governance in the Economic and Monetary Union. It is no mere coincidence that the other big state at financial risk, Italy, also hastened to apply that agreement of the Treaty before it came into force, and in November 2011 it reformed Art. 81 of its Constitution. If the occasion and reason seem more than justified, I cannot understand why the other political parties were excluded from the initiative, especially the CiU and the PNV, the majority parties in Catalonia and the Basque Country: if, from August 22, the PSOE and the PP had already secretly agreed on the text, why could they not have tried to include the CiU and the PNV in the initiative during the following days, so that it was submitted on 26 August signed by these two political parties as well? There is no evidence that they tried, and in that sense the CiU representative was right when he complained in the parliamentary debate that the PSOE-PP, by monopolizing the reform effort, were breaking the constitutional consensus,[26] however much the two complied with all the formal requirements to make the change, as the CiU had not been excluded when the Constitution was drafted in 1977-1978 or when the first reform was made in 1992.

The Content of the Reform

The former Art. 135, consisting of only two paragraphs, was limited to directing that the government should be authorized by law to issue public debt and that its repayment shall always be included in the budget:

> 1. The government must be authorised by law in order to issue public debt bonds or to contract loans.
>
> 2. Loans to meet payment on the interest and capital of the public debt shall always be deemed to be included in budget expenditure and may not be subject to amendment or modification as long as they conform to the terms of issue.

Under the new Art. 135:

> 1. All public administrations will conform to the principle of budgetary stability.
>
> 2. The state and the Autonomous Communities may not incur a structural deficit that exceeds the limits established by the EU for their member states. An Organic Law shall determine the maximum structural deficit the state and the

26 Duran i Lleida, *Diario de Sesiones del Congreso de los Diputados, IX Legislatura*, no. 269, 30 August 2011, pp. 7-8.

Autonomous Communities may have, in relation to its gross domestic product. Local authorities must submit a balanced budget.

3. The state and the Autonomous Communities must be authorized by law in order to issue public debt bonds or to contract loans.

Loans to meet payment on the interest and capital of the public debt shall always be deemed to be included in budget expenditure and their payment shall have absolute priority. These appropriations may not be subject to amendment or modification as long as they conform to the terms of issue. The volume of public debt of all the public administrations in relation to the state's gross domestic product may not exceed the benchmark laid down by the Treaty on the Functioning of the EU.

4. The limits of the structural deficit and public debt volume may be exceeded only in case of natural disasters, economic recession or extraordinary emergency situations that are beyond the control of the state and significantly impair either the financial situation or the economic or social sustainability of the state, as appreciated by an absolute majority of the members of the Congress of Deputies.

5. An Organic Law shall develop the principles referred to in this article, as well as participation in the respective procedures of the organs of institutional coordination between government fiscal policy and financial support. In any case, the Organic Law shall address:

a) The distribution of the limits of deficit and debt among the different public administrations, the exceptional circumstances to overcome them and the manner and time in which to correct deviations.

b) The methodology and procedure for calculating the structural deficit.

c) The responsibility of each public administration in case of breach of budgetary stability objectives.

6. The Autonomous Communities, in accordance with their respective laws and within the limits referred to in this article, shall take the appropriate procedures for effective implementation of the principle of stability in their rules and budgetary decisions.

Analysis of the Revised Article

Art. 135 begins by stating the principle of budgetary stability, a rule more or less implicit in the constitutions of the first liberal state[27] that had been gradually replaced by the Keynesian idea of balance within cycles, although the experience

27 Thus, the Constitution of Cadiz of 1812 established in Art. 340: 'The contributions will be proportional to the expenditure decreed by parliament for public services in all branches.'

of the twentieth century showed that this balance did not occur in reality, producing a structural deficit; thus, from the 1960s onwards quite a few constitutions (starting with several states of the USA) have echoed James Buchanan's theory of establishing a balanced budget clause in the constitution.[28] The constitutional reform can be summed up in three commitments that Spain as a whole, the state and the Autonomous Communities have made in the most important normative text:

a. To respect the limit of the structural deficit established by the EU, at present at 3 per cent of the GPD, according to Art. 126 of Treaty on the Functioning of the EU. The local authorities must submit a balanced budget and therefore cannot have a deficit. However, the entry into force of this limit for the structural deficit will not occur until 2020. This delay has been alleged as a reason to believe that there was no urgency in the reform. In my opinion, the entry into force of this limit does not mean, of course, that the other provisions of Art. 135 do not come into force in 2011. And postponing the implementation of the structural deficit limits until 2020 is to set a credible horizon, since it would have been unrealistic to think that Spain could meet European regulations overnight. It has already been noted above how difficult it would be in 2012 to comply with a deficit of 5.4 per cent.[29] Moreover, 2020 is the year when the 2009 reform of the Bonn Basic Law brings into force the prohibition of indebtedness of its Länder.
b. To respect the maximum debt permitted by the EU, 60 per cent of GDP, while at present Spain's debt is 68 per cent. According to the forecasts of the Ministry of Finance, the government debt ratio will rise to 79.8 per cent of GDP throughout 2012, although below the average of 90 per cent in the eurozone. In any case, the Spanish constitutional prohibition goes beyond the German model, which was confined to a ceiling on the deficit, but not on public debt.
c. To give 'absolute priority' to debt payments. This commitment has been criticized by the Left, which considers that if one day Spain has to choose

28 On the historical evolution of the 'golden rule' of budgetary stability in economic theory and comparative law, see M. Medina Guerrero, 'La reforma del artículo 135 de la Constitución', *Teoría y Realidad Constitucional* 29 (2012): 134.

29 While revising this work we already know that this is impossible: in the ECOFIN meeting of 10 July the EU Ministers of Finance decided to grant Spain an extension of one year to correct its excessive deficit. The new annual targets are 6.3 per cent GDP in 2012, 4.5 per cent in 2013 and 2.8 per cent in 2014. In return for this extension (and the financial aid to the banks) the government will sign a Memorandum of Understanding which is a de facto rescue and intervention in the country and which obliges the government to make new cutbacks and reforms in public spending, already announced by Prime Minister Rajoy when appearing in Congress on 11 July 2012. These measures had begun to materialize in the very long (91 pages) Royal Decree-Law 20/2012 on measures to ensure budgetary stability and promote competition.

> between paying teachers and doctors or paying the debt, the former would be left without their salaries. Far from demagogy, the truth is that the former Art. 135 had already implicitly established the priority of paying off the debt since it obliged the state to always include the payment of public debt in the Budget, and to prevent any alteration of the conditions under which it had been acquired. Reinforcing the commitment to pay with an explicit preference reassures potential buyers of government debt, making it easier to obtain new loans for the payment of teachers and doctors.

To achieve general budgetary stability, Art. 135 of the Constitution empowers the state to pass a law that will fix not only the state's and the Communities' structural deficit ceiling (Art. 135.2) but also, among other details, the coordination procedures between administrations, the responsibility of each administration to meet the deficit limit assigned to it and the manner in which to correct the hypothetical deviations that may occur (Art. 135). Given the real limitations that this organic law will mean for economic competences of the Autonomous Communities, it seems to me that, although the reform does not mention it at all, we can qualify it for ourselves as a harmonization law. Of course, as a *material* qualification, because being ordered by the Constitution its practical and informal effects mean there is no need to approve it by the special procedure laid down in Art. 150.3 of the Constitution.[30]

Among the criticisms that were made about Art. 135 are two particularly important and somewhat contradictory ones, although sometimes the same authors make them: first, it is an unnecessary law because paragraph 4 shows the exceptions to the debt and deficit ceilings in such a diffuse form that it becomes a law over which constitutional control cannot be exercised, and, second, that it establishes a liberal policy.[31] I do not share either of these objections: I do not think that the uncertain legal concepts used in Art. 135.4 are harder to clarify than many others used by the Constitution (consider, for example, the 'extraordinary and urgent necessity' that authorizes the government to dictate decree-laws). Moreover, in the case of Art. 135, it must be implemented by an absolute congressional majority, after prior public debate. Furthermore, although it is dangerous to extrapolate findings from one legal and political framework to another, the truth is that if we look at comparative law it seems that the stability clause itself has served to contain the expenditure of the states that have implemented it,[32] so that to say that it will

30 On Art. 150.3 of the Constitution, see F. Pascua Mateo 'Las Leyes de armonización: esbozo de una construcción dogmática', *Revista de Administración Pública* 167 (2005): 147-192; A. Ruiz Robledo, *Constitutional Law in Spain* (Kluwer, 2012), p. 172.

31 These criticisms are rather inconsistent because if their legal value to compel public administrations to maintain a balanced budget were null, then so too would be their power to lay down a type of political economy.

32 See, for example, A. Auerbach, 'US Experience with Federal Budget Rules', *CESifo DICE Report* 7(1) (2009) (Ifo Institute for Economic Research at the University of

not work in Spain seems at least somewhat premature. In any case, if we recall the symbolic and political value of constitutions, the *golden rule* is a statement of intent by the state and a guarantee for a balanced budget policy. In addition, we should not forget its role in the order of competences, attributing to the state an intervention tool in the budgetary spheres of the Autonomous Communities that is more specific and powerful than the Economic Planning Title of Art. 149.1.13 of the Constitution.[33]

In so far as Art. 135 establishes a liberal economic model, one must admit it is true if by that we refer to a market economy, but the statement was already in the Constitution, not only in Art. 38 ('Free enterprise within the framework of a market economy is recognized') but also in many other articles, such as the recognition of certain rights that only make sense within the market economy: private property (Art. 33), freedom to choose ones profession (Art. 35), collective bargaining (Art. 37) and so on. If it is claimed that the new Art. 135 imposes a neo-liberal policy nullifying the proclamation of the welfare state in Art. 1 and preventing left-wing policies that raise public spending, then the answer has to be clearly negative: what prevents those public spending policies (which incidentally can be very right-wing, as demonstrated by the Bush Administration's increased military spending) is that they are financed with debt and deficit. Art. 135 does not establish any expenditure ceiling. Moreover, the use of the concept of structural deficit (that is, one that takes into account the anti-cyclic stabilizers) is in line with European provisions and far from the ultra-liberal commandments of 'zero deficit'.[34]

The fact that this prevents governments from increasing the deficit and public debt beyond reasonable limits seems to me perfectly logical to the rationale of constitutionalism, limiting the power of rulers; without the restraint of the principle of balanced budget, a government may be tempted to finance many of its activities not with taxes but by loans to be paid back by future generations, committing

Munich): 41-48. For the Swiss experience of its *Schuldenbremse/frein à l'endettement* of 2001, see L.P. Feld and G. Kirchgässner, 'On the Effectiveness of Debt Brakes: The Swiss Experience', in R. Neck and J.-E. Sturm (eds), *Sustainability of Public Debt* (MIT Press, 2008), pp. 223-255.

33 On Art. 135 of the Constitution as a provision dealing with competences, see J.I. Gorospe Oviedo, 'La estabilidad presupuestaria de las Comunidades Autónomas y la reforma del artículo 135 CE', in Conde and Galván, *La constitucionalización*, pp. 339-372, at p. 360.

34 For the doctrine that considers Art. 135 one step more in 'the sovereignty of the markets' and anti-democratic, see R. Escudero Alday, 'Texto y contexto de la reforma constitucional exprés de agosto de 2011', *Eunomia* 2 (2012): 86-98. For the doctrine that rejects the description of 'liberal' of this Art. 135, see J. Tajadura Tajada, 'Reforma constitucional e integración europea', *Claves de Razón Práctica* 216 (2011): 26. For my part I would add that there was a time in which austerity was a way to put a brake on reckless capitalism, see E. Berlinguer, *Austeridad: una ocasión para transformar Italia*, intro. Julio Segura (Materiales, 1978).

the injustice of benefitting their constituents by prejudicing those to come, and in doing so, in the classic expression of Thomas Jefferson, the land would belong to the dead and not the living generations.[35] Given the social *invisibility* of the debt, I would add that it also makes it easier for people in government (national, regional and local) to appear as statesmen capable of great works without raising taxes, while their substitutes seem ineffective at politics because they have no alternative but to dedicate themselves to paying off debts they inherited from the former.

Effects of the Constitutional Reform: The New Law on Budget Stability

The only additional provision of the constitutional amendment provides that the organic law provided for in Art. 135 must be approved before 30 June 2012; one of the first measures taken by the new PP government was to pass the bill in January 2012. It also processed it very quickly in parliament, so that by 30 April, two months before the constitutional deadline, Law 2/2012 'Budgetary Stability and Financial Sustainability' was published. The law repeals all previous legislation on stability and replaces it with more rigid rules. In summary, one can reduce this lengthy law (although it has only 32 items, it occupies 23 pages of the BOE) to ten short statements:

1. All public authorities must submit a balanced budget or one with a surplus.
2. The debt of public administrations shall not exceed the value of 60 per cent of GDP stipulated in European legislation, except in exceptional cases.
3. The state, Autonomous Communities and local governments must impose a spending ceiling to be set by the Fiscal Policy Council (where the government and all communities are represented, but where the ruling party can most easily obtain a majority) taking into account EU recommendations on budgetary stability.
4. Public expenditure in all administrations cannot increase beyond the rate of growth of GDP established by EU regulations. If this limit seems a reasonable precaution to ensure a balanced budget, it is not a direct requirement of Art. 135 of the Constitution, but a mandate from the organic law. Therefore, its constitutional basis is not so much the principle of

35 Letter of T. Jefferson to J. Madison, 6 September 1789, where he wrote: 'Then I say the earth belongs to each of these generations, during its course, fully, and in their own right. The 2nd generation receives it clear of the debts and encumbrances of the 1st. the 3d of the 2nd and so on. For if the 1st could charge it with a debt, then the earth would belong to the dead and not the living generation. Then no generation can contract debts greater than may be paid during the course of its own existence … then 19 years is the term beyond which neither the representatives of a nation, nor even the whole nation itself assembled, can validly extend a debt' (available at http://press-ubs.uchicago.edu/founders/documents/v1ch2s23.html).

budgetary stability but overall economic planning (Art. 149.1.13 of the Constitution).

5. It establishes the priority of meeting the interest and principal of public debt in preference over any other expenditure, as established in Art. 135 of the Constitution.
6. The failure to achieve the aim of stability will require that a financial business plan will be presented, which allows for correction of the deviation within a year.
7. It provides different treatment in the event of a shortfall in exceptional circumstances, natural disasters, economic recession or emergency. In these cases a plan must be submitted to return to equilibrium, detailing appropriate measures to deal with extraordinary situations.
8. The law strengthens the preventive and monitoring measures for the goals of stability and debt. For example, it will report on the fulfilment of the objectives in the draft budgets, allowing preventive action against risk. It also establishes a preventive threshold of debt as a sign to avoid cash flow problems.
9. Compliance with the objectives of stability will be considered to authorize debt issues, as well as for giving grants or the signing of agreements between Communities and municipalities with the state. There will be no agreements with any administration that fails to meet the objective.
10. Sanctions imposed on Spain by the EU for stability will be assumed by the administration responsible. The law includes the EU corrective mechanisms. In case of default of a financial business plan, the administration concerned must make a deposit which may be converted into a fine if the default so requires. The Ministry of Finance will send a delegation to assess the economic situation of the defaulting administration, similar to what happens in EU countries undergoing intervention.

Concluding Remarks

The financial crisis is changing the entire Spanish political and legal framework. Let us briefly recapitulate what we have discussed so far:

a. In the strictly political sphere, the elections of 20 November resulted in the sinking of the ruling party, the PSOE, which suffered its worst result since the restoration of democracy, with only 110 seats. Conversely, the party previously in opposition, the Popular Party, achieved 186 deputies, above its previous record of 183 deputies in 2000. With this great change, the nationalist parties maintained their positions, such as the CiU (16 deputies) and the PNV (5), the resurgence of the IU (going from 3 in 2008 to 11 in 2012) and the strong growth of a new party, the UPD, which is quite critical of the organization of the Autonomous Communities (5).

b. In the field of political action neither of the two political parties in government, the PSOE first (from May 2010) and the PP after (especially with the new cuts in July 2012) have been able to develop their electoral platforms,[36] but have had to take measures to ensure the confidence of international markets and organizations able financially to help Spain. So one might be tempted to import an idea of Antonio D'Atena of the Italian government and consider that the Constitution actually existing in Spain requires that the government has a double constituency: the Congress of Deputies and the markets.[37] A group of authors[38] would also add that currently citizens no longer control the state, that sovereignty and democracy are moribund because of the markets, and other similar thoughts. I do not quite share this opinion because it does not appear to be generalized and is not applied to Finland and other much smaller countries, which logically should have lost the same or more sovereignty than Spain. If the Spanish government policy cannot carry out what it wants to do it is not because of hidden foreign conspiracies that undermine our sovereignty, but because of the many errors accumulated by the Spanish institutions, from over-ambitious investments to political control of the savings banks, that in recent years have led the state to depend to a high degree on external financing. This has led, inevitably, to some constraints on economic policy. Ordinary citizens appear to understand that it is not so much an issue of sovereignty as of poor governance, as evidenced by opinion polls suggesting in recent years that a major problem in Spain is its political class.[39]
c. The crisis has severely altered the Spanish legal system, through the reform of the Constitution and the profound changes in many laws, especially those governing the economic order. These legislative changes have been made largely by decree-laws, of which extensive use has been made as never seen before, including in areas, such as regulating the development of constitutional rights, which in pure theory were forbidden to decree-law. At the institutional level the use of decree-laws, perhaps inevitable given the urgency of the economic situation, has led to a strengthening of

36 The parties included in their programmes proposals that they knew beforehand would be impossible to fulfil, which was especially noticeable in the PP's electoral programme for the November 2011 elections, as shown in the first six months of their mandate. I have criticized this conduct as irresponsible and cynical in A. Ruiz Robledo, 'Irlanda como precedente', *Diario de Sevilla*, 9 January 2012.

37 A. Ruggeri, 'Art. 94 della Costituzione vivente: 'Il Governo deve avere la fiducia dei mercati' (nota minima a commento della nascita del Governo Monti)', *Federalisme.it* (2011): 23.

38 See the soundly-argued opinión of G. Pisarello, 'Reforma constitucional y crisis', *Jueces para la Democracia* 72 (November 2011): 3-11.

39 The third since 2010 according to the Centro de Investigaciones Sociológicas. See, for example, its barometer for May 2012; available at http://www.cis.es/cis/export/sites/default/-Archivos/Marginales/2940_2959/2944/Es2944.pdf.

government and an undervaluing of parliament. The same conclusion can be repeated for those Autonomous Communities whose governments are empowered to issue decree-laws.

d. With regard to jurisprudence, there seems to be a trend in both the Constitutional Court and the Supreme Court to take economic consequences into account in their decisions, avoiding decisions that might pose a *fiat iustitia et pereat mundus*. Without doubt, this is a responsible use of power to judge in favour of the community, but it carries the risk of weakening controls over public authorities, which can be tempted to abuse their power by the idea that in exceptional situations everything is permitted.

Chapter 6
The Constitution and the Financial Crisis in the UK: Historical and Contemporary Lessons

John F. McEldowney

Assessing the constitutional implications of the financial crisis on the UK requires an understanding of the economic impact of the crisis and the fact that it is on-going with no immediate end in sight.[1] The economic consequences are well known, with UK banks losing £122bn and the credit/banking crisis becoming one of systemic debt.[2] Julia Black has estimated that collectively governments in the USA, the UK and the EU have injected over $4.8 trillion into the support of their financial institutions.[3] The UK is currently forecast by the OECD to have the tenth highest debt of the 31 leading economies.[4] UK gross public debt increased from 46.0 per cent of GDP in 2006 to 82.2 per cent in 2010. The effects of the financial crisis on state debt are likely to be long-standing. In 2012 gross public debt is forecast to be 97.2 per cent of GDP and in 2013 to be 102.3 per cent. The UK is running a budget deficit set in 2011/12 to be £576bn, with government spending forecast to be £703bn. Primarily, the budget deficit is financed through the sale of government bonds. As of June 2012 quantitative easing reached £375bn as the Bank of England struggled to achieve economic growth in the UK economy, currently in recession.[5]

---

1 R. Tomasic and F. Akinbami, 'Towards a New Corporate Governance after the Global Financial Crisis', *International Company and Commercial Law Review* 22(8) (2011): 237-249.

2 One factor that has contributed to government debt is the support provided by the government for the banks. This took the form of share purchases, loans and guarantees, with an inevitable effect on government finances. It is hard to estimate the extent of the level of government support but it is calculated to be around 5 to 6 per cent of the deficit in 2008 and 2009.

3 J. Black, 'The Credit Crisis and the Constitution', in D. Oliver, T. Prosser and R. Rawlings (eds), *The Regulatory State* (Oxford University Press, 2010), pp. 92-128, at p. 92.

4 See HC Standard Note SN/EP/6054 government borrowing and debt: international comparisons (27 January 2012). See also HC Standard Note: SN/EP/6167 The Budget Deficit: A Short Guide (= 20 December 2011).

5 Quantitative easing is where the Bank of England prints additional funds in return for bank securities.

While the economic scale of the financial crisis is clear for all to see, there are important constitutional and regulatory effects that are addressed in this chapter. The first part provides an overview of the political and socio-economic facets of the crisis. This covers the main implications of the financial crisis on the UK's regulatory response. Failures in banking regulation have provided lessons for future regulatory strategy. The Conservative-led coalition government responded through a politically driven appraisal and re-construction of the financial regulatory system, raising questions about the legitimacy of the process, the role of experts and ultimately questions about the independence of the new arrangements. Next, the legislative reforms and fundamental rights are considered in the context of their constitutional significance. The financial crisis is also considered in terms of constitutional lessons, including the Conservative-led coalition government formed with the Liberal Democrats after the election in May 2010 because no single party could form a government. This resulted in a five-year fixed-term parliament for the first time in modern history. Constitutional innovation is apparent in the way government is now undertaken and delivered. The financial crisis has also created an opportunity to consider rights even though the role of the courts has been limited in addressing rights arising from the financial crisis itself.

Finally, there is an assessment of the longer term impact of the financial crisis on sovereignty issues associated with the UK's membership of the EU. The UK is not in the eurozone and opted out of the Fiscal Compact adopted through an intergovernmental agreement (international agreement) outside the institutional framework of the EU. This was followed by the Treaty on Stability, Coordination and Governance in the Economic and Monetary Union (TSCG) signed by 25 member states (the UK and the Czech Republic are the two exceptions).

It is clear that the UK's Constitution has shown remarkable resilience. Julia Black has observed that 'the financial crisis did not cause a constitutional crisis'.[6] It did, however, result in considerable changes to the UK's constitutional landscape, not least in the development of new techniques and processes. The financial crisis has directly affected the lives of many people, with a 30 per cent cut in public spending and severe restrictions on the public sector. Parliamentary processes have proved to be far less effective than many might have hoped. Evaluating the long-term constitutional impact is both complex and confusing. Complex, because banking regulation is difficult to assess and the new regulatory arrangements have yet to be put into place; confusing, because constitutional responses are politically driven under a coalition government, unusual in modern times, and hard to evaluate in terms of their enduring legacy.

---

6 Black, 'Credit Crisis', p. 125.

An Overview of the Political and Socio-economic Facts of the Crisis: The Crisis in UK Financial Regulation

The UK's constitutional background is distinctive from other EU member states. The UK is not part of the eurozone. Its Constitution is not to be found in a modern codified or written Constitution. There is a strong parliamentary tradition, including legal and political sovereignty, with a pre-eminence given to autonomous regulation and regulators as a major element in the constitutional checks and balances on the financial sector. The three main institutions that from 1997 were responsible for the management and regulation of the UK's financial system are the Bank of England, HM Treasury and the Financial Services Authority (FSA). The Tripartite arrangements, as it became known, were in operation during the 2008 financial crisis and have been subject to much criticism, and are in the process of being changed. The main point of the changes is to replace the FSA, with the pivotal role going to the Bank of England. This will take effect after 2012 and has echoes of past regulatory experience, which was not particularly effective, when the Bank of England was primarily the main banking regulator.[7] This role may be traced[8] back to the Bank's earliest foundation as a private institution in 1694.[9] The creation of the FSA in 1997, when the Bank of England lost its main regulatory responsibilities, came after heavy criticism of the way the Bank of England had failed to address past banking collapses. The earlier Banking Act 1979 created a statutory arrangement whereby the business of banking was to apply licensing requirements and vest formal requirements in the Bank of England in terms of granting and authorizing deposit-taking. One part of the arrangements was to ring-fence many established banking institutions and create new entry barriers and prevent competition at the fringes of their activities. In return the Bank of England hoped that through its regulatory discretion little intervention might be required and the 'self-regulatory' style would create trust and confidence in the banking system. An important component was the Basle Committee on Banking Supervision (then the G10) coordinating EU and the major world economies.

One impact of the 1979 Act was to engage the Bank of England in the refinement of financial regulation, specifically the financial stability of institutions.

7 J. Clapham, *The Bank of England 1797-1914* (Cambridge University Press, 1944); C. Goodhart, *The Evolution of Central Banks* (MIT Press, 1988); R. Cranston, *Principles of Banking Law* (2nd edn, Oxford University Press, 2002).

8 R.S. Sayers, *Bank of England Operations 1890-1914* (P.S. King and Son, 1936); R.S. Sayers, *Central Banking after Bagehot* (Oxford University Press, 1957). See also Chr. Hadjiemmanuil, *Banking Regulation and the Bank of England* (LLP, 1998).

9 The Bank of England Act 1694. See J.S. Fforde, 'Competition, Innovation and Regulation in British Banking', *Bank of England Quarterly Bulletin* 23 (1983): 363-376.

An enlargement of the Banking Supervision Division[10] was accomplished by March 1980. The admissions of overseas banks into the banking system showed how threadbare supervision was in reality.[11] The Johnson Mathey Bankers (JMB) collapse in late 1984 was startling not least because the parent bank belonged to a small number of ring-fenced gold bullion dealers but also because of accumulated losses on lending to a small number of clients of which the parent bank had been ignorant. The Bank of England decided to rescue the JMB and offered 50 per cent of the £150 million of guarantees in return for bank ownership at a token amount. The various London Clearing Banks and the other four members of the gold bullion club provided the remaining guarantees. The rationale for take-over came from a fear of loss of confidence in the banking system and undesirable consequences from a knock-on effect. Perhaps it was all out of recognition of a failure of sufficient regulatory supervision. Operating from a world of internal debate, the Bank appeared unsure and out of touch. It embarrassingly stuck to the view in public that no public money was involved when in fact it was. The result was that the Bank argued for an increased supervisory role, new powers and a mandate to regulate. What is remarkable is how the Bank of England withstood pressure for an external analysis of its role.

The Leigh-Pemberton Committee,[12] chaired by the then governor of the Bank of England, was asked by the government to undertake a report into the cause and effects of the collapse of JMB; it set the pattern for future regulation. The Committee's conclusions about regulatory weakness were that a two-tier system of regulation existed: one relaxed regime for the treatment of recognized banks and another tougher regime applied to licensed deposit-takers. A new supplementary Act to the 1979 Act was recommended and the Banking Act 1987 resulted. This included a single tier of regulation, a Board of Banking Supervision with independent members and additional powers for information gathering, including the criminalization of failure to provide information. There was also a link to European and international supervision. This also led to the completion in 1995 of the Bank's role over the system of inter-bank loans and the development of the CHAPS system of interchange between banks. There was also an attempt to provide oversight of the value of credit and risk assessment of credit lines between banks.

A critical part of bank supervision, namely the willingness of the Bank of England to act in defined circumstances of risk, emerged as a major issue of doubt following the failure of the Bank of Credit and Commerce International (BCCI). The bank collapsed on 5 July 1991 after it had accumulated deficits of many billions of pounds following widespread fraud. Despite concerns about

10 The successor of the Banking and Money Market Supervision Section of the Bank of England.

11 The collapse of the Banco Ambrosiano in 1982 is a prime example of vulnerability.

12 R. Leigh-Pemberton, *Report of the Committee set up to Consider the System of Banking Supervision*, Cmnd. 9550 (HMSO, 1985).

BCCI being voiced over many years little was done to investigate its true state of health. Many thousands of depositors lost money and the resultant political fall-out resulted in the inquiry into the collapse under Lord Bingham.[13] The Bingham Report led to recommendations that sought to strengthen investigation, communication and reporting of bank supervision. Despite political and public criticism no responsibility for regulatory failure was taken by any individual within the Bank. Particularly unobtrusive was the response of the traditional parliamentary watchdogs such as the Treasury and Civil Service Committee.[14] The Bank of England also refused to pay compensation to depositors and this became subject to legal action.

The failure of Barings Bank in February 1995 as a result of large losses due to unauthorized derivatives trading through a Singapore subsidiary caused concern that bank supervision was not effective outside the UK. On further investigation by the Board of Banking Supervision, it was revealed that the losses came from one rogue trader and that there were also shortcomings in the Bank of England's supervision. Here the Treasury and Civil Service Committee adopted a stronger criticism of banking supervision than hitherto, and questioned the appropriateness of the Bank of England as a prudential supervisor.[15]

The criticisms were deeply felt especially by the government of the day. It is estimated that the Bank had a statutory duty for over 525 institutions including 327 institutions authorized in the UK under the Banking Act 1987 and 146 institutions from other member states acting under home-state authorization. The result was an increase in staff employed by the Bank of England, and an access to specialist advice to support their abilities to operate within the confines of the Bank of England. Banking failures exposed weaknesses in regulation and, at the same time, confusion about protecting the public interest and how this was best defined. The Bingham Report[16] marked a turning point in terms of the Bank's independence and authority and marked an increasing desire for better accountability. It was also one of the few external evaluations of banking regulation.[17] The new Labour

13 Lord Bingham, *Inquiry into the Supervision of the Bank of Credit and Commerce International*, HC (1991-1992), p. 198.

14 See Treasury and Civil Service Committee, *Second Special Report, Banking Supervision and BCCI International and National Regulation: The Response of the Government and the Bank of England to the Fourth Report from the Committee in Session 1991-92*, HC (1992-1993), p. 248.

15 Sixth Report Treasury and Civil Service Committee, *The Regulation of Financial Services in the UK*, HC (1994-1995), 332-I.

16 Lord Bingham, *Return to an address of the Honourable the House of Commons dated 22nd October 1992; Inquiry into the Supervision of the Bank of Credit and commerce International* (HMSO, 1992), HC-198. See HC Deb 22 October 1992, vol. 539, cols 859-74.

17 J.F. McEldowney, 'Managing Financial Risk: The Precautionary Principle and Protecting the Public Interest in the UK', in J.R. Labrosse, R. Olivares-Caminal and D. Singh (eds), *Risk and the Banking Crisis* (Edward Elgar, 2011), pp. 449-472; J.F. McEldowney,

government created the so-called Tripartite arrangements in 1997 with the FSA, the main regulatory authority with primary regulatory responsibilities. The Bank of England remained lender of last resort and HM Treasury provided input from the Chancellor of the Exchequer. The creation of the FSA transferred to a single point of contact the supervisory responsibilities under the Bank of England and the establishment of an integrated regulator.

Legislative Reforms: The Post-crisis Structure of UK Financial Regulation and its Impact on the Constitution

Regulatory Legislation

In the aftermath of the failure of effective regulation during the 2008 financial crisis, the FSA set about reforming itself and introducing changes in its approach to regulation. The FSA came under sustained criticism for its failures, particularly in not preventing the collapse of Northern Rock and in not foreseeing the extent of the financial crisis. The election of the coalition government in May 2010 led to wide-ranging and radical reforms. The Financial Services Act 2010, introduced by the new coalition government, made substantial changes to the FSA and its powers and duties as part of wide-ranging changes to prudential financial regulation.[18] It was announced that the FSA is to be abolished and its functions split up. The FSA is to be renamed the Financial Conduct Authority (FCA) and will focus on consumer protection and market oversight. The main task of prudential supervision of banks is to be moved within the Bank of England into an independent subsidiary, the Prudential Regulation Authority (PRA) and the Financial Conduct Authority (FCA). Ellis Ferran notes:

> Likely transition costs for HM Treasury, the Bank and the supervisory authorities were initially estimated to be in the region of £50 million spread over three years, but after initial consultations, the estimated figure has been increased to between £90 and £175 million.[19]

'Defining the Public Interest: Public Law Perspectives on Regulating the Financial Crisis', in J.R. Labrosse, R. Olivares-Caminal and D. Singh (eds), *Financial Crisis Management and Bank Resolution* (Informa, 2009), pp. 103-32.

18 Some additional powers have been added including a new financial stability objective and additional enforcement powers. This includes cooperation with the Treasury, the Bank of England and other relevant statutory bodies. Disciplinary powers have also been strengthened.

19 E. Ferran, 'The Break-up of the Financial Services Authority', *Oxford Journal of Legal Studies* 31 (3) (2011): 255-480, at 456.

Throughout the current period of transition during 2012, the FSA with a staff of nearly 4,000[20] provided an important link between the old and incoming new systems prior to their gradual introduction in the coming months.

The Bank of England will be at the apex of the system of financial regulation in the UK under a system of macro-prudential regulation aimed at addressing risk and association of banking with the wider economy. Doubts have remained about the Bank of England's ability to achieve this aim, given its past regulatory history and its involvement in the 2008 financial crisis. In the past banking failures have been attributed to problems with the Bank's capacity to predict and overview systemic weaknesses. The government's belief is that a central bank focused structure for financial supervision is desirable because the central bank 'has a competitive edge due to their first hand exposure to markets and the depth of their staff's experience in the functioning of financial firms and markets'.[21] Within the Bank of England there will be a new Financial Policy Committee (FPC) with responsibility for preventing credit and asset bubbles and ensuring overall financial stability. There will be several additional advisory bodies with specific responsibilities. These include the PRA, a legally distinct subsidiary, with responsibility under the Bank of England for micro-prudential supervision of day-to-day matters relating to bank safety and soundness. Its main focus is on the prudential regulation of financial firms. The PRA will have many of the FSA supervision and enforcement powers. It will have shared responsibilities in consumer matters with the FCA, which has responsibilities for investor protection, market supervision and regulation as well as the business conduct of banks and financial services. Consumer protection will be at the centre of its main activities. Originally the FCA was to be called the Consumer Protection and Markets Authority (CPMA) but after initial consultations it was renamed the FCA (Financial Conduct Authority).

The FCA inherits many of the FSA's responsibilities but the main test of the FCA will be to ensure consumer protection amid changes in derivates trading as a consequence of changes in the USA. The role of the Bank of England will be paramount through providing the necessary guidance to negotiate the regulation of exchanges, the payment systems for derivates and the facilities for securities and derivatives – all of which fall within the remit of the FCA. The PRA and the FCA were intended to have their own independent enforcement powers but this seems to have been modified with the FCA taking the lead role and having additional powers to enforce consumer rights. The new structure of regulation provides the Bank of England with a pivotal role. It is unclear how this will work in practice, specifically the interrelationship between the Bank of England, the FCA and the PRA.

---

20 FSA, Annual Report 2010/11, pp. 99-100.

21 'A New Approach to Financial Regulation: Judgement, Focus and Stability (Presented to Parliament by Command of Her Majesty) July 2010', Cm 7874, para 2.14; available at http://www.hm-treasury.gov.uk/d/consult_financial_regulation_condoc.pdf.

The main driver of the changes is not only the politics of abolishing the FSA but a strong political engagement to create a new system of regulation.[22] To what extent will the new arrangements have operational independence? How will the FCA be held to account? The changes mark an important break from the Tripartite system and a major change in the regulatory architecture which raises a fundamental question about the desirability of giving primacy to the Bank of England. The key issues, however, go to the suitability of the Bank of England to have regulatory pre-eminence. As the central bank, it also has to retain pre-eminent responsibility to oversee money and payments systems and retains the role as lender of last resort. It will also continue to have ultimate responsibility for systemic risk. Given the responsibilities and burdens of regulatory oversight, undoubtedly there are questions as to how the Bank of England is to act as the major financial regulator.

There remains largely unresolved the question of how best to address the current size and allocation of the large High Street banks.[23] The coalition government set up an independent Banking Commission under the chair of Sir John Vickers to inquire into the structures of British banks.[24] Its task was to assess the arguments relating to 'too big to fail', namely the desirability of breaking up the large banks in the public interest. The Commission's interim report and final report concluded that the major banks should be split up, separating the high risk part of the banks from those that are less risky. Legislation is under consideration to implement the Vickers Report. There are two bills before parliament, the Financial Services Bill, to introduce the new regulatory regime, and the Banking Reform Bill to implement the Vickers Commission and to split up the banks between the high risk and the less risky.

Frustrations over the regulation of the financial sector have also encouraged MPs to consider how the Bank of England governor should be appointed in the future. For example, a private members' bill[25] is currently before parliament on the approval of any Bank of England governor being subject to the House of Commons Treasury Select Committee. This follows the precedent set by the Budget Responsibility and National Audit Act 2011 which requires the Chancellor of the Exchequer when appointing the chair to the Office of Budget responsibility to seek the consent of the Treasury Committee of the House of Commons. This is also consistent with the appointment of the Comptroller and Auditor General with the agreement of the Public Accounts Committee.

---

22 See Ferran, 'Break-up of the Financial Services Authority', 455.

23 ICB, Interim Report, Consultation on Reform Options, April 2011. See HC 1069 19th Report Treasury Committee: Independent Commission on Banking 2010-2012.

24 Leigh-Pemberton, *Committee set up to Consider the System of Banking Supervision*.

25 House of Commons: Research Paper 12/35 *Bank of England (Appointment of Governor) Bill 8 2012-13* (3 July 2012).

Tougher Regulatory Sanctions?

An important aspect of regulatory control is the use of criminal and civil sanctions. The operation of civil sanctions through fines and warnings has not proved effective and there is considerable public support for strengthening regulatory powers including the use of the criminal law. This is a key issue in the recent LIBOR scandal, discussed in more detail below. Since the 2008 financial crisis the FSA, influenced by the Turner Review,[26] has adopted a more robust approach to regulation than in the past.[27] Sections 401 and 402 of the Financial Services and Markets Act 2000 give the FSA similar powers to other prosecution authorities.[28] Section 401 is directed at prosecutions that specifically arise for offences found within the Financial Services and Markets Act 2000. For example, under section 307 of the Financial Services and Markets Act 2000 the FSA may prosecute for making false or misleading statements – often associated with causing share price inflation and ultimately collapse of the share market. Section 402 is broader and applies to offences outside the Financial Services Act 2000 but where there is a need to prosecute related to maintaining market confidence in the public interest. The broader remit captures offences that fall within money laundering offences under Part V of the Criminal Justice Act 1993 and related regulations. Taken together the FSA has considerable scope to prosecute, especially when practices that fall under the generic term of 'market manipulation' are considered. Lacking a clear definition, the term can be interpreted to cover various ways in which the capital market can be distorted or inaccurately adjusted to produce an outcome that leads to loss of investor and market confidence. The fragility of markets and their sensitivity is at the heart of the problem of setting a clear definition. At stake, however, is the idea that market efficiency is being put in jeopardy. Market abuse is also covered by the 1993 Act to include insider dealing, inaccuracy in information and its misuse. Insider dealing is also a specific offence under Part V of the Criminal Justice Act 1993. This has proved a controversial and difficult offence, not least for the collection of evidence to prove it, as well as for the jury to understand its complexity. The link between insider dealing and its damaging effects on financial markets is also contentious. The LIBOR misdeeds fall outside the criminal prosecution powers of the FSA but the Serious Fraud Office is currently investigating allegations of criminal wrongdoing, strongly denied by Barclays.

In addition to the criminal jurisdiction of the FSA, outlined above, it has a large civil jurisdiction for imposing civil sanctions for market abuse under section

26 Lord Turner, *The Turner Review: A Regulatory Response to the Global Banking Crisis* (FSA, 2009).

27 See Travers Smith Regulatory Investigations Group, 'FSA Enforcement Action: Themes and Trends', *Compliance Officer Bulletin* (2011).

28 The Director of Public Prosecutions, HM Revenue and Customs and the Serious Fraud Office.

118 of the Financial Services and Markets Act 2000. This is enforced by the FSA through its own specialist tribunal. Consequently, insider dealing falls within the jurisdiction of the tribunal as set out in the Market Abuse Directive[29] under the Financial Services and Markets Act 2000 (Market Abuse) Regulations 2005.[30] The use of civil sanctions is consistent with the direction favoured by the EU and it is also part of a wide-ranging debate on the use of civil sanctions and their application in the regulatory process in the UK,[31] as explained above. As recently as 3 August 2010 the FSA fined the Royal Bank of Scotland £5.6 million for failing to have adequate systems in place to apply UK financial sanctions over screening procedures to prevent money laundering. The National Audit Office (NAO) noted how important[32] civil sanctions had become to the work of the FSA and this remains the case today.

Initially the FSA was not active in pursuing criminal prosecutions. Only in 2005 was the first criminal prosecution against market abuse taken[33] and this was successful. Even by 2007 there had been no insider dealing prosecutions taken by the FSA under the Criminal Justice Act 1993. This may have reflected a policy approach to use prosecutions sparingly or recognition of the high evidential burdens required to mount successful prosecutions. Jury trial and the complexity of financial instruments and markets may also have inhibited the use of prosecutions. Difficulties of detection are also evident in such cases. The fear of detection and the threat of criminal prosecutions may also act as a deterrent. Monitoring and surveillance are likely to be easier if the threat of criminal prosecutions is not aggressively pursued.

The banking crisis has changed the FSA's approach. Following the Turner Review, the FSA adopted a more intensive supervisory model in its attempts to redress past regulatory shortcomings. The use of fines and prosecutions was intensified. *The Economist* noted:

> That year [2009] saw a big change in the level and nature of fines imposed by the FSA: £34.9m ($54.6 m) compared with £22.7m in 2008 and just £5.3m in 2007.[34]

---

29 Directive 2003/6/EC.

30 SI 2005 No. 381.

31 R. Macrory, *Regulatory Justice: Sanctioning in a Post-Hampton World: A Consultation Document* (Cabinet Office, May 2006) and *Regulatory Justice: Making Sanctions Effective* (Cabinet Office, November 2006).

32 NAO, *The Financial Services Authority: A review under Section 12 of the Financial Services and Markets Act 2000*, HC 500 Session 2006-07 (27 April 2007), 49, noted that from 2001-2002 there were an average of 200 cases each year dealing with money laundering and other breaches of the financial standards. At para 4.63 2005-06, 17 cases involving financial penalties totalling £17.4 million, £14 million of which was for one market protection case and £505,000 related specifically to financial crime.

33 *R.* v. *Rigby, Bailey and Rowley* [2005] EWCA 3487.

34 *The Economist*, 27 March 2010, p. 81.

In fact the FSA is getting tougher and more vigilant. At the end of March 2010 a large investigation into insider dealing resulted in the arrest of six people, among them employees of Deutsche Bank, BNP Paribas and Moore Capital, a large hedge fund. This accompanied large-scale penalties against a former interest rate trader at Merrill Lynch (a ban of at least five years) and the prosecution of a former stockbroker at Cazenove. The FSA has hired an additional 460 staff and the largest banks have been allocated 15 officials permanently stationed at their headquarters. No one can doubt that regulation is likely to be more intense.

Recent Court of Appeal decisions in *R.* v. *Rollins* and *R.* v. *McInerney*[35] secured an important extension of prosecution power. The Court of Appeal accepted that the FSA had powers to prosecute beyond sections 401 and 402 of the Financial Services and Markets Act 2000 to include sections 327 and 328 under the Proceeds of Crime Act 2002. Although there were not specific powers of investigation in relation to the 2002 Act, this did not prevent prosecutions being taken, notwithstanding that the offences were outside the FSA's powers of investigation. This is a major shift in the FSA's role. Richards LJ accepted that for many years the FSA did not claim the power to prosecute for offences other than those that it had an express power over. In July 2007 the FSA stated for the first time that it could prosecute in areas where in the past it may have lacked express powers.[36] This reinforces the change in attitude adopted by the FSA.

The Walker Review,[37] undertaken by Sir David Walker and published in November 2009, makes important proposals for the establishment of Board Risk Committees and the appointment of chief risk officers at senior executive levels in appropriately listed banks and insurers. This is to reinforce the firm's own due diligence and to ensure more effective scrutiny at Board level.[38] The FSA's own Business Plan 2010/11 is indicative of the robust approach planned by the FSA that includes deterrence in enforcement, changing the culture of supervision, implementing the reforms advocated by the Turner Review and creating a link between regulation and financial stability.

There have been a number of high profile prosecutions that underline a robust approach to regulation. The FSA's Annual Review for 2008/09 reported that the FSA imposed a record £27.3 million in financial penalties compared to an average of £14 million over the previous five years, with an increase in FSA investigations and inquiries. The approach taken is indicative of the FSA's new directions. Selective cases are investigated and effectiveness in terms of public profile and

35 [2009] EWCA Crim 1941; [2010] 1 All ER 1183.

36 FSA, 'Decision Procedure and Penalties Manual and the Enforcement Guide', PS07/12 (July 2007).

37 Sir David Walker, *A Review of Corporate Governance in UK Banks and other Financial Industry Entities* (26 November 2009); FSA, 'Effective Corporate Governance (Significant Influence Controlled Functions and the Walker Review)', CP10/3 (January 2010).

38 See Recommendation 23 of the Walker Review.

stakeholder awareness are overriding principles. Considerations include whether the alleged misconduct poses a serious risk to the objectives of the FSA; if the nature of the allegation is sufficiently serious or not; if there is actual or potential consumer loss or detriment; if there is evidence or risk of financial crime or market abuse and whether there is an FSA priority to raise standards in that sector over the issue raised.

There is also a priority given to taking cases against individuals rather than against firms. This also reinforces the approach that the threat of criminal prosecutions is a deterrent against market abuse and might include custodial sentences. Three insider dealing cases were begun in 2009 concluding with two convictions and a custodial sentence. There are also a number of investigations into mortgage fraud resulting in 23 mortgage brokers being found guilty with penalties of over £100,000 in fines.

The future of criminal prosecutions depends on the development of a network of information and strategies to combat market manipulation and abuse. General market misconduct needs to be addressed through the successful prosecution of high profile hard cases and also a public awareness and debate about strategy and how the public interest is to be protected. This debate is likely to be controversial and includes the question of the granting of immunities in return for evidence, whistle-blowing within the city and even the use of 'supergrasses' for collecting evidence. There are dangers in malicious motives giving rise to unjust prosecutions and considerable doubts about the effectiveness of such strategies[39] in the light of human rights considerations and protections afforded to the accused. There is also a debate over whether civil or criminal sanctions are to be given priority and which is likely to be most cost-effective and offer adequate deterrence.

The FSA prosecution policy has further intensified. Fines are regularly levied and the scale of activity has increased. In 2009 the then Director of the Fraud Prosecution Service, a specialist unit of the Crown Prosecution Service, was made Chief Criminal Counsel and this gave the FSA added specialist experience.[40] In recent years the experience and publicity of high profile prosecutions and fines has shaped changing perceptions about the FSA and its competence. It remains to be seen whether the FCA, the new organization that will take over the FSA's role, will act in a similar way. The ingoing Chief Executive has undertaken a review of the adequacy of the UK's civil and criminal sanctioning powers.

The LIBOR Crisis and Future Regulation

The on-going nature of the financial crisis has not abated in recent times. The revelations at the end of June 2012 that Barclays Bank was involved in 'rigging'

39 G. Wilson and S. Wilson, 'Market Misconduct, the Financial Services Authority and Creating a System of "City Grasses": Blowing the Whistle on Whistle Blowing', *Company Lawyer* 67 (2010): 80.

40 FSA, *Annual Reports on Criminal Prosecutions* (FSA, 2008).

the LIBOR rate has led to the bank being fined £290 million, a historic amount, the resignation of its Chairman and Chief Executive, and various investigations into the conduct of the Bank.[41] Barclays cooperated with the regulators and strongly denies any wrongdoing and breaches of the criminal law. It is believed that there are other UK banks currently under investigation. The government has promised amendments in the current legislation going through parliament to take account of any recommendations, including the use of criminal sanctions in respect of misrepresentations made on the LIBOR rate.

It is clear that future developments in legislative reforms will have to take account of the current crisis in confidence in the regulatory system. Three comments may be made. First, there is a strong demand for greater public accountability over the banking sector. Second, there is a noticeable distrust in expert systems and a growing frustration with public institutions. Third, the role of parliamentary scrutiny has weakened considerably given the reputation of MPs following the corruption scandals over MPs' expenses. The setting up of an independent inquiry into the LIBOR scandal was controversial: the government favoured the use of the Treasury Committee; the opposition favoured a judge-led independent inquiry. In the event the government view prevailed and the Treasury Committee will report by the end of 2012.

There is also considerable interest in reclaiming the public money invested in the banking sector. The taxation of banking as part of the coalition agreement through a bank levy is high on the political agenda. Setting the rate of the levy is variable and dependent on the calculation of the necessary tax yields, but the bank levy rate is likely to raise £2.2bn in 2012/13 and £2.7-2.8bn over the following four years.[42]

Constitutional Lessons from the UK Experience of the Financial Crisis

The evaluation of the main constitutional lessons from the financial crisis is an on-going debate and focuses on the accountability process both during and after the crisis. Constitutional lessons are to be found in a number of areas: the operation of parliamentary systems of accountability, the role of rights, the formation of coalition government and the impact of fixed term parliaments.

Impact of the Crisis on the Political System and Party System

Assessing the impact of the financial crisis on the political and party system is quite difficult. The election in May 2010 resulted in no single party being able to form a government. After much deliberation, a Conservative-led coalition

41 *The Economist*, 6 July 2012.

42 House of Commons, 'Taxation of Banking', Commons Library Standard Note SN05251 (11April 2012).

government was formed with the Liberal Democrats.[43] This is the first coalition government in modern times. The election result was a rejection of the Labour government under Gordon Brown, blamed by many for the UK's large debt and a failure to deliver strong economic growth. Some regarded the Labour government as responsible for the financial crisis in the UK and the failures in the Tripartite system of financial regulation, particularly over the collapse of Northern Rock PLC. Widespread speculation prior to the election that there would be a hung parliament proved to be justified. Considerable effort was undertaken to provide for that eventuality in terms of setting out the procedures to be followed and the timetable to be taken. Attention was given to the drafting of the Cabinet Manual setting out the rules and procedures in the event of a hung parliament, which was supported by the House of Commons Justice Committee. In the light of the May 2010 experience the Cabinet Manual was re-drafted and published in December 2010. These unusual steps were in part motivated by the need to have in place as soon as possible after the election a strong government and in part influenced by the political uncertainties that might lead to financial market instability. As Professor Robert Blackburn suggested, this was a change to conventional practice particularly in the role and function of the civil service, required to facilitate political negotiations on the formation of the government.[44]

The coalition government took the step of creating a policy document that sets out its main policies and legislative programmes, *The Coalition: Our Programme for Government*.[45] This is a fundamental document that provides the basis for the next five years of the expected life of the coalition government. This is in line with one of the major impacts of coalition government, the passage of the Fixed-Term Parliaments Act 2011, taken under a time-tabling procedure in the House of Commons[46] that sets the period for the Bill to be debated and agreed. The impact of the new Act is to limit the term of the parliament to five years including arrangements for calling the election in May 2015. Early parliamentary elections may be held either through a vote of no confidence in the government, within 14 days of such a vote in the House of Commons, or a vote by at least two-thirds of all MPs in favour of an early election. The Act provides detailed provision

43 House of Lords, 'Debate on 20th January: Constitutional and Parliamentary Effect of Coalition Government', Lords Library Note 2011/002 (17 January 2011).

44 R. Blackburn et al., *Who Governs? Forming a Coalition or a Minority Government in the Event of a Hung Parliament* (Hansard Society and the Study of Parliament Group, 2010).

45 HM Government: *The Coalition: Our Programme for Government* (2010). Generally see R. Hazell and A. Paun (eds), *Making Minority Government Work: Hung Parliaments and the Challenges for Westminster and Whitehall* (Institute for Government and the Constitution Unit, 2011).

46 House of Commons, 'Timetabling of Constitutional Bills since 1997', Commons Library Standard Note SN/PC/06371 (29 July 2012).

on dissolution of parliament if required before the expiry of the five-year period. Dissolution may be triggered if 55 per cent or more of the House votes in favour.

The Act places a long standing royal prerogative of dissolution on a codified statutory framework. The coalition government has also introduced a major constitutional innovation, proposals for having recall elections for MPs as part of the coalition agreement. The proposals are contained in the Draft Recall Bill 2011. The operation of recall of an individual MP may be triggered by an MP being convicted of an offence and receiving a custodial sentence of 12 months or less, or where the House of Commons in exercising its disciplinary functions resolves that an MP should be recalled.[47] The Bill is currently being debated and is expected to become law in late 2012.

A further impact of the financial crisis is the publication of a revised version of the Cabinet Manual for the first time. Written by the then head of the Civil Service and Cabinet Secretary, the Cabinet Manual,[48] in draft form before the May 2010 election, was published in December 2010. The Cabinet Manual contains a detailed guide of the main rules, procedures and workings of government. The guide is an important constitutional document and broadly modelled on the New Zealand experience, where a similar document has been in operation for some time. As a work of reference it is the first attempt to have in a published form the workings of government. In effect the unwritten parts of the UK's Constitution are being gradually transformed into a written form.

The internal workings of the government also reflect coalition government. Key ministerial offices have been shared with the coalition partners with the Deputy Prime Minister, a Liberal Democrat, having to work alongside a Conservative Prime Minister. Party political tensions are in evidence over some of the key issues surrounding human rights and membership of the EU. The party political issues surrounding two political parties sharing power in government are contained in the *Coalition Agreement for Stability and Reform* published on 20 May 2010. Some key issues that divided the two political parties in the past are addressed. This includes the promise of a referendum on the change in the electoral system from first past the post to an Alternative Vote (AV) system (this was subsequently held and defeated); the renewal of Trident but the agreement for the Liberal Democrats to look for alternatives; nuclear power stations but allowing the Liberal Democrats to oppose this policy; married couples' tax allowances, but allowing the Liberal Democrats to abstain; higher education funding, but allowing the Liberal Democrats to abstain in certain circumstances.

There are also areas where it was necessary to ensure that the unelected House of Lords does not try to vote down at second or third reading a government bill that has been approved in the House of Commons. The so-called Salisbury Convention has been applied. This is intended to avoid a clash between Commons and Lords.

---

47 See House of Commons, 'Recall Elections', Commons Library Standard Note SN05089 (8 October 2012).

48 HM Government, *The Cabinet Manual* (1st edn, TSO, 2011).

There have also been some changes in parliamentary working practices. Seating in the Commons represented government and opposition. The front bench now comprises the two coalition parties. The architecture of the House of Lords has proved to be more complicated and this has required some reconfiguration, including the order of speakers and additional seating. The Coalition Agreement also promises reform of the House of Lords into a wholly or partially elected house, but with a smaller size of no more than 300 members. There is a bill before parliament currently being debated on Lords reform.

Parliamentary Accountability

Limited parliamentary debate was possible during the height of the crisis and the rescuing of Northern Rock. The Bank of England's powers to manage the crisis under the Banking Act 2009 limited parliamentary oversight. Stabilization options were not subject to parliamentary scrutiny as the legal powers did not require prior authorization or parliamentary legislation. There are also questions about the effectiveness of various constitutional actors including select committees. Criticism of the Bank of England has already been noted, especially in terms of the debate over transparency and effectiveness. Doubts remain as to how the Bank of England will develop its new role after the FSA is disbanded.

The Treasury has been the subject of criticism that it failed to predict the financial crisis and take the relevant steps to avert its consequences. A recent internal review of the Treasury's management response to the financial crisis, undertaken by Sharon White, makes a number of findings and recommendations.[49] The findings included recognizing the additional support provided within the Treasury and the workload attended to by Treasury officials. Lessons gained include better contingency planning and mobilization, establishing better links between financial stability and macroeconomic policy, continuous monitoring of financial risks and procurement of external advisers where required. Various recommendations are included to strengthen the workings of the Treasury. Crisis management is at the heart of the strategy with proactive risk assessment as part of a new management style. Salaries for civil servants also need to be addressed in a department where there is an average annual turnover of 25 per cent of staff. Retaining expertise is challenging and difficult especially when the private sector attracts higher salaries and more attractive employment opportunities. Organizational challenges remain for the future including clarity about protecting the taxpayers' interests through risk assessment and evaluation.

The success of the government's financial reforms will depend on providing sufficient integration with the Bank of England and the new regulatory authorities. Drawing together the different strands of constitutional impact is challenging. Much can be made of the advice received within the civil service and made

49 HM Treasury, *Review of HM Treasury's Response to the Financial Crisis* (March 2012).

available to Ministers. Tension between public sector advice and private sector expertise may leave regulatory agencies struggling to compete. Perhaps the greatest constitutional problem is to make the civil service more reactive and better trained to contend with private operators and their expertise.

Austerity budgets within national systems add to the pressure on democratically elected governments to balance popular support with external pressures for fiscal responsibility. National interests protected by constitutional authority have set up tensions within the EU.

In order to strengthen UK supervision of the financial sector and ensure that there is sufficient oversight, the UK initially adopted a Fiscal Responsibility Law. This provides a strengthening of debt arrangements, but unlike those in Germany the UK arrangements stop short of an enforceable constitutional debt brake. Germany's so-called 'debt brake' is a constitutional mechanism that seeks to ensure that fiscal policy is legally immune from direct political interference and bid for debt-funded public spending. Eurozone countries have adopted a similar approach to Germany through the Fiscal Compact, a mechanism to constrain debt and borrowing .The Fiscal Compact was established for 26 out of the 27 EU member states (with the exception of the UK) and adopted through an intergovernmental agreement (international agreement) outside the institutional framework of the EU. This was followed by the Treaty on Stability, Coordination and Governance in the Economic and Monetary Union (TSCG), signed by 25 member states (the UK and the Czech Republic are the two exceptions).

The UK's Fiscal Responsibility Act 2010 strengthened the Treasury Code of Fiscal Responsibility and parliamentary scrutiny by requiring the Treasury to undertake a number of key measures: from 2011 to 2016 the Treasury must ensure that public sector borrowing as a percentage of GDP is reduced from the previous year; overall by the end of the financial year 2014, the Treasury has a duty to ensure that borrowing is reduced by at least a half from the financial year 2010; to secure sound finances, the Treasury has duties to make good reductions in applying the fiscal stability principles to the public finances; the Treasury must make regular progress reports to parliament to ensure that the strategy to provide reductions in borrowing and sound finances are secured in the relevant Economic and Fiscal Strategy Reports and Pre-Budget reports.

The Act provided parliament with the potential to vote on the government's medium-term fiscal plans including proposed borrowing and debt totals. The Fiscal Responsibility Act 2010 has been replaced by the Budget Responsibility and National Audit Act 2011 with a new Charter for Budget Responsibility setting out the Treasury's rules for the constraint of debt. There are debt management objectives and targets for fiscal policy, otherwise known as the fiscal mandate. This supersedes the previous arrangements. There is to be an annual Financial Statement and Budget Report containing the details of the government's policy. The coalition government has adopted two fiscal rules to constrain government behaviour. The Fiscal Mandate states that the structural current budget must be forecast to be in balance or in surplus at the end of the five-year parliament; the supplementary target states that public sector net debt as a share of national income should be falling by a fixed date of 2015/16. Meeting the above requirements will be hard and unpredictable. Under the new legislation the coalition government set up the independent Office of Budget Responsibility (OBR) under the Budget Responsibility and National Audit Act 2011 to ensure compliance. There is considerable uncertainty in achieving these goals because of many variables such as oil prices, the stability of the eurozone, the performance of the economy and income receipts. In constitutional terms the creation of the Office of Budget Responsibility is an innovation marking out the necessity for an independent body to oversee the government's handling of the economy and to act as a check on the Treasury. This serves to underline one of the foundations of UK government accountability.

The financial crisis has had profound effects on the way banks are regulated and the effectiveness of constitutional scrutiny. It is important to consider these questions in the context of banking regulation in the UK, that is the soon to be replaced Tripartite arrangements under the Financial Services and Markets Act 2000 – the Bank of England, the Treasury and the FSA. The coalition government made major architectural changes to this tripartite arrangement of financial regulation including making the Bank of England the key financial regulator with the abolition of the FSA and the splitting up of its functions. This adds considerable uncertainty especially in the unproven nature of these changes. Political tinkering is much in evidence in choosing the most appropriate form of regulation and whether this will prove effective is very much open to discussion. Could outcome-based regulation offer a more effective form of regulation or is the government's desire to return to a light touch form of principles-based regulation moving the goal posts once more?

Since March 2009, the Bank of England has been active in pursuing a policy of quantitative easing (QE). This is undertaken by the governor of the Bank of England, with the tacit agreement of the Chancellor of the Exchequer. The reporting mechanism is through the Monetary Policy Committee (MPC). The governor of the Bank of England may be called before the Treasury Committee or the Public Accounts Committee and questioned, but this is very much after the event. Total amounts of QE are £325bn to 9 February 2012,[50] with an additional £50bn in June 2012 making a total of £375bn.

Overall there have been some improvements on the work of select committees of the House of Commons, known as the Wright Committee Reforms (named after its chairman former Labour MP Tony Wright). There is now a Backbench Business Committee. Chaired by a member of a non-governing party and composed of members elected by secret ballot, it is intended to reflect more cross-party voices outside the direct patronage of the Whips. This is designed to strengthen parliamentary scrutiny over the executive. This is the first business committee of

50 House of Commons, 'Quantitative Easing', Commons Library Standard Note SN/EP/4997 (22 March 2012).

any kind established by the House to give backbench MPs an opportunity to bring forward debates of their choice.

Rights and Judicial Oversight

The unwritten nature of the UK's Constitution leaves little opportunity for constitutional review by the courts. Judicial review provides an important forum to consider the legality of public bodies. The Human Rights Act 1998 has strengthened judicial oversight but stops short of allowing the courts to overturn an Act of Parliament. A declaration of incompatibility allows the courts to declare an Act of Parliament incompatible with the European Convention of Human Rights (ECHR) but it is for parliament to determine whether to remedy the incompatibility through amending legislation. The Conservative-led coalition government has an ambivalent attitude to human rights and has set up a Commission on a British Bill of Rights. On the ECHR, the coalition has been highly critical of the Strasburg-based European Court of Human Rights.[51]

The courts have been limited in their role over the financial crisis. The clearest example of a legal challenge came with the nationalization of Northern Rock PLC, which left many shareholders aggrieved as their compensation payments did not meet their expectations and in many cases no compensation was payable at all. The government case was that over £54bn of taxpayers' money had been invested in the bailout of Northern Rock in the form of loans and guarantees. The Bank of England as the creditor of last resort argued that in 2008 the application of an Order to nationalize Northern Rock was simply acting on the reality of the situation. Northern Rock was unable to provide sufficient funds to meet its creditors. The government acted in the public interest and did so as representatives of the taxpayers to ensure that financial support was sufficient to meet the needs of Northern Rock. Compensation was payable to shareholders, but this was subject to a scheme administered by a valuer. In many cases the valuation scheme resulted in no compensation being payable.

The shareholders argued that their shares should be valued at more than £4 each and they formed an association and sought judicial review against the Treasury's decision to nationalize.[52] The application of the scheme left many shareholders with nothing or virtually nothing for their shares; given the financial problems that the bank was suffering, its share price was also non-existent. The claimants argued that they had been debarred from making representations to the valuer and were unable to query or contribute to the fairness of the assessment. The Court rejected the shareholders' arguments and held that the decision to nationalize and make valuations of the shares was not one that came from government policy but simply

51 House of Commons 'The UK and Reform of the European Court of Human Rights', Commons Library Standard Note SN/IA/6277 (27 April 2012).

52 See unreported judicial review, 19 February 2009.

from the facts that had arisen in the specific circumstances of Northern Rock.[53] Northern Rock was nationalized to ensure that it was retained as a going concern and this was achieved through the issuing of loans. The claim in the British courts, including an appeal to the Court of Appeal, failed even though many shareholders received no direct compensation. The shareholders also argued that when Northern Rock was nationalized it was not insolvent and many shareholders were prepared to have their shares held for a long term. The Court of Appeal took the view that the design of the compensation scheme was reasonable and took account of the value of the shares based on the fact that Northern Rock was unable to pay its debts without government financial support.

The shareholders also took their case under the ECHR.[54] The main arguments were similar to those raised in the British courts, but they argued that under Art. 34 and Rules 45 and 47 of the Court that state nationalization should give rise to compensation. The state's justification was based on the claim that there had been considerable financial support to ensure the survival of the company. The shareholders argued that they had been treated unfairly and disproportionally. All the arguments were rejected. Northern Rock was sold to Virgin in November 2011, ironically one of the main bidders that had been unsuccessful in 2008.

The courts have not been active in the aftermath of the financial crisis, reflecting their limited jurisdiction to review the merits of policy-making. This is an important aspect of the UK's system of constitutional checks and balances.

Sovereignty Issues: The UK's Membership of the EU and Attitudes to the Treaty on Stability

UK attitudes to the current financial crisis have impacted on public perception of the EU. The Conservative-led coalition government has increased its scepticism of EU legislation and the implications for the UK. In December 2010, the coalition government adopted new Guiding Principles for EU legislation. The Guidelines provide an alternative to adopting EU legislation in order to secure UK interests. The aim is to enhance UK competitiveness and ensure the minimum of regulation.[55] Consequently the UK has adopted an increasingly sceptical approach to the TSCG. Largely this is a matter of political discussion and was undertaken without prior parliamentary debate. Reservations about the TSCG arise because of a perceived threat to national sovereignty not least because of the operation of the

53 Cases such as *Beyler* v. *Italy* 33202/96 no. 10 (2001) 33 EHRR 52 ECHR were considered.

54 *R (on the application of SRM Global Master Fund Lp, RAB Special Situations (Master) Fund Limited; Dennis Grainger and others* v. *The Commissioners of Her Majesty's Treasury* [2009] EWCA Civ 788.

55 House of Commons, 'How the UK Government deals with EU Business', Commons Library Standard Note SN/IA/6323 (10 May 2012).

QMV principle on financial services whereby no single country has an absolute veto. Historically the UK has been able to object to measures when required by working closely with countries such as the Netherlands, Sweden and Finland in the form of a blocking group. The only exception to QMV is the proposed financial transaction tax, which as a taxation measure requires unanimity. The UK regards the Fiscal Compact as having profound implications for a country's autonomy.[56] The main issue is whether the national budgetary discipline that is provided in the Fiscal Compact is a practical and workable reality in the context of the politics of national parliaments. The sovereignty of the state is under threat if the Fiscal Compact is applied too rigorously. There are some doubts over the efficacy of ensuring that the rules relating to budget deficits are taken into the form of a written constitution or given legal effect that is enforceable in the courts. There are also some doubts that the TSCG is needed at all. It is arguable that most of the powers might be already found in the existing treaties.[57] Underlying the issues raised are questions of democratic legitimacy even though it is accepted that EU treaties and EU law would take precedence over the TSCG requirements. There is also a role for the national parliaments that needs to be taken into account. The general conclusion is that the TSCG cannot take precedence over the other EU treaties. The UK is also concerned that the Court of Justice will be given jurisdiction over the TSCG. As guardian of the TSCG this would be the first time the Court has jurisdiction over a non-EU European Inter-governmental Agreement at the request of member states.

Aside from the TSCG, there is the European Stability Mechanism (ESM), intended to replace the existing EFSM. The UK is part of the ESM even though not in the eurozone, and intends to support the setting up of a permanent stability mechanism. The EU (Approval of Treaty Amendment Decision) Bill (HL) 2011 makes it possible for the UK to support the ESM but subject to statutory arrangements within the UK.[58]

56 Eurozone states have to introduce into their law or constitutions the requirement that the annual structural deficit does not exceed 0.5 per cent of nominal GDP; member states that breach a 3 per cent deficit limit will face automatic sanctions at EU level; the EU Commission will give oversight to national budgets and make recommendations; the European Stability Mechanism would be brought into operation once member states represented 90 per cent of the capital commitments ratified on Treaty change; EU members would pay extra funds ($200bn) into the IMF to part-finance bailouts; the EU Council President would publish reports on progress and there would be regular eurozone summits.

57 Arts 5-7, Directive 2011/85.

58 House of Lords, 'European (Approval of Treaty Amendment Decision) Bill HL Bill 3 2012-13', Lords Library Note 2012/019.

The Impact of the Financial Crisis on the Regulatory Debate and Constitutional Theory

The impact of the financial crisis in the UK has raised questions about the type of regulation and how regulatory theory engages with effective outcomes. Many of the banks are under quasi state ownership with large amounts of public money at risk. Politically motivated regulatory reforms may have uncertain outcomes and may vary from light touch to more substantive forms of tougher review. Defining each of the regulatory approaches is not easy. Many overlap with each other. The terminology is often imprecise. Many of the terms are based on economic concepts that do not easily translate into legal regulation. In vogue at present is responsive regulation. This involves a blend of persuasion and coercion. Expectations may be met by adjusting the form of review when required. Smart regulation suggests that in different ways consumers may act through markets, civil society and other institutions. Risk-based regulation is based on the premise that intervention is needed in the event of non-compliance. This is based on an evaluation of the degree of risk. There is also a calculation based on the regulatory body's ability to seek compliance. In terms of resources and responsibilities this may influence the approach to be taken. Meta-regulation involves some form of responsibility shared with the regulated organizations. Risk management is undertaken by the individual organization.

Warning of the dangers of adopting a principles-based approach for financial regulation, Julia Black[59] identified a number of concerns including the generality with which the principles are drafted; the call for qualitative assessment rather than quantitative analysis; the diversity and breadth of their application; that the principles assume behavioural standards; that breaches of the principles are largely based on fault and it is assumed that through enforcement sanctions will be controlled. There is an underlying assumption that competitive tendencies between the banks will result in the market applying competition principles that will complement principles-based regulation. In fact the idea of principles-based regulation is to encourage market forces rather than act as an impediment. This assumes that large banks may be too big to fail or that if a poorly performing bank does fail, it will be rescued by powerful competitors who will ensure that the market is self-adjusting. It was largely unforeseen that systemic weaknesses even among large banks might threaten the system as a whole.

There are clear risks associated with the principles-based approach. Complex legal obstacles when seeking to enforce the rules may come from technical and divergent interpretations of EU rules. Vagueness and ambiguity may arise over the delegation of so much discretion to the firms themselves as interpretations can vary. It is possible that there may be a lack of certainty in the standards that are being

59 J. Black, 'Tensions in the Regulatory State', *Public Law* (2007): 58-73. See also T. Prosser, 'Models of Economic and Social Regulation', in Oliver, Prosser and Rawlings, *Regulatory State*, pp. 34-49, at p. 48.

applied and if and when they are to be enforced. There may be a proliferation of rules to the point that they may be ignored or simply contested. Minimum standards and best practice may become blurred and impossible to apply. Unpredictability in enforcement and inadequate training, knowledge and skills of the regulators or those being regulated may make the rules impossible to apply, and accountability issues may arise. This may occur through inadequate consultation or a degree of institutional capture of the regulators by the industry they regulate.[60] There is an increasing need to identify and reinforce the public interest in the future of regulation especially since the taxpayer is seriously exposed through the support given to the UK's banks.

The NAO's report, *Delivering Regulatory Reform* (February 2011), sets the future direction of regulatory reform. The report makes clear that regulation is a 'key tool' used by departments to achieve policy objectives:

> Complying with regulation can create costs, for example, for businesses. The cost of compliance can be a direct cost, such as licences or buying equipment to comply with regulation, often known as the policy cost. Regulated entities also face indirect costs, for example the time spent understanding legislative requirements, which are usually referred to as administrative burdens.[61]

It is clear that the direction of regulatory reform towards 'tougher' financial regulation has to be reconciled with the general approach adopted by the coalition government that regulation should be minimal with active steps to reduce regulation and regulatory burdens. The government has set up a new Cabinet Committee, the Reducing Regulation Committee, established in May 2010, to ensure that there is a robust case for any new regulations. Regular steps are taken to monitor departmental implementation of this policy. This takes effect in the following way: the system of 'one in one out' applies where the cost of new regulation must be compensated for by a corresponding cut; a policy for departments to challenge the costs and the need for regulation; the use of 'sunset clauses' to end tick-the-box systems and require that regulations should automatically expire after a certain time period; rolling review programmes of current approaches to regulation; and ensuring that additional costs and burdens are being controlled.

The impact of policy is intended to ensure that any regulatory reform strikes the right balance between the benefits of regulation and its costs. Improvements are on-going to the 'better regulation' agenda and place emphasis on improving the regulatory and policy-making framework; the coalition government is operating under the assumption that current levels of regulation are excessive and reducing regulation for business is one of its key commitments.

---

60 J. Black, M. Hopper and C. Band, 'Making a Success of Principles-based Regulation', *Law and Financial Markets* (2007): 191-206.

61 NAO, C&AG, Department for Business, *Delivering Regulatory Reform*, HC 758 Session 2010-11 (17 February 2011), 4 (NAO, 2011).

The lessons from the crisis are partly regulatory and in favour of more robust forms of accountability. Financial elites trusted with regulatory day-to-day stewardship failed. The legitimacy of their role and function is open to doubt and the need for participation and transparency has shown strains in the traditional role of parliamentary oversight. The movement within the eurozone towards greater institutional oversight over national banks and treasuries is resisted within the UK. Equally compelling is increased regulatory supervision and vigilance supported by penalties and deterrence against wrongdoing. Cultural change is widely recognized as being required yet the means to achieve this is uncertain and vague. As Carol Harlow has noted, there is 'no "one-size-fits-all"'[62] and the need for different values and public inclusion are remarkably important in the design and operation of more effective scrutiny and improved policy-making.

Conclusions

Clear constitutional lessons from the UK's experience of the financial crisis are difficult to provide. This is partly because of the strong political agenda set by the government of the day, which overshadows much of the debate and analysis. It is also difficult to assess many of the changes as the arrangements for the replacement of the FSA are on-going. The problem with the recent reforms and general approach is that the changes are untested. The financial crisis has managed to raise issues about the legitimacy of the regulatory structures and the system of regulation in terms of the role of law, expert systems and independent regulation and regulators. Rule-based systems and legislative solutions are applied too readily without an appropriate diagnosis and analysis driven output. As Carol Harlow has explained:

> Legitimacy is always contingent and contestable; different circumstances require different answers; no one answer is sufficient. Much depends too on the eye of the beholder. Elites favour élite theories of delegated legitimacy based on effectiveness and expertise, in part reflecting their own élite status and … are sometimes surprised to find that others feel differently. Representative democracy is untidy and often ineffective, yet it seems to claim a greater degree of public support … there is no 'one-size-fits-all' solution.[63]

It is clear from this chapter that prudent financial regulation requires the correct institutional support as well as the appropriate regulatory techniques. In the lead up to the 2008 banking crisis, the UK adopted various forms of 'principles'-based regulation. Held responsible for many of the regulatory failures, principles-based

---

62 C. Harlow, 'The Concepts and Methods of Reasoning of the New Public Law: Legitimacy', LSE Legal Studies Working Paper 19/2010, p. 38.

63 Ibid., pp. 37-38.

regulation was heavily criticized by the FSA, which favours outcomes-based regulation and a general strengthening of regulatory oversight. Learning from past mistakes, the FSA adopted a more robust approach to prosecutions than it had in the past, and a greater vigilance in terms of improving and maintaining better operational risk controls. Strategic planning engages with financial companies to develop their own risk-based systems of assessment.

As Julia Black has observed, 'Meanwhile, other regulators are climbing on the PBR [principles-based regulation] bandwagon just as it appears to be abandoned by its main proponents.'[64] The UK example has proved how over-reliance on a particular version of regulation led to a systemic failure to regulate effectively and contributed to the UK banking crisis and the need to nationalize Northern Rock. Perhaps one of the most interesting aspects of the UK's experience is the separation of the regulatory architecture from the type of regulation to be deployed. There is much confusion and even contradiction in the present thinking, leading to some uncertainty and lack of clarity as to how regulation is to be viewed in the future. Even the terminology is inexact. Principles-based regulation is out of favour but is likely to reappear in different guises and fresh terminology.

The coalition government's recent White Paper refers to a 'new, more judgement-focused approach' to prudential regulation.[65] There is considerable uncertainty as to whether this will work in practice. The technical detail is important. It is certainly intended to be more robust than the past but it largely relies on the pre-existing handbook and evaluations. This leaves a lack of clarity over the future type of regulation and how the new regulatory system that replaces the Tripartite arrangements will work. The vulnerability of the new system is its link to political influence and oversight. Doubts remain about the effectiveness of the Bank of England as part of the new architectural support for effective financial regulation. The past history of the Bank of England in such matters is not reassuring. The dislocation and inevitable cultural changes brought about by major new institutional arrangements will need some time to settle. This is not to suggest that it is inevitable that the Bank of England will fail to live up to the expectations placed upon it but more that it might be wrong-footed by events when speed is of the essence and political sensitivity at its height. The weight of political influence may not always serve the new arrangements well. The FSA has gained a great deal from the aftermath of the 2008 financial crisis and it is disappointing that uncertainty remains about its legacy. The FSA had not lived up to its hyped world 'pre-eminence' but equally it contributed to a single line of command for all financial institutions as a 'single point of contact'. The abolition of the FSA marks a major turning point. The transition to the new arrangements will see the FCA covering many of the FSA's responsibilities in the conduct of business supervision and Prudential Regulation Authority authorized firms will be

---

64 J. Black, 'The Rise, Fall and Fate of Principles Based regulation', LSE Working Paper 17/2010, p. 3.

65 'A New Approach to Financial Regulation', para 1.13.

subject to FCA oversight. This will lead inevitably to complication and perhaps even boundary disputes.

There is no perfect regulatory system and no ideal regulatory model. The current uncertainties in financial markets make the UK's introduction of its new institutional regulatory architecture particularly risky. Added to this there is confusion about how 'light touch' regulation can be made more effective. The expected splitting up of different parts of the banking industry following the Vickers Report will inevitably test the new arrangements. Even if this proposal is not fully implemented there remains the question of how to regulate banks that are too big to fail. The role of the governor of the Bank of England will be critical to the success of the new arrangements. There are also issues about the Bank's accountability and the role of parliament. The role of the Chancellor of the Exchequer and Treasury in terms of political influence and policy-making is also critical.

The financial crisis has also raised questions about the financial arrangements for public money to support private and market-led institutions. At the same time there has been an increasing Eurosceptic approach to EU membership and an awakening of national sovereignty. The UK is outside the euro and it also opted out of the European Council's discussion of a Fiscal Compact in December 2011. The statement agreed by the euro area heads of state was supported by 26 of the 27 EU member states with the exception of the UK. This was followed in January 2012 by a new Treaty on Stability, Coordination and Governance in the Economic Monetary Union which was not agreed to by the UK. There remain divided opinions on the UK's position. Isolation is favoured by some but criticized by others. This should not distract us from learning from the UK's response to the financial crisis in terms of its own constitutional arrangements as well as its relationship with Europe.

Finally, there are questions about the lasting nature of the various constitutional changes introduced by the coalition government. There is a detectable movement in favour of codifying much of the unwritten procedure and practice of government into a written form such as the Cabinet Manual. Growing Euroscepticism and the possibility of a referendum may lead the UK in a different direction far from other member states. Systems of parliamentary scrutiny and accountability appear inadequate to the task of robust scrutiny, leaving many to question the future economic stability of the UK banking system. The coalition arrangements have created a new synergy in policy-making. The financial crisis has afforded an opportunity to reconfigure the state in its relationship with the citizen. Consequently, issues about legitimacy and the rule of law set frequent challenges for the authority of government and policy-makers. Regulators and regulation are likely to be the most challenged aspect of our constitutional arrangements with uncertain outcomes that are hard to predict, such is the rapidly changing nature of the financial crisis.

PART III
Second Path: Submission

Chapter 7
The Impact of the Financial Crisis on the Greek Constitution

Xenophon Contiades and Ioannis A. Tassopoulos

Setting the Scene

The financial crisis made a late yet imposing appearance in Greece. The beginning of the crisis can be traced back to the autumn of 2009, when the centre-right government of the New Democracy Party called early elections. 'Greek statistics', that is numbers juggling by the government, account for the remarkable distance between the official deficit figure for the year 2009, which was 5.4 per cent of GDP, and the Eurostat estimation of it a few months later at 15.4 per cent. Greek society was therefore caught utterly by surprise and the new government of the centre-left PASOK Party, led by George Papandreou, was faced with unprecedented challenges.

This sudden disillusionment can be explained by the outstanding growth performance of Greece from 1996 to 2008, when the average annual growth of real GDP according to Eurostat amounted to 3.8 per cent. Factors contributing to this were the liberalization of the credit markets, the growth of the shipping and tourism industries, the deregulation of telecommunications and other product markets, the fiscal stimulus of the 2004 Olympic Games and the steady inflow of funds from the EU. However, beneath this boost lay serious structural weaknesses both in the economy and in the political system. In the realm of the economy such weaknesses were the eurozone–Greece inflation differential, the low level of competitiveness and foreign direct investment, and the persistently large trade deficit.[1] Perhaps of even greater importance were the political and institutional flaws, mainly corruption and lack of efficiency in public administration, clientelism as well as populist political practices, which translated into the adoption and implementation of policies based on criteria strictly related to electoral and partisan strategies.[2] The repeated failure of reforms, which halted any attempt to rationalize the state

1 M. Mitsopoulos and Th. Pelagidis, *Understanding the Crisis in Greece: From Boom to Bust* (Palgrave Macmillan, 2012).

2 Ch. Lyrintzis, 'The Changing Party System: Stable Democracy, Contested "Modernization"', *West European Politics* 28(2) (2005): 242-259.

mechanisms and the regulation of the economy, was a lingering problem both before and after the crisis.[3]

Since the beginning of 2010 the crisis has accelerated at a rapid pace. The first sign appeared in December 2009, when Greece's credit rating was downgraded from A− to BBB+ for the first time in more than a decade. In March 2010 a radical austerity package was adopted, consisting mainly of tax increases and wage and pension cuts. Faced with the danger of default, as the austerity measures taken were deemed inadequate by international markets, in April Greece requested the activation of an EU/IMF bailout package. The first bailout loan, granted to Greece in May 2010, was accompanied by the signature of a memorandum, whereby Greece undertook the obligation to tackle its budget deficit through the introduction of severe budget cuts. A series of legislative packages followed, imposing unprecedented austerity measures as well as introducing reforms; yet their actual implementation proved to be much harder than anticipated. A large part of this legislation was challenged before the courts with regard to its constitutionality, which inevitably triggered a heated constitutional debate.

One year later, in June 2011, in the midst of general strikes and violent clashes between police and protestors, the Papandreou government, apparently under tremendous pressure, narrowly won a confidence vote and parliament approved a five-year austerity package. In July the EU leaders agreed on a €109bn bailout for Greece. In October 2011 new general strikes and violent protests broke out, while on 26-27 October a second bailout loan, which reduced Greece's debt by 50 per cent, was agreed on by EU leaders, the IMF and banks. As the adoption of new harsh measures was due, Prime Minister Papandreou decided to hold a referendum to request the opinion of the people on the conditions of the new agreement. Under immense pressure exerted by the French and German leaders, by his own party and by the opposition parties as well, Papandreou called off the referendum on 3 November. As a vote of confidence was pending in parliament and Papandreou was faced with the eminent danger of losing it, a constitutional absurdum occurred: the Prime Minister won the vote of confidence under the unprecedented condition that he would subsequently resign, so that a coalition government could be formed. One week later, on 11 November, an interim coalition government was indeed formed with the participation of PASOK, New Democracy and a far right-wing party, the Popular Orthodox Rally (LAOS). The new Prime Minister, Loukas Papademos, was a highly regarded technocrat, ex-vice-president of the European Central Bank. The government's main task was to lead the country to elections, while ensuring that Greece would abide by its commitments regarding the debt restructuring.

Although elections were due for late 2013 according to the Constitution, that is, four years after the previous elections, it was evident that early elections would be called. In February 2012 violent riots broke out again as parliament approved new

3 K. Featherstone and D. Papadimitriou, *The Limits of Europization: Reform Capacity and Policy Conflict in Greece* (Macmillan, 2008).

harsh austerity measures. Forty-three MPs who belonged to the two major parties voted against the measures and as a consequence they were expelled from their parties, and thus the ruling coalition's governing majority was greatly reduced.[4] The second bailout package was finalized on 21 February 2012 and extended from €109bn to €130bn. In April 2012 the debt restructuring was complete and general elections were announced for 6 May.

The elections turned out to be the next act in the drama, as the two major pro-bailout parties, PASOK and New Democracy, who in the 2009 general election had obtained 43.9 per cent and 33.5 per cent of votes respectively, were reduced to a 13.2 per cent and 18.9 per cent, failing thus to obtain the majority of seats. SYRIZA, the coalition of left-wing and far left political parties, quadrupled its power and came second, gaining 16.8 per cent of the popular vote. It is noteworthy that 2012 was the fifth consecutive year of recession for the Greek economy – unemployment rates rose from 11.1 per cent in February 2010 to 22.5 per cent in April 2012, and the income of Greek citizens suffered a shrinkage amounting to 25.3 per cent. Thus the result of the election was an expression of dismay against the political parties held responsible for the situation. The basic feature of the election was fragmentation: seven political parties entered parliament, including for the first time a party of the extreme right (the ultra-nationalist Golden Dawn).

The impossibility of forming a government led to the announcement of new general elections for 17 June 2012. If in the Greek elections of 6 May the prevailing mood was that of anger against the austerity measures and punishment for the established political parties, the elections of 17 June were generally acknowledged, both in Greece and abroad, to be of historical magnitude. Just one week after the announcement of European economic assistance to Spain, on 10 June 2012, Greece's position in the eurozone was at stake, threatening to aggravate the debt crisis with a new dramatic episode in case of a Greek exit. There was a marked contrast between the electoral campaigns of the two elections. In the campaign leading to the May elections, a series of incidents of public heckling of the politicians of the two major parties caused concern for a possible escalation during the second campaign; but with the serious exception of physical violence by an MP of the Golden Dawn Party, the prevailing mood on the way to the elections of 17 June was in general quite phlegmatic, stating in clear terms their dilemmatic nature, also highlighted by public statements of European political leaders and officials.

This time the New Democracy Party received 29.66 per cent of the votes, electing 129 deputies; SYRIZA got 26.89 per cent and 71 seats; PASOK 12.28 per cent and 31 seats; the right-wing populist party of Independent Greeks 7.51 per cent and 21 seats; the Golden Dawn 6.92 per cent and 18 seats; the pro-

4 The Greek Parliament is comprised of 300 members. On constitutional law in Greece, see X. Contiades and A. Fotiadou, 'Constitutional Law in Greece', in L.F.M. Besselink, P.P.T. Bovend'Eert, H. Broeksteeg, R. de Lange and W. Voermans (eds), *Constitutional Law of the EU Member States* (Kluwer Law International, 2013).

European Democratic Left 6.26 per cent and 17 seats, and finally, the Communist Party of Greece 4.50 per cent and 12 seats. The three parties with unwavering pro-European agendas (New Democracy, PASOK, Democratic Left) formed a coalition government under the head of New Democracy's leader Antonis Samaras, with the mandate to guarantee the country's place in the eurozone, effectuating the necessary structural reforms, while at the same time renegotiating and easing up the austerity measures, which had stifled economic growth.

Litigating against the Memorandum and the Austerity Measures

The Greek Legal Order Sanctions the Memorandum and Encounters the Troika's Novel Institutional Setting

The main legislative piece of the first Greek bailout is Law 3845/2010, entitled 'Measures for the Implementation of the Mechanism in Support of the Greek Economy from the Member-States of the Eurozone and the IMF'. Parliament discussed the draft of the law in an extremely tense socio-political environment. The law has been qualified by some deputies as the most important one since 1974, when the dictatorship of the Colonels collapsed.

The structure and the form of Law 3845/2010 are rather atypical. Art. 1 referred to the 'Mechanism for the Consolidation of Greek Economy' described in four attachments, which were an integral part of the law. Attachment I was the 'Statement by the Heads of State and Government of the Euro Area' of 25 March 2010, regarding the creation of a mechanism 'to take determined and coordinated action, if needed, to safeguard financial stability in the euro area as a whole'. Attachment II was the 'Statement on the Support to Greece by Euro Area Member-States' of 11 April 2010, providing among others that

> The Commission, in liaison with the ECB, will start working on Monday April 12th with the International Monetary Fund and the Greek authorities on a joint programme (including amounts and conditionality, building on the recommendations adopted by the Ecofin Council in February). In parallel, Euro area member states will engage the necessary steps, at national level, in order to be able to deliver a swift assistance to Greece.

Attachment III was the 'Memorandum of Economic and Financial Policies' of 3 May 2010, while Attachment IV contained the 'Technical Memorandum of Understanding'. Arts 1 and 2 of the law provided authorizations for the implementation of the programme. Other provisions concerned a number of public spending cuts in areas such as social security and salaries, and new taxes, for example higher TVA, a special contribution by private companies and so on.

The Memorandum reflected the 'determined and coordinated action to safeguard financial stability in the euro area as a whole' (Statement 3.25.2010), engaging national authorities (the Greek Government and the Bank of Greece), European authorities (the European Commission, the European Central Bank, the euro-member states and the European Council) and the IMF. The unprecedented events of spring 2010 led to the creation of a totally novel, at the time, and quite complex institutional setting. The Statement of 25 March 2010 provided that: 'As part of a package involving substantial IMF financing and a majority of European financing, Euro area member states are ready to contribute to coordinated bilateral loans ... For the future, surveillance of economic and budgetary risks and the instruments for their prevention, including the Excessive Deficit Procedure, must be strengthened.' In the mechanism of the Greek bailout, the member states of the eurozone were both partners and debtors. This dual capacity is also reflected in the strong conditionality and the ultimate ratio logic of the Greek bailout.[5] In addition, the monitoring and surveillance of the Greek economy was undertaken by the Troika (the European Commission, the ECB and the IMF), that is a combination of European authorities and an international organization. Originally this structure was tried in the financial assistance to Greece as an ad hoc mechanism.

Subsequently, however, the aforementioned mechanism took a general but temporary form with the European Financial Stabilization Mechanism (EFSM), founded on 7 June 2010. Next, the euro area member states signed the European Stability Mechanism (ESM) treaty on 2 February 2012. The ESM is a permanent structure, in the form of an international financial institution based in Luxembourg, whose purpose is, according to Art. 3 of the Treaty, 'to mobilise funding and provide stability support under strict conditionality, appropriate to the financial assistance instrument chosen, to the benefit of ESM members which are experiencing, or are threatened by, severe financing problems, if indispensable to safeguard the financial stability of the euro area as a whole and of its member states'.[6]

The technicalities described above are useful because they reflect the way the EU moves on and develops through a combination of intergovernmental agreements with the community method. If that were the 'methodology' of the Greek bailout there would be nothing particularly novel or exceptional about it (leaving aside, of course, the unexpected prospect of a default by a eurozone member state). But this time things looked quite different, uncertain and obscure. They were aggravated by the presence of a non-European player, the IMF, who gave the whole enterprise the distinctive aura of globalization at its best. The sovereign debt crisis pushed Europe into a phase of experimentation.

The Greek parliament, in voting Law 3845/2010 incorporating the Memorandum and the other aforementioned attachments, 'sanctioned' from the

5 The Council of the EU on 21 July 2011 decided (par. 3) 'to lengthen the maturity of future EFSF loans to Greece' and 'to provide EFSF loans at lending rates equivalent to those of the Balance of Payments facility (currently approx. 3.5 per cent [instead of the higher original interest rate]), close to, without going below, the EFSF funding cost'.

6 See www.consilium.europa.eu/uedocs/cms_data/docs/pressdata/en/ecofin/127788.pdf.

point of view of the domestic legal order the various acts through which political actors (other than the Greek state) cooperating in the Greek bailout had tried to invest in the appropriate legal form and to ground their political decisions as provided in the basic legal instruments (treaties, charters and so forth) out of which they derived their authority. The fundamental constitutional question regarded the legal significance of this parliamentary sanction, which in turn depended on the exact legal nature of the composite scheme, resulting from the concurring and coordinated action of Greece, the EU's entities, the IMF and the member states.

In voting Law 3845/2010 with its attachments, what was the Greek parliament called to sanction? Merely an international treaty made up ad hoc for the case of Greece? A new form of international cooperation, setting, if successful, a precedent to be applied in other problematic eurozone countries of the European periphery? One step forward on the long way to European integration towards the end of economic government, with the participation of the IMF being merely a technocratic addition, plus of course its contribution in financial aid? Possibly, these questions were not mutually exclusive but in any case they were boiling down to a more fundamental dilemma: was the Greek bailout scheme primarily an international treaty between debtors or an agreement between the partners of the eurozone? As the final scheme implicated both a loan agreement *and* decisions of the EU organs and the eurozone, opting for one horn of the dilemma was a matter of perspective, calling for the interpretation of the legal and political situation. J. Rubenfeld uses the metaphor of a marriage to describe the shift from 'international *cooperation* to international *governance*': 'The EU is an instance of an international "marriage" of this sort. Through the EU, various states merge themselves in a special way with one another, pledging to take each other's opinion and interests into account in their most important decisions, and vowing to submit themselves to supranational governance bodies to manage their affairs.'[7] The parties in a prenuptial agreement may hope not to resort to their agreement, but, just in case, they have set in advance the terms of divorce. Yet the heart of constitutional law is political unity, which is in principle indissoluble. In the USA no bankruptcy of a state could lead to its exit from the Union; but of course it took the American Civil War for recession to become unthinkable, like the dismemberment of the limbs from the body. By contrast, separation is always an open possibility in a marriage, constituting therefore a quite different metaphor for political unity in the EU than the organic and anthropomorphic vision of the nation-state.

In the Greek crisis, separation was openly discussed in the complex and ambivalent political relationship of partners and lenders/debtors. Naturally, some people focused on the continuation of Greece's participation in the eurozone (that is on partnership) as a consequence of the bailout, while others focused on the terms and conditions of a possible default (that is on the termination of partnership), among them Greece's waiver of sovereign immunity under English law for the

7 J. Rubenfeld, 'Unilateralism and Constitutionalism', *New York University Law Review* 79 (2004): 1971-2028, at 2023.

loans of the bailout. Moreover, the representatives of the Troika, the technocrats monitoring the Greek programme of structural reforms and of fiscal and economic policies described in the Memorandum, whose positive report was necessary for the payment of each new instalment of the loan, made very clear the restrictions to sovereignty inextricably bound up with the financial assistance to the country.

In the Penumbras of Sovereignty: The Memorandum before the Greek Council of State

The dubious legal nature of the Greek bailout was brought under the judicial scrutiny of the Greek Council of State, which plays an important centralizing role in the diffused system of constitutional review in Greece, because it has general jurisdiction over the petition for the annulment of administrative acts, according to the French model of the Conseil d'Etat, in the first and last degree. The petitioner, who took the initiative to challenge the constitutionality of the law, was the Bar of Athens in collaboration with other institutions such as the National Union of Public Servants and the Union of Journalists, as well as other persons, who were also litigants in the case. Their petition technically asked the Court to annul administrative acts which executed the cuts and other austerity measures included in the Memorandum between Greece and the Troika as a precondition to continue the subvention of the Greek economy. However, the emphasis was placed on the constitutional provisions guaranteeing popular sovereignty in the international relations of the state – that is in the Greek bailout, the international commitments, agreements and obligations undertaken by the Greek government as a result of the negotiations with the IMF, the ECB and the EC. According to Art. 28.1 of the Constitution, an international treaty ratified by parliament becomes legally superior to statutory law, while Art. 28.2&3 of the Constitution provides the foundation for the participation of the country in the European integration process. The ratification of Greece's accession treaty was voted invoking as constitutional *sedes materiae* Art. 28, without further specification; but according to the prevailing theory it meant a combined application of both paras 2 and 3 of Art. 28, on a cumulative basis of the positive procedural requirements of three-fifths of the total number of parliamentary votes and of the negative material limits of respect for human rights, democracy, equality and reciprocity.

The gist of the petitioners' argument before the Greek Council of State was that the Memorandum, incorporated in Law 3845/2010, although it made concessions of sovereignty and transferred state competences to international organizations (that is the Troika), was not voted in with the necessary enhanced majority of three-fifths of votes, as provided by Art. 28 of the Constitution, and did not fulfil the requirement of Art. 28 that such concessions and transfers promote the public interest, to the extent that the economic policies of the Memorandum were highly dubious and contested. In addition, the argument continued, the austerity measures per se, such as the economic burdens they placed on the shoulders of public servants and pensioners, cutting salaries and pensions horizontally on an allegedly disproportional scale, violated the negative material limits of Art. 28 and especially the constitutional value of human dignity, which guaranteed the minimum level of subsistence.

The Court was squarely faced with the duty to render a diagnosis on the legal nature of the Memorandum and its quite atypical incorporation in Law 3845/2010 in a series of Attachments. Legal certainty and the rule of law render obligatory predictable, clear and secure classification according to the established sources of positive law. J. Raz notes that 'a law is authoritative if its existence is a reason for conforming action and for excluding conflicting considerations'.[8] As already said, however, the Memorandum was a novel and therefore unclassified creature in the legal universe, unknown to traditional legal taxonomy, which provides the template to subsume the various legal instruments and acts under the appropriate legal category. What should the Court do with the Memorandum's legal uncertainty?

The cause of legal complexity was that the Troika-components had legally uneven relations with the Greek legal order, being placed at different levels in the hierarchical pyramid of the sources of law. With regard to EU law the Court seemed ready to recognize that it prevailed even over the Constitution. But, of course, this was inconceivable for the IMF, whose treaty had only supra-statutory validity. What about their offspring, the product of their coordinated activity, the Memorandum? There were various logical combinations available to analyse this tripartite-plus-one(Greece)-relationship, but the critical question concerned the 'European connection'. Depending on its presence or absence, the legal characterization changed. The reason is that the Greek Constitution's conception of sovereignty is fundamentally bipolar, recognizing in principle national and European governance. But nothing similar to the Troika-mechanism exists in the EU Treaties or in secondary EU law. From the point of view of the Greek Constitution, the Troika-mechanism and Memorandum were in the penumbras of sovereignty, between the Greek state, European institutions (Commission, ECB) and an international organization (IMF). Conceived in the grey zone of ambivalence between Greece's debtors (in international loan agreements) and partners within the EU, it could hardly be identified with either, being rather a legal and political hybrid. In the American case of *Griswold* v. *Connecticut*,[9] Justice Douglas invoked the 'penumbras and emanations' of various provisions of the American Constitution to justify the novel right of privacy in American constitutional law. But this interpretive exercise of the Supreme Court moved in the unexplored zones of the constitutional text, not in the penumbras of sovereignty and the uncharted oceans of international relations.

If legal formalism is unhelpful, then functionalism may offer a way out in the quest for a relatively objective legal qualification. Here, however, functionalism's contribution could be limited. It is politically open what will happen in the case that the Troika does not give the green light, while monitoring the programme.

8 J. Raz, *The Authority of Law* (Oxford University Press, 1979), p. 29.

9 381 U.S. 479 (1965).

Most likely Greece will default. And then what is going to be the course of Greek–European relations? Assuming that it is possible to separate the legal identity of lender from that of partner, would this mean that the former does not affect the latter; that what will stop is the financing of Greece's current unbalanced budget, covering, however, pre-existing sovereign debt? These are inherently political questions, accepting only political answers.

The Memorandum Decision of the Greek Council of State

In the seminal Memorandum case, the Council of State rendered its judgment 668/2012, supported by the great majority of its members. The Court rejected even the applicability of Art. 28 of the Constitution, which concerns the transfer of sovereignty and of constitutional competences following an international treaty or agreement, because, according to the Court, the Memorandum was not an international treaty, but a political programme, which came out of the cooperation and planning of the Greek government with the Troika, setting targets to be achieved and policies to be implemented in due time.[10] The incorporation of this

10 The court rejected the argument that the requirement of a supermajority of three-fifths of votes in parliament falls into the category of *interna corporis*, that is that it is a procedural and not a substantive matter. This distinction is all the more important, given that the Greek courts do not have the power to review procedural constitutionality, that is whether parliament kept all the procedural niceties and ramifications regarding the preparation and voting of legislation, but only the substantive unconstitutionality. The ground for the exclusion of procedural unconstitutionality is basically to prevent the involvement of the courts in the *interna corporis* of parliament, infringing therefore its institutional autonomy. Three judges were of the opinion that the question of the three-fifths majority cannot be addressed because, to begin with, there is no transfer of sovereignty to international organizations as required by Art. 28.2 for its application. In any case, in their view, the court would not review whether a law was voted by the plenary session or a section or parliament, a question with which the case of the supermajority was analogous. Three judges were of the concurring opinion that the Memorandum was an international treaty but Art. 28.2 was not applicable because there had been no transfer of sovereignty to international organizations. Three other judges held the concurring opinion that the Memorandum was a preliminary agreement to conclude loan-contracts between states.

There were also *dissents*. A vice-president of the court was of the opinion that the Memorandum is an international treaty which should be ratified by three-fifths of parliament. Another six judges, including one of its vice-presidents, held that the Memorandum was an international agreement, which does not fall into any of the known categories of law-making by the EU, being the product of a source of law that is not established or recognized. Moreover, the incorporation of the Memorandum into the statute as such was not adequate for ratification because it was the draft of an international treaty, and not the treaty itself. Two other judges also held with a similar argumentation that the Memorandum was an international agreement triggering the application of Art. 28. A vice-president held that there is infringement of legislative authority because of the fact that parliament is confronted with a fait accompli. Seven judges held that Greece does not legislate freely as

political programme in statutory law hardly affected its nature. Beyond the specific rules of Law 3845/2010, which enacted the cuts in the salaries and pensions, the various other provisions of the Memorandum, setting goals and courses of action to be pursued, did not cause any immediate legal consequences affecting existing legal rights and duties. Under established principles of public law, parliament, which voted in Law 3845/2010, could not preclude future majorities from changing or even abandoning the Memorandum's political programme. In any case, the Memorandum was not self-executing and the legal implementation of the Memorandum's policies and provisions would have to be enacted through one of the recognized and accepted legal sources of established public law. The Court refused to make assumptions or predictions about the legal nature of the Memorandum that would go beyond its 'rule of recognition',[11] that is the Greek Constitution, which defined its jurisdiction and role. The Court's holding that it would review the measures of the Memorandum as soon as they were enacted in one of the valid sources of Greek law was the legal aspect of the same coin, complementing the nature of the Memorandum as a non-justiciable political programme. This legal qualification of the Memorandum amounts in essence to the endorsement of the doctrine of political questions by the Council of State. It is a classic example of judicial self-restraint on matters of international relations, implicating foreign policy.

This landmark decision, however, should be placed in the wider context of the Council of State's profile and identity. Since 1929, this prestigious court has built its authority on exercising rather rigorous judicial review of the constitutionality of law, while avoiding in general judicial activism (with the significant exception of its jurisprudence on the protection of the environment). In the Memorandum case, self-restraint was not only legally sound and justified in principle, but in addition corresponded to the tradition of the Court. In full awareness of its institutional role, the Court was cautious not to frustrate legislative reforms without giving free leeway to the legislature. The Court indicated that it would enter into a dialogue with the legislator, making it clear that even legislative measures taken under the pressure of the crisis should not violate the principle of proportionality.

Nevertheless, in the past the Court had the opportunity to review legislative measures in times of financial crisis. The Constitution guarantees state intervention, including the power to plan and coordinate economic activity in the country with the aim of securing growth in all sectors of the national economy (Art. 106.1). Invoking the general interest, the jurisprudence of the Council of State recognizes ample authority in the state in regulating the economy. Constitutional limits in the economic intervention of the state come from the application of the principle of proportionality.[12] However, given that the starting point of the analysis is the

provided by Art. 28.3, but under the pressure of the euro group. Finally, a number of judges held that there was a violation of human dignity.

11 See H.L.A. Hart, *The Concept of Law* (Oxford University Press, 1961), p. 92.

12 See, for example, Council of State (in plenum) 2125/1977, 1149/1988.

constitutional affirmation of the state power to take measures for the sake of the economy, the Court applies in essence what would be called in the USA the mere rationality test,[13] rejecting only measures that are obviously unreasonable and arbitrary.[14]

Characteristically, the Council of State has reversed its position, accepting in judgment 1620/2011 that because of the financial crisis the national interest justified the reduction of the interest rate for state debts to 6 per cent instead of the general interest rates of 8.75 per cent to 12.5 per cent. The Court invoked implicitly the reason of state, stating that 'the financial crisis has acquired, due to its unprecedented magnitude, the dimensions of a national crisis'. The Court cited, in this respect, the legislative record of Law 3845/2010, where a default is associated with severe economic, social and even national consequences.

Obviously in the Memorandum case the state interest was beyond doubt. The state had activated its international alliances to secure its funding, and the austerity measures appeared causally connected with the achievement of this goal, being hardly separable from the broader context of the Greek bailout. It was far from obvious that the Memorandum, that is the outcome of a polycentric negotiation, could be reversed by courts substituting their evaluation of the national interest in place of the politically responsible government and the democratically elected parliament. Finally, the climax of the public interest escalated to the European membership of the country, which the Constitution recognized as a vital end (Arts 28 and 80). Human dignity set the ultimate limit to the austerity measures, in case of excessive cuts to pensions and salaries. But the threat to the public interest was imminent and pressing. If the law were not voted in, the country might default in a few days.

Admittedly, the constitutional consequences of the Court's judgment regarding the merely political nature of the Memorandum were a bit strange and awkward. Because, legally speaking, what was the Greek Parliament doing by voting in the Memorandum? In the light of the Court's decision, the answer seems to be that the parliamentary majority of the time voted in a political programme, although according to the Constitution it is the government's and not the legislature's competence to define the political direction of the country (Art. 82 Greek Constitution). Political programmes fall within the political responsibility of Cabinet under the scrutiny of parliament expressed in specific constitutional forms of confidence-vote (Art. 84 Greek Constitution). Parliamentary support for a governmental policy hardly ever takes the form of statutory incorporation of the political programme in question. Conversely, it turned out that parliament did not ratify an international agreement, giving the Memorandum a supra-statutory force

13 *Williamson* v. *Lee Optical Co.* 348 U.S. 483 (1955), discussed in G. Gunther, *Constitutional Law* (11th edn, Foundation Press, 1985), p. 472.

14 Council of State 3665/2005, 4175/1998 plenum, 2522/2000, 24/2011 (limitation to the exercise of legal profession); 441/2011 (price fixing without consideration of minimum cost); 1731/2011 (liberalization of the profession of road transports).

as provided by Art. 28 of the Constitution. In conclusion, the specific legal import of Law 3845/2010, incorporating the Memorandum, has been surprisingly limited. More significant was the explicit political support of the austerity programme by the representatives of the people, the idea being that once endorsed in its totality the implementation of the programme by concrete legal acts, though open to constitutional challenge before the courts, would face lesser political hurdles.

The Court's judgment in the Memorandum case confirms the tendency of the Greek judiciary to abide by legal forms, retaining on the surface its political detachment and coolness in the midst of tumultuous events. *Fiat justitia pereat mundus*? That would be too idealistic. The underlying reason for this judicial self-restraint lies more likely in the quite unusual continuity and stability of the Greek state's fundamental constitutional identity, despite political discontinuities caused by catastrophic historical occasions such as dictatorships, occupations or wars. Every time that a grave crisis occurred, causing the disruption of normal political life and constitutional continuity, the country was returned to more or less the same version of the constitutional form of government, with smaller or larger modifications, which, however, did not bring into question the essential principles: a parliamentary democracy of European type, based on free general elections, under the rule of law.

Fundamental Rights before Courts

Austerity measures caused the limitation of numerous constitutional rights for the Greek Constitution enshrines a long list of social rights, while it also protects collective autonomy, the right to work and freedom to unionize. The serious concerns expressed about the deterioration of rights protection in the report of the International Labour Office's High Level Mission to Greece are characteristic. According to the report, freedom of association and collective bargaining, equality and non-discrimination, and social security protection are severely endangered.[15] Litigation questioning the constitutionality of measures was an inevitable consequence of the financial crisis.

The most important among the crisis decisions, the Memorandum case, beyond sovereignty issues answered claims that there had been violations of several constitutional rights. In upholding the constitutionality of wage and benefit cuts the Council of State employed an elaborate construction of the proportionality test, to offer a detailed analysis of the constitutionality of the impugned measures. The Court accepted that the measures interfered with property rights enshrined in Art. 1 of the First Protocol ECHR and stated that nonetheless the general package of measures taken in response to the Memorandum and to ameliorate the fiscal

15 International Labour Office, Report on the High Level Mission to Greece, Geneva, 22 November 2011. See also A. Koukiadaki and L. Kretsos, 'Opening Pandora's Box: The Sovereign Debt Crisis and Labour Market Regulation in Greece', *Industrial Law Journal* 41(3) (2012): 276-304.

situation of the country pursues a serious aim and serves the general interest. The Court thus proclaimed that, due to the above, the review of the contested measures by the Court would be marginal. Nevertheless what it actually did was the exact opposite: it exercised a rigorous version of proportionality, exhausting all three tiers of the test, in a more sophisticated application than usual. The Court entered also the *stricto sensu* considerations, something it rarely does, as it traditionally avoids expediency evaluations as a demonstration of self-restraint. Yet, this rigour was a means to verify and enhance the proportionality of the impugned measures. In examining necessity the Court was satisfied by the mere existence of other measures, that is that the impugned measure was part of an overall package of measures aiming to reform the Greek economy. The Court thus deactivated the ad hoc character of the examination of necessity, as it did not engage in the juxtaposition of a particular measure with other available measures that could serve a particular goal. Absence of an aim more specific than the general deficit control aspiration rendered the examination of necessity impossible in practice.

What is more, the Court employed a reversal of the burden of proof, stating that it is up to the rights claimants to show evidence that the legislator took into consideration the wrong elements and facts in drafting the measures under review. By so doing it frees the legislator from the obligation to justify measures infringing fundamental rights, which is the very minimum expectation imposed by proportionality during a severe crisis. A paradoxical self-restraint underlies this decision, where the Court proclaims that it shall only exercise marginal review and employs contrarily a rigorous version of proportionality to support the legislative choices. Underlying this paradox is the reluctance of the judge to interfere with the policies drafted by the legislator to deal with the crisis, in a context where the loan agreements were challenged as a whole and an unconstitutionality ruling would be perceived, both favourably and unfavourably, as declaring the unconstitutionality of the Memorandum at large.[16]

In the exact opposite direction was a Justice of the Peace of Athens ruling (Decision 599/2012), which found wage and pension cuts unconstitutional as they resulted in the disproportional limitation of collective autonomy protected by the Constitution and International Labour Treaties. The Court placed much importance on the necessity tier of proportionality, the fulfilment of which dictates that the measure has obviously temporary character. According to the Court, the severity of the aim does not remove or lessen the legislator's obligation to prove the necessity of the measure. Although delivered from a low-ranking court, in the context of diffused constitutionality review, this decision gained enormous publicity. Perhaps the difference between the two decisions, which are widely juxtaposed, lies exactly in the enormous burden judges of a supreme court feel reflecting on the potential political consequences of their rulings and the impact

---

16 See X. Contiades and A. Fotiadou, 'Social Rights, Proportionality, and the Financial Crisis: A Comment on Council of State 668/2012' [in Greek], *Revue Hellénique des Drois de L'Homme* 53 (2012): 27-51.

of the decision on the image of the court itself, a pressure that is not so strong in lower courts. Thus the difference in the approaches does not lie only in their legal reasoning, but in the way self-restraint is linked to the system of judicial review and the tradition of a particular court.

Judicial self-restraint of the Council of State in the Memorandum case aimed at safeguarding judicial review of prospect measures implementing the Memorandum, while preventing the immersion of the Court in the muddy waters of economic globalization and international politics. For example, in judgment 693/2011 the Court was willing to apply more strictly than before the constitutional limitations on the retroactivity of taxes, while, in other cases, the judiciary struck down administrative measures which threatened to cut the electric power from households that did not pay a special fee on real property, in the invoices of electricity. When faced with a far more specific question of constitutionality the Council of State did invalidate the impugned measure (Decision 1972/2012). The Court ruled on the constitutionality of a property tax named 'Special Duty on Buildings Powered by Electricity'. This levy was put on electric bills so that its collection could be administered by the electric company, that is the Public Power Corporation and all other providers of electricity. The Court found that the imposition of the tax itself was not contrary to the Constitution nor was its collection via the electric companies. What, however, constitutes a violation of the Constitution is cutting off the electricity to non-paying taxpayers. The pressing need to take urgent measures to cut Greece's deficit due to the crisis and the temporary character of the measure lie at the heart of the rationale of accepting the constitutionality of the measure since, according to the Court, the principles of equality and proportionality are not violated and the limitation of property rights enshrined in Art. 1 of the First Protocol ECHR is not disproportional. Cutting off the electricity, however, is a disproportional intervention to freedom of contract, because no serious reasons for inducing via legislation changes to the terms of the contracts between providers and clients exist, since legislative interventions are irrelevant to the content of the contract itself and aim to goals that lie totally outside the contract.

The first reactions of Greek courts faced with challenges against austerity measures show that the judiciary is trying to find a balance between self-restraint and guaranteeing rights. The affirmation that rights are indeed infringed by the legislative efforts to deal with the crisis and the application of proportionality show that not all limitations of fundamental rights will be tolerated by courts. Nonetheless, what the judiciary seems unwilling to do is to take it upon itself to put serious obstacles in the way of the enforcement of the obligations undertaken towards international lenders and to respond to challenges against the Memoranda brought as quasi class actions and pursuing their overall invalidation on a large variety of grounds. The Council of State has never been an activist court, nonetheless it does exercise rigorous constitutionality review, and the odds are that it will navigate through the crisis with extreme caution.

The Impact of the Crisis on the Political System

For the assessment of the impact of the financial crisis on the Greek political system one should take into account their interplay. The crisis profoundly affected the functioning of the political system of the Third Greek Republic (established in 1974), interrupting the regular and predictable alternation in power of strong one-party governments formed by either one of the two major historical parties of the country (New Democracy and PASOK), with the Communist Party of Greece being the third factor in the system, representing the Left.

The Background of the Crisis

Tracing the origins of the socio-political context of the crisis leads back to the restoration of democracy in 1974, which signalled the beginning of a new era in which parliamentarism and the rule of law were established, democratic normality becoming gradually a self-evident reality, while new political forces emerged. Following a short period (1974-1981) during which polarized pluralism lingered on from the pre-dictatorship years, a polarized two-party system was consolidated and two parties rotated in and out of government. From 1981 until the crisis broke out the two major parties monopolized power: in all the 11 general elections held their combined percentage was somewhere between 77.5 per cent and 87 per cent. This political configuration was an expression of the Left–Right cleavage, and seemed to have acquired stability and the capacity to resist any crisis. The electoral system has, since 1974, provided for 'reinforced proportionality', according to which the party coming first in number of votes obtained the absolute majority of seats in parliament if its nationwide percentage was approximately 40 per cent. During the only period in which an electoral law introduced pure proportional representation (June 1989 to April 1990) political polarization was further increased and two short-lived coalition governments were formed, whose function only stressed the absence of a cooperative ethos and consensual political culture in Greece, where the satisfaction of electoral clienteles has been traditionally the main political priority.

Populist practices, clientelistic networks and patronage are the standard hurdles for the modernization of the Greek state, society and economy. These also constitute the deeper causes undermining the function of democracy and explaining the lack of effective response at the outbreak of the financial crisis. Since the mid-1970s, especially after 1981, the public sector has been enlarged and public administration subordinated to the political parties. The two major political parties became bureaucratic cartel parties, offering state jobs and state-related benefits to their voters, and party patronage dominated all areas of public administration, penetrating the private sector as well.[17] At the level of public discourse, discussions

17 T. Pappas, 'The Causes of the Greek Crisis are in Greek Politics'; available at: www.opendemocracy.net.

over the sustainability of Greece's model of economic development were never quite high enough in the political agenda, to the extent that the two major political parties hardly pursued a consistent programme and a systematic plan of action for the implementation of the necessary economic reforms. The discourse of social justice remained dangerously hollow, imprecise and indiscriminating. Greece did not cultivate the political and administrative ethos of analysing rationally and critically the actual contribution of the various sectors of Greek society to public welfare for the assessment of the legitimacy of economic claims.

Equally negative were the attitudes towards the evaluation of actual performance in fulfilling duties and obligations. Corruption and lack of meritocracy were an inherent part of the system, but were swept under the rug, or silently tolerated for as long as wages kept rising and redistributive income policies appeared to boost the economy and the general well-being. European money from the structural funds was not invested in the modernization and development of the Greek economy, so as to liberate Greek society from economic stagnation. It has been common knowledge that growth was based on consumption, unsupported by the real productive capacity of the economy. Political apathy was subtly cultivated in that context, and the credibility of the political class was being gradually eroded. A curious laxity and permissiveness developed, cultivating a culture of limited accountability and embedding a sense of impunity, even in serious cases of mismanagement in the public sector. The sudden wake-up resulting from the implementation of the harsh austerity measures that began in 2010 caused an earthquake in the political system, which was already suffering from a severe crisis of political representation.[18]

The Effects of the Crisis

The established party system was swept away by the crisis. The two major parties broke down as the majority of their populist factions either created new parties (the Independent Greeks to the Right) or turned to other parties of the Left. Furthermore, the relatively mild far right-wing party of the Popular Orthodox Rally gave way to the radical extreme right, nationalistic and xenophobic party of the Golden Dawn. Moreover, PASOK's political hegemony in the centre-left political hemisphere diminished, with SYRIZA becoming the new pole of attraction.

The new political landscape emerged out of three interrelated factors: first, the responsibility of the established parties for the crisis, because of the way they were running the political system up to the crisis; second, the inability of the two traditional parties to manage the crisis efficiently and the failure of the Memoranda, that is of the austerity measures, which plunged the Greek economy into deep recession; and third, the unequal distribution of the social cost of the crisis through horizontal cuts in wages and pensions, as a result of persistent tax evasion and

18 Y.Z. Drossos, 'Greece: The Sovereignty of the Debt, the Sovereigns over the Debts and some Reflections on Law', IGLP Working Paper Series, 2011/7.

corruption. Greek society has been criticized for the poor level of implementing structural reforms in the economy, but the combined result of the two elections of 6 May and 17 June 2012 amount in a way to an impressive structural reform of the party system, at least as much as it depended on the people and not on the politicians. There was a mandate for continuity within the eurozone, but also a call for a coalition government, and for new policies that would be able to revitalize the economy, alleviating the immense social costs of the crisis for the most vulnerable parts of society. Undoubtedly, the electorate was correct in finding a causal relationship between the crisis and the malfunctions of the political system and of the established parties. The financial crisis rendered the pathologies of the political system transparent, seriously undermining its legitimacy.[19]

The financial crisis put an end to the alternation in power of the two major parties, which had been taking place in the context of a Westminster-type polarized democracy, where strict party discipline is the rule. The first symptom of the crisis regarding the functioning of the political system was the formation of a coalition government with the participation of the two major parties (originally with the additional participation of a smaller party, which subsequently withdrew) under a technocrat Prime Minister. This government was formed with the agenda of ratifying and implementing decisions taken by the eurozone countries and the IMF, despite the fact that the governing centre-left party, PASOK, still had the majority of seats in parliament.

The second symptom of a looming political crisis was that a great number of parliamentarians of both major parties were expelled from their parties when they voted down the pro-Memoranda policies (retaining in the plurality of cases their seats and becoming independent MPs). This happened because the parliamentary votes were subject to the rule of party discipline. Extensive 'rebellion' to party discipline implied that the political system was undergoing a major transformation, but prior to the general election of May 2012 the political class failed to realize the imminent changes.

An important consequence of the crisis was the fragmentation of the party system. Although in the general election held in October 2009 five political parties entered parliament, they became eleven before the end of the parliamentary term in April 2012, as six new parties were formed with the participation of the MPs who had abandoned the political party they were elected with. In the elections of 6 May 2012, the fragmentation of the party system was confirmed with the entrance of seven political parties to parliament, none of which received more than 20 per cent of the vote. It is noteworthy that this thoroughly novel picture emerged notwithstanding the 3 per cent threshold of the general vote that is required by the electoral law for a party to achieve parliamentary representation. The lack of a political culture of cooperation between the political parties, and perhaps most significantly the absence of a clear popular mandate in the elections of May 2012

19 Ch. Lyrintzis, 'Greek Politics in the Era of Economic Crisis: Reassessing Causes and Effects', GreeSE Paper No. 45, Hellenic Observatory Papers, LSE (March 2011).

regarding the country's political direction to handle the crisis, led inevitably to new elections.

As a consequence of the dilemma over Greece's European future, within the short interval of the two elections a new polarization emerged, around New Democracy, representing the pillar of Greece's traditional pro-European political agenda, and SYRIZA, offering the hope of a fresh socio-political start away from the austerity measures of the Memoranda. The motivating force behind this renovated (but less pervasive) polarization was the trophy of 50 parliamentary seats bequeathed by the electoral law to the first party, which thereby was going to be the winner of the elections by definition, even if it surpassed the second party by only a handful of votes. The second elections of 2012 confirmed the new distribution of power among the political parties. The same seven parties represented in parliament in the elections of 6 May were again present in parliament following the elections of 17 June.

Clearly the party system has entered an era of transformation, with fluidity being the dominant characteristic. The substitution of the Left–Right cleavage by the pro-Memoranda–anti-Memoranda dichotomy, despite its temporary character, marked an important shift from traditional narratives and political identities. The fabric of political parties started to tear apart through the appearance of multiple cleavages cutting through the pre-existing one.

The New Political Cleavages

During the Third Republic two different political cultures had developed in Greece, one associated with populism and the other with progress and modernization.[20] The most striking feature has been their symbiotic and simultaneously antagonistic,[21] if not overtly hostile, relationship within the dominant political party of the time, PASOK.[22] The cynic would say that this symbiosis is due to the fact that together they were able to form a winning coalition within Greek society. The populists were able to secure popular support, while the modernizers met the demands of progress in the context of European integration and promised the fulfilment of the aspirations of a highly educated middle class. In any case, however, the opposite ideological poles within PASOK (and the basic socio-political forces backing them) were relatively well crystallized, and this self-awareness was surely an alleviating factor checking the most odious consequences of PASOK's populism. Indeed, the equilibrium between the two groups was more stable than one would

---

20 See N. Diamandouros, 'Politics and Culture in Greece, 1974-91: An Interpretation', in R. Clogg (ed.), *Greece, 1981-89: The Populist Decade* (St. Martin's Press, 1993), pp. 1-25, at p. 7.

21 Ibid.

22 See M. Spourdalakis, 'PASOK in the 1990's: Structure, Ideology, Political Strategy', in J. M. Maravall et al. (eds), *Socialist Parties in Europe* (Institut de Ciències Polítiques i Socials, 1991), pp. 157-186.

assume on the basis of the profound cultural diversity between the ideal types of the elitist pro-European modernizer and the populist diehard party-member. There was a crucial convergence between PASOK's two flanks[23] on Europe's democratic inheritance, and a mutual understanding, going beyond strong personal sentiments, of their complementary relation in the dialectic of democratization and progressivism.

As a result, the prevailing political culture of Greece's Third Republic, being an amalgam of diverse, partly antagonistic and partly convergent elements, is a complex and dynamic synthesis, and any effort to reduce it to a simple mechanism or to a single factor is bound to fail. The financial crisis and the virtual bankruptcy of the Greek state brought the breakdown of the established dialectic between populism and modernization in the country, permanently destroying the pre-existing balance. This was the underlying reason for the breaking up of the two major political parties. Under that prism, the necessity of a new ruling coalition among the European and modernizing forces across the political spectrum seemed to be inevitable, exposing Greece's political system to the different logic and modality of a consensual pattern of democracy.

Constitutional Reform Dialogue

The crisis triggered a heated and interesting academic and political dialogue with regard to the revision of the Constitution. The fact that this dialogue did not lead to an actual constitutional revision should be attributed to the mandatory five-year time lapse, provided for by the amending clause, before reopening the revision process. Therefore, given the fact that the previous revision was concluded in May 2008, a new one could only begin in May 2013. But George Papandreou, as Prime Minister, and his successor in the leadership of PASOK, Evangelos Venizelos, employed the language of 'constituent power' along with other commentators and the media. The underlying idea was that a new constitution, suitable to meet novel demands, would be necessary for the new era that followed the political closure of the post-dictatorial Third Republic as a result of the virtual bankruptcy of the state and the arrival of the Troika. The debate acquired specificity through the strong use of constitutional reform narratives as part of the electoral campaign in April 2012. In particular the two major political parties included elaborate analyses of constitutional reform proposals in their agenda, the centre-left PASOK going so far as to propose a total revision. These discussions, however, did not take into account the reversal of the bipartisan political system, under which constitutional revisions had been a game monopolized by the two major parties.

---

23 And, it should be added, also of the centre-right, given the presence of a 'popular right' within the New Democracy Party.

In any case, a central aspect of the political and constitutional dialogue is whether the need for constitutional reform still persists after the collapse of the established bipartisan system in the two general elections of 2012. Are the risks of the concentration of power in the hands of an omnipotent Prime Minister, leading a disciplined one-party majority in parliament, dramatically reduced by the political guarantees of the actual sharing of power within a multiparty coalition government? Are additional legal guarantees still necessary? Or, could it be the case that constitutional reform might provide a way out of the crisis?

Many constitutional scholars pointed out in the course of this debate that the Constitution was not to blame for the crisis, and that the required institutional changes could be achieved through the normal law-making process. Nevertheless, others felt that a constitutional change would create the impetus for a new start, a turn of the political page. More specifically, three distinct tendencies were crystallized in that debate. The most radical approach from a constitutional point of view invited the exercise of constituent power, welcoming the prospect of an altogether new constitution or, if that were not possible, an acceptable compromise would be a deep and extended revision of the Constitution. The second tendency was in support of a limited constitutional amendment to rectify strictly those provisions that were deemed to be problematic, also introducing changes necessary to tackle the financial crisis. Yet, for others, the crisis in Greece was primarily administrative and managerial, reflecting the dismantling of public administration after decades of populist excesses, corruption and lack of meritocracy; therefore, the focus should be on the institutional and structural weaknesses of the state, which could be addressed through legislative reforms or through the implementation of already existing legislation that remained nevertheless inoperative. In this last view, the emphasis on the Constitution was an attempt to distract the attention from the real causes of the problem.

The discussion on the propriety of a constitutional amendment was reinvigorated somewhat unexpectedly by the statement of the Euro Area Heads of State or Government, according to which a balanced budget rule should be introduced in member states' national legal systems at constitutional or equivalent level, containing also an automatic correction mechanism that will be triggered in the event of deviation.[24] In Greece, any constitutional amendment had to be postponed until 2013; but beside the five-year interval between two consecutive amendments, an immediate source of concern was the further loss of sovereignty as a result of the constitutionalization of such a fiscal rule. Scepticism concentrated on the practical feasibility of adhering by such a rule, whose failure could undermine the Constitution's normative power, and on the excessive narrowing of political manoeuvring in matters of public finance and fiscal policy, inscribing into the Constitution neo-liberal economic policies, which could curtail the scope of democratic decision-making excessively.

---

24 See Statement by the Euro Area Heads of State or Government of 9 Dec 2011, para 4.

Another area of proposals for reform was much more familiar: how to enhance constitutional checks and balances. Old ideas acquired new pertinence in the crisis – for example the empowerment of the President of the Republic to become a true veto player and the quest for ways to halt the tendency not to exhaust the four-year legislative period in an effort to avoid the responsibility of unpopular reforms.[25] Other bolder ideas included the incompatibility between the office of Members of Parliament and Ministers, but also the very opposite, that is the limitation of the omnipotence of the Prime Minister through prohibiting the appointment of Ministers who are not Members of Parliament. Of course, the disentanglement of the judiciary from the executive, through the abandonment of the problematic selection of the head of the judiciary by the Cabinet, could not be missing from the proposals for constitutional reform; here, the suggestion was to involve parliament in the process of selection through enhanced majorities.

The final area of interest regarded constitutional changes to the political system itself. Prominent in this respect was the excessive constitutional immunity of the Members of Government from criminal liability, due to a very short prescription period. Other proposals made by most political parties sought to safeguard the transparency of party finances, to cut down the number of MPs and to ensure that the opposition was guaranteed the right to commence a parliamentary investigation through the creation of a parliamentary investigation committee.

In the light of the aforementioned discussions, the excessive constraints on formal constitutional change in Greece became once more conspicuous. The burden of a turbulent constitutional history in combination with the dominant tradition of legal positivism had consolidated a cumbersome procedure of revision for the sake of constitutional continuity and stability.[26] Consequently, arguments for the relaxation of formal limitations were revived. At the operational level of the regime, the fragmentation of the party system has already influenced the revision process, making necessary new mechanisms for the building of consensus,[27] because a constitutional reform is no longer the business of two dominant political parties. With the crisis still simmering, it is hard to say which one of the aforementioned tendencies over the propriety of a constitutional revision is going to acquire momentum eventually. It is certain, however, that the financial crisis will be the catalyst for serious and profound changes in the political development of the country.

25 In this respect, some argued that the dissolution of parliament, if it failed to elect the President of the Republic with three-fifths of the total number of deputies, was unnecessary, suggesting instead direct election by the people.

26 See X. Contiades and I. Tassopoulos, 'Constitutional Change in Greece', in X. Contiades (ed.), *Engineering Constitutional Change: A Comparative Perspective on Europe, Canada and the USA* (Routledge, 2013), pp. 151-178.

27 For an analysis of the interaction between the political party system and constitutional revision mechanisms, see X. Contiades and A. Fotiadou, 'Models of Constitutional Change', in X. Contiades (ed.), *Engineering Constitutional Change*, pp. 417-468.

Impact of the Crisis on the Perception of the Constitution

A paradox typical of the Greek perception of the Constitution has re-emerged during the crisis. Despite the absence of a strong culture of constitutional patriotism, due perhaps to the ethnic and religious homogeneity of Greek society, the Constitution played the role of an emblem during the turbulent period of democracy's crises (1936-1974) and, consequently, constitutional narratives were quite influential in public discourse. Strict application of constitutional legality and full respect for the rules of the game have been taken for granted only since 1974. After the turning point of the first constitutional revision ever effected in Greek history 'by the book', that is by meticulous application of the applicable rules, in 1986, the Constitution had no enemies to fear. Its normative meaning can even grow through judicial interpretation rather than through the upheaval of great historical events, culminating in constitutional moments. This does not mean that the Constitution is relegated to the background of everyday politics. Universities, trade unions, the mass media, private persons and so forth continue steadily to invoke the Constitution in their public discourse against harmful legislative measures and governmental policies. Obviously, constitutional argumentation served as first rate ammunition against the radical austerity measures and the structural reforms pursued according to the Memoranda.

The perception of the Constitution in Greece by scholars, judges and citizens is best reflected in the first reactions regarding the constitutionality of the first Memorandum in May 2010. Scholars were divided between those who passionately advocated the complete and thorough unconstitutionality of the Memorandum and others who held firmly the opinion that it passed constitutional muster in all respects. This controversy found its way to the Council of State in the case over the constitutionality of the Memorandum, discussed above. The reception of the Court's judgment was equally split, depending not only on the assessment of its ratio decidendi, but also on the prevailing attitudes on judicial activism and judicial self-restraint. Some scholars supporting judicial activism applauded the Court's self-restraint under the rationale that the contested issues were primarily of a political nature. Contrariwise, other scholars who stressed democracy over constitutionalism strongly criticized the ruling, which disappointed them with its mild scrutiny. But what looks superficially as an inconsistency may turn out to have a rather clear logic: in the Memorandum case the supporters of the traditional nation-state held a conception of the Constitution as an instrument of popular sovereignty and expected national courts actively to defend the Constitution and the domestic legal order from foreign infringements on national sovereignty; therefore, judicial activism of the national courts in the Memorandum case would contribute, in their view, to defending democracy. Conversely, for others, who took seriously the transfer of sovereignty by the Constitution of the member states to the EU and emphasized the obligation of domestic courts to act as European courts when applying EU law, the other side of judicial self-restraint by national courts was an activist attitude favouring further European integration. Thus, this discussion does not necessarily align to the different question of judicial activism and the counter-majoritarian difficulty in issues of domestic constitutional law, since the way in which the Memorandum case was greeted by constitutional theory was ambivalent and inconsistent with the attitude many scholars previously had as to the role of judges with regard to the Constitution.

The Council of State rejected the arguments that the Memorandum violated the Constitution, leaving to the political process and in particular to parliamentary elections the making of the great political decisions for the resolution of the financial crisis. The Court opted to be a rather polite and soft conversation partner to the legislator, however it did establish itself as one. An overall evaluation of reform proposals implies the existence of a will to abide by fundamental rights protection despite their shrinkage. That betrays an enduring faith in the importance of their constitutional protection despite its temporary (or thus perceived) inability to effectively shield a number of rights, such as social rights, collective bargaining and so on.

Nevertheless, the Greek crisis mostly affected the legitimacy of the political process, the role of political parties as institutions with a vital say in political representation and of course the political class of the country, which suffered severe political blows particularly up to the general election of 6 May 2012. Indeed, the overabundance at the height of the crisis of proposals for constitutional revisions reflected in a way the attempts by the politicians to regain momentum by taking the political initiative on the more grandiose themes of constitutional law.

Conclusions

Despite its many negative aspects, the Greek crisis and more broadly the European sovereign debt crisis offered a unique opportunity to the EU to fulfil one of the strongest, and seemingly hardest to attain, aspirations of European *political* integration: the creation of a European public sphere, where Europe would play a pivotal role in people's life and a European leadership would address a European audience about Europe's common political and economic future. Given the critical situation in Greece, the political leaders of Europe and the political players influencing the Greek crisis acquired an unprecedented publicity and pre-eminence.

Greece's and Europe's political systems became intertwined in a novel manner. Despite the fact that Greece reduced its public deficit from approximately €24bn to €5bn in a very short time, that the Greek economy has been plunged into deep recession for the fifth consecutive year and that the austerity measures have harshly affected the income of the Greek population, the reluctance of Greek political elites to commit themselves to economic reform and to the implementation of structural changes has caused frustration and strained the relationships between Athens and the European centres of power. In an understandable strategy against the expansion of the crisis from its Greek epicentre to other countries of the European periphery vulnerable to the pressure of the markets, Greece was repeatedly and emphatically set aside as a special and unique case. No doubt the country's ineffective public administration offered ample room for this stigmatization.

The financial crisis brought about in Greece severe consequences with regard to the constitutional and political order. Parallel to the culmination of the financial crisis, constitutional issues began to pop up at an accelerating pace, as the transformative impact of the crisis led to the imposition of various limitations to fundamental rights and triggered the restructuring of the political party system.

Fundamental rights have come to a crucial turning point. Ever since the restoration of democracy, constitutional rights have seemed to follow a path towards more protection. New facets were continuously added through constitutional revisions and judicial interpretation, and focus was put on remedying problems and expanding protection. This evolution has come to a halt as austerity measures have caused serious threats to rights, and reasons for alarm regarding the protection of the environment, discrimination and racism have started to become apparent. Whether rights will withstand these endangerments and the role the judiciary will play, trying not to cross the line of activism and yet retain the role of guarantor of constitutional rights, are in a process of determining the future of Greek constitutionalism.

As lingering pathologies in the organization of the state can no longer be swept under the carpet, and shifts and changes in the party system are in the path of producing new balances that may require a different ethos of consent, a new landscape is being formed. The critical elections of 17 June 2012, the coalition government formed by the pro-European political parties across the political spectrum, from the Right to the Left, and the expression of impatience and anger at the record level of unemployment, particularly among the younger generation, are a clear sign of the epochal changes in the political life of the country.

An overview of the way in which the three branches responded to the pressing challenges created by the outbreak of the crisis outlines this emerging landscape. The legislator reacted promptly, hastily drafting legislation and adopting measures that may cause informal change to the Constitution. The judge demonstrated a remarkable degree of self-restraint, nonetheless entering the discussion and showing that although the crisis created a type of emergency that justifies limitations of rights nonetheless not every infringement will be upheld as constitutional. The executive sought to enhance the legitimacy required to implement harsh austerity measures through engaging technocrats in key government positions and by forming coalitions between parties of a different political pedigree.

The heated constitutional reform discussions that have been taking place throughout the crisis show that if it were not for the hurdles placed in the way of constitutional revision by the demanding amending formula of the Greek Constitution, the Constitution itself would have been subjected to important and perhaps spontaneous and hastily drawn alterations. How it will function remaining intact is up to the constitutional players. Reflection on the stringency of the formula itself and the way it has impacted the operation of the Constitution in the new emerging context are among the tests the crisis has imposed on the political and constitutional order.

Chapter 8

The Sovereign Debt Crisis and the Constitution's Negative Outlook: A Portuguese Preliminary Assessment

Jónatas E.M. Machado

The present economic and financial crisis emerged like a perfect storm, causing panic and extreme devastation on a transnational scale. Its causes are as numerous as they are complex, having political, legal, economic and social underpinnings. Some point to concurring and sometimes contradictory factors.[1] In the absence of centralized political and economic leadership, the level of constitutional, political and economic readiness to deal with such an emergency situation varied according to very different levels of awareness, social attitudes, political culture and institutional fitness.

Portugal felt the first effects of the crisis immediately in 2008. It tried to resist for several years, only to request a bailout from the EU and the IMF in April 2011, after Greece and Ireland. The crisis is certainly complex, and will be with us for many years to come. Economists themselves were stunned by its dimension, and will spend the next decades rethinking their models.[2] Its impact on constitutions and constitutional law, significant as it may be, is still unfolding and will take many years to assess. It is too important to be ignored. In this chapter we will explore some of the constitutional causes and consequences of the Portuguese sovereign debt crisis.

Am I the Constitution's Keeper?

The Guardian of the Constitution

European constitutional scholarship has been fascinated by the debate between Hans Kelsen and Carl Schmitt, at the end of the Weimar Republic, about the

1 A discussion of the initial phases of the crisis can be found in J. Foster and F. Magdoff, *The Great Financial Crisis: Causes and Consequences* (Monthly Review Press, 2009), pp. 11ff.; C.M. Reinhart and K. Rogoff, *This Time is Different: Eight Centuries of Financial Folly* (Princeton University Press, 2009), pp. 208ff.

2 O. Blanchard, D. Romer, M. Spence and J. Stiglitz (eds), *In the Wake of the Crisis, Leading Economists Reassess Economic Policy* (MIT Press, 2012), pp. 7ff.

guardian of the constitution (*Hüter der Verfassung*).[3] Being a written document, the normative force of a constitution depends on a specific institutional guarantee. So the question inevitably arises: who is the guardian of the constitution? Is it the president of the republic or the constitutional court?

Schmitt was a German conservative scholar with strong views about politics, law and constitutionalism. In his view, in the vortex of the legal order one finds the President, the one with the power and the responsibility for taking decisions in exceptional times. Schmitt viewed the legal system more in terms of history, culture and tradition. Beyond the legislative, executive and judicial institutions that dominate the discussions on the principle of separation of powers, someone has to personify the political community in times of crisis. It is up to the president to perform that task. Kelsen was a renowned Austrian Jewish legal scholar who developed a positivist, formalist and hierarchic view of the legal system, in which the validity of each norm derived from its conformity with a norm of higher rank. The constitution would be the superior norm of a pyramid-shaped legal system and should be protected by a constitutional court specialized in abstract judicial review of legislation. Kelsen's pure theory of law provided a system that could be adopted by any state, regardless of ideology and politics, and understood by any bureaucrat and judge.

If the Portuguese Constitution of 1976 is any indication, neither Kelsen nor Schmitt have won the debate. On the one hand, the Portuguese Constitution claims to be more than just the basic norm of a hierarchically structured legal system. It comprises a substantive commitment to civil and political rights and to economic, social and cultural rights, as proclaimed by the Universal Declaration of Human Rights, as well as to democracy, the rule of law and social justice. On the other hand, although the Constitutional Court has played a significant role in interpreting and applying the Constitution, neither the Court nor the current Portuguese President – an economist and former Prime Minister – were able to provide the legal and financial control mechanisms needed to engage in *preventive constitutional law*, so as to protect the Constitution and its core ideals and principles in times of crisis. The Schmitt/Kelsen debate may have distracted constitutional scholars from crucial aspects of the political, institutional and legal systems.

Constitutionalism and Financial Justice

The Constitutional Court plays an important role in assuring the primacy of the Constitution, in protecting fundamental rights against the majoritarian legislature and reinforcing the mechanisms of representative democracy. But one of its main tasks is to protect the political and social rights against powerful economic interests. However, the crisis has shown that constitutional judicial review, important as it may be, is not enough to secure these goals. The crisis brought to the forefront the

3 C. Schmitt, *Der Hüter der Verfassung* (Mohr, 1931); H. Kelsen, *Wer soll die Hüter der Verfassung sein?* (Grunewald, 1931).

intimate relationship between political and constitutional self-determination, on the one hand, and the fiscal and financial foundations of democratic government, on the other.

This relationship is as old as modern constitutionalism itself. We can find it explicitly acknowledged already in the 1215 Magna Charta.[4] Moreover, both the American and French revolutions had an important connection with issues such as sovereign debt, taxation decisions and economic and social justice. In America the revolutionaries fought for the principle of 'no taxation without representation', revolting against taxes levied by the British government.[5] In France the Third Estate fought against the tax privileges and immunities of the clergy and the nobility, advocating the abolishment of entitlements of the rich and powerful classes, the confiscation of their illegitimately acquired property and the rebuilding of a new economic order based on the democratic right to participate in the decision-making about taxation and public spending control.[6] Today, powerful economic and financial interests, associated with giants such as Lehman Brothers, AIG, J.P. Morgan, Goldman Sachs, Moody or Fitch, have endangered the right of millions of people around the world to a decent livelihood, giving rise to transnational protest movements such as the Indignados or Occupy Wall Street.[7]

Political and social rights and the operation of democratic institutions have costs that must be supported by all members of the political community on a fair basis.[8] A sound financial condition is crucial not only to ensure the enforcement of political and social rights, but also to guarantee the possibility of democratic self-government and political independence. However, the need to respond to a deregulated financial system, built upon the free market fallacy,[9] was a major factor in generating an uncontrolled sovereign debt which, in the bailed-out member states, led to abrupt spending cuts in social programmes and considerable

4 Arts 12-15.

5 J. Cummins, *Ten Tea Parties: Patriotic Protests That History Forgot* (Quirk Books, PA, 2012), pp. 11ff.

6 D. Stasavage, *Public Debt and the Birth of the Democratic State: France and Great Britain 1688-1789* (2nd edn, Cambridge University Press, 2008), pp. 130ff. Art. 14 of the Declaration of the Rights of Man and of the Citizen, of 1789, provided that 'All the citizens have a right to decide, either personally or by their representatives, as to the necessity of public contribution; to grant this freely; to know to what uses it is put; and to fix the proportion, the mode of assessment and of collection and the duration of the taxes.' Art. 15 established that 'Society has the right to require of every public agent an account of his administration.' The same principles are found in Arts 12-15 of the French Constitution of 1791.

7 A.J.A. Nunes, 'Uma Leitura Crítica da Atual Crise do Capitalismo', *Boletim de Ciências Económicas* LIV (2011): 1.

8 S. Holmes and C. Sunstein, *The Cost of Rights* (W.W. Norton, 1999), pp. 35ff.

9 J. Sachs, *The Price of Civilization: Reawakening American Virtue and Prosperity* (Random House, 2011), pp. 27ff.

loss of sovereignty. As such, this problem acquired an inescapable constitutional relevance.

On the other hand, a civic republican framework implies that private interest groups should be unable to capture the legislative, administrative and judicial institutions and processes, as well as contractual, fiscal and taxing powers, to advance their own economic and financial benefits at the expense of the public good. Modern constitutionalism was set up as a way of limiting and diffusing power. Today many financial institutions have more power than many states, being able to inflict severe costs on a substantial group of them, while lacking in credibility, transparency, deliberation, accountability and contestability.[10] The political theory of thinkers such as Locke, Montesquieu or Kant must now target these giant private entities.[11]

One area where this can be especially important are the disturbing trends of contracting out of some important public functions and the proliferation of public-private partnerships (PPPs), both national and international, in terms which had a major impact on the public interest and common good. In Portugal a large number of PPPs have been 'negotiated' by past governments in areas such as infrastructure, health and education, in a way that allocated the commercial and financial risks almost entirely to the state. Both parliament and the Court of Auditors failed to control these 'negotiations' effectively. The public and even the auditing institutions had no information about their true financial terms. As a result, it is estimated that PPPs will cost the Portuguese taxpayers billions of euros in the next decades.[12]

Democratic self-government is only possible when economic liberty and private property are protected within a framework of social and financial justice, and when effective and accountable mechanisms are put in place. Solving the current situation will probably require the revival of constitutional doctrines such as *social contract*, *public interest*, *eminent domain* and *ministerial criminal liability* as a way to curb the promiscuity between public figures and private interests.[13]

Building a Transparency and Accountability Network

In the words of economist Guillermo Ortiz, 'the great crisis was a massive institutional failure, involving financial institutions, regulators, rating agencies, and international organizations'.[14] As far as Portugal is concerned, assuring the

---

10 Nunes, 'Uma Leitura Crítica', 112ff.

11 A. Corbett and P. Spender, 'Corporate Constitutionalism', *Sydney Law Review* 31 (2009): 147-161.

12 There is an important study on this subject by former Court of Auditors Judge C. Moreno, *Como o Estado Gasta o Nosso Dinheiro* (Caderno, 2010), pp. 99ff.

13 D. Custos and J. Reitz, 'Public-Private Partnerships', *American Journal of Comparative Law* 58 (2010): 555-584.

14 Blanchard, Romer, Spence and Stiglitz, *In the Wake of the Crisis*, p. 19.

supremacy of the Constitution requires more than just the contributions of the President or of the Constitutional Court, important as they may be. It requires a system of checks and balances able to engage in *preventive constitutional law*.

The current crisis has shown the design flaws of the institutions that were in place, preventing them from effectively foreseeing and avoiding the crisis. That casts a dark shadow of doubt over the last three decades of Portuguese constitutional theory, law and practice. Constitutional law, like economics and finance, is now going through a credibility crisis. It is up to constitutional scholarship to come to terms with this problem, point out the constitutional failures and emphasize the constitutional relevance of several other institutions and organs when it comes to guaranteeing the possibilities of constitutional self-government.

A credible government, with a credible Prime Minister, transparent policy-making, sound accounting standards and a pattern of publicity, is a very important aspect of the institutional framework. During the years before the crisis, Portugal was governed by a socialist Prime Minister involved in all sorts of accusations of wrongdoing concerning his private, professional and ministerial dealings. For various reasons, the judicial investigations around these accusations were never conclusive. After losing the elections, in the aftermath of the crisis, far from being held accountable, he moved to Paris where he is allegedly living the good life.[15] In the future, political morality, premised on human dignity and social justice and the fight against corruption, should dominate institutional design and function.

Equally important is a parliament in which opposition parties have access to the relevant information and are able to engage in thorough assessments of public policy. The lack of an effective parliament control proved to be particularly damaging in the light of the wide discretion of the majority-backed executive in contracting out public functions through expensive and unbalanced PPPs. The lack of enforcement of constitutional and legislative limitations on public power delegation meant that important constitutional functions were captured by powerful special interests, imposing an *odious debt* on the Portuguese taxpayer. In the aftermath of the bailout to Portugal parliament is creating several inquiry commissions to investigate different factors that led to the financial crisis.[16]

Another area of concern should be '*political party financing and governance*'. Although the crisis has not yet resulted in the rise of extreme left-wing or right-wing political parties, only through increased levels of participation, transparency and accountability within political parties can that be averted. Following scandals involving the promiscuous relationship between several politicians and some bankrupt private banks, between politicians, secret services and private interests,

---

15 Newspapers report that the family of former PM Socrates has millions of euros in Gibraltar. '383 milhões em offshores', *Correio da Manhã*, 6 December 2011; available at http://www.cmjornal.xl.pt/detalhe/noticias/exclusivo-cm/383-milhoes-em-offshores-215912803.

16 CPIs, BPN and PPPs. See http://www.parlamento.pt/ComissoesAR/Paginas/default.aspx.

along with the irregular acquisition of university degrees at some private universities by former and current Members of Government, the general public has the perception that the main political parties are dominated by a few opportunists who started their political careers in the political parties' youth groups and became specialists in courting private interest groups and unlawfully conducting financial operations for the gain of their party and themselves.[17]

Important also is the role of the Portuguese Central Bank. Besides being a part of the European System of Central Banks and the Euro System, the Portuguese Central Bank has an important role to play in the supervision of the financial institutions and the enforcement of banking laws. Unfortunately, the prevailing opinion is that its overpaid administration shirked its responsibilities before and during the crisis, failing to detect and prevent huge financial debacles in two private financial institutions with significant connections to the main political parties and the current President of the Republic. It is now being reformed in order to be given stronger teeth.[18] As far as the Attorney General is concerned, being nominated by the President of the Republic on the basis of a government proposal did not give him the unquestionable political independence or the power and resources to investigate and prosecute corruption at the highest levels of political authority.

It also became clear that the Court of Auditors has an important constitutional function to perform when it comes to protecting state sovereignty, popular self-government and civil and political rights. These are dependent not only on the subordination of lower norms to the higher norms, but also on the public authority to engage in public expenditure, budget deficit and public debt control. The Court of Auditors must be given access to all the relevant information along with the ability to engage in effective control of budget-and-deficit-sensitive contracts and expenses. A recent change in its statute acknowledged this reality.[19] Administrative courts must also play a stronger role in the future. With their injunctive powers, they must make sure that government, including local governments, public enterprises and even private contractors, do provide complete, relevant and truthful financial and performance information, so that their activities are effectively assessed.[20]

17 'Lusófona deu sede para as eleições de Passos Coelho', *Expresso*, 9 July 2012; available at http://expresso.sapo.pt/lusofona-deu-sede-para-as-eleicoes-de-passos-coelho=f738394.

18 Decreto-Lei 31-A/2012, 10-2.

19 Lei 61/2011, 7-12.

20 When relevant constitutional issues are at stake, we should follow the path recommended in *Clarke* v. *Tri-Cities Animal Care and Control Shelter*, 144 Wash. App. 185, 181 P.3d 881 (2008), in spite of objections such as those in J.A. Ware, '*Clarke v. Tri-Cities Animal Care and Control Shelter*: How did Private Businesses Become Government "Agencies" Under the Washington Public Records Act?', *Seattle University Law Review* 33 (2010): 741-776.; the same general concern is dealt with in J. Freeman and M. Minow (eds), *Government by Contract: Outsourcing and American Democracy* (Harvard University Press, 2009).

The need for heightened scrutiny of budgetary policy and public finances has led to the creation of a Superior Council of Public Finances,[21] an independent body, with five senior members plus 15 experts, nominated by the government on the basis of a joint proposal by the Central Bank and the Court of Auditors. Two of the senior members may be foreigners, preferably nationals from EU member states. Its job is to elaborate periodical public independent reports on macroeconomic outlook, budgetary policy and financial control. The Council has not been operating long enough for its effectiveness to be evaluated.

Another important aspect has to do with a free press and an uninhibited, robust and open sphere of public discourse. The public has the right to know the relevant facts about government activity and to discuss politics, policies and politicians, so as to make informed decisions when it comes to selecting and evaluating public officials. The Portuguese Constitution guarantees the rights of freedom of expression and information, as well as the political and economic independence of the mass media (Arts 37-39). In reality, though, there is still a long way to go. On the one hand, the over-interpretation, by national courts, of personality rights or secrecy of judicial proceedings in defamation lawsuits has stifled investigative journalism, which is essential to democratic self-government.[22] The ECtHR has held Portugal responsible, several times, for violations of the rights of freedom of expression and information in cases where the discussion of issues of public interest was at stake.[23] Moreover, too many journalists have a precarious labour status within the media, with little independence to raise and report controversial issues. On the other hand, in recent years, significant evidence has been reported about attempts by successive governments to control and influence the media. Even today, there are some signs of impermissible pressure on journalists by political and economic interests, both national and foreign. This endangers the Constitution, as it prevents the free and open discussion of relevant matters of public interest. The independent agency for the regulation of the mass media (ERC),[24] which itself complains about being subject to external pressure, must play a more active role in protecting the media from public and private power.

Political sovereignty and democracy depend on the ability of a political community to ensure its economic and financial independence. Many public and private institutions, organs and entities, along with an informed public opinion, play a constitutional role of the highest order. The protection of the Constitution rests on the existence of a fully functional 'accountability network', based on the

21 Lei 54/2011.

22 J. Eichhoff, *Investigativer Journalismus aus verfassungsrechtlicher Sicht* (Mohr, 2010), pp. 12ff.

23 *Publico et. Al.* v. *Portugal*, App. 39324/07, ECHR, II, 07/12/2010; *Colaço Campos Damaso* v. *Portugal*, App. 17107/05, ECHR, II, 24/04/2008, *Mestre and Sic, S.A.* v. *Portugal*, Apps. 11182/03 and 11319/03, ECHR, II, 26/07/2007; *Lopes Gomes da Silva* v. *Portugal*, App. 37698/97, ECHR, IV, 28/12/2000.

24 Lei 53/2005.

principles of transparency and integrity.[25] The guardians of the Constitution are the same citizens it is intended to protect.

Constitutions' 'Dirty Little Secret'

The Standard Model

Traditionally, written constitutions are intended to be the ultimate expressions of democratic self-government. According to this standard model, the constitution is closely connected to the idea of popular and state sovereignty, being the fundamental norm of the legal system. It provides for a set of values, principles and goals that should direct the political community as a whole, including a catalogue of fundamental rights that protect citizens from abusive exercises of both public and private power. It establishes some basic principles and rules according to which the economic system is supposed to function, and institutionalizes a set of legislative, administrative and judicial powers with the responsibility of enacting the necessary laws and regulations, enforcing them and adjudicating legal disputes. According to the standard model, it is up to the courts, especially to some kind of constitutional court or chamber, to guarantee the supremacy of the constitution.

International and European Revisions to the Standard Model

After the Second World War and the Holocaust, the standard model has gradually been turned upside down. Sovereignty and constitutionalism have been affected by the transformation of international law which started with the Charter of the United Nations (1945), the Nuremberg Military Tribunal (1946) and the Universal Declaration of Human Rights (1948), and led to the creation of several regional human rights courts and the development of international criminal law. Nowadays, international institutions and international law establish global regulatory parameters in many domains, through treaties, resolutions, technical standards, codes, regulations, customs and so forth.[26] Sovereignty, statehood and even democratic decision-making power have been radically transformed and subjected to legal international constraints.[27] In this context many scholars speak of a process of constitutionalization of international law.

25 F. Bignami, 'From Expert Administration to Accountability Network: A New Paradigm for Comparative Administrative Law', *American Journal of Comparative Law* 59 (Fall 2011): 859-908.

26 M. Sterio, 'The Evolution of International Law', *Boston College International and Comparative Law Review* 31 (2008): 213-256.

27 M. Sterio, 'A Grotian Moment: Changes in the Legal Theory of Statehood', *Denver Journal of International Law and Policy* 39 (2011): 209-238, at 237.

European integration has been another major factor of sovereignty transformation. EU law has become part of the law of the land in each member state. It is directly applicable and enforceable in national courts of law. In the realms of EU competence its norms cannot be overridden by national constitutional considerations. Currently it is up to the Treaty of the EU, the Treaty on the Functioning of the EU and the Charter of Fundamental Rights to regulate major parts of legislative, administrative and judicial activity within the EU.[28]

National sovereign institutions and processes have undergone a process of *functional unfolding* and dynamic change currently serving both national and European constitutional tasks. The parliaments of the member states are now part of a network of parliaments, along with the European Parliament, in a layered democratic system. National governments are represented in both the European Council, through the heads of state or government, and in the different formations of the Council at a ministerial level. The national courts have long been co-opted by the European Court of Justice to engage in European jurisdiction and are now EU courts in a broader sense. They cannot apply national laws contrary to EU law, and must defer to the Court of Justice whenever they come across doubts about the meaning or the validity of EU law provisions. They also must hold the member states responsible for injuries caused by serious violations of EU law, including those committed by national supreme courts themselves. The national central banks are an integral part of the European System of Central Banks. Through this and other factors, national constitutions have been confined to a marginal role, and their supremacy has slowly eroded. They are now part of a *multilevel constitutionalism*.[29] The most problematic aspect of this new reality is the development of a kind of *constitutionalism without sovereignty*.

Constitutions in Denial?

What is remarkable is the extent to which national constitutions remain silent about this radical transformation of the institutional, legal and political landscape. It is almost as if they are in a state of denial, clinging to old notions of people, state, sovereignty, constitution, constitutional law and even constitutional patriotism. It is as if they are trying to conceal the 'dirty little secret' of having to relinquish their original claims about popular self-government and the supremacy and autonomy of constituent power. The structural changes that have taken place in international and European law cannot really be accounted for by successive constitutional revisions.

In the case of the Portuguese Constitution, only a few provisions mention international law or the process of European integration. The reading of the Constitution in isolation would still convey the idea that we are dealing with a

28 C. Nowak, *Europarecht nach Lissabon* (Nomos, 2011), pp. 83ff.

29 I. Pernice, 'The Treaty of Lisbon: Multilevel Constitutionalism in Action', *Columbia Journal of European Law* 15 (2009): 349-408, at 352.

fully sovereign state, whose legislative, administrative and judicial functions are performed by the national parliament, government and courts. We would still think that the Constitutional Court plays an important role in assuring the Constitution's status as higher law. This intense constitutional silence goes a long way to maintaining an impression, if not an illusion, of sovereignty.

However, the bailing out of Portugal by a Troika of the IMF, the ECB and the European Commission, with the background support of the G8 and G20, reflects the reality that the Constitution, its institutions and procedures are totally unable to provide the appropriate framework for public power to deal with a financial crisis of cataclysmic proportions. Real power lies elsewhere. The Constitution has long ceased to be the *panton genethla*, that is the 'mother of all' sovereign powers. When one reads the Portuguese Constitution, one feels a bit as though one is visiting the ruins of an ancient Greek temple, being able to stare with awe and amazement at the statue of the 'goddess sovereignty', to touch its remaining forms and to imagine its long lost sceptre. But EU member states cannot easily retreat to old notions of sovereignty and constitutionalism, and refuse new and deeper forms of regional and international integration.

Sovereignty and the Wet Footprint

Wet Footprint Anxiety

When flying over the ocean, civil aviation and corporate pilots normally use the expression 'wet footprint' to designate the area from which they would not be able to glide to the origin or destiny airport, should they lose an engine. When flying within the 'wet footprint', pilots will usually pay close attention to the engine and every noise it makes. Any strange noise will be a potential reason for alarm, because they know that if anything goes wrong with the engine and they cannot repair it while flying, their range decreases and they will end up landing (or crashing) in the water, or going swimming. The best option is to do all one can to try to solve the problem before that. To a certain extent, we can use this analogy to understand what went wrong in the present crisis.

Sovereignty Lost

For several decades, European integration required the transfer of important parts of state sovereignty to the EU. In fact, that's what the EU is all about. Currently, the EU has a clear political dimension, including common security and external affairs, along with cooperation in matters of internal administration. The purpose of this transfer of competences was to create a more politically, economically and socially integrated Europe.[30] Although subject to the principle of conferral,

30 Nowak, *Europarecht*, pp. 87ff.

or enumerated powers, EU competences have consistently been expanding. Nowadays, a significant part of the legislative and administrative activity of the states consists of implementation and execution of legislative and non-legislative acts of the EU. European integration has long permeated the domains of trade and economic relations between states. As this process reached deeper levels, the internal market came to be seen not only as a way to foster economic efficiency and growth, but also as a means to establish a social market economy and to promote European citizenship and fundamental rights.

The impact of these developments in the economic and financial realms became particularly clear during the sovereign debt crisis, although some effects were already apparent well before that. One immediate consequence of the internal market rules was the deactivation of the Portuguese economic constitution, without any formal revision or revocation. Furthermore, the internal market, with its freedoms of movement of goods, workers, services and capital, its rules on common agricultural and fisheries policy and its norms on competition law, including those concerning state aids, substantially reduced the ability of member states to protect their primary, secondary and tertiary production sectors. Internal market freedoms, along with transport and communications infrastructures, allow enterprises of a given member state to distribute their products in different states without establishing themselves in the states' territories. The economies of scale thus generated tend to benefit large economic corporations from rich member states at the expense of small businesses from poorer and less developed ones.

Left to the erratic movements of the market, stronger enterprises gradually become stronger, and weaker enterprises easily become weaker. Internal market rules prevent weaker member states from adopting policies and measures protecting national products, enterprises and industries, and make it harder for them to protect their tax base. Although corporate, personal income and property taxation are still within the exclusive competence of the member states, there are important restrictions to their use in order to prevent protectionist abuses. The creation of the Economic and Monetary Union and the euro eliminated the ability of the states to engage in expansionary monetary policy, so as to prevent recession and to foster economic growth and employment.

Constitutional and European Law Failure

The above-mentioned situation would not be entirely problematic, from a constitutional stand point, in a context of economic growth, social development and low unemployment rates. It would have provided enough time for the EU to integrate politically and economically at a gradual pace, giving the states sufficient room for constitutional adaptation. However, in a time of severe economic and financial crisis, it left many member states powerless to avoid the causes and mitigate the consequences of the crisis. National constitutions were not able to provide the political, institutional and procedural resources to face the emerging problems. This was aggravated by the absence of effective means to control public spending at the member state level. An excessive emphasis on constitutional judicial review, as a way to ensure the supremacy of the constitution, left many areas of constitutional significance without sufficient control mechanisms. This was the case in areas such as public spending, public borrowing, PPPs, public management, financial auditing and the operation of the financial system. These areas proved to be essential to the safeguarding of popular self-determination and independence, and thus to constitutionalism itself. They were largely neglected.

This *constitution failure* was aggravated by the fact that the sovereignty that has been lost at state level was not entirely regained at EU level. Some of it leaked in the process. The rejection of the European Constitutional Treaty in 2006 was a relevant development in this sovereignty spill. Although it did not yet provide for the creation of a Federal European State, the project of the European Constitutional Treaty attempted to introduce the sort of sovereignty symbology and constitutional rhetoric that would inevitably have a transformative impact on the nature of the EU and of its legal system.[31] One cannot say for certain if that would be sufficient to deal with the present crisis, since the project maintained the delimitation of the competences according to the principle of conferral and lacked a strong institutional base. However, it seems fair to suggest that it would probably have allowed for more margin of manoeuvre in appealing to implied and inherent powers in a crisis situation.

The European Court of Justice had already recognized the substantive constitutional nature of the primary law of the EU, as far as it purports to ground, regulate and limit the exercise of sovereign prerogatives at the European level. Even today, the constitutional nature of the Treaties and the Charter of Fundamental Rights is widely acknowledged, if only with a derived constitutional character. However, it seems entirely plausible that if the EU were based on a treaty with formal constitutional clout, it would have found itself with more room for moments of constitutional transformation, such as those that took place in the USA with the New Deal, after the Great Depression.[32] The crisis of the 1930s led to the creation of the welfare state and strong regulatory agencies. It is not yet clear if the present crisis will be able to generate institutional transformations of comparable scale. This is because the Lisbon Treaty was a less ambitious alternative, as far as constitutionalist pretensions are concerned. Its formal constitutional nature was explicitly rejected, reducing the transformative and interpretative possibilities when dealing with a major crisis.

This means that EU legislative, administrative and judicial institutions lacked crucial competences and interpretative resources that would have enabled them to deal effectively with the current financial crisis. Furthermore, the Stability and Growth Pact has long been practically deactivated after Germany and France decided not to comply with its limits of 3 per cent and 60 per cent of

31 Ibid, pp. 60ff.

32 B. Ackerman, *We the People: Transformations*, vols I and II (Harvard University Press, 1991, 1998).

GDP for budget and public debt, respectively, and the Council closed the door to infringement procedures. The EU institutions themselves did not have enough policy-making instruments and financial control mechanisms to prevent the crisis or to avoid its dispersion. The absence of a common and consistent economic and fiscal policy has rendered the EU incapable of promoting balanced economic growth, if necessary through fiscal transfers of money from the richest parts of Europe to the poorest ones. There is no Treasury Department with an EU budget and the ability to collect European income taxes and to issue bonds at a European level, much like federal states do.

Dealing with the most serious financial and economic crisis since the New York Stock Exchange Crash of 1929 and the Great Depression became especially difficult. On the one hand, the states could not go back to their lost sovereign powers and introduce trade barriers, engage in import substitution, industrial policy, promotion of local agricultural and fisheries, export subsidization, credit expansion, currency devaluation and so on. Although these instruments are far from a panacea, they could have been used, at least to a certain extent, to prevent or mitigate the most serious consequences of the crisis. On the other hand, it was impossible for the EU to move forward to a more integrated, almost federal, political, economic and financial system, at a fast enough pace to allow it to solve the crisis. In the current phase of European integration, the ECB and the national central banks were forbidden from extending credit to the member states or directly buying their bonds, which meant that the ECB could not operate as a lender of last resort.

The EU and member states were caught in the 'wet footprint'. They could not go back to traditional state sovereignty constitutionalism, nor could they move forward to new forms of quasi-federal constitutionalism. The alternative was to buy some time and to glide for as long as possible while trying to fix the problem before crashing and falling apart. In the end, both the member states and the EU had difficulty dealing with the crisis. Constitutionalism without sovereignty proved to be a major problem in times of crisis.[33] The sovereignty that had been lost at the European level was captured by stronger states (for example France and Germany), powerful financial institutions (for example rating agencies, investment banks, hedge funds, private equity corporations), as well as by sovereign and private funds (for example from China, Angola, Brazil and Qatar). This, in turn, reinforced sovereignty erosion, and constitutional and European failure.

Constitutions are not Created Equal

In the current economic and financial crisis the rate of the sovereign debt became somehow linked to the rate of sovereignty itself, as well as to the normative value

33 This shows the relevance of the scholarly discussion in P. Dobner and M. Loughlin (eds), *The Twilight of Constitutionalism?* (Oxford University Press, 2010).

of the corresponding national constitution. That this seems to be the case can be confirmed through the comparative analysis of the approaches of the German Federal Constitutional Court towards the Bonn Constitution and of the Portuguese Constitutional Court towards the Portuguese Constitution of 1976 in the wake of the crisis.

The German Constitution: Premium?

In its decision on the constitutionality of the Lisbon Treaty,[34] the German Federal Constitutional Court took a strong position defending the primacy of the German Basic Law (*Grundgesetz*). It received a constitutional complaint (*Verfassungsbeschwerde*) questioning the constitutionality of the Lisbon Treaty based on the right to vote of German citizens, enshrined in Art. 38 of the *Grundgesetz*, broadly understood so as to include the right to prevent any erosion of the powers of the German Parliament through deeper European integration. Understandably, the democratic principle plays a central role in the argument of the Court. It is expressly linked to the values of human dignity, freedom and equality that are the foundations of the German Basic Law. However, the principle of democracy is used as a reason for increasing the powers of the Lower House, and not so much as a framework in which there could be room for further European integration.

On the contrary, the German Federal Constitutional Court appeared to be very suspicious of the democratic pedigree of the European Parliament, as well as of the democratic viability of the whole European project.[35] It went on to determine some core subjects which are reserved for national sovereign decision-making, including nationality, national security, the use of force, budget and fiscal policy, family and privacy, criminal procedure, education, culture, religion, language and so on. These subjects structure the identity of the German people, and are the basis of its constitutional identity. It is up to the Federal Constitutional Court to enforce the respect for German identity and to make sure the European institutions do not overstep their competences.[36] In the eyes of the Court, sovereignty and constitutionalism seem to be inextricably linked with a state, a people and a national constitution.

The processes of Europeanization, globalization and constitutionalization seem to be too nebulous and unpredictable to be considered politically and constitutionally relevant by the Court. The possibility of constitutionalism without state borders seems to be totally implausible. The EU, described as a mere

34 See Nowak, *Europarecht*, pp. 69ff.

35 F. Schorkopf, 'The European Union as an Association of Sovereign States: Karlsruhe's Ruling on the Treaty of Lisbon', *German Law Journal* 10(8) (2009): 1219-1240, at 1225.

36 D. Halberstam and Chr. Möllers, 'The German Constitutional Court says "Ja zu Deutschland!"', *German Law Review* 10(8) (2009): 1241-1257, at 1242.

association of sovereign states, can move forward to deeper integration only to the extent that it does not disturb the primacy of national constitutions, parliaments and constitutional courts. What's more, the German Federal Constitutional Court does not stop itself from putting forward its own limited vision of the nature, meaning and future of the process of European integration. In its view, deeper integration will be a threat to the sovereignty of Germany. Within the standard model of state sovereignty and national constitutionalism, the reasoning and conclusions of the Court may seem entirely logical. It is also fair to say that it is too soon to affirm that the EU is the prime locus of sovereignty, or of the *competence of competences*. The primacy of the Treaties over national constitutional and internal law is still limited to those areas in which there has been an explicit and clear transfer of powers. The states undoubtedly still play a primary role in the process of European integration.

However, one may ask if allowing for national constitutional courts to have the last word, especially those of stronger countries, really serves the process of European integration and the functional capacity of the EU. It is also doubtful that the interests of European citizens will be best served by that state of affairs. There is no doubt that the German Federal Constitutional Court is still very influenced by the standard model of state-centred sovereignty, popular self-determination and constitutionalism.[37] Because of this, many feared that after the Lisbon Treaty decision the German Federal Constitutional Court would threaten not only the ability of the EU to cope with the sovereign debt crisis, but also the future of European integration itself.

So far, in both its provisional and final decisions on the Greek bailout, the German Court has relented slightly. It underlined the importance of economic and financial stability, it acknowledged the role that Germany necessarily plays in the stabilization of the eurozone and it showed a reasonable deference towards the decision-making powers of the executive. The case responded to a constitutional complaint presented by conservative politicians, jurists and economists, who argued that the Financial Stability of the Monetary Union Act, and the Guarantees within the Framework of the Monetary Stability Act, which regulated the German participation in the bailout of Greece through a European Financial Stability Fund,[38] violated their right to vote and the principle of democratic representative supremacy. The plaintiffs argued that these acts would threaten the budgetary and fiscal competences of the Lower House and its reserved powers on matters essential to the German polity. They also argued that a hypothetical devaluation of the euro, caused by the bailout, would violate their property rights. The Court argued that the EU Treaties, while providing for a monetary union based on financial and price stability, do not interfere with the budgetary competences of the national parliaments. The Court held that in matters as delicate and complex as this one, it must show reasonable deference to the executive and legislative powers,

37 W. Frenz, *Handbuch Europarecht, Institutionen und Politiken*, VI (Springer, 2011), pp. 3ff.

38 Council Regulation (EU) 407/2010.

and review only the most extreme and obvious violations of the Constitution. It argued that the acts under judicial review did not render Germany dependent on automatic mechanisms of unlimited liability. According to the Court, the scope of the guarantees, as far as their amount, duration and repayment are concerned, is defined in a clear and precise way, and also requires precise guarantees from Greece of a budgetary, fiscal and economic nature. Adopting an attitude of judicial self-restraint, the Court pleased itself with the approval of guarantees by a parliamentary budgetary committee.

However, according to the Treaties, it is up to the European Court of Justice, and not the constitutional courts of the 27 member states, to play a central and final role in clarifying the boundaries of national and EU competences.[39] Besides, the problem with the German Court's approach, even in its more European friendly tone, is that it deliberately excludes the possibility of an EU constitutional alternative to national state constitutionalism. Democracy at the European level is perceived as a threat to 'real' democracy at the national level. By doing so, while trying to keep the discussion about constitutionalism, sovereignty and popular self-determination connected to the states, it ends up placing it within a realm of European member states' constitutional law and politics, in which strong inequalities between states abound.

This means that most member states will be unable to afford the type of strong national constitutionalism that the German Constitutional Court advocates for Germany. If national constitutions, and not the EU Treaties, are placed in the centre of gravity of the EU, what will happen is that politically and financially stronger states, such as Germany and France, with larger *constitutional mass*, will be able to generate an enormous gravitational pull that will allow them to capture weaker states, hold them firmly in their orbit and ultimately deactivate and disintegrate their weak constitutional structure into small fragments. The result will not be particularly edifying from the point of view of the principle of democracy and the rule of law. Nor will it help their recovery in a sustainable way. Both the EU and its weaker member states will be total and permanent losers in this process.

The Portuguese Constitution: Subprime?

A 'Troika' consisting of the IMF, the European Commission and the ECB was called to bailout Portugal and send its representatives to supervise a fiscal adjustment programme. Even before that, some austerity measures had already been implemented, such as the adoption of retroactive taxation. In itself, the calling for a bailout and the arrival of the Troika was a symptom of serious constitutional failure. It meant that the institutional system that had been in place for the last three decades was not able to create the oversight mechanisms necessary to prevent an

39 A. Pliakos and G. Anagnostaras, 'Who is the Ultimate Arbiter? The Battle over Judicial Supremacy in EU Law', *European Law Review* 36(1) (2011): 109-123.

escalation of sovereign debt. As we have seen, it was also a European integration failure.

Since the beginning of the sovereign debt crisis, the Portuguese Constitutional Court has been confronted with retroactive taxation and salary and pensions reductions. In the summer of 2010 there was a first round of retroactive taxation. Although the Constitution explicitly forbids retroactive taxation (Art. 103.3), the Constitutional Court has limited this prohibition to authentic retroactivity, and upheld the new tax on the grounds that it was merely retrospective and was necessary to accomplish compelling fiscal objectives.[40]

Critics say the Court accepted the mere invocation of necessity, without requiring any technical or factual demonstration of an absence of less restrictive alternatives. This retroactive tax was followed by the creation of another extra tax rate of 2 per cent on income earned in 2011. Another measure was the unilateral reduction of salaries of public servants and other public sector employees by between 5 and 10 per cent. This unilateral pay cut, in many cases violating specific contract provisions, totally blurred the legal difference between tax, fee and contribution, amounting to a de facto tax on a specific group of citizens, without any regard for constitutional principles such as contract, ability to pay, equality, vertical and horizontal equity, legal certainty and so on. The Constitution establishes the principle that all citizens must bear the cost of public spending according to their ability to pay determined by the filing of a tax return. This principle has been violated. Although the exceptionality of the economic situation was used as a ground for these measures, the fact is that there was no formal declaration of a state of emergency, according to the rigorous procedure of Art. 19 of the Portuguese Constitution.

Concerning salary reductions of between 5 and 10 per cent, included in the budget for 2011,[41] the Portuguese Constitutional Court[42] held that they are necessary to comply with both the Stability and Growth Pact and the conditionality required by the Memorandum of Understanding signed between Portugal and the Troika.[43] The Court held that, even though parliament has not said so explicitly, the pay cuts are just a part of a larger adjustment programme, extending between 2010 and 2013, having a budgetary nature. This means that these measures are

40 Constitutional Court, Decision 399/2010.

41 Act 55-A/2010.

42 Constitutional Court, Decision 396/2011.

43 Portugal: Memorandum of Understanding on Specific Economic Policy Conditionality, 3.5.2011. In fact we are dealing here with several legal instruments signed by the Portuguese government and the IMF, the ECB and the European Commission, based on their respective constitutive treaties, of which Portugal is member, and on Regulation 407/2010, and the Decision 2011/344/EU about financial assistance to Portugal. These legal instruments are deemed to be in force, as they are based on international treaties directly applicable in the Portuguese legal order by means of Art. 8.2 of the Portuguese Constitution and have not been subject to litigation.

of necessity transitory, being valid only on an annual basis, even if they would unavoidably be repeated in the 2012 and 2013 budgets. What's more, the Court stated that there is no constitutional right not to have a salary reduction and that there is a compelling state interest in fiscal adjustment that outweighs the principle of legal certainty. It also held that the transitory targeting of public servants and public sector employees is an adequate, necessary and proportional measure to achieve tangible results in the short run, explicitly stating that those who are paid with public monies have a status of special duty towards the public interest.[44] As such the 2011 budget pay cuts were upheld.

The 2012 budget[45] introduced a further salary cut, consisting of the Holiday and Christmas subsidies of public sector workers.[46] For many of them, the 2011 and 2012 budgets represented a sudden cumulative pay cut of around 25 per cent, with a substantial disruptive impact on the financial lives of many families. Since they had settled expectations of income, many had committed themselves to long-term credit contracts (for example mortgages) which they will now have trouble fulfilling. This deliberate targeting of public sector workers with such an intense salary reduction immediately raised concerns based on the legal certainty, equality and proportionality principles and their corollaries of prohibition of arbitrariness and discrimination. The existence of less restrictive alternative means seemed plausible to many. Moreover, some public sector workers turned out not to be affected by them, when working in some regions (for example Azores), independent public institutions (for example the Portuguese Central Bank) or public enterprises operating in competitive markets, a result which introduced a further sense of inequality, injustice and arbitrariness. The situation became especially delicate when the Members of the Government started suggesting that the pay cuts would last many more years than expected, if not eliminated altogether. The Portuguese Constitutional Court had upheld the discriminatory targeting of public sector workers and pensioners only if it was a provisional solution.

When asked to initiate abstract constitutional judicial review proceedings on the 2012 budget, the Portuguese Ombudsman declined, explaining that there were already pending proceedings with the Portuguese Constitutional Court on the same subject. These proceedings had been started by left-wing MPs, including a minority of MPs of the Socialist Party, defecting against the official party line. However, in its Opinion clarifying its position on the issue, the Ombudsman raised

44 This statement seems to consider public sector salaries as mere subsidies, and not as a right to a deserved pre-specified payment for work done (work-for-pay exchange). Interestingly enough, the Constitutional Court doesn't apply the same reasoning to all those private enterprises that have contracts with the state (for example utilities, construction, public-private partnerships) and are also paid with public monies.

45 Act 64/b/2011.

46 These were first established in 1980 by Executive degree with legislative force (Decreto-Lei 496/80). Art. 25 of Budget 2012 extended this cut to retired pensioners, of both public and private sectors.

concerns of equality and proportionality, underlining that the public servant's special duty towards public interest has a strictly functional meaning, and does not create a special pecuniary duty to finance public expenditures. At the same time, it affirmed the existence of least restrictive alternatives, such as distributing the burden among all citizens. In its Opinion, the Ombudsman explicitly acknowledged an 'effective crisis in the value of the Constitution', precisely at a time when the citizens' fundamental rights face a high level of danger.[47]

The Constitutional Court to the Rescue

This sample of case law illustrates that while some member states are able to appeal to their own constitutions to slow down the process of European integration and democratic decision-making and evade a more European approach to the sovereign debt crisis, in other member states the crisis is putting constitutional jurisdiction under increasing pressure, in the face of higher risks of indeterminacy, arbitrariness, inequality and injustice. In Portugal, what seemed at first to be an ailing Court made a resounding comeback.

In its most recent decision, on abstract constitutionality control of Budget 2012 salary and pension cuts, the Constitutional Court[48] was sensitive to the same line of reasoning followed by the Ombudsman. It affirmed that in both the private and the public sectors, the existence of a 14-month pay is an integral part of the annual salary of workers. It also acknowledged that the targeting of public servants and pensioners for substantial salary reductions violates the principle of equality of all citizens in the face of public burdens and its corollary that all citizens, with their different categories of income, must contribute to cover public expenditures according to their ability to pay. According to the Court, this *discriminatory targeting* of certain groups leaves unscathed the income of many other citizens, irrespective of its nature and absolute and relative size. The Court found it irrelevant that public servants and pensioners are paid by public monies, assuming that these come from all the taxpayers, including public servants and pensioners themselves. It is up to all citizens, in the public and private sectors, to pay for public goods and services, according to their ability to pay.

The Court held that any compromising of the principle of equality in the distribution of sacrifices among the totality of the citizens cannot but be temporary. It acknowledged that because of these and previous salary cuts, some of the targeted groups would instantly lose more than one-quarter of their annual salaries, which it saw as a violation of the principles of equality and proportionality when read and interpreted in the light of their semantic interplay. Interestingly enough, the

47 'Provedor de Justiça, Orçamento do Estado para 2012: a suspensão do pagamento de subsídios de Natal e de férias'. The Ombudsman took time to discuss the pension cuts of retired pensioners, including those of the private sector, which he considered unconstitutional.

48 Constitutional Court, Decision 353/2012.

decision did not discuss the *status* of unilateral pay cuts, as opposed to a special tax, nor its impact on the ability to pay or on the social rights of individuals and families. The Court's decision stated that the necessary compliance with the Troika Programme of Financial Assistance does not justify such an unequal and disproportional measure. Its objectives must be achieved through a more fair distribution of the burdens among the people. However, in order not to impair the achievement of the government's financial goals, the Court left the 2012 budget cuts untouched, prescribing a substantial change of policy from the 2013 budget on, something which turned out to be controversial. Important as this decision may be, it risks creating more problems than it solves if the necessary mechanisms of sound public management and effective financial control are not put in place.

This puts the Portuguese Constitutional Court under enormous strain. It is not clear how long it will resist the pressure. While delaying a larger constitutional role to European institutions, stronger member states are able to export negative constitutional externalities not only to the EU but also to more vulnerable member states. At the EU level, economic policy-making decisions need a defined centre of sovereignty and legitimate democratic authority, or else the chances for political and economic development and the future of European cooperation and integration may be downgraded.

Shattering the Constitution

Once the sovereign debt of a country is placed on negative outlook by a rating agency its whole constitutional and institutional framework is called to deal with this delicate new status. In reality, the constitution may suffer a serious impact. In a sense, the sovereign debt crisis has placed the Portuguese Constitution on negative outlook. The institutional and legal system is going through a credibility crisis, since it was not able to prevent the sovereign debt crisis. This is true at both European and national levels. European integration deprived member states of monetary and fiscal competences and policy instruments that could have been used to protect national individuals, corporations, goods and services. This loss has not been compensated by a gain in sovereign powers by the EU. The general public is now suspicious of a political and legal system that was unable to prevent the crisis or protect them from it.

Fundamental Rights' Negative Outlook

This strong sentiment of constitutional doubt and frustration is particularly felt in the domains of fundamental rights, including social rights, where there is a serious risk of a *promise v. performance* debacle. After the Carnations Revolution of 1974, the Portuguese Constitution of 1976 was premised on values and principles of social justice, social rights, social security and the subordination of economic interests to democratic political power (Arts 1 & 2).[49] It is true that several constitutional scholars warned that it was not enough to have a catalogue of social rights in the Constitution for them to be truly effective. However, the revolutionary hope of the 1970s, strengthened by the accession to the European Community in the 1980s, led to a firm conviction that social rights and conditions were here to stay and would significantly improve.

Several years ago there was some discussion about changing the status and content of the economic, social and cultural rights. In September 2010 the social democratic party (PSD) made a constitutional revision proposal which, among other things, did away with the rights to free universal education and health care and made it easier to fire workers. This proposal met with a strong reaction from the left-wing parties, such as the socialists (PS), the communists (PCP) and others (for example the BE), who made their own counter-proposals, as well as from public opinion. Many public figures of the PSD considered this proposal a neo-liberal market-oriented betrayal of the party's original social democratic ideals.

Since a constitutional amendment requires two-thirds of the parliamentary votes and is thus impossible without agreement between the PSD and the PS, MPs, realizing the debate on constitutional revision was going nowhere, and could even backfire, decided to close it.[50] It has now been mute for more than a year. However, a strong programme of public spending cuts will certainly take a toll on economic, social and cultural rights, without formally revoking them. The challenge is to make the necessary public spending cuts without infringing essential dimensions of these rights. The Memorandum signed with the Troika is often cited, in the preface of the newly enacted legislative acts, as a justification for the adoption of restrictive measures. These touch many civil and social rights. Here we can discuss but some examples.

As far as the right of access to justice is concerned, there has been a significant increase in judicial fees applying retrospectively to pending judicial proceedings.[51] Although the purpose is to ensure the sustainability of the judicial system and prevent excessive delay of judicial proceedings, this risks leaving many people without an effective right of access to justice and judicial protection, since one has to have a very small income to be able to benefit from legal help. This led the president of the Portuguese Bar Association to claim that this new regime treats justice as a luxury item, violating the constitutional right of access to justice.[52] The

49 J.J. Gomes Canotilho and V. Moreira, *Constituição da República Portuguesa Anotada*, I (Coimbra, 2007), pp. 195ff.

50 The constitutional revision debate was closed by the Parliament Commission on Constitutional Revision on 31 March 2011, in a meeting that lasted only four minutes. Diário da Assembleia da República, II Série, RC, 31-3-2011.

51 Lei 7/2012.

52 Marinho Pinto diz que custas judiciais são uma 'brutalidade'; available at http://www.tsf.pt/PaginaInicial/Portugal/Interior.aspx?content_id=1203546.

recent plan of the Minister of Justice to close more than 50 courts throughout the country only exacerbated these concerns.

The domain of workers' rights and social security is another example. Although the Constitution guarantees the right to work and requires the government to promote full employment policies, the government has just recently made firing easier and unemployment is at an all-time high.[53] Moreover, it has abruptly suspended the regime of flexibility of retirement before the age of 65 with no regard for the principle of settled expectations and for the rights of participation of the representatives of the workers.[54] These and other measures (for example restrictions to collective bargaining) claim to reduce transaction costs in the labour market, boost productivity and guarantee the sustainability of social security in the face of increasing life expectancy. However, their negative impact on the sense of dignity and self-worth of the rising number of unemployed is a matter of great concern.

The right to housing is threatened by massive foreclosures and rising property taxes. Thousands of Portuguese families have had to give up their houses after defaulting on their mortgages and property taxes.[55] Single and divorced mothers have suffered a serious blow, since banks and landlords often look at their financial situation with suspicion.[56] The unprecedented social dimension of the problem suggests it requires a political and legislative solution. Financial markets and residential housing markets, far from being natural and neutral entities, were legal creations of the state.[57] The government must protect citizens from decades of institutionalized unequal bargaining power, information asymmetries, illusory contractual freedom and equality, and several other market and government failures, in a way that is 'consistent with minimum standards for social and economic relationships in a free and democratic society'.[58] This is especially important since the Portuguese Constitution creates a positive duty, on the part of the state, to guarantee the right to housing by means of a comprehensive housing policy aimed at securing affordable houses for both homeowners and tenants.[59]

The right to health has also been impaired by severe spending cuts in the national health service, accompanied by the increase of the so-called moderating

---

53 Lei 53/2011.

54 Decreto-Lei 85-A/2012.

55 DECO pede protecçāo para famílias com dificuldade em pagar a casa; available at http://rr.sapo.pt/informacao_detalhe.aspx?fid=25anddid=60714.

56 M.R. St. Cyr, 'Gender, Maternity Leave, and Home Financing: A Critical Analysis of Mortgage Lending Discrimination Against Pregnant Women', *University of Pennsylvania Journal of Law and Social Change* 15 (2011): 109-141.

57 D.K. Hart, 'Contract Law Now – Reality Meets Legal Fictions', *Hart University of Baltimore Law Review* 41 (2011): 1-81, at 30ff.

58 J.W. Singer, 'Things That We Would Like to Take for Granted: Minimum Standards for the Legal Framework of a Free and Democratic Society', *Harvard Law and Policy Review* 2 (2008): 139-159.

59 Gomes Canotilho and Moreira, *Constituição*, pp. 832ff.

fees aimed at discouraging the excessive use of the system.[60] Again, the justification for these spending cuts and higher fees is the sustainability of the national health service. Taken together, these and other restrictive measures may undermine human capital, social cohesion, trust and citizenship. People in general feel their constitutional social rights are being sacrificed to pay, to a large extent, for ruinous public-private deals involving special interest groups and enforced by the state.

Constitutional Nihilism?

These are but some examples of how the crisis is impacting fundamental rights, placing them on negative outlook. In Portugal this has caused a major crisis of faith in the Constitution and constitutional law. As in the theodicy discussions, the constitution may be good, but it is not all powerful to prevent economic and financial evil in the world and deal with it. It is probably too early to slip into constitutional nihilism and conclude, with Nietzschean overtones, that 'the Constitution is dead and we have killed it'.[61] In its above-mentioned decision, the Constitutional Court was a beacon of hope and direction. But there is no doubt that recent events have severely undermined constitutional trust and weakened the public perception of the primacy and normative force of the Constitution, while at the same time imposing very high *demoralization costs* on individuals. Such a landscape may frustrate the political, economic and social goals that current European and national policies purport to achieve.

Conclusions

The way the current sovereign debt crisis is being fought has had a major impact on constitutions and constitutional law, allowing for some preliminary observations. First, major constitutional failures in the institutional systems of governance and control have contributed to aggravation of the crisis. More attention must be given in the future to constitutional, political and economic reality and to the development of governance standards for all EU member states that deal not only with financial affairs, but also with the effectiveness of checks and balances, party financing and governance, and the fight against corruption.[62]

The crisis caught state sovereignty and the state constitutional law in the *wet footprint*. On the one hand, states could not go back to traditional forms of sovereign crisis management, while on the other, they couldn't move forward, at a fast enough speed, to a more European form of cooperative crisis management.

---

60 Decreto-Lei 113/2011.

61 Remembering 'Gott ist tot, Gott bleibt tot und wir haben ihn getötet', from Friedrich Nietzsche, *Die fröhliche Wissenschaft*, 1882, III, sec. 125.

62 'Money, Politics, Power: Corruption Risks in Europe, Transparency International'; available at http://www.transparency.org/enis/report (accessed 6/6/2012).

This constitutional stalemate proved to be a major problem, creating a sort of constitutional and sovereignty vacuum.

The crisis also made it clear that while stronger states were fighting to protect their own constitutional systems and democratic forms of government, they were making it harder for the EU to move forward to deeper levels of integration, while at the same time forcing weaker states to relinquish their own capacities of democratic self-government along with fundamental rule of law principles. All this, along with the shattering of social and labour rights, has generated serious constitutional imbalances and has led to a major crisis of faith in constitutionalism. Policy-makers may be underestimating the damage that their decisions are causing to fundamental rights, democracy and the rule of law.

PART IV
Third Path: Breakdown

Chapter 9

Breaking and Making Constitutional Rules: The Constitutional Effects of the Financial Crisis in Hungary

Zoltán Szente

Although Hungary was the only post-communist country that did not adopt a new constitution during its transition to democracy in 1989/1990, after a peaceful negotiating process between the ruling communist party and the democratic opposition parties and movements, the existing Constitution of 1949 was fundamentally revised in 1989, bringing about fundamental changes in Hungarian constitutional law. In reality, the general revision of the Constitution changed almost all the important parts of the basic law to such a degree that many refer to it as 'an actually new constitution'.[1] As a result of these changes, Hungary became a multiparty parliamentary republic with constitutional safeguards of fundamental rights. The country, where all governments completed their four-year mandate from 1990, and where, until 2006, the former opposition parties could always form a government after the general elections, was regarded as a stable constitutional democracy.[2] This stability was supported not only by institutional guarantees, such as an effective Constitutional Court or some special constitutional procedures (like the constructive non-confidence motion preserving the position of the incumbent government), but also by solid economic growth since the mid-1990s. Hungary was admitted into the EU in 2004, and expressed its intention to also join the eurozone in the near future. Nevertheless, whereas in the 1990s the country was seen as a champion of democratic and economic development in the Eastern and

1 A. Jakab, 'The Republic of Hungary: Commentary', in R. Wolfrum and R. Grote (eds), *Constitutions of the Countries of the World* (Oceana, 2008), p. 8.

2 See, for example, P. Paczolay, 'The New Hungarian Constitutional State: Challenges and Perspectives', in A.E. Dick Howard (ed.), *Constitution Making in Eastern Europe* (Woodrow Wilson Center Press, 1993), pp. 21-55; I. Szikinger, 'Hungary's Pliable Constitution', in J. Zielonka (ed.), *Democratic Consolidation in Eastern Europe*, vol. I: *Institutional Engineering* (Oxford University Press, 2001), pp. 409-415; G. Halmai, 'Ungarn', in A. von Bogdandy, P.C. Villalón and P.M. Huber (eds), *Handbuch Ius Publicum Europaeum*, Band I: *Grundlagen und Grundzüge staatlichen Verfassungsrechts* (C.F. Müller, 2007), pp. 695-700.

Central European region, there appeared more and more signs of its political and economic problems.

Under the circumstances of a growing political legitimacy crisis after 2006, the world economic and financial crisis had devastating effects not only on the economic development of the country, but also on its constitutional arrangements. Soon after the parliamentary elections of 2010, when the new government majority adopted a new Constitution, and a number of laws on the constitutional system, Hungary became the focus of the attention of the international community, as a country where constitutional democracy is deteriorating. The question evidently arises as to how the downfall of democracy in Hungary is connected to the deep economic crisis which broke out in the autumn of 2008. In this chapter, I will also examine ways of managing the effects of the economic and financial crisis on constitutional institutions and processes in Hungary.

The Effects of the Global Financial Crisis on Hungary's Economy

The constitutional effects of the global financial crisis can hardly be understood without knowing the nature and basic symptoms of the economic impacts of the depression. Some constitutional amendments, legislative measures and even certain institutions and procedures initiated by the new Constitution were direct reactions to the special effects of the crisis and to the political developments induced by these impacts.

Hungary is a small, open economic system, highly dependent on the trends of the world economy. At the time of its accession to the EU, in 2004, Hungary undertook to make all necessary efforts to comply with the so-called Maastricht criteria, which are needed to introduce the euro. Hungary's GDP amounts to about 65 per cent of the average gross national product of the EU countries. Although the rate of economic growth was above the EU average between 1997 and 2006, the results of the economic catch-up policy have never been clear, since the country has had financial accounting problems since its accession. Since 2004, the European Commission has proceeded with an excessive deficit procedure because of the long-standing unbalanced budget of the country.

The crisis brought about serious economic depression almost immediately after its outbreak in the autumn of 2008, and sharply increased the financial risks of the country. Economic performance turned into a recession, as the loss of GDP was almost 7 per cent in 2009. The economic depression caused financial destabilization, which had spill-over effects reducing investor confidence and negatively affecting the foreign exchange rate of the national currency (forint, HUF) and a weak demand for government securities and bonds.

Financial stabilization was the central concern of consecutive governments, although they proceeded with different economic policies. In order to ensure liquidity in domestic financial markets, the socialist government concluded a €20bn financial stabilization package with the IMF and EU in November 2008, undertaking strict conditions, like fiscal consolidation and a reform of the financial sector. In April 2009, a new socialist government was formed, when Ferenc Gyurcsány was replaced by Gordon Bajnai. The Bajnai government launched an economic austerity programme, reducing public expenditure and increasing government incomes. After the general elections of 2010, the new, rightist coalition government, led by Viktor Orbán, unsuccessfully asked the European Commission for an exemption from keeping the deficit target of 3.8 per cent of GDP and a goal of less than 3 per cent in 2011, undertaken by the former socialist governments. It led to a difficult financial situation, since the corporate tax cut and the introduction of a flat-rate income tax of 16 per cent were cornerstones of the political programme of the rightist coalition, which was unwilling to abandon these policy measures, because the promises of the tax cuts and the creation of new jobs helped the rightist parties to oust the socialist party associated with economic restrictions and corruption.

Thus, the new government found itself in a tense financial situation, in which it desperately had to seek additional budget revenues for keeping Hungary's commitments to the EU in its convergence programme. As a response to the rising financial risks, the Orbán government discontinued the policy lines of the former government, and instigated a so-called 'unorthodox' economic policy with the application of unexpected policy measures, instead of traditional and well-admitted instruments. But the actions taken by the new regime did not prove to be successful; in fact, in autumn 2010 the government terminated the agreement concluded by the Gyurcsány government with the IMF and the EU. This was fuelled by a new political stance, emphasizing national sovereignty and announcing a 'freedom fight' for economic independence. The new taxation policy (imposing 'crisis taxes' in certain sectors) and the financial restrictions undermined investor confidence even more than before. By the beginning of 2012, the public debt, as a result of the continuously worsening exchange rate of the forint (it slumped by around 20 per cent in the second half of 2011), had increased to 84 per cent of GDP. According to all relevant data, the risk of Hungarian state bankruptcy grew dramatically. Moreover, the biggest ratings agencies downgraded Hungary's debt to 'junk' status, that is to a non-investment grade, invoking further deterioration of the country's financial position. All these events forced the government in November 2011 to invite the IMF and the EU back for talks about a so-called 'standby agreement' to provide a financial 'safety net' for Hungary.

Political Background

When the world economic and financial crisis began in autumn 2008, the Hungarian economy was in a particularly bad situation because of the unsustainable welfare policy of the consecutive socialist governments since 2002, which had slowly but surely undermined the financial balance of the country. Economic growth dramatically slowed after 2006, so it was already slowing before the crisis. Besides that, just a few months before the crisis broke out the socialist-liberal coalition government was dissolved when the liberal Alliance of Free Democrats left the coalition. So, at the beginning of the global financial crisis in 2008, the country was in a highly vulnerable financial situation and had a weak government in political terms. The economic pitfall swept away the controversial Prime Minister Ferenc Gyurcsány with his cautious institutional reform plans. The governing socialist party, instead of opening the way to general elections, took the chance of forming a new government, consisting partly of experts and technocrats, partly of party politicians. Although this government, led by Gordon Bajnai, successfully pursued a crisis management policy for a year, it was politically weak, since it needed the support of the socialist party, and it had to cope with great unpopularity. The former rightist opposition party, Fidesz, and its satellite Christian Democratic Party, won a landslide victory in the parliamentary elections of 2010.

The new government acquired a two-thirds majority. The supermajority of governing parties is not unprecedented in Hungary; in 1994, the first left-liberal coalition gained 72 per cent of parliamentary seats. Yet this time, the two-thirds majority is sharply different, because the general elections of 2010 restructured the whole party system in Hungary; two 'system changing' parties, the conservative MDF (Hungarian Democratic Forum, the major government party between 1990 and 1994) and the liberal Alliance of Free Democrats (coalition partner of the socialist party between 1994 and 1998, and 2002-2009) fell out of the parliament, while two new parties, the liberal LMP and the extreme right Jobbik, entered the National Assembly. Thus, a new party system appeared, with the dominant position of Fidesz facing a divided opposition, with two democratic parties and a radical one.

Certainly, there were deeper reasons for the upset of the political balance. As a result of the ineffective and corrupt politics of the socialist government, in the 2000s a new style of opposition politics evolved (for example taking politics out of parliament to the streets, and founding easily moveable, active local groups). The poor performance of the left-liberal coalition government and a series of corruption scandals caused social unrest, which led to street riots after a secret speech of the Prime Minister was leaked.[3] The rightist opposition, under the unquestioned leadership of the charismatic Viktor Orbán, successfully exploited this situation and in 2008 initiated a national referendum torpedoing some important public policy measures of the Gyurcsány government. The first effects of the unfolding world economic crisis sealed the fate of the socialist government. All these events contributed to the destruction of public confidence in political institutions in general, and especially in the government. Empirical studies show that since

3 The speech was given by Gyurcsány to the members of the parliamentary faction of the socialist party. In that speech, the Prime Minister admitted that his government had lied about the financial situation of the country in order to win the impending parliamentary elections. In Hungary, the term 'speech of Őszöd' (after the place where the speech was given) has become a byword for political lying.

the early 2000s, the popularity of the extreme right has been growing in parallel with an increase in distrust of political institutions.[4] To sum up, public cynicism, disappointment and moral outrage generated by the incompetent and corrupt socialist governments, supplemented by the effects of the world economic crisis, caused voters to become disillusioned and opened the way for the 'revolution of the ballot boxes'.

Whatever the reasons for the results of the parliamentary elections in 2010, they produced an extremely strong government with a mandate to make changes in politics. Seemingly, this was just in time; the crisis management needed a politically capable central government, and the second Orbán government (Orbán was first Prime Minister between 1998 and 2002) did not hesitate to use its power. In spring 2011, parliament, in the absence of the two democratic opposition parties (which, protesting against the 'destruction of the rule of law', boycotted the whole constitution-making process), approved a new Constitution of Hungary. The 'unorthodox economic policy' of the government was already being pursued on this new constitutional basis. No doubt, the world economic crisis had an impact on the new constitutional rules, and the new legal frameworks have provided unprecedented perspectives for the economic policy of the executive power.

The Economic and Financial Provisions of the New Constitution

As we have seen, the two-thirds majority gave a constitution-making power to the rightist coalition government in 2010, and the governing parties did not hesitate to use this power to accomplish their political objectives. They were able to rewrite the entire text of the Constitution, including its rules concerning public economy and finance. Notably, the old Constitution contained only a few provisions on these issues.[5] These rules bore the imprint of the age in which they were made; while the reference to 'the right to work' was rooted in the original text of the Constitution of 1949, the principle of 'social market economy' was added to the text in 1989. Thus, there was a real demand to consider these provisions and to complete them with the constitutional regulation of state intervention and the guarantees of a well-balanced national economy.[6]

4 P. Krekó, A. Juhász and Cs. Molnár, 'A szélsőjobboldal iránti társadalmi kereslet növekedése Magyarországon', *Politikatudományi Szemle* 20 (2011): 53-79.

5 T. Drinóczi, *Economic Constitution and Economic Rights* [in Hungarian] (Dialóg Campus, 2007), pp. 72-75.

6 B. Molnár, Zs. Gyombolai and A. Téglási (eds), *Economic Basic Rights and the New Hungarian Constitution* [in Hungarian] (Az Országgyűlés Emberi jogi, kisebbségi, civil- és vallásügyi bizottsága, 2011).

New Economic and Taxation Principles

According to these expectations, the Constitution of 2011 contains some new principles and mechanisms for public finance, in particular relating to the state budget and debt management. It is surprising, at the same time, that the general reference to the 'market economy', which was put in the preamble of the previous text, is missing from the new one, although the relevant jurisprudence of the Constitutional Court was based on that principle. Instead, the new Constitution stipulates only that '[t]he economy of Hungary shall be based on work which creates value and freedom of enterprise'.[7] The anachronistic 'right to work' clause of the old Constitution was left out of the new text. Besides that, the new Constitution requests a balanced, transparent and sustainable budget management.

The new constitutional regulation has also brought about a change in taxation principles: whereas the Constitution of 1949/1989 required distribution of tax burdens based upon the ability to pay principle, the Constitution of 2011 declares that every person should 'contribute to satisfying community needs to the best of his or her capabilities and in proportion to his or her participation in the economy'.[8] The new conservative government's political intention behind this change was apparently to introduce a flat-rate personal income tax (applying 16 per cent rate for all incomes), instead of the progressive income tax.

Debt-ceiling Rules

Undoubtedly, the most important innovation of the new Constitution is to establish debt-ceiling provisions, restricting the budgetary power of parliament. These rules require the legislature not to adopt a state budget act that allows the state debt to exceed half of GDP. Moreover, as long as the state debt exceeds this limit, parliament must adopt debt reduction measures. Deviation from these rules is possible only under a special legal order, and if there is a significant and enduring national economic recession to the extent required for redressing the balance of the national economy. If parliament fails to follow these provisions, the new Constitution entitles the government to collect statutory revenues yearly on a pro-rata basis in accordance with the expenditure targets defined by the state budget act.[9]

Similar restrictions are also imposed on the economic policy-making of the executive power. According to Art. 37 of the new Constitution, during the implementation of the state budget act, 'no debt or financial obligation may be assumed that allows state debt to exceed half of Gross Domestic Product' or 'to exceed its level in the previous year'. Remarkably, the new debt-ceiling provisions soon proved to be too rigid, especially with the vulnerable financial position of the

7 Art. M, para 1 of the Constitution of 2011.

8 Art. XXX, para 1 of the Constitution of 2011.

9 Art. 36.4-6.

country, in which the central government has only limited capacity to reduce the level of state debt. Therefore, new constitutional legislation – whose legal nature and relationship with the new Constitution is not clear – postponed the entry into force of these rules until 2014.

Surprisingly, the restriction of the budgetary power of parliament and the debt-ceiling regulations are not supported by independent institutional safeguards. The new constitutional rules remove public finance issues from judicial control.

Restricting Judicial Control over Public Finance

As we will see below, when the government majority encountered the controlling power of the Constitutional Court, it immediately reduced the Court's power of constitutional review.[10] It is worth noting that for two decades the Constitutional Court had been the most effective and strongest counterbalance to the executive.[11] Just a few months after its formation, the new coalition government, using its two-thirds majority, transformed the process of nomination of justices to the Constitutional Court. Since then, the membership of the parliamentary committee responsible for the nomination has no longer been based on parity, but reflects the party-strength in the National Assembly. Whereas the earlier regulation required a compromise between the parties to nominate justices (because of the two-thirds majority requirement), since the autumn of 2010 the government parties have been able to elect their own nominees. It is not only a theoretical option: in 2010 two justices, and in the spring of 2011 five more, were elected by government party MPs, ignoring the protests of the opposition parties.[12] In this way, the government managed to place its loyal supporters in the judicial body, reaching a stable majority.[13] The personal control of the Court was extended by the new Constitution, empowering parliament to elect the head of the Court (before that, he

---

10 Act No. CXIX of 2010 [modifying the Constitution of 1949/1989 to restrict the constitutional review of public finance laws].

11 See, for example, H. Schwartz, *The Struggle for Constitutional Justice in Post-Communist Europe* (University of Chicago Press, 2000), pp. 87-108; L. Sólyom and G. Brunner, *Constitutional Judiciary in a New Democracy: The Hungarian Constitutional Court* (University of Michigan Press, 2000); G. Halmai, 'The Hungarian Approach to Constitutional Review: The End of Activism? The First Decade of the Hungarian Constitutional Court', in W. Sadurski (ed.), *Constitutional Justice, East and West: Democratic Legitimacy and Constitutional Courts in Post-Communist Europe in a Comparative Perspective* (Kluwer International Law, 2002), pp. 189-211.

12 One of the reasons for the protests was that some nominees failed to comply with the qualification conditions set by law.

13 For example, one of the new justices, Stumpf, was a Minister in the first Orbán government between 1998 and 2002, and an adviser to the Prime Minister just before his nomination in 2010; another one, Balsai, was a forerunner MP of Fidesz before his election.

or she was elected by the justices themselves).[14] After that, in autumn 2010, with the scope of constitutional review badly reduced, the new Constitution finalized this restriction in the constitutional text. Since then, the Court has been able to review and annul the budgetary laws, the acts on taxes, duties, pensions, customs or any kind of financial contributions to the state only if they violate the right to life and human dignity, the right to the protection of personal data, freedom of thought, conscience and religion, and the rights related to Hungarian citizenship. In theory, this is a temporal provision, since the new Constitution upholds this restriction of the Court's power as long as state debt exceeds half of GDP.[15]

Although removing some issues from judicial review is not unprecedented in Europe,[16] the elimination of constitutional review as an institutional guarantee from all public finance issues, even for only a deemed transitional period, raises the assumption that the constitutional constraints of the executive power can be put aside in economically difficult times. This kind of constitutional regulation appears to give an unlimited entitlement to the executive power, allowing even an unconstitutional economic or financial policy. The condition of the revival of constitutional review, that is the reduction of state debt below half of GDP, is unjustified and hardly a defensible legal position, because the level of protection of fundamental rights should not depend on economic indicators.

Judicial power has been curtailed in other ways as well, since a special provision of the new Constitution prescribes a general interpretive principle not only for the Constitutional Court, but also for the ordinary courts, saying that '[t]he interpretation of the Basic Law and other laws shall be based on the assumption that they serve a moral and economical purpose corresponding to common sense and the public benefit'.[17] This provision seems to suggest the unconditional preference of particular moral and economic needs and interests over legal aspects, which can bring about legal uncertainty in judicial practice. This assumption is strengthened by another provision requesting that, 'in the course of performing their duties', the Constitutional Court and the ordinary courts are obliged to respect the principles of balanced, transparent and sustainable budget management.[18] There is some concern that these provisions appear to favour budgetary interests above any other interests, including the requirements of the rule of law. Nevertheless, the application of these interpretive principles can hardly be controlled by the

14 The political motivation for these changes can be demonstrated by the fact that they were enacted by modifying the old Constitution, that is not waiting for the effect of the new Constitution. Otherwise, the Constitutional Court, in its old composition, would have been able to decide on some politically hot issues, and elect its own president for three years.

15 Nevertheless, having regard to the rate of state debt which is permanently over 80 per cent, the restriction will surely be long-standing.

16 K. Wheare, *Modern Constitution* (Oxford University Press, 1966), p. 102.

17 Art. 28 of the Constitution of 2011.

18 Art. N, para 3 of the Constitution of 2011.

executive power, so probably they will not have any effect on the jurisprudence of the courts.

Curbing the Freedom of Action of Future Governments – Constitutional Protection for Policy Measures

Already the legislation curbing the Constitutional Court's power has attracted wide-ranging domestic and international criticism of Hungarian constitutional politics. The constitutional provisions that cemented some economic policy measures of the current rightist coalition government sparked new concerns. The new Constitution prefers the 'general state pension system based on social solidarity', vis-à-vis private pension funds, which were abolished by the incumbent coalition government. Similarly, the new Constitution requires a two-thirds parliamentary majority for changes to key tenets of economic policy, such as taxation or family care, reducing the freedom of policy-making and the scope for fiscal adjustment of all future governments. All these requirements are in conflict with the inherent logic of parliamentary democracy, because they make it impossible for future governments, having a simple majority, to realize their own economic programmes in these fields.[19]

The Restriction of the Budgetary Power of Parliament

The rightist constitution-makers were ready to restrict the freedom of action of following governments in other ways as well. While the new Constitution more or less retained the previous structure of separation of powers, it has recognized the constitutional status of the Budget Council, which is 'an organ supporting parliament's legislative activities and examining the feasibility of the state budget'. But it is not a purely advisory body, since its prior consent is required for the adoption of the state budget by parliament. Although the Council may refuse to give consent only in specified cases (for example if the budget bill would allow state debt to exceed half of GDP), its decision may not be reviewed or annulled, so it will have a real veto right, which is an exceptional restriction of parliament's budgetary power. This absolute veto power of the Budget Council might be the sword of Damocles hanging over a possible leftist government after 2014 as well, because for a couple of years all the three members of the Council will be party soldiers of the conservative government. The veto power of the Budget Council can threaten the existence of the next governments because the new Constitution gives a new power to the President of the Republic to dissolve parliament (and simultaneously announce elections) if it fails to adopt (and to get approved by the Budget Council) a state budget for the running year by 31 March. Since the Head of State, János Áder, is a veteran and loyal politician of the major governing party

19 Venice Commission, 'Opinion on the New Constitution of Hungary', Opinion no. 618/2011 (2011), para 24, 6-7.

Fidesz (and is the personal choice of the Prime Minister, Viktor Orbán), this party will have the ability to dismiss the next government.

Conservative Economic Philosophy of the Constitution

As the constitution-makers were not reluctant to curb the freedom of action of future governments, they also ensured that the new Constitution reflects some of their values and priorities. For example, the whole approach of the chapter on fundamental rights seems to be suffused with a conservative social philosophy, which connects the justification of rights with the accomplishment of civic duties. It can be exemplified by the title of the whole chapter 'Freedom and Responsibility' or by a curious provision that adult children are 'obliged to look after their parents if they are in need'. The new Constitution declares that 'every person shall be obliged to contribute to the community's enrichment with his or her work to the best of his or her abilities and potential'.

At the same time, the new Constitution clarifies the constitutional nature of social and economic rights as state aims, instead of recognizing them as rights. Although it might seem to be a decrease of protection, it brings the regulation closer to practice; the old Constitution, for example, declared simply the right to work (as a remnant of its original text, dated 1949), without any enforceable right.

The new Constitution emphasizes the importance of national assets and the empowerment of the legislature to determine the range of exclusive economic activities of the state. The new Constitution also refers to the principles of social responsibility of the property right and the right to enterprise.[20]

The 'Unorthodox' Economic Policy of the New Government and its Constitutional Implications

Soon after the EU refused to approve Hungary's exceeding of the promised budget deficit in 2010, the Orbán government announced a so-called 'unorthodox economic policy' in order to keep the budget deficit under the requested limit. This term refers to the unusual policy measures and instruments employed to increase budget revenues, abandoning the traditional methods of economic recovery. A lot of policy measures that are components of this sort of economic policy do not have any constitutional implications, even if they have generated heavy political and economic disputes. Although the centralization of state economic resources (emphasizing the importance of national assets),[21] the increase of the economic activity of the state and its property share in the so-called 'strategic

20 For a detailed description of the constitutional regulation, see Zs. Halász, 'Public Finances', in L. Csink, B. Schanda and Zs. Varga (eds), *The Basic Law of Hungary: A First Commentary* (Clarus Press, NIPA, 2012), pp. 288-294.

21 See, for example, Act No. CXCVI of 2010 on the national assets.

enterprises' (in the biggest Hungarian oil company or in the 'national airline') and economic protectionism (for example preferring Hungarian companies in public procurements) can raise some concern as to whether they are compatible with the rules of EU law, they do not cause primary constitutional problems. Similarly, the increase of state intervention in the national economy and the systematic destruction of welfare services can be criticized, but basically, they are not constitutional issues. Nevertheless, certain actions taken by the government and statutes approved by parliament have led to constitutional conflicts.

The Nationalization of Private Pension Fund Savings

One of the most disputed economic measures of the Orbán government was the diversion of the assets of private pension funds. From 1998, certain parts of employees' mandatory pension contributions were paid to several private pension funds for completing the state-run pension system.[22] These funds had about three million members and collected almost three trillion HUF (about 10 per cent of the Hungarian GDP). In autumn 2010, parliament adopted a law to divert private pension contributions to the state budget temporarily for the next 14 months.[23] The law also contained a set of provisions to force people to leave the private pension funds, and return to the state pension scheme, prescribing that people who opted to stay in the private funds would lose their future pension claim from the state, even though their employer is bound to pay social security contributions for them in the future. It was a strange provision that only those private pension fund members who wished to stay in their respective funds needed to express their wishes, while all assets from the savings of the returning members were automatically shifted to the state budget.

Although a part of this extraordinary government revenue was spent to reduce the state debt, it was in fact a nationalization of the assets of the private pension funds (or the confiscation of their members' savings). The whole process was very strange in a democratic society, since central government threatened to deprive many citizens of their future pension claims, unless they decided as the government wished.[24]

It is more important for this study that the process raises not only moral (and political) concerns, but constitutional problems as well. Under the legal threat of

22 According to this system, the private pension funds would have paid 30 per cent of the total pension of their members, while the remaining 70 per cent would have been covered by the state.

23 Act No. CLIV of 2010.

24 Only about 10 per cent decided not to go back to the state pension system, but even their contributions were shifted to the state budget after 14 months. In 2012, a new law withdrew the threat and guaranteed the future pension claims of those who remained in private pension funds. It was a widespread view that the expulsion of the private pension fund members from the state pension would be harsh discrimination against them.

depriving future pension claims of citizens, even if their employers are obliged to pay social security contributions for them, the decision of the private pension fund members to return to the state pension system is obviously not a voluntary one, and it cannot be seen as an expression of their free will. If this is the case, the constitutionality of government measures can be questioned, since the pension savings are protected by the Constitution in the same way as property rights. This has been the permanent interpretive practice of the Constitutional Court since the early 1990s. In 1992, and in 1993 in a more detailed form, the Court found that reversions and certain other rights have the same function as property (that is the provision of the material basis of personal autonomy) and, therefore, the constitutional protection of property has to be applied to them as well.[25] This became a consistent jurisprudence of the Court,[26] which implicitly declared that pension savings are included in the rights that are protected in the same way as property rights.[27] The relevant constitutional rule states that the state guarantees the right to property and the expropriation of property is permitted only in exceptional cases, in the public interest, and only in cases and in the manner stipulated by law, with the provision of full, unconditional and immediate compensation.[28] The new Constitution contains the same rules on property rights.[29]

It is arguable whether the takeover of the savings of private pension funds members is a procedure equivalent to expropriation, because the state gives a safeguard for paying full pensions for those who pay social security contributions (though the government has not undertaken the value guarantee of the contributions, as the private funds did). But a partial limitation of property rights needs a justification that requires concrete public interest as the legitimate objective of the limitation, which must be proportional to its legitimate ends.[30] Since none of these conditions were met when the central government forced the private pension funds members to turn their savings over to the state budget, all relevant provisions would probably have been declared unconstitutional by the Constitutional Court.

The Retroactive Taxation of Severance Payments

Another highly controversial measure was a law that imposed a 98 per cent tax on the extreme severance payment, with retroactive effect. Fidesz, the major governing party, during the election campaign had promised to review the

25 Decision 17/1992 (III 30) ABH 1992, 108 of the Constitutional Court; 64/1993 (VI 3).

26 1138/B/1995. ABH 1996, 555-556, 51/2001 (IX 15) ABH 2007, 661, 109/2008 (IX 26) ABH 2008, 909.

27 867/B/1997. ABH 2003, 996, 1010.

28 Art. 13.1&2 of the Constitution of 1949/1989.

29 Art. 13.1&2 of the Constitution of 2011. The only difference is that the Constitution refers also to the social responsibility that the property entails.

30 42/2006. (X 5) ABH 2006, 529, 50/2007 (VII 10) ABH 2007, 994-995.

'unabashed' severance payment in state-run enterprises, after some scandalous payments had been revealed. When the party came to power, one of its first actions was to implement this promise, and the new parliament adopted a statute imposing special tax on severance payments against good morals (*contra bonos mores*) and paid from the state budget. An extra high tax rate (98 per cent) was determined, imposed retroactively, from the beginning of the current 'tax year' (that is from 1 January 2010). Since the retroactive taxation was expected to be found unconstitutional as it violates the principle of the rule of law,[31] the government majority modified the old Constitution (of 1949/1989) allowing *ex post facto* tax-imposing legislation in the case of incomes acquired against good morals.[32]

The law was attacked by many, claiming that it violates the principle of proportional contribution to public revenues, because the new statute, in determining the tax rate, ignored the income and wealth of the taxpayers. Furthermore, it was also criticized for violating the right to property, because the regulation met neither the requirement of public interest nor the principles of necessity and proportionality. The Constitutional Court found that while the modified Constitution allowed the retroactive tax-imposing legislation, the new law incorrectly defined severance payment as being against good morals, once it had been paid according to law.[33] It is worth noting that the annulment of the retroactive tax-imposing law gave a handle for the government majority to curtail the Court's power of constitutional review in public finance cases.

At first sight, this truncation of the Court's powers was only political revenge for an unfavourable decision, but it proved to be a long-term strategy neutralizing the Court's controlling role. The real objective could be to prevent the Court from striking down the aforementioned nationalization of private pension fund savings, arguing that without the takeover of the assets of these funds, the budgetary deficit would jump to about 7 per cent instead of the 3 per cent to which Hungary had committed itself towards the EU.

After the Constitutional Court struck down the 98 per cent tax, parliament again imposed a 98 per cent tax on any income over two million forints received either as a retirement package or as severance pay in the last five years in the government sector paid to state and local government leaders and chief executives of state and local government-run companies. The minimum level of payment to which the tax had to be applied was raised to 3.5 million HUF, but also with a retroactive effect to 2005. The constitutional text was accordingly amended again, allowing unlimited retroactive taxation of any income coming from the state budget.

The new law had also been sent to the Constitutional Court, and the Court, within its recently restricted jurisdiction, and under the political pressure upon it, found a compromise: while it declared that the law's sanctioning of the severance

31 903/B/1990. ABH 1990, 250-251.

32 See also K. Kovács and G.A. Tóth, 'Hungary's Constitutional Transformation', *European Constitutional Law Review* 7 (2011): 192-193.

33 184/2010 (X 28).

payment paid since 2005 was unconstitutional, it upheld retroactive taxation if it extends only to the beginning of the current tax year.[34]

Imposing Special 'Crisis Taxes' on Certain Economic Sectors

As the introduction of a flat-rate income tax and the reduction of corporate tax significantly decreased budget revenues, central government had to fill this gap in order to keep the state budget in balance. Therefore, in October 2011, additional so-called 'crisis taxes' were introduced in the banking, telecommunications, energy and retail sectors for a limited, three-year period, until the long-term structural changes were made.[35] In theory, the government wanted to save the country's population, the poorly-financed domestic small and middle-sized private companies from this tax burden and therefore the sectoral extra taxes targeted only companies of substantial profitability. Nevertheless, the tax base was not the net profit of the concerned companies, but was made up by their turnover from taxable activities. The rate of tax is different in the various sectors, and depends on the amount of the annual turnover. The projected revenues from the introduction of this tax were HUF161bn (approximately €588 million) for 2010, and similar revenues were expected (and later implemented) for 2011 and 2012.

The introduction of the crisis taxes did not cause a constitutional dispute in Hungary, because, as we have seen above, the Constitutional Court's power of constitutional review of public finance laws was extremely restricted. Nonetheless, the regulation seems to violate the equality principle, a basic constitutional tenet for several reasons. First, the new taxes were applied only to certain types of economic activity. Thus, the distribution of tax burdens was highly uneven, since certain taxpayers had to pay significant taxes, while others were hardly troubled at all. Second, the crisis taxes predominantly affected foreign companies, raising the suspicion of indirect discrimination. Third, in contrast with the official explanation, the tax base was turnover, rather than profitability, which could also lead to discriminative and unfair treatment of companies.

It is to be noted that the new Constitution enshrines the principle of equality before the law for 'every person';[36] the Constitutional Court, on the basis of the similar provision of the Constitution of 1949/1989, extended the effect of the anti-discrimination principle to the entire legal system,[37] as 'legal persons' belong to the category of 'every person'. Certainly, it is another question whether the Court, in its new composition, will uphold this extensive interpretation of the constitutional text or not. Most probably, the Court will not examine the particular case of crisis taxes, referring to the lack of relevant competence. Still, the question was put on the European agenda, as 13 leading European firms asked the European

34 37/2011 (V 10).

35 Act No. XCIV of 2010.

36 Art. XV, para 1 of the Constitution of 2011.

37 61/1992 (XI. 20), ABH 1992, 280.

Commission in 2011 to sanction Hungary over the special sectoral taxes, arguing that the selectively imposed crisis taxes violate the principle of equality within community rules.

Setting Fixed Exchange Rates for Private Loans

Not surprisingly, beyond the general worsening of the state budget's situation, the population also suffered directly from the effects of the global economic and financial crisis. Perhaps the most dramatic effect was the rapid and non-retrievable indebtedness of those people who took out loans in foreign currency a couple of years before the crisis. As a result of general mistrust of the national currency, a great number of households took up Swiss franc denominated (mortgage) loans, which made them extremely vulnerable to the global financial crisis, as the forint exchange rate against the Swiss franc has continuously and significantly fallen in the last few years, and the mortgage on their homes or other debt burdens have become unbearable for them. Notably, the indebtedness of a portion of the population was not only an additional economic problem but a phenomenon with many political implications as well.

The government took several measures to ease the situation of the indebted people and to help them to retain their properties. One of these steps was the setting of a fixed exchange rate for loans in foreign currency taken during the boom years before 2008.[38] Although the reason for the regulation had a strong moral justification, namely the division of the burden between the creditors (the banks) and the debtor (the citizens), it also raised some worries about its compatibility with constitutional principles. The first concern relates to the alleged violation of the freedom of contract, which prevents the state from encroaching on private contracts. Notably, this is an unenumerated right, without any explicit textual base, recognized only by the practice of the Constitutional Court. According to its jurisprudence, private contracts are protected by the (also unenumerated) principle of *clausula rebus sic stantibus*, allowing change to the content of contracts only in the case of a fundamental change of circumstances that could not be foreseen when the contract was concluded.[39] As a matter of fact, it could have been argued that there was a significant and unpredictable change of circumstances since the date of signing of these contracts, but, as we have seen, the new Constitution excluded any constitutional review of the issue.

Another concern relates to the disproportionality of the distribution of burden between the contracting parties, because in fact the law forced the banks to cover all the losses resulting from the national currency's depreciation.[40] As in other

38 Act No. LXXV of 2011.

39 32/1991 (VI 6) ABH 1991, 151-154, 160.

40 For example, the law set an exchange rate of 1 SF to 180 HUF, equivalent by and large to the currency exchange rate before the world economic crisis, while the real currency exchange rate was about 1:240 when the law came into effect.

cases, this question could not be considered fair procedure by constitutional review.

Conclusions

In studying constitutional change under the conditions of the global economic depression, the case of Hungary can be highly interesting, because the government, with its constitution-making supermajority in parliament, has had an extraordinary mandate to manage the impacts of the crisis. This situation offers a good opportunity to observe the behaviour of an almost unrestricted executive power.

As to one of the research questions of this study, that is how the constitutional transformation of Hungary was connected to the effects of the economic and financial crisis, it can certainly be said that the constitutional system changed considerably during the crisis. The adoption of a new Constitution, the extensive economic and constitutional legislation, and the establishment (and transformation) of some public power institutions give enough evidence of this finding. However, the new constitutional rules cannot be explained by the effects of the global economic and financial crisis, even if sometimes they were referred to as an excuse for unpopular and restrictive measures. It was hypocrisy; the new rules of the game were not reactions to the worsening economic conditions but, rather, they were adjusted to the ambitions for power of the governing parties at the expense of the fair rules of competing for governmental power in a democratic society. This was made possible by the landslide election victory and, as a consequence, the overwhelming parliamentary majority of the government parties. In other words, the major variable of the comprehensive and deep constitutional changes is the two-thirds constitution-making majority of one political camp, which was used to consolidate the governmental power of the political right for a long time.

For the other research question, that is whether the decline of Hungarian constitutional democracy is a corollary of the global economic crisis, the answer is also negative. Analysing the constitutional changes, it must be said that neither the process of constitution-making nor the content of the new Constitution is fully compatible with the well-entrenched values of modern European constitutionalism. The new constitutional legislation has significantly reduced the quality of democracy and has led to a democratic deficit. In general, the institutional balances of executive power have considerably weakened. Some of them have lost their independence or some of their control powers. The party soldiers of the government parties occupy the leadership of all independent institutions (with the exception of the National Bank) from the Constitutional Court to the State Audit Office, for prolonged periods of six to twelve years. But all these changes took place independently from the global financial crisis; they were the products of the hostile political relationships between the parties and the two-thirds majority of the government coalition. Still, they have also affected the way that central government reacted to the effects of the economic depression.

Though the government followed traditional aims in handling the economic and financial impacts of the global crisis, it used 'unorthodox' means and instruments to manage it. While the reduction of government expenditure, the raising of budget revenues and certain administrative reforms are usual methods of coping with economic difficulties, the retroactive tax-imposing legislation, the imposition of special taxes, the nationalization of citizens' savings and the intervention in private contracts are to be seen as extraordinary measures even in times of financial crisis. As we have seen, some of these measures were highly controversial from a constitutional point of view.

Notably, the whole process was performed more or less in a formally constitutional way. Still, the procedural correctness has led to a deterioration in the level of constitutional democracy. So the differentiation between material and formal concepts of constitution(alism)[41] and between substantive and procedural democracy seems to be legitimate, at least under such conditions as exist in Hungary.

Unfortunately, in Hungary, there is a great chance that the deterioration of the rule of law and constitutional culture will have long-term impacts. Whereas in the current situation the rules of the Constitution can easily be changed whenever the coalition government so wishes, the qualified majority requirement of any constitutional change will make the Constitution very inflexible if the government does not have a two-thirds majority in parliament. Therefore, it will be difficult to modify the existing system of separation of powers, and to replace the partisan office-holders in the controlling institutions. The conservative public policy, set in stone by the new Constitution, could also cause many problems for future governments.

The incoherence of the new Constitution causes another problem. It occurred several times between 2010 and 2012 that when a particular policy measure of the government encountered constitutional obstacles, its parliamentary majority, with a formal amendment, incorporated it into the constitutional text. Although this method eliminated the current constitutional difficulty, it produced some inconsistencies in the Constitution.

The final lesson of this case study is that extraordinary political circumstances, such as the gaining of a supermajority or a constitution-making power by a political camp, can pose a bigger threat to democracy than an economic or financial crisis. And together, they may create a challenge to even a consolidated democracy.

41 See, for example, H. Kelsen, *General Theory of Law and State* (Harvard University Press, 1946), pp. 124-125; G. Champagne, *L'essentiel du Droit Constitutionnel*, 1: *Théorie générale du Droit Constitutionnel* (Gualino, 2001), p. 24; A. Katz, *Staatsrecht. Grundkurs im öffentlichen Recht* (C.F. Müller Juristischer, 1994), p. 167.

Chapter 10

The Impact of the Financial Crisis on Icelandic Constitutional Law: Legislative Reforms, Judicial Review and Revision of the Constitution

Björg Thorarensen

The Collapse of the Icelandic Financial System and its Multifarious Impact on Constitutional Law

Following rapid growth of the Icelandic economy for several years, based mainly on the expansion of the country's largest commercial banks following their privatization in the early years of the twenty-first century, the situation had deteriorated in 2007. The consequences were felt suddenly and very severely in Iceland at the end of September and in the first days of October 2008. The collapse of the Icelandic financial system in the autumn of 2008, and the ensuing economic crisis, brought about a variety of unexpected consequences and unprecedented questions involving Icelandic constitutional law. A number of legal complications evolved with respect to the winding up of the Icelandic banks and other financial institutions, not to mention the wide and drastic implications of the collapse for the nation's economy.

The crisis triggered a heated debate on the foundations of Icelandic society and its government, as well as widespread protests, particularly against the government and parliament but also against other state institutions responsible for control in the financial market. A Special Investigation Commission was elected by the Icelandic Parliament, the Althing (*Althingi*), at the end of 2008, by Act 142/2008, to investigate the events that led to the collapse of the three main banks in Iceland and to seek to answer questions as to what caused their failure. The Commission issued an extensive report with its findings in April 2010. It analysed the reasons why the financial situation of the country's three largest commercial banks had deteriorated steadily from 2007 onwards, and criticized both the banks and the country's government, singling out the government for its failure to take action towards the banks, which expanded very rapidly, and for various decisions on economic management. The report also provided explanations for the economic difficulties facing the three banks and the entire society at the beginning of October 2008. Among other things, it pointed out that the total obligations of these banks in the first half of 2004 had amounted to the equivalent of over half of Iceland's GDP, but had increased enormously in just four years to the equivalent of over nine times the country's GDP by mid-2008.[1] The social benefits of the investigation were obvious, not least in identifying how to prevent such a calamity from happening again.[2]

A new office of a Special Prosecutor was established by Act 135/2008. It was given the task to investigate suspicions of criminal conduct in the period preceding or in connection with the collapse of the Icelandic banks, connected to the activities of financial undertakings and other legal entities or individuals, and to follow up on these investigations by prosecuting those concerned.

For the first time an impeachment procedure was initiated based on the main findings of the Special Investigation Commission. The Althing decided in September 2010 to issue an indictment against the former Prime Minister of Iceland for negligence in office by not having reacted properly to the processes leading to the collapse while he was in office.[3] On 23 April 2012, the Court of Impeachment of Iceland (*Landsdómur*) pronounced its judgment and convicted the former Prime Minister on one of the four counts he was accused of, namely for not having held ministerial meetings according to his duties under Art. 17 of the Constitution in order to discuss and form a government policy to react to the serious problems confronting the Icelandic bank system and the national economy in 2008.

Highly complicated legal issues of European and international law evolved in relation to the so-called Icesave-savings. The Icelandic bank Landsbanki Íslands had offered online savings accounts under the 'Icesave' brand operating in the United Kingdom and the Netherlands. This created one of Iceland's most difficult diplomatic disputes, which still remains unresolved. The main question was whether the Icelandic state should bear responsibility and issue a state guarantee for the Depositors and Investors Guarantee Fund of Iceland towards the governments of the United Kingdom and the Netherlands, to comply with their alleged obligations under the European Economic Area (EEA) Agreement.

1 Extracts from the report in English are published on the website of the Althing at http: www.sic.althingi.is. See also M.J. Flannery, 'Iceland's Failed Banks: A Post-Mortem of 9 November 2009', Appendix 3 to the report, accessible at the website.

2 E.G. Gunnarsson, 'The Icelandic Regulatory Responses to the Financial Crisis', *European Business Organization Law Review* 12(1) (2011): 1-39, at 15.

3 Art. 14 of the Constitution reads as follows: 'Ministers are accountable for all executive acts. The Accountability of the Ministers shall be established by law and Althingi may impeach Ministers on account of their conduct in office. The Court of Impeachment has competence in such cases.' The punishable conduct of Ministers is further defined in the Ministers' Accountability Act 4/1963 and more detailed provisions on the composition, quorum and procedure of the Court of Impeachment are laid down by Act 3/1963. The system is based on similar model to that stipulated in Arts 14 and 16 of the Constitution of Denmark (*Rigsretten*).

The President of Iceland took a crucial role in this issue by twice applying his constitutional power to refuse to sign legislation passed by the Althing to issue a state guarantee in relation to Icesave. In accordance with Art. 26 of the Constitution, the two Acts were put into referendum, the former in 2010 and the latter in 2011, and rejected by the nation on both occasions.[4] This has given rise to a lively debate in Iceland on the authority of the President of Iceland to refuse to sign bills, and to put them to referendum.[5] Since its adoption in 1944, Art. 26 had never been applied by previous Presidents of the Republic, even though it was accepted in theory that the President had the authority to do so in extraordinary situations. This has now raised a new debate in constitutional law and political theory in Iceland on the role and powers of the President, and the need to redefine his authority in this respect, as well as the constitutional dilemma that has evolved between parliament and the President.[6]

This chapter will address two different aspects of the relationship between the Constitution and the economic crisis in Iceland. The first will focus on legislative reforms resulting from the bank collapse, which restricted constitutionally protected property rights, and how the Icelandic courts exercised their constitutional review in this respect. Accordingly, the chapter will provide an analysis of how the so-called 'Emergency Act' adopted by the Althing on the day of the collapse, 6 October 2008, restricted the property rights of creditors who did not belong to the group of owners of deposits, since the claims of the latter where changed into priority claims in the winding up of the Icelandic banks. In a series of court cases,

4 The issue is now pending before the European Free Trade Association (EFTA) Court, as the EFTA Surveillance Authority filed a case against Iceland in December 2011 seeking a declaration that Iceland had failed to comply with Directive 94/19/EC on deposit guarantee schemes and the EEA Agreement, with respect to its obligation of non-discrimination. See further information on the events leading to the Icesave dispute in Gunnarsson, 'Icelandic Regulatory Responses', 25-34 and J. Danielsson, 'The Saga of Icesave', Centre for Economic Policy Research Policy Insight 44 (January 2010); available at http://www.cepr.org/pubs/policyinsights/CEPR_Policy_Insight_044.asp.

5 Art. 26 of the Icelandic Constitution reads as follows: 'If the Althing has passed a bill, it shall be submitted to the President of the Republic for confirmation not later than two weeks after it has been passed. Such confirmation gives it the force of law. If the President rejects a bill, it shall nevertheless become valid but shall, as soon as circumstances permit, be submitted to a vote by secret ballot of all those eligible to vote, for approval or rejection. The law shall become void if rejected, but otherwise retains its force.' The provision replaced a previous provision on the authority of the King to veto legislation. It has been suggested that the idea behind the new Art. 26 in 1944 was inspired by Art. 73 of the German Constitution (Weimar Republic) of 11 August 1919, then in force, according to which a law passed by the Reichstag had to be presented in a plebiscite, if the Reich President decided so, within a period of one month.

6 On the historical origin and constitutional theories related to Art. 26, see F. Magnusson, 'Opening Pandora's Box: The Refusal of a President to Sign a Bill from Parliament', *Zeitschrift für öffentliches Recht* 65(2) (1 June 2010): 203-224, at 205.

the Icelandic courts had to assess the constitutionality of the Emergency Act with respect to property rights of creditors and the principle of equality.

The latter part of the chapter will focus on how the crisis affected general support for revising the Constitution, as public debate resurfaced in Iceland on reform of the Constitution following the collapse. The focus will be on the reasons for the debate, and the new routes of the reform process that were decided by the enactment of an Act on a Constitutional Assembly in 2010. In this new exercise, great emphasis was put on the involvement of the public and seeking the views of the nation so that they could be reflected in the Constitution. The Act established a consultative Constitutional Assembly with 25 members elected by direct personal elections, without participation of politicians or political parties. The Assembly was given the role of submitting proposals on a review of the Constitution to the Althing.

The Enactment of the Emergency Act and Constitutional Review

Main Elements of the Act

On 6 October 2008, the Prime Minister introduced to the Althing a bill 'Authorizing Treasury Disbursements due to Unusual Financial Market Circumstances etc.' The bill was a response to economic difficulties that had arisen in the preceding months, and was adopted with great haste on the same day as Act 125/2008.[7] From the outset it was called the 'Emergency Act', referring to the extraordinary circumstances of the financial market, considered equivalent to an emergency situation. The Act contained 13 material provisions, mainly amending other legislation related to the financial market.

First, the Act provided for disbursements from the Treasury, including an authorization to allocate funds under the extraordinary and very unusual circumstances of the financial market, to establish new financial undertakings or to take over such undertakings or their estates in full or in part.

Second, several provisions were added to Act 161/2002, on Financial Undertakings, which among other things authorized the Financial Supervisory Authority to take special measures if it deemed them necessary due to exceptional circumstances or events, with the aim of limiting loss or risk of loss on the financial market.

Third, and most importantly for this chapter, Art. 6 of the Act added a new paragraph to Art. 103 of Act 161/2002, which read as follows: 'Upon the winding-up of a financial undertaking, claims to deposits, as defined in the Act on Deposit Guarantees and an Investor Compensation Scheme, shall enjoy priority as referred to in the first paragraph of Art. 112 of the Act on Bankruptcy.'

---

7 The Act is accessible in English translation at http://eng.forsaetisraduneyti.is/news-and-articles/nr/3037.

It is evident that the time available to prepare the Act was extremely short, with only a few days for the drafting of the main portion of the bill. Its Explanatory Notes were extremely brief, and the debate in parliament only took a few hours.[8] From the explanations provided, it was clear that the proposed legislation was seen as emergency legislation taken to prevent the banks in Iceland from closing and the payment system from freezing or collapsing and ceasing to function. Around this time a run had begun on the Icelandic banks, and on Friday, 3 October 2008, cash withdrawals from banks in Iceland amounted to ISK5.5bn, compared to withdrawals of ISK200 million on a normal Friday. Runs had also begun on their branches abroad. The authorities in the United Kingdom raised strong objections to the activities of the Icelandic banks' subsidiaries there, and prepared actions against them.[9]

By the measures provided for in Act 125/2008, the idea was both to protect the interests of the general public, the continued functioning of banking activities and payment systems in the country, and to ensure that all deposits in banks in Iceland would be secure and that the state would be authorized to intervene in the management of financial undertakings if they were heading for failure. The Act took immediate effect, and in the following three days the Icelandic authorities availed themselves of the authorizations it provided. Accordingly, the Financial Supervisory Authority took the powers of shareholders' meetings in all the country's largest commercial banks: Landsbanki Íslands, Glitnir Bank and Kaupthing Bank. Their Boards of Directors were dismissed and a Resolution Committee appointed for each of them.[10] At the same time three new banks were established on the basis of the collapsed banks, which bore the names of the older ones prefixed by 'New'. Their financial basis was laid out in particular with the transfer of assets to them from the old banks, but also with financial allocations from the Icelandic Treasury. The new banks also took over certain obligations of the old ones, primarily deposits in the banks in Iceland. Deposits in their branches abroad, which were in the UK and the Netherlands in particular, including the Icesave brands of Landsbanki Íslands, were not transferred to the new banks, however. All the three older banks were placed in liquidation on 22 April 2009, and boards of winding-up were appointed for each of them.

8 Alþingistíðindi, A-deild 2008, þskj. 80 [Parliamentary Gazette-A, doc. No. 80].

9 Under the Landsbanki Freezing Order of 8 October 2008, the UK Treasury went on to freeze the assets of Landsbanki Íslands and assets belonging to the Central Bank of Iceland, and the Government of Iceland relating to the Landsbanki. The order was issued on the basis of provisions in the Anti-terrorism, Crime and Security Act 2001 and was made because the Treasury believed that action to the detriment of the UK's economy (or part of it) had been or was likely to be taken by certain persons who were the government of or resident of a country or territory outside the UK. The decision to apply the Anti-Terrorist legislation to freeze the assets of Landsbanki in the UK was strongly protested and criticized by the Icelandic authorities.

10 See further on the impact of the Emergency Act, Gunnarsson, 'Icelandic Regulatory Responses', 5-13.

The Alleged Violations of Property Rights and the Supreme Court's Judgment

A number of banks and other financial institutions throughout Europe, many of which had lent the Icelandic banks billions of euros, claimed that the legislation, specifically the clause redefining the claims of owners of deposits in brands located in Iceland as priority claims, violated both their property rights and the principle of equality. The fact that deposits in domestic bank accounts, which altogether amounted to ISK2.7 trillion (approx. €16.1bn), were paid as priority claims before general claims resulted in considerable losses for other creditors. In a series of cases filed by creditors before the Icelandic courts, they claimed that Art. 6 of Act 125/2008 was unconstitutional as it violated Art. 72.1 of the Constitution of Iceland, which protects the right to property as one of the core human rights of the Constitution.[11] Furthermore, they claimed that their rights under Art. 1 of the First Protocol ECHR and Art. 65 of the Constitution on non-discrimination (cf. also Art. 14 ECHR and Art. 40 of the EEA Agreement), had been violated.

On 28 October 2011, the Supreme Court of Iceland pronounced 11 judgments, each of which dealt with one or another aspect of the core constitutional question described above, and each of them having a number of plaintiffs. In the following, the leading judgment in this group, in case 340/2011, will be explored to cast some light on the arguments in relation to the constitutionality of the Act and to analyse how the Icelandic courts applied and interpreted the provisions of the Constitution and the ECHR.[12] The plaintiffs in case 340/2011 were 64 creditors, the largest group being German banks, as well as other owners of claims to the bank Landsbanki Íslands, who maintained that they had suffered financial loss due do the Emergency Act.

The Supreme Court closely analysed the difficulties that gave rise to the adoption of Act 125/2008, to be able to assess in this regard the objectives and actions the legislature had decided to undertake, and to conclude whether they had acted beyond the boundaries of the Constitution. It pointed out that the three large commercial banks proved to be incapable of withstanding the shocks when they came. They were no longer viewed with confidence, and their formerly easy access to credit was now closed. Furthermore, depositors' distrust of the banks

---

11 Art. 72.1 of the Constitution reads as follows: 'The right of private ownership shall be inviolate. No one may be obliged to surrender his property unless required by public interests. Such a measure shall be provided for by law, and full compensation shall be paid.'

12 The case was filed against Landsbanki Íslands, presented by its winding-up board. The Icelandic state was not a party to these 11 cases. According to Icelandic constitutional theory it is the responsibility of the courts to decide whether specific statutory provisions, which are disputed, violate the Constitution and there is no procedural necessity for the Icelandic state to be a party to the case. A conclusion by courts to the effect that an Act is deemed to be in violation of the Constitution would result, in such circumstances, in the Act being disregarded but could not imply a decision on the possible liability of the state for damages.

had reached a stage where a run had started on the banks. It was evident that the government and the Althing considered it impossible to refinance the banks with Treasury funds, and thereby enable them to continue operation. The situation in the financial markets, furthermore, meant that the possibility of the state obtaining financing abroad quickly became practically non-existent. In accordance with the above, the Supreme Court accepted that without a rapid response by the legislature and government, a collapse of banking activities and breakdown of the country's payment systems was imminent. Nor was there any doubt that such a situation would immediately or very soon have had disastrous consequences for the general public and all economic activities in the country. The Emergency Act was therefore adopted under very serious and pressing circumstances for the entire Icelandic society.

The Court accepted the contention of the plaintiffs, that their claims rights were *property*, under the meaning of Art. 72 of the Constitution and the First Protocol ECHR. It therefore needed to be resolved whether the provisions of Art. 6 of the Emergency Act involved such violation of the plaintiffs' rights, as is considered to be expropriation, or such restriction on property rights that it violated the provisions of Art. 72 of the Constitution on property rights and Art. 65 on the principle of equality. In this regard a number of aspects had to be assessed concurrently, such as the cause of the actions taken, their objectives and consequences, the nature of these measures and how general and widespread was their application.

The Court analysed the possible legitimate expectations of the plaintiffs. It recalled the legislature's assumption that it was authorized to alter the priority of claims in liquidation without constitutional provisions limiting its scope to do so. This assumption had repeatedly been manifest in legislation, from 1974 onwards, when statutory provisions were amended on priority ranking of claims in insolvency liquidation and probate so that priority claims have been variously broadened or narrowed, with a resulting impact on the ranking of other claims, to the advantage or disadvantage of their owners. Accordingly, the plaintiffs could not rightly have expected the legislature not to take action in this respect to their disadvantage and the legislation did not infringe their rights retroactively.

The allegations that equal treatment of creditors had been distorted by Art. 6 of the Emergency Act were twofold: first, that it implied direct and indirect discrimination against general creditors who, prior to the adoption of the Act, had the same ranking in priority as depositors; and second, that the legislature had discriminated between creditors on the basis of nationality or their status in other respects. The Court compared the two groups of creditors, the deposit owners on the one hand and other general creditors on the other, and whether they had equal status. The Court's view was that general creditors were not comparable to deposit owners, taking into account the nature of the claims, different means to react to financial difficulties of banks and the necessity that deposit owners are confident that their savings are secure. If the deposits were felt to be unsecure, this could initiate a run on the banks with serious consequences for the stability of the financial market, and could potentially cause economic collapse. Accordingly, these groups of creditors were not comparable. Nor had the legislature discriminated between creditors on the basis of nationality or their status in other respects, as it was clear that the legislation applied equally to all deposit owners in banks in Iceland without any regard to their nationality or their status in other respects. The same arguments applied with respect to the prohibition of discrimination under Art. 40 of the EEA Agreement. Accordingly, the claim of the plaintiffs that Art. 65 of the Constitution and Art. 14 ECHR were violated was rejected.

As regards the objectives of Art. 6 of the Emergency Act, the Supreme Court accepted the view that there were tangible reasons for giving deposits special status in the inescapable settlement among those parties with direct interests at stake in the indebted financial undertakings. In this regard, it had been demonstrated that, prior to the adoption of the Act, a run on the banks had begun due to depositors' loss of confidence. New banks were established in Iceland on the basis of the former banks in direct continuation of the entry into force of the Act, and the old banks' deposits in Iceland had been transferred to the new banks. To achieve the objective of a functioning banking and payment system, the legislature deemed it necessary to grant priority to deposits in the winding-up of financial undertakings and thereby instil in depositors confidence in the new banks and stop the run on the banks which had already begun. In doing so, the bank run had been stopped and had subsequently subsided over the course of the following two to three weeks. The contention that the objective of Act 125/2008 of maintaining functioning banking activities and payment systems in Iceland, and of securing deposits in banks in Iceland, had been achieved remained unrefuted in the Court's view. Accordingly, there were objective reasons underlying the legislature's decision to grant priority to deposits. Furthermore, as regards the question of proportionality, the Court noted that more lenient options with less consequence for the creditors would not have achieved the legitimate objective of avoiding a bank run. The assessment by the government and the legislature had been that the Icelandic state had no possibility of refinancing the banks and this was the only option available at that time. The Court accepted the wide margin of appreciation that the legislature had to be given under the extraordinary and perilous circumstances that had arisen. With regard thereto, the allegation that the legislature's adoption of Act 125/2008 comprised a violation of the principle of proportionality was rejected.

In resolving the constitutionality of the Emergency Act, the Court reiterated the legislature's extensive scope in assessing the necessity of the measures provided for in the Act, in circumstances where great risk had jeopardized the existence of the entire society due to the chain reaction of the collapse of the largest commercial banks, which could have ended with the collapse of the country's entire economy. Under these circumstances, the legislature was not only entitled but above all obliged by its constitutional responsibility to ensure the welfare of the general public.

In accordance with all the above arguments, it was evident, in the view of the Court, that in the actions concerned in the parties' dispute, the legislature did not exceed its authority according to Art. 72 of the Constitution and Art. 1 of the First Protocol ECHR.

Assessment of the Judgment in the Light of Existing Theory of Icelandic Constitutional Law on Property Rights and the ECHR

The judgments reviewing the constitutionality of the Emergency Act were the subject of great attention and debate in Icelandic society, not least within the legal profession. The financial interests at stake were enormous and unprecedented. The amounts claimed by general creditors to the Icelandic banks were estimated in September 2008 to be approximately ISK7 trillion (€44bn), the largest group of creditors being German banks holding one-third of these claims.

One may contemplate whether the Icelandic courts were affected by great pressure in the light of the interest at stake. There would clearly have been drastic consequences had Art. 6 of the Emergency Act been declared unconstitutional. It is therefore interesting to assess the application of relevant constitutional provisions in the light of previous court practice. It should be noted that the Icelandic courts have been relatively active, compared to courts in other Nordic countries, in exercising their role of judicial review, particularly following a complete revision of the human rights provisions of the Icelandic Constitution in 1995 by constitutional Act 97/1995.[13]

Examining the conclusion of the Supreme Court in case 340/2011 regarding the limits of the legislature to restrict property rights, it appears that a classical approach is applied according to Icelandic constitutional theory and practice. This approach has been developed in court practice for decades concerning general restrictions of property rights, for instance cases relating to withdrawal of official licences for certain occupations, limitation of fishing rights and reduction of pension rights. Accordingly, an assessment is first made to establish whether a restriction of property right is a *deprivation of property* or expropriation, for which full compensation should be paid, or whether it is a *general restriction* of property rights not creating a right to compensation. The main criteria that have been applied when assessing whether general restriction is justified are the following: first, it must be stipulated by statute law; second, it must be general in nature and not aimed directly or indirectly at a small group; third, it must have a legitimate objective, usually the public interest; and fourth, a proportionality test is performed, that is there should be a reasonable relationship of proportionality between the means employed and the aims pursued. Finally, the courts have acknowledged that the legislature has a wide margin of appreciation when choosing the means to pursue certain objectives in the fields of social and economic policies.

In the last decade, Icelandic courts have been more influenced by the interpretation methods of the ECtHR when assessing conditions for restrictions

13 B. Thorarensen, *Constitutional Law: Human Rights* [in Icelandic] (Codex, 2008), pp. 65-68.

of property rights. According to Art. 1.2 of the First Protocol ECHR, the right to peaceful enjoyment of possessions shall not impair the right of a state to enforce such laws it deems necessary to *control the use* of property in accordance with the *general interest* or to secure the payment of taxes or other contributions or penalties.[14] The case law from the Strasburg Court illustrates the wide scope of margin of appreciation that may be enjoyed by member states when regulating the use of property according to Art. 1.2. However, it will determine whether a fair balance was struck between the demands of the general interests of the community and the requirements of protection of the individual's fundamental rights.[15] This means that the Court investigates the lawfulness and the proportionality of the controlling measures, apart from the lawfulness in national law of the measures of control, and the state must show that the fair balance is satisfied, that the burden which falls on the individual is not excessive and that the measures are not disproportionate.[16]

It is apparent from the judgments of the Supreme Court in the cases on the Emergency Act that all these considerations were explored. The Court thoroughly argued each step in its assessment before it concluded that the enactment of Art. 6 of the Emergency Act was not in violation of the Constitution. The elements that the Court took into account in the proportionality test, and concurrently the assessment of the legislature's margin of appreciation, are particularly noteworthy. In that respect, the Court not only accepted the wide margin of appreciation of the legislature to select the means to pursue the aim but also basically confirmed that no other means were available, by stating that lenient options with fewer consequences for the creditors 'would not have achieved the legitimate objective to avoid a bank run'.

The Supreme Court did not go as far as suggested by the defendant, as a reserve claim, to confirm that a formal *situation of emergency* had emerged in Iceland justifying derogation of constitutional rights. In Icelandic constitutional theory it is acknowledged that an unwritten principle exists in emergency situations where temporary exceptions from the Constitution may be justified. No written provisions on this issue can be found in the Icelandic Constitution, similar to many other

14 See one of the leading judgments on the interpretation of Art. 1, First Protocol ECHR and the distinct rules it comprises in ECtHR, 21 February 1986, Case 8793/79, *James and Others* v. *the United Kingdom*, para 37.

15 D.J. Harris, M. O'Boyle and C. Warbrick, *Law of the European Convention on Human Rights* (2nd edn, Oxford University Press, 2009), pp. 687-688.

16 In the case of *Kjartan Ásmundsson* v. *Iceland*, the ECtHR looked into the discriminatory character of the control of use of property according to Art. 1.2, First Protocol ECHR since general rules related to interference with pension rights had affected the applicant in a particularly concrete and harsh manner. The Court stated that even having regard to the wide margin of appreciation to be enjoyed by the state in the area of social legislation, it cannot be justified by the legitimate community interests relied on by the authorities, when an individual is made to bear an excessive and disproportionate burden of measures to control use of property. ECtHR, 12 October 2004, Case 60669/00, para 45.

European constitutions and Art. 15 ECHR. It appears, on the other hand, from the judgments regarding the Emergency Act that the extraordinary and serious situation, despite not being defined as a time of emergency within the meaning of Art. 15 ECHR, justified extraordinary measures which resulted in extensive restrictions of property rights of general creditors. This was the conclusion from weighing the interests of general creditors against the pressing interest of the nation. In this respect, the Court referred to the *constitutional responsibility of the legislature* to ensure the welfare of the general public, which is a novelty in Icelandic constitutional law.

If the ECtHR is confronted with the question as to whether the Emergency Act violated property rights of creditors according to Art. 1 of the First Protocol ECHR, one may speculate as to the outcome. With regard to the case law of the Strasburg Court, it can first be maintained that the Court has not dealt with applications comparable to the Emergency Act cases. The extraordinary situation the Icelandic authorities faced in the autumn of 2008, and the objective of the means employed by enacting Art. 6 of the Emergency Act, would, in the view of the Strasburg Court, undoubtedly provide an unusually wide margin of appreciation of the Icelandic legislature when regulating the use of property according to Art 1.2 of the First Protocol. The field of legislation in this case relates to economic measures and legitimate and pressing community interests involving an element of emergency. Underlying the Court's approach of granting wide discretion is the core of the *subsidiary principle*, which means that the national authorities are generally in a better position than an international supervisory body to *strike a balance* between the interest of the community and the protection of the individual's fundamental rights. As the Court's emphasis on the subsidiary principle has clearly increased in recent years, this would be an important factor in its assessment.[17]

Revision of the Icelandic Constitution and the New Constitutional Reform Process

Reasons Underlying Demand for Constitutional Reform

As mentioned at the outset, the collapse of the Icelandic financial system in 2008 initiated an awakening in the foundations of Icelandic society and its government. This public debate brought to light some pressing questions regarding the meaning of democracy. Furthermore, a certain background must also be taken into account as an important factor in reviving the debate concerning reform of the Icelandic Constitution.

---

17 B. Thorarensen, 'Strengthening of the Principle of Subsidiarity of the European Convention on Human Rights', in A. Eide, J.Th. Möller and I. Ziemele (eds), *Making Peoples Heard: Essays on Human Rights in Honour of Gudmundur Alfredsson* (Martinus Nijhoff, 2011), pp. 271-292, at p. 286.

The starting point is that large parts of the Constitution adopted in 1944, especially as regards the executive powers and its relation to the Althing, as well as provisions on the judiciary, have remained more or less unchanged from the time that Iceland received its first constitution from the King of Denmark in 1874, with subsequent additions made in the Constitution of 1920.[18] In 1944 Iceland decided to break the union with Denmark and establish a separate republic. Because of the special circumstances that prevailed at the peak of the Second World War only minimal amendments were made to the Constitution with the purpose of giving effect to the transformation from constitutional monarchy to a republican form of government with a directly elected President. This was particularly through the establishment of the office of a President to replace the monarch; the decision was made to postpone any comprehensive revision until a more favourable time. Constitution No. 33/1944 took effect on 17 June 1944, following a referendum where it was approved with approximately 95 per cent of the vote. In the same referendum, the Icelanders decided to discontinue the union with Denmark, also with approximately 97 per cent of the vote. Over 98 per cent of the voters participated in the referendum.[19]

Despite assurances to the contrary by the Althing, a comprehensive review of the Constitution has never taken place. Since 1944 a number of initiatives have been made to reach that aim, without result. The work has always become stranded owing to a lack of political consensus. Nevertheless, a number of limited changes have been approved to the Constitution, the most important involving reorganization of the electoral system, the working procedures of the Althing in 1991 and a new human rights chapter in 1995.[20] Important provisions of the Constitution, however, remain unchanged, and do not reflect the current reality regarding the executive branch and the work of the government, nor do they adequately ensure separation of the executive and legislative branches, or the role of the Althing in supervising the executive. It does not mention key concepts, such as 'democracy', 'nation', 'parliamentary rule' and 'state government'.

More importantly, the Constitution does not provide a clear picture of where the executive powers of the state are in fact vested or what the division of functions is between the President of the Republic and the government in exercising executive

18 The Constitution of the Kingdom of Iceland No. 9/1920 was adopted after Iceland was granted sovereignty in 1918, and recognition of its equal status in union with Denmark under the same king, through a special agreement, the Union treaty, and the Danish-Icelandic Union Act adopted in both states.

19 A translation of the current Constitution of 1944 is available at www.government.is/constitution/.

20 Constitutional Acts 56/1991 and 97/1995. In the latter amendment a complete revision was made to the human rights chapter of the Constitution. A number of new human rights provisions were added, and older ones were rephrased and modernized. In this, the ECHR and the main human rights treaties of the United Nations, to which Iceland is a party, were chiefly used as models.

powers, nor does it clearly stipulate the role of the Prime Minister as the leader of the government and the general role and powers of the state government.[21]

The points of debate that came up when the Althing decided last year, for the first time, under Art. 14 of the Constitution, to indict the former Prime Minister before the Court of Impeachment for negligence in the course of events leading up to the collapse of the financial system, put to the test the definition of the constitutional role and position of the Prime Minister. The Court of Impeachment convicted the former Prime Minister in its judgment of 23 April 2012 for gross negligence and violation of Art. 17 of the Constitution for not having convened government meetings in order to form a policy to discuss and react to the severe situation in the banking system in 2008.

Some are of the opinion that the Constitution can be blamed for playing a role in the collapse of the banks and the economic crisis in Iceland. It is certainly an exaggeration to say that causes of those events can be traced to the flaws of the Constitution. There are, nevertheless, direct links between the economic crisis and the public demand for constitutional reform. The collapse of the banks and the economic crisis resulted in a call for a certain degree of reassessment of values and a need for some form of reckoning with the past. As a matter of fact, one of the consequences of the crisis was an unprecedented lack of confidence in both the political parties and the elected representatives of the nation in the Althing to make decisions on important public affairs, and finding a way to restore this confidence is in itself a separate matter for concern.

This is the main reason that yet another attempt was made to reform the Constitution, this time with a completely different approach. The decision was made to involve the nation directly in the reform process. An important factor in that context was that the Icelandic nation has, in fact, never drawn up its own constitution. A reference was made to the fact the Icelandic Constitution was originally established unilaterally by a Danish king without any substantive discussion whatsoever as to what sort of constitution the nation wanted or on what fundamental values it should be based. The minimal amendments made in 1944 for the foundation of the republic had the effect that the Constitution is a fusion of, on the one hand, the constitution of a kingdom resting on a heritage of absolute monarchy, where the crown was the supreme institution, and, on the other hand, a republic based on parliamentary rule with a nationally elected president. Whereas the politicians had failed to prepare the long promised revision, this was an opportunity for the nation to adopt a constitution that would not have the features of a unilateral royal decree, but would be a covenant on the organization of the state and the position of its citizens, deriving from the nation itself.

---

21 In the report of the Special Investigation Commission it was pointed out *inter alia* that the Prime Minister, as the leader of government, had not fulfilled his duties to inform other ministers about the situation. See further English summaries of the Committee's report in Chapter 2, Executive summary, 10; available at http://sic.althingi.is/.

A parliamentary election was held in Iceland on 25 April 2009, following strong pressure from the public as a result of the Icelandic financial crisis. The Social Democratic Alliance and the Left-Green Movement gained an overall majority of seats in the Althing and formed a coalition government which took office on 5 May 2009. The Independent Party, a centre-right party, which had been in power for 18 years, lost a great deal of its support.

The Constitutional Assembly

One of the goals stipulated in the new government's agenda was to establish a special Constitutional Assembly with the task of revising the Constitution. On 16 June 2010, the Althing passed Act 90/2010 on the Constitutional Assembly (ACA) following a heated political debate.[22] The main opponents, including most of the members of the Independent Party, argued that this was not the right time to revise the Constitution, which was wrongly blamed for being part of the reason for the collapse of the banks. However, the main opposing argument was that it should be the task of the already existing nationally elected representatives, the Members of the Althing, to revise the Constitution, not a new elected forum.

According to Art. 1 of the ACA, a consultative body, the Constitutional Assembly, was given the role of reviewing the Constitution and submitting to the Althing a draft legislative bill for a new constitution. The Assembly was instructed to specifically address the following: the foundations of the Constitution and its fundamental concepts; the organization of the legislative and executive branches and the limits of their powers; the role and position of the President of the Republic; the independence of the judiciary and their supervision of other holders of governmental powers; provisions on elections and electoral districts; public participation in the democratic process, the timing and organization of a referendum, including a referendum on a legislative bill for a constitutional act; transfer of sovereign powers to international organizations and the conduct of foreign affairs; environmental matters, including the ownership and utilization of natural resources.

According to the ACA, a separate personal election was to be held to the Constitutional Assembly in order to select 25 delegates. The Assembly was to be convened on 15 February 2011, and was to complete its work by 15 June 2011 at the latest.

The Roles of the National Forum and the Constitutional Commission

In order to ensure careful preparation of the Constitutional Assembly and further involvement of the public in the proposed project, the ACA provided that the Althing should elect seven members of a Constitutional Commission with an

22 The Act is accessible in English at http://thjodfundur2010.is/other_files/2010/doc/Act-on-a-Constitutional-Assembly.pdf.

independent status. The Commission was entrusted with the task of preparimg and organizing a National Forum on constitutional matters. Participation of approximately one thousand people was assumed for the National Forum, selected by means of random sampling from the National Population Register. The National Forum was to endeavour to call for the principal viewpoints and points of emphasis of the public concerning the organization of the country's government and its constitution. Furthermore, the Commission was to collect material on constitutional matters and present ideas on amendments to the Constitution for the Assembly.

The National Forum was held on 6 November 2010, following extensive preparations and detailed organization of the Constitutional Commission, and was completed in a single day. The Forum was attended by 950 people from all over the country, selected at random from the National Register. Obviously, careful preparations were needed to collect together the viewpoints of a thousand people concerning the foundations of governmental organization and state power. The main conclusions were divided into separate but broadly framed themes, grouping together the viewpoints of the participants, reflecting some basic values that they wished to see form the basis of Iceland's new constitution themes.[23]

The Election to the Constitutional Assembly and its Nullification

The next major step in the process was the election to the Assembly. There was great interest in running, as candidates and the conditions for running were not strict. The result was that 522 candidates put themselves forward. This unexpectedly large number of candidates caused a number of difficulties with regard to both the promotion and the execution of the election, as it became clear that it would be impossible to use traditional ballot papers. Voters were permitted to select up to 25 candidates. The election to the Constitutional Assembly took place on 27 November 2010, when 25 delegates were elected to the Assembly: 10 women and 15 men. It was a cause for great disappointment, however, that participation in the election was much less than expected, with only about 36 per cent of the electorate turning up at the polls. This was considerably short of the normal turnout in elections to the Althing, where participation generally exceeds 80 per cent. Among the reasons suggested for the low turnout was that the large number of candidates in the election made it difficult for voters to pick candidates from the great number of largely unknown people. As candidates had no connections with political parties, only acting in their own personal capacity, it seemed to be difficult for voters to assess which policy they were presenting. Another possible reason was that the nation's interest in the whole exercise was perhaps not as much as expected and clearly there was not a general political consensus on this new path of reform.

---

23 Further description of the Forum and its conclusions are available at http://www.thjodfundur2010.is/english/.

It turned out, as predicted by many, that the great majority of the elected candidates were those who were previously known faces in society, partly from public debate in relation to the crisis. Accordingly, among the candidates selected, there was little representation from the areas outside Reykjavik, and participation in the election was also considerably lower in these areas. It was clear that the election to the Constitutional Assembly differed from other public elections held in Iceland in several respects, including the fact that delegates were elected by direct personal election. Some special rules were adopted in the ACA to reflect special voting methods. However, according to the ACA, the provisions of the Act on elections to the Althing should apply to the Constitutional Assembly elections to the extent that they were applicable. This applied to the general provisions of the Act on elections to the Althing regarding the principles of a secret ballot. According to the ACA there was a special procedure for protest, which provided that any protests concerning the election should be resolved directly by the Supreme Court.

The election to the Constitutional Assembly was protested on the grounds of various alleged defects in its execution. Eventually, complaints were brought forth. In particular, it was contended that the secret ballot rules of legislation on general elections had been violated, as the specially designed ballot papers had been sequentially numbered, so that it was possible to trace them to voters; in addition, polling had not taken place in enclosed booths, as required; further defects were also mentioned, but there is no need to describe them here in further detail.

On 25 January 2011, the Supreme Court ruled that owing to various defects in the conduct of the election, the election was nullified. The Court referred to the responsibility of the legislature to lay down clear and detailed rules on the conduct of public elections, taking into account the circumstances resulting from their unique nature. In the Court's opinion, the public authorities had not been entitled to deviate from clear statutory instructions on the conduct of the election in the light of the large number of candidates or new procedures deemed suitable because of the introduction of electronic tallying. The defects in the conduct of the election held on 27 November 2010 to the Constitutional Assembly were, as such, considered collectively, and accordingly the Court found no alternative but to nullify the election.

Establishment of the Constitutional Council and its Proposals

As one can expect, this conclusion was a blow to the entire process, and it was obvious that the Assembly would be unable to start its work on 15 February 2011, as intended. So, what recourses were available? The main options discussed were whether a new election should be held to the Constitutional Assembly, which would have incurred significant cost, apart from the risk of an even smaller voter turnout, or whether other recourses would be more feasible. In brief, the eventual conclusion was that the Althing, by a Resolution passed on 24 March 2011, decided that the 25 candidates elected to the Constitutional Assembly should be invited to take a seat on a council appointed by the Althing, the Constitutional Council, which was given the role of submitting proposals to the Althing on a review of the Constitution, in the same manner as the Constitutional Assembly had been intended to do. This decision of the Althing was criticized on the grounds that it constituted a circumvention of the decision of the Supreme Court. Others pointed out that, on the contrary, the decision of the Supreme Court would be observed by admitting the invalidity of the election, but this could not prevent the Althing from appointing as its advisors the individuals elected to the Assembly. There was little consensus on the direction that the matter took, and it was likely to weaken the outcome of the whole project, by undercutting the initial idea underlying the Constitutional Assembly that specially elected representatives of the nation should be given the task to write a new constitution.

The Constitutional Council was finally convened in early April 2011. At its first meeting, it took delivery of a detailed report prepared by the Constitutional Commission over the preceding nine months. The report summarized the principal points of focus that had emerged at the National Forum in November 2010. It also included reasoned proposals from the Constitutional Commission regarding amendments to the Constitution that would, among other things, reflect the conclusions of the National Forum.

The Constitutional Council faced an extremely difficult task. It was working in an environment of heated political argument, and it was fundamentally different in nature from a lawfully elected assembly. This novel experiment of providing direct public access to the drafting of a constitution and creating a broad consensus on the foundation of the Icelandic constitutional structure had therefore taken a different direction than originally intended. But in the short time accorded to the Council, less than four months, it succeeded in organizing its work well. It split itself into three working committees, each entrusted with specific issues.[24] At the end of July 2011, the Constitutional Council submitted its proposals to the Althing on a new constitution in the form of a legislative bill. The bill was unanimously approved by all delegates of the Council.[25]

The Material Proposals of the Constitutional Council

The Constitutional Council's bill assumes a number of changes from the current Constitution, without proposing any fundamental changes in the constitutional organization, which in fact was never its intention. Among the notable aspects of the proposals is the presentation of various fundamental concepts of the constitutional organization in clear language, making the Constitution more

24 See rules of procedures adopted by the Council available at stjornlagarad.is/english/rules-of-procedure/.

25 An English version of the bill of the Constitutional Council is available at the Council's homepage: http://stjornlagathing.is/other_files/stjornlagarad/Frumvarp-enska.pdf.

understandable and accessible to the general public. A preamble describes the common values and certain noble goals that all governments should attempt to achieve. This strengthens the image of the Constitution as a national covenant.

There are numerous improvements in the proposal, in particular a proposal on strengthening the position of the Althing and its supervisory control over the executive, duties of Ministers towards parliament and new provisions to strengthen the independence of the courts. The proposals include clearer and more detailed rules on the executive branch, the position of the government and new methods for the formation of government. The position of the President of the Republic is redefined to some extent, and this position no longer resembles that of a king in a monarchy, as in the current Constitution. Provisions on foreign affairs and international treaties are now included in the Constitution in a separate chapter. They include, *inter alia*, the authorization for parliament to delegate state power to international organizations established with treaties to which Iceland is a party.

As might have been anticipated, opinion is divided on the proposals of the Constitutional Council. They bear the marks of having been prepared in a very short time, and some of the proposals appear not to have been carefully considered, lack harmonization in some aspects and may be difficult to apply as legal text. There is an impression that the reason that a consensus could be reached was that many proposals entered the eventual draft without objective discussion or challenge and without careful scrutiny of their possible consequences. The phrasing of some provisions is unclear and padded with ambiguous concepts, however likely to gain popular support for declaring noble objectives. This applies in particular to some of the new provisions in the human rights chapter, where it is particularly important for the rules of law to be phrased carefully as guidance for the courts of law, which apply these rules and interpret them in individual legal cases. This is accompanied by imprecise wording and a use of concepts that, for instance, departs from the traditional meaning of the same concepts in international human rights conventions, such as the ECHR. Other provisions are too specific and precise instead of laying down general principles, and they are doomed to early obsolescence.

The proposals attach great weight to means to enhance direct democracy and new recourses available to force a referendum, including referendums on controversial legislation passed by the Althing. This is in line with developments in most other European states. The reasons underlying the increased pressure to hold referendums are, however, possibly attached to the present and vast distrust of politics and political parties in Iceland.

In light of the emphasis on expanding direct democracy, it comes as a surprise that the proposals for a new constitution do not assume that its entry into force should be subject to approval in a national referendum. This represents a certain contradiction of the fundamental principle that the nation itself should be the source of the constitution, and a regression from the previous order, where the current Constitution could only enter into force if approved by a majority of the electorate, as was done in 1944. On the other hand, the Council suggested that its proposals should be put to referendum with a consultative conclusion before their handling in the Althing. This would aim at further legitimization of the proposals, and be more likely to tie the hands of politically elected representatives.

The Handling of the Council's Proposals and their Present Status

As recounted earlier, the Constitutional Council submitted proposals for a new Constitution to the Althing in July 2011. Since that time, the task has been in the hands of the Althing. After all, the proposals were meant to be advisory and subject to the present rules related to amendments of the Constitution.[26] The proposals were discussed widely in society, among the public, in the media and among scholars of law and political science. It did not come as a surprise that the proposals would need to be amended or redrafted in some aspects after only four months of work. It was a great achievement, however, to produce a comprehensive document by individuals with little or no experience in legislative work, and indeed who had been chosen for the task precisely because of their distance from political participation.

The handling of the situation by the Althing since the summer of 2011 has been disappointing. As the main opposition party, the Independent Party, which had been against the appointment of the Council from the outset, had no hesitation in criticizing strongly the material proposals, the coalition parties, the Social Democratic Alliance and the Left-Green Movement, hesitated at the next step. The proposals were referred to one of the Standing Committees, the Constitutional Affairs Committee. The Committee called a number of people, including members of the Council, legal experts and others, to discuss the proposals. No advice or assistance from legal experts or drafters was planned to elaborate the work, and neither proposals nor formal opinions were sought. Through the whole winter it seemed as if it was problematic for the coalition parties to take a stand on the proposals and discuss their substance. Instead of further preparing and processing the task with the aim of introducing a bill, the majority of the Committee felt it was more timely to put the proposals into a consultative referendum, and ask whether they should be used as a basis for further work in revising the Constitution. Furthermore, some general questions were suggested, to seek the opinion of the voters, such as on constitutional provisions related to defining natural resources as national property, equal voting rights and popular initiative. A great dispute arose between the political parties related to this step of the procedure. The criticism was mainly that an advisory referendum at this stage would be aimless: first, as it had always been the intention to prepare a constitutional amendment on the basis

26 According to Art. 79 of the Constitution, proposals to amend or supplement it call for a special procedure, similar to other Nordic constitutions. If the proposal is adopted, the Althing shall immediately be dissolved and a general election held. If the Althing then passes the resolution unchanged, it shall be confirmed by the President of the Republic and come into force as constitutional law.

of the proposals and second, because the questions suggested were too ambiguous and open-ended. Finally, a decision was reached in May 2012 that a consultative referendum would be held in the autumn of 2012.

Assessment of the Task and Likelihood of Success

The creation of the Constitutional Assembly, which later became the Constitutional Council, is based on the core concept of constitutional theories on the constituent power of the people and at the same time connected to the initial ideas of constitutional assemblies of the nineteenth century. But the noble ideal aimed at in the beginning has not been achieved, and there are signs that it will not be fruitful in the end. In the following, some suggestions will be made as to the reasons why.

First, as explained at the outset, the idea to move the task of constitution-making away from the political forum to elected representatives in a special body was based on the great distrust that emerged in Iceland towards politicians and political parties following the bank collapse. Defining constitution-making as a non-political issue, and distancing it entirely from the political forum, is, however, impossible in a democratic system. At the end of the day, political involvement must come into play, and the political forces in the country must take a stand on the substance of a new constitution before it is adopted. The involvement of the people at the initial stages, reflecting their will in the preparation and drafting of a new constitution, is indeed a positive step. It strengthens its democratic foundation and legitimacy, as well as being likely to create greater consensus in society on the document. It may put pressure on the political parties to finalize the task that they had not completed since 1944. However, expecting the representatives in the Constitutional Council to draft a comprehensive and complete document was unrealistic.

Second, a closely connected point related to the doctrine of the constituent power of the people is that one must distinguish between the involvement of the people in preparing a constitution and influencing which elements it should contain, on the one hand, and adopting a constitution, on the other hand. Following the drafting by the Constitutional Council, a phase in the procedure which should now be over, the legislative part should have been continued in the Althing. To fulfil the requirement of constituent power of the people, the document on the foundation of Icelandic society should be subject to the final approval of the nation in a referendum with a binding conclusion. The representatives in the Constitutional Council lost sight of this fundamental element in their proposals.

Third, the consensus aimed at by establishing the Assembly is unlikely to be achieved. This is partly due to the extremely low turnout in the election to the Assembly in 2010, but more importantly due to the nullification of the election by the Supreme Court in January 2011. Inevitably this caused the Council, which replaced the Assembly on the basis of a parliamentary resolution, to lose its popular legitimacy. Furthermore, the strong opposition of the largest opposition party in parliament indeed made the Council a creature of a political nature, supported only by the coalition parties, and therefore splitting the nation into two groups.

Fourth, and most importantly, the Althing failed to react to the proposals when they were submitted, and the coalition parties have refrained from taking any position in relation to their substance. This has resulted in hesitation on how to proceed and how to introduce and handle a bill for a new constitution. This fact, along with the most recent debate concerning the consultative referendum on the proposals of the Constitutional Council, has created great ambiguity in the current situation and how to conclude the exercise.

Concluding Remarks

This chapter has illustrated some examples of how the financial collapse and economic crisis has affected different constitutional aspects in Icelandic society and the legal system. They are among the demanding questions that have confronted Iceland since 2008 in this area, as discussed in the first part of the chapter. It is evident that the crisis initiated a debate and development in Icelandic constitutional law theory and practice which has been, and will become, the source for numerous articles and extensive legal research in the coming years, as well as a number of court cases. Despite having being a most unfortunate experience in itself, the financial crisis has offered new and interesting opportunities for scholars in the field of constitutional law to develop new theories and seek new solutions to unprecedented problems. It is important to share this experience with other nations and assess the lessons that can be learned from it.

Apart from the value that the crisis created for constitutionalists, it is safe to assert that it also had an important impact on public awareness of fundamental issues. Never before has there been such extensive public discussion in Icelandic society of what the Constitution means and its core concepts; this has increased both understanding and sensibility of its value, and it has also encouraged people to take a position on important matters that form the foundations of democratic society.

PART V
Fourth Path: Stamina

Chapter 11
The United States Constitution and the Great Recession

Mark Tushnet

Perhaps because of the US role in the world economy, perhaps because of the US Constitution's age, perhaps because of its flexibility, the Great Recession occasioned relatively little in the way of constitutional development, much less crisis, in the United States. The first factor gave the United States more room to manoeuvre in its response to the Recession. The Constitution's age meant that it lacked provisions on fiscal matters that are more common in more modern constitutions. And its flexibility allowed creative adaptation within the Constitution's framework. As Chief Justice Charles Evans Hughes put it in what is perhaps the most widely quoted – and, despite its brevity, perhaps the most insightful – statement about the Constitution in crisis times, 'While emergency does not create power, emergency may furnish the occasion for the exercise of power.'[1]

This chapter examines two constitutional episodes in the US response to the Great Recession. The first section deals with the application and practical irrelevance of the doctrine that Congress cannot delegate legislative authority to executive officials. The second examines the proposal made during the political negotiations over raising the statutory ceiling on the debt that the United States could accumulate, that the President could unilaterally raise the debt ceiling. The conclusion steps back from those episodes to analyse briefly the constitutional consequences of the hyperpolarized politics on the United States, and in particular the suggestion that hyperpolarized politics leads to increasing presidential power.

The Practical Irrelevance of the Non-delegation Doctrine

As financial markets began to seize up in 2008, the Bush administration looked for ways to ensure the continued availability of credit. Understanding that financial institutions held large amounts of unrecoverable debt, which limited their ability to extend credit, officials in the Department of the Treasury began to develop a plan that would allow the US government to take over these 'troubled assets', as they were known. The proposal came to be described as a programme to 'bail out' the banks by taking over the worst of their assets.

1 Home Building & Loan Ass'n v. Blaisdell, 290 U.S. 398, 426 (1934).

Events proceeded more rapidly than planning, though, and in September the Treasury Department had to present its legislative proposal. The proposed statute it sent to Congress was only three pages long. It gave the Secretary of the Treasury extremely broad authority to take over troubled assets. Section 2(a) gave the Secretary the authority 'to purchase … on such terms and conditions as determined by the Secretary, mortgage-related assets from any financial institution'. Section 2(b) authorized 'such actions as the Secretary deems necessary to carry out the authorities in this Act, including, without limitation' signing contracts and 'issuing such regulations and other guidance as may be necessary or appropriate to define terms or carry out the authorities of this Act'. Section 3 stated, 'In exercising the authorities granted in this Act, the Secretary shall take into consideration means for (1) providing stability or preventing disruption to the financial markets or banking system; and (2) protecting the taxpayer.'[2]

These provisions were obviously quite broad, and constitutional scholars might have noted that they raised an old-fashioned constitutional question: did the proposal give so much discretion to the Secretary to flesh out the details of the bailout programme that the Secretary became in effect a legislator rather than an executive official? Long-standing doctrine held that Congress could not delegate legislative authority to executive officials. The doctrine itself had been fleshed out, though, because everyone agreed that Congress could enact programmes giving executive officials general directions to be made more precise by the executive officials themselves. As the doctrine had developed, the requirement was that Congress state an 'intelligible principle' to guide the executive officials' discretion. The 'considerations' in Section 3 were Congress's attempt to do so. But, was 'providing stability or preventing disruption' while 'protecting the taxpayer' an intelligible principle?

The Supreme Court had not pursued one obvious path to answering that question. Along that path the courts would ask whether the considerations ruled out any remotely plausible programme the Treasury Secretary might develop. If not – and on the face of the statute it is not clear that it would rule out any such policy – the courts would conclude that the considerations did not state an intelligible principle. The Court pursued a different path, more oriented to precedent than to fundamental principle. In its most recent major non-delegation decision the Court dealt with a provision authorizing the Environmental Protection Agency to set certain air quality standards subject to the requirement that the standards 'are requisite to protect the public health' 'with an adequate margin of safety'.[3] The question for the Court was whether this requirement stated an intelligible principle. The lower court that dealt with the case thought that it did not, because essentially any level – from zero exposure to exposures that cause substantial but

2 For the text, see http://blogs.wsj.com/economics/2008/09/20/treasurys-financial-bailout-proposal-to-congress/.

3 Whitman v. American Trucking Ass'ns, Inc., 531 U.S. 457 (2001).

not catastrophic harm – could be defended on the ground that it protected the public health with an 'adequate' margin of safety.

The Supreme Court disagreed with the lower court's conclusion that the statute failed to state an intelligible principle, but its mode of analysis was distinctive. The Court compared the standard at hand to standards it had approved in prior cases. These included standards saying that the executive officials' rules could not be 'unduly or unnecessarily complicated' or that the prices they set should be 'generally fair and equitable and will effectuate the purposes' of the price control act. Similarly, the Court had upheld statutes that directed executive officials to adopt regulations that were 'in the public interest'. The Court said in the air quality case that if *those* provisions stated intelligible standards, so did the air quality statute. 'Requisite to protect the public health with an adequate margin of safety' was at least as precise as 'in the public interest'.

As a matter of law, Section 3's considerations were, again, at least as precise as those in the air quality statute or the other statutes the Court said stated intelligible principles. So, as a matter of doctrine the Treasury Department's three-page proposal would have almost certainly been constitutional had it been enacted.

But it was not enacted. Rather, members of Congress derided the proposal precisely because it was so short, for such a significant intervention in the national economy. Eventually the statute grew from three to 157 pages, with many provisions setting out details that the three-page proposals would have left to the Treasury Department. Here the Constitution may have played a *political* rather than a legal role. Members of Congress understood that broad delegations of authority channelled power to the executive branch, while narrower ones kept more power in legislative hands. The idea of non-delegation, more than stated constitutional doctrine, affected the development of the bailout policy.

As enacted, the bailout statute, the Troubled Asset Relief Program (TARP), defined 'troubled assets' in these terms: '(A) residential or commercial mortgages and any securities, obligations, or other instruments that are based on or related to such mortgages ... the purchase of which the Secretary determines promotes financial market stability; and (B) any other financial instrument that the Secretary ... determines the purchase of which is necessary to promote financial stability'. Provision (A) was the key to the bank bailouts. Provision (B) was something of a mopping-up clause, which clearly would cover other troubled assets banks held but that might have been overlooked in the rush to enact TARP.

But, the second provision by its own terms clearly extended to 'financial instruments' other than mortgages and instruments derived from mortgages. When major automobile manufacturers faced bankruptcy, Congress refused to bail out the automobile industry. Contending that bankruptcies in that industry would have a severe adverse effect on the economy, the Obama administration pressed TARP into a service that Congress had not contemplated. Critics noted not only Congress's refusal to bail out the industry, but TARP's other provisions, which appeared to limit the Secretary's authority to purchase assets from banks, credit unions and insurers. No mention of manufacturing companies could be found in the TARP statute. The Obama administration took the position that TARP did allow it to bail out the car companies. Why? Because each one was associated with an entity that loaned money to car purchasers. General Motors, for example, had within its corporate structure the General Motors Acceptance Corporation (GMAC). For the Obama administration, these lending organizations were financial institutions within TARP's definition, and so TARP allowed the automobile bailouts. Although some aspects of the automobile bailouts were subject to litigation, no one challenged in court the Obama administration's interpretation that the TARP statute's definitions covered GMAC and then the entire corporation.

The story of the bank and automobile bailouts illustrates some aspects of the US constitutional system that were triggered by the Great Recession: the particular irrelevance but political significance of the non-delegation doctrine and the President's ability to invoke broad delegations of authority to implement programmes that he favours but that Congress refuses to enact. Importantly, these were not experienced as *changes* in the constitutional system but, as Chief Justice Hughes said, as the occasion for exercising power already understood to exist.

The Debt-ceiling Crisis

During the summer of 2011 the United States faced a debt-related crisis, which was ultimately 'resolved' by adopting legislation that effectively moved the date on which the crisis would recur until after the 2012 elections. As a result of the crisis, though, some bond rating agencies downgraded the United States' credit rating, thereby increasing the cost of borrowing.

The crisis arose from the fact that the United States, like most nations, regularly runs a deficit in its operations. To finance those operations it must borrow money. The government as a whole can control the amount it must borrow in several ways. The most straightforward, of course, is through spending and tax policy. When Congress appropriates money, it sets an amount that will have to be financed either through taxes or borrowing. The amount of borrowing depends on the amount raised by taxes. But, there are two reasons why relying on the combination of spending and taxes might not control the amount of borrowing. First, the amount of taxes collected will fluctuate depending on the overall state of the economy. Budgeters can attempt to predict the amounts that taxation will raise, but their projections will inevitably be inaccurate. When they are, borrowing may be needed to complement the amount taxation brings in. Second, and probably more important, legislators are reluctant to raise taxes to pay for new programmes. Of course they could deal with this by not spending money on new programmes, but they also have strong electoral incentives to continually propose new programmes, so that they can claim to their constituents that they have 'delivered' something the constituents value.

So, to have some control over borrowing Congress has regularly adopted legislation specifying the total amount of indebtedness the US government can incur – so-called 'debt-ceiling' legislation. Such legislation prohibits the government from issuing bonds – indebtedness – whose total exceeds the debt ceiling. The Department of the Treasury then estimates the date on which the existing obligations – appropriations authorized by Congress for substantive programmes, and interest on existing debt – would exceed the debt ceiling. At that point Congress can respond. In theory it could do so by rescinding scheduled spending or even by repudiating existing debt. The latter, it is generally thought, would be disastrous for the US economy, because bondholders would liquidate their holdings and demand higher rates of interest on loans in the future. The former is politically impossible. In consequence, as the government's indebtedness approaches the debt ceiling, Congress has routinely raised the ceiling.

In the summer of 2011 the usual scenario did not play itself out in the usual way. Republicans, who controlled the House of Representatives and were highly disciplined as a party, insisted that they would not vote to raise the debt ceiling unless Democrats agreed to sharp reductions in spending for programmes important to the Democratic Party and its constituents, and refused to consider additional taxes as a way of insulating some of those programmes against reduction.

On its face the impasse over the debt ceiling was a 'mere' political problem, not a constitutional one. It might be described as an example of 'constitutional hardball', though: a departure from previously taken-for-granted norms of appropriate political behaviour, used as part of a larger political strategy to transform the day-to-day assumptions that allow any political system to operate smoothly.[4] Some academics, mostly identified as liberals, came up with a novel constitutional theory to deal with the impasse. The Fourteenth Amendment to the US Constitution was adopted after the Civil War ended. Its primary effect since its adoption has been through its first section, which guaranteed fundamental rights against violation by state governments. Other sections dealt with additional aspects of the reconstruction of the overall government system after the Civil War. Section 2 addressed the risk that Southern states would deny emancipated slaves the right to vote, by specifying that state representation in the House of Representatives would be reduced in proportion to the disqualification of male citizens over the age of 21, and Section 3 disqualified from national public office anyone who, after having held such an office before the Civil War, supported the rebellious Confederacy.

Section 4 became the focus of the discussion of the debt ceiling. It provides:

> The validity of the public debt of the United States, authorized by law, including debts incurred for payment of pensions and bounties for services in suppressing insurrection or rebellion, shall not be questioned. But neither the United States nor any State shall assume or pay any debt or obligation incurred in aid of insurrection or rebellion against the United States, or any claim for the loss or

4 For a somewhat more complete discussion of constitutional hardball, see M. Tushnet, 'Constitutional Hardball', John Marshall Law Review 37 (2004): 523-553.

> emancipation of any slave; but all such debts, obligations and claims shall be held illegal and void.

Section 4's overall purpose is apparent on its face. The second sentence says that the national government did not intend to assume responsibility for paying the debts incurred by the defeated Confederacy. The first sentence guards against the possibility that Congress in the future would repudiate pensions awarded to soldiers who had fought for the Union. But, of course, its language is broader, referring generally to 'the public debt'.

Liberal academics asked, 'What actions by Congress constitute "questioning the validity" of the national debt?' They focused on interest payments on existing debt and appropriations for entitlement programmes, the latter analogous, they argued, to the pensions expressly mentioned in Section 4.[5] Consider what would happen were the government's borrowing obligations to exceed the debt ceiling. The Department of the Treasury would structure its payments from existing resources – essentially, taxes as they were collected – to pay interest on existing debt first, entitlements second. It would effectively repudiate only 'discretionary' spending, refusing to pay for projects that Congress had authorized but that had not yet begun.[6] At some point, though, the revenue coming in from existing taxes would be insufficient to cover the costs of interest payments and entitlements. The academics argued that Section 4 barred the repudiation of any portion of the national debt, because such repudiation amounted to 'questioning' the public debt. And, they argued, legislative action or inaction that would have the predictable consequence of repudiating the debt also amounted to 'questioning' the public debt.

The Supreme Court had rarely addressed the meaning of Section 4, but at least one of its decisions lent some support to the proposition that Section 4 reached beyond its origins in the Civil War and its focus on repudiating debt incurred to defeat the Confederacy.[7] Still, I believe that most legal scholars found the argument I have sketched implausible. For them, Section 4 dealt with Civil War debt and express repudiation, nothing more.

My description of the argument that Section 4 had some bearing on the debt-ceiling question has been incomplete to this point. Assuming that it did,

---

5 Social Security, the national pension system for all Americans, and Medicare, the national health care system for the elderly, are exemplary entitlement programmes. The term 'entitlement' is used because all Americans (or all the elderly) are automatically qualified to receive benefits from the programmes.

6 I believe it was uncertain where payments on existing contracts would be on the schedule, but I assume that they would be, roughly, third in line.

7 Perry v. United States, 294 U.S. 330, 354 (1935) (although §4 'was undoubtedly inspired by the desire to put beyond question the obligations of the Government issued during the Civil War, its language indicates a broader connation', including 'whatever concerns the integrity of the public obligations').

what could be done about the situation? The usual remedy for constitutional violations in the United States is a judicial order directing the violator to stop violating the Constitution or to take action to prevent a violation from occurring. Essentially everyone agreed that remedy was unavailable. No one thought that the courts would order Congress and the President to come to some agreement to raise the debt ceiling.[8] So, the suggestion was, the President on his own could direct the Treasury Department to issue bonds in an amount sufficient to cover existing obligations, without regard to the debt ceiling. The best argument for that position, and it was a weak one, was this: Section 4 placed the President under a constitutional duty to avoid debt repudiation, while Article II required him to 'take Care that the Laws be faithfully executed'. Among the laws he had a duty to execute were laws authorizing new projects. So, the argument went, the President faced a conflict of duties, and was entitled to take action, not otherwise prohibited by the Constitution, to eliminate the conflict.[9]

President Obama expressly stated that he lacked the power to borrow money without congressional authorization. And, in any event, given the legal uncertainty associated with the Section 4 argument and, even more, with the lawfulness of the proposed presidential action, bondholders would inevitably demand higher interest rates, which is precisely the effect of debt repudiation anyway.

The conflict was resolved politically, by deferring ultimate action. Congress enacted a statute with one face-saving provision and one substantive one. The face-saving provision authorized the President to raise the debt ceiling three times before 1 January 2013. Republicans apparently believed that doing so would impose political costs on the President. It did not; President Obama issued the required statements with essentially no political consequences or even attention paid.

The substantive provision was serious. Congress created a bipartisan committee with members from both the House of Representatives and the Senate, charged with devising a budget plan. If the committee failed to develop a plan and Congress did not approve one on its own, spending would automatically change on 1 January 2013. Spending would be affected by a 'sequestration' of already appropriated funds, reducing spending on all projects, including defence and national security, by 50 per cent. Nothing was said about taxes, but they would be automatically

8 The technical obstacles to such a ruling were insurmountable in any event. It was impossible to identify a person who would be a proper defendant subject to an order from the courts; the courts could not act in a timely manner; and more.

9 One difficulty with the argument is that unilateral presidential action might indeed be prohibited by a constitutional provision stating that Congress has the power 'To borrow Money on the credit of the United States', Art. I, §8, cl. 2. This does not expressly state that the President may not borrow money on the nation's credit, but at least one other provision in Article I, authorizing the suspension of the privilege of the writ of habeas corpus, is universally understood as allocating the power to suspend to Congress and prohibiting the President from suspending the writ unilaterally.

affected as well, though not by the new agreement. During the Bush administration Congress approved a series of cuts in tax rates. To avoid the accurate appearance that these cuts would permanently increase the deficit, they were scheduled to expire in ten years. That period ended during the Great Recession, and President Obama agreed to a one-year extension of the cuts, pushing the expiration date to 1 January 2013. So, unless Congress and the President agreed on a budget plan, the tax cuts would automatically expire and revenues to the government would increase. No one believed that this combination of tax increases and indiscriminate spending cuts made good policy sense. The thought behind these provisions was that the threat of going over the 'fiscal cliff', as it came to be described, would induce Republicans and Democrats to agree on a budget plan. The bipartisan committee failed to do so, and as of fall 2012 an agreement had not materialized.[10]

Hyperpolarized Politics and the Constitutional Structure

The debt-ceiling crisis has a modest but revealing connection to the Great Recession. The mere fact that the statutory debt ceiling had to be raised did not result from the Recession.[11] Well before the Great Recession the government's debts routinely approached the debt ceiling, and just as routinely Congress raised the ceiling. The Great Recession's role in the 2011 debt-ceiling crisis arose from the Recession's effect on politics. Conservatives mobilized against President Obama almost from the moment of his election. They capitalized on the unpopularity of some of his administration's responses to the Recession, such as the bank bailouts and the Keynesian stimulus programmes Congress enacted. During the summer of 2010, in anticipation of that fall's elections for Congress, conservatives organized the Tea Party, an extremely conservative faction within the Republican Party. Republicans won control of the House of Representatives in the November elections, and its Tea Party members played a dominant role within the Republican House caucus. They were adamantly opposed to government spending and to increasing federal taxes, and they used the occasion of the debt-ceiling legislation

10 By the time this chapter is published we will know whether President Obama was re-elected. If he was, there will still be some question about the possibility of achieving a long-term solution to the budget issue, given rules in the Senate that make it quite difficult for a simple majority to move legislation forward. That same problem will affect actions by a President Romney as well, on the assumption that the Democrats retain enough seats in the Senate to obstruct his proposals.

11 The Recession may have pushed forward the date on which the ceiling would be reached because of the Recession's effects on revenues and because of the spending associated with Keynesian stimulus programmes aimed at reducing the Recession's depth and length.

to insist on their agenda. Because they would not compromise on either spending or taxes, Republicans provoked the crisis.[12]

The debt-ceiling crisis is diagnostic of the present structure of US politics, which can be described as one in which hyperpolarized political parties operate almost like parliamentary parties, but within a separation-of-powers system in which legislative rules give the minority party a near-veto over policy. The effects are predictable and straightforward: legislative gridlock and an accretion of power, within quite broad limits, to the Presidency. As legal scholars Eric Posner and Adrian Vermeule have argued, Carl Schmitt provides better though imperfect guidance to those who would try to understand contemporary policy-making in the United States than the more imperfect James Madison.[13]

Hyperpolarization emerged in the United States from a combination of structural logic, demographic changes and political strategy. Its foundation is the first-past-the-post system of electing members of the House of Representatives from single-member districts.[14] As is well known, such a system conduces to the emergence of two dominant parties in each district. Starting quite early on, national political leaders organized these local parties into two national parties, which became loose coalitions of local parties that existed primarily for presidential elections. After a presidential election, the parties 'disintegrated' in Congress into local factions again. National policy-making thus became a system of deals made among a set of factions that constantly rearranged themselves as different policy issues came before Congress.

The national political parties did have some influence on policy-making because their role in presidential elections gave the party names a certain 'brand name' quality. For example, after the New Deal a person who ran as a Democrat in a state or district election was more likely to be roughly 'liberal' than one who ran as a Republican, because the parties' presidential candidates were, again roughly, liberal and conservative. But, there were conservative Democrats and liberal Republicans through much of the late twentieth century.

In the last quarter of that century, though, the parties became more coherent ideological organizations at the state and local levels. One indication is the disappearance of 'moderate' Republicans and 'conservative' Democrats. Studies of votes cast in Congress show that, as of 2010 or so, the parties had completely

12 Democrats, in contrast, were willing to reduce spending, though with great reluctance, but insisted on some offsets through increased taxes. Democrats, that is, were willing to compromise; Republicans were not.

13 E.A. Posner and A. Vermeule, The Executive Unbound: After the Madisonian Republic (Oxford University Press, 2011).

14 This system is not required by the US Constitution. Single-member districts are required by a federal statute. The US Supreme Court has interpreted the Constitution to require that congressional districts within each state have as close to equal populations as is possible, with deviations from strict equality justified only by the sheer impossibility of doing better. (The standard for state legislative districts is more forgiving.)

separated, with the most conservative Democrat more liberal than the most liberal Republican.[15] The sorting was well advanced before that.

The causes of this ideological sorting are not entirely clear. Most observers believe that an important cause lies in an interaction between districting practices and the way in which candidates for office are selected. In most jurisdictions within the United States, districts are drawn not by specialized and independent commissions, as occurs in other nations with district-based elections, but by legislatures or, sometimes, bodies dominated by partisan appointees. As a result, district boundaries are drawn to achieve political advantage. Most observers of the process believe that politically influenced boundary drawing aims at producing a substantial number of 'safe' seats for each party – ones where victory by one or the other party is highly likely no matter who the candidates are or what the issues are.[16] The proliferation of safe seats interacts with candidate selection in 'primary' elections, where voters who identify themselves as Republicans or Democrats select their party's candidate, again by plurality vote. These primary elections attract a relatively small number of voters, and both political logic and empirical studies suggest that those who do vote are likely to be the most partisan party members. Here partisanship means that voters in Democratic primary elections are more liberal than Democrats as a whole and, inevitably, more liberal than the average voter, and conversely for Republicans. The effect, overstated here to bring out its central features, is that elections pit extremely liberal Democrats against extremely conservative Republicans, in districts some of which are guaranteed to produce a Democratic victory and some a Republican one. The result is a House of Representatives consisting of extremely liberal Democrats and extremely conservative Republicans.

Districting cannot be the full story, though, because a similar separation of the parties has occurred in the Senate. Here one part of the story appears to be 'sorting' by voters themselves, which occurs as people move to states where they find the *political* atmosphere congenial.[17] Another factor seems to be the increased role of national political party organizations in supporting – and therefore influencing the selection of – local candidates. The incentives of the national party organizations are mixed: they want to win, but they also want to ensure that the party 'brand name' means something. So, they will tend to support electable candidates who do

---

15 'An Update on Political Polarization (through 2011) – Part IV', voteview blog; available at http://voteview.com/blog/?p=349 (accessed 28.8.2012).

16 Districting to maximize safe seats poses something of a puzzle. One might think that partisan boundary-drawers would want to maximize the number of districts in which the chances of one party's victory were slightly better than the others, rather than attempting to guarantee victory. To the extent that there is a solution to this puzzle, it may be that maximizing the number of safe seats serves as something like an insurance policy against an election in which one party wins every seat by a narrow margin.

17 This sorting can occur at the district level as well, and may have some modest effects in elections for the House of Representatives.

a reasonable job of conforming to the views held by the national party leadership. That leadership's views, in turn, are shaped by the general orientation of the party's presidential candidates.

Combine these elements and the structure of US policy-making begins to emerge. As represented in Congress, the political parties are largely ideologically unified and opposed to each other – in a word, they are polarized. The polarization is reinforced by internal legislative rules that allow the party leadership to exercise substantial discipline over individual Representatives and Senators. They can place members on 'good' or 'bad' committees, for example, or recruit them into secondary leadership positions. But, because the members are already likely to be quite ideologically homogeneous, express exercise of this sort of discipline is rare. Overall, then, the parties in Congress act almost like parties in parliamentary systems do. As suggested earlier, this is a relatively recent development.

Two additional features are worth mentioning before turning to *hyper*polarization. First, although elected separately from members of Congress, the President has become the leader of his party in Congress. He sets the policy agenda and, if his party controls both the House of Representatives and the Senate – an important qualification, of course – his policies are the focus of legislative attention. In this way the President has come to resemble a Prime Minister in a parliamentary system, though without the guaranteed control of the legislative process that Prime Ministers have.

Second, the Senate's rules effectively give the minority a veto over legislative action. On the formal level, the Senate's rules allow for 'extended debate', commonly known as the filibuster, meaning that Senate leaders cannot insist on a vote on a proposal unless they terminate debate, and that termination can occur only if 60 Senators agree. Achieving a filibuster-proof majority is extremely difficult.[18] Until quite recently, Senate norms counselled against routine use of the filibuster. Those norms appear to have changed, though, as a result of polarization and, more important, hyperpolarization.

By 'hyperpolarization' I mean an almost absolute refusal by both parties to accord political legitimacy to the other party's programmes. Again the sources of hyperpolarization are not entirely clear. The best accounts locate its sources in the presidency of Ronald Reagan. Reagan offered a programme of substantial retrenchment of the existing New Deal/Great Society constitutional order.[19] Both because of his administration's relatively weak commitment to that transformation

18 Many close observers of the Senate believe that even reforming the filibuster rule would not do much to eliminate minority vetoes. The reason is that the business the Senate must do increased quite substantially in the late twentieth century. The only way to do much of the work is through unanimous consent to waive ordinary rules of proceeding. (For example, the ordinary rules require that committees not hold meetings when the full Senate is meeting, unless the Senate consents.)

19 For an earlier discussion, see M. Tushnet, The New Constitutional Order (Princeton University Press, 2004).

and because of Democratic opposition to it, Reagan's administration achieved relatively little in the way of retrenchment. The ideology of a Reagan Revolution became embedded in the Republican Party, where activists came to believe that a majority of the American people actually supported their programme of retrenchment and were frustrated by their inability to implement it. Their next opportunity came during the presidency of Bill Clinton when, for the first time in decades, Republicans briefly became the majority party in both the House and the Senate. Again they attempted to implement the Reagan Revolution as they had come to understand it, and again they were frustrated, this time by the fact that they did not hold the Presidency. Their third chance came with the election of George W. Bush. That too ended in failure. Part of the reason was that during President Bush's first term in office Democrats never truly conceded that he was the legitimate President of the United States. More important, Democrats controlled the House and Senate during some of Bush's presidency, and blocked the legislative initiatives most closely linked to the Reagan Revolution. And, of course, eventually the wars that President Bush initiated became extremely unpopular, damaging his political position overall.

In brief, then, these are the sources of hyperpolarization: the US system of elections and the frustration of partisans at their inability to advance their policy positions through legislation. What are its effects?

Carl Schmitt gave the answer: the accretion of power to the executive. Hyperpolarization means that Congress cannot enact policy through ordinary legislation, however much its members have incentives to get *something* done. The debt-ceiling crisis is exemplary: provoked by Republicans' insistence that federal spending be reduced and taxes remain unaffected, the crisis ended up with legislation deferring any final decision until 2013 and, perhaps more revealingly, putting in place a 'solution' universally regarded as unsound policy that would go into effect automatically, that is without any additional legislative action. Members of Congress want to enact policy, because doing so has both political and policy benefits, but they cannot. The President also wants to put policies in place, for the same two reasons – political benefit and policy soundness. But, unlike Congress, the President *can* implement his policies, through the exercise of his powers as President.

For present purposes it is unnecessary to explore the constitutional limits to exercises of presidential power not specifically endorsed by Congress.[20] What matters is that, as the bailout story shows, Congress has enacted statutes that delegate broad discretionary power to the President. Sometimes those delegations occurred generations ago, sometimes they occurred more recently, including responses to the Great Recession. The theory of the modern administrative state

20 President George W. Bush made extremely expansive claims of presidential power arising out of his constitutional role as Commander in Chief. The legal culture generally rejected those claims, but it continues to view some exercises of 'pure' presidential power as constitutionally permissible.

endorses such delegations on functional grounds of timeliness and expertise. Take the bailouts. Events were moving quite fast, bankruptcies were looming within days and Congress simply could not have enacted detailed legislation quickly enough. Nor could Congress know enough about the specifics of the affected economic sectors or about the situation facing individual banks and other entities to develop sensible entity-by-entity legislation. So, the theory holds, generous delegations of authority are functionally necessary in the modern state.

More recently scholars have begun to analyse how these delegations produce what now-Justice Elena Kagan called, in a brilliant article, 'Presidential Administration'.[21] Kagan wrote in the early 2000s, well before the Great Recession, and she described a phenomenon somewhat different from the pure accretion of executive power. But her deep insight was that the modern administrative state gave presidents the opportunity to gain political advantage from the broad delegations characteristic of that state. And, though hyperpolarization had not yet fully emerged when Kagan wrote, hyperpolarization gives presidents reasons to seize on that opportunity rather than futilely attempt to implement policy through legislation.

As Posner and Vermeule argue, this is all quite Schmittian.[22] They note, though, that Schmitt focused on the *legal* constraints on the exercise of expansive executive power, and argued that legal constraints were inevitably ineffective. Posner and Vermeule largely agree, pointing out, for example, that the non-delegation doctrine has no real purchase in law, as the use of bank bailout legislation to rescue the automobile industry shows. Other examples of presidential administration suggest that legal constraints do matter.[23] Consider, for example, President Obama's response to the inability of Congress to enact a statute – known as the DREAM Act – regularizing the legal status of people who were brought to the United States when they were children and have lived law-abiding lives since then. President Obama announced that he had directed the relevant federal agency to forgo deporting people who fit the DREAM Act's criteria. This was justified as a class-based decision about the agency's enforcement priorities, and as such falls well within the ordinary scope of delegated administrative discretion. But, the President's order does not fully regularize status, and does not provide everything

21 E. Kagan, 'Presidential Administration', Harvard Law Review 114 (2001): 2245-2385.

22 It should not be surprising, then, that Posner and Vermeule urged President Obama to invoke Section 4 of the Fourteenth Amendment to ignore the debt ceiling and issue the necessary bonds. See E.A. Posner and A. Vermeule, 'Obama Should Raise the Debt Ceiling on His Own', New York Times, 22 July 2011.

23 Reviews of Posner and Vermeule make this point. See, for example, R.H. Pildes 'Law and the President', Harvard Law Review 125 (2012): 1381-1424; S. Prakash and M. Ramsey, 'The Goldilocks Executive', Texas Law Review 90 (2012): 973-1008; A.A. Huq, 'Binding the Executive (by Law or by Politics)', University of Chicago Law Review 79 (2012): 777-836.

the DREAM Act would have. And, perhaps more important, as an exercise of executive discretion it can be undone by a successor President. Legal constraints do exist on some exercises of presidential administration.

For Posner and Vermeule, though, the legal constraints are generally weak, as Schmitt asserted. But, they argue, Schmitt overlooked the fact that accretion of power to the executive is limited by *political* rather than legal factors. So, for example, for them it is analytically significant that Secretary Paulson's three-page bailout proposal was replaced by a somewhat more detailed one: the political and (for them therefore) the legal culture would not accept a delegation as completely unstructured as the three-page one was.

Conclusions

The Great Recession had relatively little direct resonance in US constitutional law.[24] The problems of governance it generated were handled relatively easily within the existing constitutional framework, in large part because the US interpretive tradition readily accommodates new responses to new problems. The debt-ceiling crisis occurred because of political hyperpolarization rooted in the interaction between constitutional structure, political incentives and political ideology, but the episode is more revealing about hyperpolarization than about the Constitution itself. The bailout legislation indirectly illuminates some aspects of presidential administration, the Schmittian theme in contemporary US constitutionalism, with weak to non-existent constitutional constraints in the non-delegation doctrine and quite modestly stronger political constraints on delegating discretion to the President.

Unlike the situation in other nations, then, the Great Recession rippled through the US economy without significant effects on the US constitutional order. Rather, the US government's response to the Great Recession illustrates some fundamental characteristics of that order.

24 An index of this might be the complete absence (as far as I know) of discussions of the Great Recession's effects on constitutional law in any of the leading texts on constitutional law.

Index

Bajnai, Gordon 247
balanced budget principle 28-30, 214
  Greece 29
  Hungary 29
  Italy 28, 48, 90, 91, 92, 94, 96-8, 100, 112
  and social rights 23
  Spain 28-9, 155, 162-3
  and state sovereignty 29
  US 29
Basle Committee on Banking Supervision 169
Bērziņs, Andris 137
bricolage, financial crisis-induced 12-13, 14
Bush, George W. 298

Clinton, Bill 298
constitutional hardball 52, 55, 56
  definition 54
  US 291
constitutional moment 2, 5, 50, 52
  Greece 216
  Iceland 55
  Ireland 55
  New Deal as 1, 54
  transformative 54
constitutions
  and GFC (2008)
    adjustment 47-50
    balanced budget principle 28-30, 214
    breakdown 50-51
    changes 4-5
    coalition and technocrat governments 21
    collective bargaining 37
    constitutional reactions vs crises 52-6
    factors influencing 56-8
    four paths forward 46-52
    constitutional reforms 22-30
    constitutionalism, challenge to 40-42, 112
    emergency and legal doctrines 35-7
    executive 17-19, 45
    expectations 58-9
    fundamental rights 31-2
    judiciary, interpretive shifts 10-14, 45
    legislatures 14-17, 45
    party systems, changes 20
    political system 19-22
    politicians, distrust of 19
    powers, reallocation of 44-6
    proportionality, transformations of 32-5
    social rights, deterioration 37-8
    stamina 51-2, 56
    state sovereignty before courts 38-40
    submission 49-50
    symbolic function 42-4
    welfare policies 112
    see also individual countries
  and state sovereignty 226, 227, 231, 233, 241

Economic and Monetary Union (EMU) 27, 89, 90, 138, 157, 168, 183, 229
Einaudi, Luigi 94
European Constitutional Treaty (2006) 230
European Convention on Human Rights (ECHR) 31, 34, 38, 185, 186
  and Iceland 268, 269, 270, 273
  and property rights 271-2, 273
European Court of Human Rights (ECtHR) 34, 41, 185
  and Portugal 225
European Court of Justice 227, 230, 234

European Financial Stabilization Mechanism (EFSM) 199
European integration, and state sovereignty 38, 77, 78, 228
European Stability Mechanism (ESM) 28, 187, 199
Eurozone sovereign debt crisis 3, 89

Fianna Fáil, Ireland, fall from power 65, 67
Fiscal Compact (TSCG) 28, 29, 44, 47, 93, 168, 183, 187, 192 *see also* balanced budget principle

Germany, constitution, and Lisbon Treaty (2007) 232-4
Global Financial Crisis (2008) *see* Constitutions, and GFC (2008)
Great Depression (1929) 1, 230, 231
Greece
  austerity measures 196, 206
  bailout loans 196, 197
    constitutional issues 198-201
    Council of State scrutiny 201-6
  balanced budget principle 29
  coalition government 18, 198
  collective bargaining 37
  Communist Party of Greece 209
  Constitution
    and bail out loans 198-201
    perception of 216-17
    reform, dialogue 30, 213-16
    rights, limitation of 206-8
  constitutional moment 216
  consumption 210
  corruption 195, 210
  Council of State 11, 12, 36, 39, 45, 216
    role 201
    scrutiny of bailout loans 201-6
  credit rating, downgrading 196
  economy
    growth 195
    recession 197, 210, 217
  elections 20, 197-8, 211
  eurozone crisis 197
  GDP, growth 195
  Golden Dawn Party 197
  New Democracy Party 195, 196, 197, 209, 212
  Olympic Games (2004), stimulus of 195
  party system
    collapse 210-11
    fragmentation 211-12
  PASOK Party 195, 196, 197, 209, 210
  political cultures 212-13
  political system 209
  Popular Orthodox Rally (LAOS) 196, 210
  proportionality 33
  riots 196
  sovereignty issues 39, 214
  SYRIZA coalition 197, 210, 212
  technocrat government 21
  trade deficit 195
Gyurcsány, Ferenc 247, 248

Hughes, Charles Evans 287
Hungary
  balanced budget principle 29
  Constitution
    breakdown 50-51, 55
    debt-ceiling rules 250-51
    economic and financial provisions 249-54
    economic philosophy 254
    economic and taxation principles 250
    incoherence 261
    judicial control of finance 251-3
    parliamentary budgetary powers, restriction 253-4
    policy measures, protection for 253
    revision 24-5, 245
  Constitutional Court 35, 245, 257-8
  crises taxes, imposition of 258-9
  democratic deficit 260-61
  economy
    and GFC (2008) 246-7, 248, 260
    growth 245, 246
    recession 246, 247
  fixed exchange rates, private loans 259-60
  GDP 246
  party system, restructuring 248
  political institutions, distrust of 248-9

private pension funds, nationalization 255-6
severance payments, retroactive taxation 256-8
stabilization measures 246-7
technocrat government 21
welfare policy, unsustainability 247

Iceland 3, 55
banks
amount claimed from 271
collapse 263, 275
new, establishment of 267, 270-71
run on 267, 269, 270
coalition government 276
Constitution
'crowd-sourcing' 24, 50
and ECHR 268, 269, 270, 273
history 274
new, proposals 16, 23-4
reform, demand for 274-6
Constitutional Assembly
elections to 277-8
establishment 276
Constitutional Commission 276-7
Constitutional Council, proposals 279-83
constitutional moment 55
Court of Impeachment of Iceland 264
crisis legislation 15
Denmark, union 274
early elections 20
Emergency Act 266-7
constitutionality of 268-71
emergency doctrines 35
Icesave 264, 265
Independent Party 276
National Forum 277
National Population Register 277
political parties, distrust of 24
Presidential powers 18
Prime Minister, impeachment 21, 264, 275
property rights
and EHCR 271-2, 273
violation of 268-71
Special Investigation Commission 21, 263, 264
Special Prosecutor 264
Supreme Court 268
and Emergency Act 272
Indignados 221
International Monetary Fund (IMF) 3, 65, 196, 199, 200, 201, 202, 211, 219, 228, 234, 246, 247
Ireland
banks, bailout 65, 79, 84
and the CAP 64
Celtic Tiger period 63, 64
Central Bank Reform Act (2010) 18
Constitution
adjustments 27, 47-8
and Fiscal Treaty (2012) 76-8
Joint Parliamentary Committee on 70
constitutional moment 55
constitutional reform, proposals 68-9
corporate governance, failures 75-6
economy, chronology 64-5
Electoral Commission 18
proposals 72
emergency doctrines 35
emigration 64
Financial Regulator, failures 73-5
Fiscal Advisory Council 18
Freedom of Information Act 72-3
governing party, collapse 20
individual rights 66, 79-80
international rescue agreement 65
Irish Fiscal Advisory Council 72
judicial
activism 63
pensions 82, 83
judiciary, and elites 86-7
legitimate expectations 80-83
National Asset Management Agency (NAMA), bank debts 84-6
Ombudsman for the Public Service 71-2
Parliament 69-70
planning control, failure 76
politicians, distrust of 19, 21-2, 70, 87
post-Tiger years 63, 64
public debt 64
public service salaries, reduction 65, 79
rental values, fall 82

Seanad, proposal to remove 71
and Single European Treaty (1987) 77
sovereignty issues 39, 76
unemployment 64
Italy
'Alitalia case' 36, 105
balanced budget principle 28, 48, 90, 91, 92, 94, 96-8, 100, 112
Berlusconi government, collapse 21, 90, 99, 100, 101-3
Christian Democratic Party 90
'Clean Hands' investigations 90
coalitions 99
Constitution
adjustments 48, 90-91
and European obligations 93
GFC impact 91-9
principles 112
threats to 112
Constitutional Court 35, 36, 95, 96, 104, 105-6, 107, 108, 113
crisis legislation 15
decree-laws 15-16
economic crises 89
electoral system, reform 99
fundamental rights 32
government
form 99
of technocrats 21, 99
Monti government 103-4
political crisis 100
President, role 99
public debt 89, 90, 94-5
public spending
and cost of additive judgments 110-12
and social rights 108-9
and state-region relations 106-8
sovereignty issues 98
Stability Law 102, 103, 104

Kagan, Elena, Justice 299
Kelsen, Hans 112, 219, 220

Latvia
budget cuts 116
Constitution
amendments 48, 136-40
reform proposals 27-8
separation of powers 115
Constitutional Court 11, 32-3, 35-6, 38-9, 115, 116, 118-19, 133-4
case law 121-8
complaints filed 122
and fundamental rights 121
legal certainty principle 125-6
legislature, dialogue 126-8
role in GFC (2008) 121-3
and socially responsible state 123-5
Constitutional Law, Presidential Commission 119
EU law, primacy 115
external debt 116
fiscal discipline 29, 115
GFC (2008) 116-17
compensation law 135-6
fiscal discipline, reforms 138-40
legislation 132-4
policy planning 131-2
political system, reforms 136-7
Presidential role 129-31
reforms triggered by 131-6
IMF loan 117
inflation 116
National Audit Office 115, 116
population, decline 117
Presidential powers 18-19
attempts to increase 136-7
dissolution of Parliament 130-31
ultimatum to Parliament 129-30
sovereignty issues 38-9, 117-20
Lehman Brothers 221
collapse 3, 141
Lisbon Treaty (2007) 230, 233
and German constitution 232-4

Madison, James 295
Magna Charta (1215) 221
Mortati, Costantino 94

New Deal, as constitutional moment 1, 54

Obama, Barack 299
Occupy Wall Street 221
Orbán, Viktor 247, 248, 249
Ortiz, Guillermo 222

Papandreou, George 195, 196, 213
Portugal
bail out 219, 228, 234
Carnations Revolution (1974) 238
Central Bank, role 224
Constitution
amendment, attempts at 239
crisis 223, 241
features 220, 238-9
reform 30
Constitutional Court 11, 12, 34, 36, 49, 228, 235-6
equality principle, temporality of 237-8
role 220
constitutionalism, and financial justice 220-22
Court of Auditors, role 224
early elections 20
and ECtHR 225
health rights 240-41
housing rights, threat to 240
justice, access to 239-40
Ombudsman 236-7
pay cuts 235, 236
politicians, distrust of 19, 49, 224
press freedom 225
proportionality 33
social rights 240
sovereignty
loss of 228-9
Superior Council of Public Finances 225
property rights, and ECHR 271-2, 273
Public-Private Partnerships (PPPs) 222

Reagan, Ronald 297-8

Schmitt, Carl 219, 220, 295, 298, 299, 300
social rights 10, 91, 206, 238-9
and balanced budget principle 23
costs 221
downgrading of 30, 37-8, 49, 106, 143, 241
justiciability of 38, 41
as positive rights 108
protection of 51, 93, 107, 109, 112, 217, 220
and public spending 108-9
Spain
balanced budget principle 28-9, 155, 162-3
banks, bailout 142
Constitution
adjustments 48
GFC (2008), effects of 144-54
judicial interpretation 149-54
popular reactions 144
reforms 154-63, 164-5
Constitutional Court 37, 48, 156
credit agency rating 142
crisis legislation 15
economy, decline 141-2
elections 20, 141
GDP, fall 142
GFC (2008) 144-65
austerity measures 143
decree-laws, use 145-9
and mortgage payments 144-5
and Workers' Statute 146
politicians, distrust of 20
public debt 143
public spending, increase 142
recession 142
Socialist Party 141
unemployment 142-3
Stability and Growth Pact 230, 235
state sovereignty 23
and balanced budget principle 29
and constitutions 226, 227, 231, 233, 241
erosion 5, 10, 40, 44
and European integration 38, 77, 78, 228
scrutiny by courts 38-9

Treaty on Stability, Coordination and Governance *see* Fiscal Compact

UK
Backbench Business Committee 16
Bank of England
Banking Supervision Division 170
Financial Policy Committee (FPC) 173
governor, appointment of 174
role 17, 169, 171, 172, 173

bank failures
  Bank of Credit and Commerce International 170-71
  Barings Bank 171
  Bingham Report 171
  Johnson Mathey Bankers 170
bank losses 167
Banking Act (1979) 169
Banking Act (1987) 170, 171
Banking Act (2009) 182
Banking Commission 18, 174
budget deficit 167
Budget Responsibility and National Audit Act (2011) 183
Cabinet Manual, revision 18, 26, 47, 180, 181
CHAPS system 170
coalition government 18, 21, 26, 168, 172, 179-80
Constitution
  adjustments 47
  and GFC (2008) 179-92
  nature of 169
  possible codification 192
  resilience 168
Draft Recall Bill (2011) 26
ESM membership 187
Financial Conduct Authority 17, 172
  role 173, 191
financial regulation 172-4
  constitutional importance 26-7, 188-90
  outcomes-based 191
  principles-based 190-91
  sanctions 175-8
Financial Services Act (2010) 172
Financial Services Authority (FSA) 169, 173
  abolition 174
  civil sanctions 175-6
  criminal sanctions 175
  criticism of 172
Fiscal Compact
  opt out 168, 183
  reservations about 186-7
Fiscal Responsibility Act (2010) 16, 183
Fixed-Term Parliaments Act (2011) 26, 47, 180-81
Human Rights Act (1998) 185
judicial review 185
Leigh-Pemberton Committee 170
LIBOR rate, rigging 21, 175, 178-9
MPs' expenses, scandal 19, 179
Northern Rock
  collapse 172, 180
  nationalization 34, 182, 185-6
Office of Budget Responsibility (OBR) 184
parliamentary accountability 182-5
political system 179-82
Prudential Regulation Authority (PRA) 172
  role 173, 191-2
public debt 167
quantitative easing 167, 184
recall elections, proposals 21, 181
sovereignty issues, and EU 186-7
Treasury 169, 172, 182, 183
Turner Review 175
Vickers Report 192
US
  bailouts
    banks 287, 299
    car companies 290
  balanced budget principle 29
  Congress 297, 298
  Constitution
    and debt-ceiling crisis 290-94, 298
    and hyperpolarized politics 295, 297-300
    informal changes 2, 51, 57
    robustness 51, 52, 56
  constitutional hardball 291
  Dodd-Frank Act (2010) 18
  DREAM Act 299-300
  Federal Reserve 18
  New Deal 295
    as constitutional moment 1, 54, 230
  non-delegation doctrine, irrelevance of 288-90
  party system
    branding 296-7
    ideologies 295-6
  Senate 297
  Tea Party faction 20, 294-5

Troubled Asset Relief Program (TARP) 289-90

Vanoni, Ezio 94
Venizelos, Evangelos 213

Weimar Constitution, collapse 1, 2

Zapatero, Jose Luis Rodriguez 141, 143
Zatlers, Valdis 129-30, 136-7

For Product Safety Concerns and Information please contact our EU representative GPSR@taylorandfrancis.com
Taylor & Francis Verlag GmbH, Kaufingerstraße 24, 80331 München, Germany

www.ingramcontent.com/pod-product-compliance
Ingram Content Group UK Ltd.
Pitfield, Milton Keynes, MK11 3LW, UK
UKHW022012180926
475701UK00003B/316
* 9 7 8 1 1 3 8 2 5 5 7 0 8 *